PUBLISHING THE HISTORY PLAY IN THE TIME OF SHAKESPEARE

During the early modern period, the publication process decisively shaped the history play and its reception. Bringing together the methodologies of genre criticism and book history, this study argues that stationers have – through acts of selection and presentation – constructed some remarkably influential expectations and ideas surrounding genre. Amy Lidster boldly challenges the uncritical use of Shakespeare's Folio as a touchstone for the history play, exposing the harmful ways in which this has solidified its parameters as a genre exclusively interested in the lives of English kings. Reframing the Folio as a single example of participation in genre-making, this book illuminates the exciting and diverse range of historical pasts that were available to readers and audiences in the early modern period. Lidster invites us to reappraise the connection between plays on stage and in print, and to reposition playbooks within the historical culture and geopolitics of the book trade.

AMY LIDSTER is a Departmental Lecturer in English Language and Literature at Jesus College, University of Oxford. She is co-editor of *Shakespeare at War: A Material History* (Cambridge University Press, forthcoming), and her work has appeared widely in books and journals, including *Old St Paul's and Culture* (2021), *Shakespeare Survey*, *Shakespeare Studies*, and *Renaissance Drama*.

PUBLISHING THE HISTORY PLAY IN THE TIME OF SHAKESPEARE

Stationers Shaping a Genre

AMY LIDSTER

Jesus College, University of Oxford

CAMBRIDGE
UNIVERSITY PRESS

CAMBRIDGE
UNIVERSITY PRESS

Shaftesbury Road, Cambridge CB2 8EA, United Kingdom

One Liberty Plaza, 20th Floor, New York, NY 10006, USA

477 Williamstown Road, Port Melbourne, VIC 3207, Australia

314–321, 3rd Floor, Plot 3, Splendor Forum, Jasola District Centre, New Delhi – 110025, India

103 Penang Road, #05–06/07, Visioncrest Commercial, Singapore 238467

Cambridge University Press is part of Cambridge University Press & Assessment,
a department of the University of Cambridge.

We share the University's mission to contribute to society through the pursuit of
education, learning and research at the highest international levels of excellence.

www.cambridge.org
Information on this title: www.cambridge.org/9781009044493

DOI: 10.1017/9781009043656

© Amy Lidster 2022

First published 2022
First paperback edition 2024

A catalogue record for this publication is available from the British Library

ISBN   978-1-316-51725-3   Hardback
ISBN   978-1-009-04449-3   Paperback

For Nathan and Sandra

Catalogue

Figures

Acknowledgements

My greatest thanks are to Sonia Massai for her unwavering support of this project throughout its various manifestations: from a PhD proposal to a dissertation and, finally, to a book. The brevity of these Acknowledgements cannot do justice to her incisive feedback, encouragement, and friendship, and it has been through this help that my research has, to adapt Genette, 'made a book of itself'. I am also particularly grateful to Lucy Munro, my second supervisor, and my PhD examiners, John Jowett and Tiffany Stern, without whom this book – and, indeed, my wider research practices – would be much poorer. All remaining errors are, of course, Compositor E's.

This project began at desks 154 to 159 in the Rare Books reading room of the British Library and came to an end during lockdown. Despite all the solitary hours of working in silence, it really reflects a collaboration with colleagues and students over the years. King's College London could not have been a better home for my research during this time, and I have been exceptionally fortunate to be surrounded by inspiring and generous colleagues of whom there are too many to name. Special thanks go to Gordon McMullan and Daniel Starza Smith for their advice, collegiality, and readiness to offer support. My ideas in this book have also benefited immensely from the London Shakespeare Seminar series, which I had the pleasure to attend (religiously!) over the past six years.

The guidance, scholarship, and friendship of other colleagues in the field of early modern studies have been crucial to me. Paulina Kewes's work was the first inspiration and catalyst that set me on this journey back in 2014 and I am thankful for her continuing support and camaraderie in my new home at Jesus College, Oxford. Kim Gilchrist, fellow history-play enthusiast and co-conspirator, helped me, amidst countless coffee and pub breaks, to figure out what I think about 'history', and Nicole Mennell was always ready to exchange ideas, read drafts, and be an academic partner in crime (#shakeass17). Peter Blayney generously shared his ideas on the geography of Paul's Cross Churchyard with me, and Shakespeare's

Globe gave me the opportunity – and a vote of confidence – to present my research on _King Lear_ at St Austin's Gate as one of the 2017 'Youths That Thunder'. I am indebted to the speakers at 'Changing Histories: Rethinking the Early Modern History Play', a conference that I co-organized with Kim Gilchrist in 2019, for their important papers that prompted me to revise my own ways of reading 'histories', and to Aaron Pratt and fellow participants of 'Collecting Shakespeare', held at the 2019 meeting of the Shakespeare Association of America in Washington, DC. My research is also richer for the exciting work carried out by the 'Before Shakespeare' project and the invigorating conversations we had at their 2017 conference. Finally, thanks go to Shanyn Altman, Tamara Atkin, Shani Bans, Sally Barnden, Matthew Blaiden, Callan Davies, Jennifer Edwards, Robbie Hand, Ben Higgins, Gabriella Infante, Andy Kesson, Roberta Klimt, Sarah O'Malley, Jennifer Richards, and Chris Stamatakis who have listened to research conundrums, shared their own work, and/or occasionally lightened the mood.

The main research for this project was generously funded by the London Arts and Humanities Partnership (LAHP) through a PhD studentship; without this financial assistance, I doubt that my book would be appearing in print at this time. I am also grateful to the LAHP for an additional award that enabled me to attend the 2017 meeting of the Shakespeare Association of America in Atlanta as a Next Generation Plenary speaker and to present ideas that are now included within Chapter 2 of this book. Thanks also go to the Society for Renaissance Studies, the London Shakespeare Centre, and the Arts and Humanities Research Institute at King's College London for funding the conference 'Changing Histories'.

I would like to thank Emily Hockley at Cambridge University Press for her patience and assistance with this book, George Laver and Ken Moxham for their contributions and attention to detail, and the anonymous Press readers whose constructive and thoughtful comments have vastly improved the final version. Material from two chapters has already been published elsewhere. Some research from Chapter 2 features in my 2018 _Shakespeare Survey_ article, 'At the Sign of the Angel: The Influence of Andrew Wise on Shakespeare in Print'. A section of Chapter 3 appears as 'Publishing _King Lear_ (1608) at the Sign of the Pied Bull' in _Old St Paul's and Culture_, edited by Shanyn Altman and Jonathan Buckner (Palgrave Macmillan, 2021). I am grateful for the kind permission to reproduce the material here. Thanks also go to librarians at the British Library, Folger Shakespeare Library, Huntington Library, and Harry Ransom Center –

and to the Aeon team at the Huntington for speedily fulfilling digital image requests.

Finally, this book would not exist were it not for the support, love, and understanding of my family. To my mother, Sandra Lidster, I owe countless thanks – among them, for always supporting my plots 'conceived in discontentedness' and for encouraging me, all those years ago, to look again (and again) at what I was writing. To my partner, Nathan Jones, I owe the 'greater part of happiness': he has patiently lived with this book for as long as I have and has steered me away from 'idle preoccupation' to see the beauty of life outside academia. For these and many more unpayable debts, this book is dedicated to them, with gratitude.

Note on the Text

As this book concentrates on early modern publication practices and the production of texts, I quote exclusively from the early printed witnesses of the works under discussion. I silently expand contractions, regularize the long -s and -vv, but otherwise retain the original spelling, punctuation, and capitalization for all pre-1800 texts. After an initial footnote, further references to these texts appear parenthetically. Unless otherwise stated, all dates accompanying the titles of works refer to the date of first publication, rather than composition or first performance. Titles of lost plays are given in quotation marks. In my main discussion and Appendix, I give all early works a standardized, modern-spelling title, while references in the footnotes and bibliography retain original spelling. I adopt this principle to avoid the hierarchy that would be implied by using original spelling for lesser-studied works and modern titles for well-known ones (such as *Richard II* for *The Tragedie of King Richard the second*, as it was first published in 1597). Here, I apply the same principle to all titles.

Abbreviations

Arber	Edward Arber (ed.), *A Transcript of the Registers of the Company of Stationers of London, 1554–1640 A.D.*, 5 vols. (London, 1875–77; Birmingham, 1894)
DEEP	Alan B. Farmer and Zachary Lesser (eds.), *DEEP: Database of Early English Playbooks* Created 2007. http://deep.sas.upenn .edu
Greg	W. W. Greg, *A Bibliography of the English Printed Drama to the Restoration*, 4 vols. (London: Oxford University Press for the Bibliographical Society, 1939–59)
ODNB	*Oxford Dictionary of National Biography* (Oxford: Oxford University Press, 2004) online ed. http://oxforddnb.com
SRO	Giles Bergel and Ian Gadd (eds.), *Stationers' Register Online*, CREATe, University of Glasgow. http://stationersregister.online
STC	A. W. Pollard and G. R. Redgrave (eds.), *A Short-Title Catalogue of Books Printed in England, Scotland, and Ireland and of English Books Printed Abroad, 1475–1640*, 2nd ed., rev. W. A. Jackson, F. S. Ferguson, and K. F. Pantzer, 3 vols. (London: The Bibliographical Society, 1976–91)
Wiggins	Martin Wiggins, in association with Catherine Richardson, *British Drama 1533–1642: A Catalogue*, 8 vols (Oxford: Oxford University Press, 2011–)

Introduction
'To the great Variety of Readers'

When Shakespeare's First Folio reached the bookstalls in 1623, it became the first collection printed in the prestigious folio format to feature plays exclusively from the commercial stages.[1] It was also the first collection to construct and advertise history as a clearly defined dramatic genre. The Folio divides its plays – eighteen of which had not been printed before – into three theatrical genres, which are indicated by the 'Catalogue' (omitting *Troilus and Cressida*) and also by the title of the collection – *Master William Shakespeare's Comedies, Histories, and Tragedies*. The Folio selectively collects its 'Histories', excluding, for example, the Scottish history of *Macbeth* and classical histories, such as *Julius Caesar*, and arranges them according to the historical order of English kings, rather than the plays' order of composition. By doing so, the collection effectively publishes its own statement about the parameters of the genre: the history play's proper subject is English monarchical history after the Conquest.

This design was not, of course, undertaken by Shakespeare, who died in 1616. It was the product of a collaboration between Shakespeare's former colleagues John Heminges and Henry Condell and the syndicate of stationers who invested in the project – William and Isaac Jaggard, Edward Blount, William Aspley, and John Smethwick. The Folio categories are therefore a retrospective division propelled by the publication process – and specifically by *this* publication venture, which has had an immense (and sometimes unproductive) influence on critical approaches to early modern history plays. Rather than revealing something inherent about the form, style, subject, or ideology of Shakespeare's plays that dramatize the past, the Folio division offers a *reading* of them, and its construction reflects the interests and strategies of those who took part in its publication. The impact of this venture cannot be overstated: the Folio's design has subsequently entrenched critical expectations about the generic

---

[1] Ben Jonson's *Works* (1616) contains poetry, masques, and entertainments, alongside his plays.

identity of Shakespeare's plays and those of other early modern dramatists. *Publishing the History Play in the Time of Shakespeare* aims to show that the publication process, rather than simply reflecting established views and exempla of dramatic genres, has played a crucial role in constructing them. Publication agents have defined, shaped, and marketed history plays in ways that have affected the experiences of 'the great Variety of Readers' – from early modern to modern.[2]

A key premise of this study is that genre offers mediating frameworks through which writers and readers create meaning, but it involves a kind of participation that, as Jacques Derrida proposes, 'never amounts to belonging'.[3] Statements about genre are part of the 'aftermarket' of plays in print and are subject to revision and reappraisal.[4] Many of the Folio 'Histories', such as *Richard II*, are described as tragedies in their earliest single-text editions, which demonstrates the mutability of genre labels. The cultural capital that Shakespeare and his plays subsequently accrued, however, has led to the 1623 Folio being used uncritically as a touchstone, rather than as a single and not necessarily representative example of participation in categorizing dramatic 'kinds'. Andy Kesson proposes that the Folio has standardized generic expectations of comedies, with the effect of marginalizing and problematizing the plays of other dramatists.[5] Similarly, in relation to its 'Histories', Gary Taylor argues that the 'posthumous Shakespeare folio [has] retrospectively conquered, solidified, legitimized and singularized the genre'.[6] Many history-play studies have concentrated on the plays listed in the Folio's catalogue, defined the genre (explicitly or implicitly) as the dramatization of English monarchical history, and developed a rise-and-fall narrative trajectory that is tied to Shakespeare's *oeuvre* and typically identifies the 1590s as the heyday of the history play, arguing

---

[2] William Shakespeare, *Comedies, Histories, and Tragedies* (London, 1623; STC 22273), A3r.
[3] Jacques Derrida, 'The Law of Genre', trans. Avital Ronell, *Critical Inquiry*, 7:1 (1980), 55–81 (p. 65).
[4] Peter Berek, 'Genres, Early Modern Theatrical Title Pages, and the Authority of Print', in *The Book of the Play: Playwrights, Stationers, and Readers in Early Modern England*, ed. Marta Straznicky (Amherst and Boston: University of Massachusetts Press, 2006), pp. 159–75 (p. 160).
[5] Andy Kesson, 'Was Comedy a Genre in English Early Modern Drama?', *British Journal of Aesthetics*, 54:2 (2014), 213–25.
[6] Gary Taylor, 'History, Plays, Genre, Games', in *The Oxford Handbook of Thomas Middleton*, ed. Gary Taylor and Trish Thomas Henley (Oxford: Oxford University Press, 2012), pp. 47–63 (p. 51). See also Adam G. Hooks, 'Making Histories: or, Shakespeare's Ring', in *The Book in History, the Book as History: New Intersections of the Material Text*, ed. Heidi Brayman, Jesse M. Lander, and Zachary Lesser (New Haven and London: Yale University Press, 2016), pp. 341–74.

for its swift decline in the early seventeenth century.[7] Lawrence Danson claims, for example, that 'it would only be a small exaggeration to say that "history play" is the only genre [Shakespeare] actually invented'.[8] Insightful reappraisals in chapters and collections by Michael Hattaway, Richard Helgerson, Paulina Kewes, Teresa Grant, Barbara Ravelhofer, Gary Taylor, and Adam Hooks have challenged the enduring critical emphasis on Shakespeare's English histories and assumptions about the uses and ideology of history plays.[9] However, no study has yet concentrated on publication and the fact that the ways in which plays make books of themselves encourage particular interpretations of them and their genres.[10]

Publishing the History Play in the Time of Shakespeare is the first book-length study of history plays to examine the genre through the publication process, an approach that crucially recovers evidence for early readings of these plays and their position within the period's historical culture and the geopolitics of the book trade. In doing so, it draws on the methodologies of genre criticism and book history, bringing together two areas of study that are often considered separately. This method is vital for history plays because of the overlooked and outsized influence of the publication process in creating expectations for a dramatic genre that, unlike the

---

[7] See E. M. W. Tillyard, *Shakespeare's History Plays* (London: Chatto & Windus, 1944); Lily B. Campbell, *Shakespeare's 'Histories': Mirrors of Elizabethan Policy* (San Marino, CA: Huntington Library, 1947); Graham Holderness, *Shakespeare's History* (Dublin: Gill and Macmillan, 1985); Phyllis Rackin, *Stages of History: Shakespeare's English Chronicles* (Ithaca: Cornell University Press, 1990); Graham Holderness, *Shakespeare Recycled: The Making of Historical Drama* (Hemel Hempstead: Harvester Wheatsheaf, 1992); Paola Pugliatti, *Shakespeare the Historian* (Basingstoke: Palgrave Macmillan, 1996); John W. Velz (ed.), *Shakespeare's English Histories: A Quest for Form and Genre* (Binghamton, NY: Medieval & Renaissance Texts & Studies, 1996); Neema Parvini, *Shakespeare's History Plays: Rethinking Historicism* (Edinburgh: Edinburgh University Press, 2012); Ralf Hertel, *Staging England in the Elizabethan History Play: Performing National Identity* (London: Routledge, 2014).

[8] Lawrence Danson, *Shakespeare's Dramatic Genres* (Oxford: Oxford University Press, 2000), p. 87.

[9] Michael Hattaway, 'The Shakespearean History Play', in *The Cambridge Companion to Shakespeare's History Plays*, ed. Michael Hattaway (Cambridge: Cambridge University Press, 2002), pp. 3–24; Richard Helgerson, 'Shakespeare and Contemporary Dramatists of History', in *A Companion to Shakespeare's Works, Volume II: The Histories*, ed. Richard Dutton and Jean E. Howard (Oxford: Blackwell, 2003), pp. 26–47; Paulina Kewes, 'The Elizabethan History Play: A True Genre?' in *Companion to Shakespeare's Works*, ed. Dutton and Howard, pp. 170–93; Teresa Grant and Barbara Ravelhofer (eds.), *English Historical Drama, 1500–1660: Forms outside the Canon* (Basingstoke: Palgrave Macmillan, 2008); Taylor, 'History'; and Hooks, 'Making Histories'.

[10] For other ways of approaching Shakespeare's genres, from the early modern period through to contemporary performance, see Anthony R. Guneratne, *Shakespeare and Genre: From Early Modern Inheritances to Postmodern Legacies* (New York: Palgrave Macmillan, 2011). For a linguistic analysis of genre using DocuScope, see Jonathan Hope and Michael Witmore, 'The Hundredth Psalm to the Tune of "Green Sleeves": Digital Approaches to Shakespeare's Language of Genre', *Shakespeare Quarterly*, 61:3 (2010), 357–90.

classically derived comedy and tragedy, lacks established discursive parameters. Indeed, the term 'history play' was not in use during the period, the
preferred descriptor being 'a history' or 'histories'. Because of the overlap
between 'history' as a dramatic category and as an emerging field of
enquiry about the past, the over-dominance of the Shakespearean model
of English history inhibits our access to the period's historical culture,
including the evidence of trans-temporal and transnational exchanges that
take place within and across publications (including plays) that address
some kind of historical past.

This book concentrates on the publication of history plays from the
commercial stages during Shakespeare's 'time' – that is, from the early
1590s (when his working career in London was beginning) to the publication of the Folio in 1623. The reasons for this time frame are twofold:
first, to re-evaluate the generic markers of Shakespeare's plays in print,
showing how they are part of competing discourses of genre, rather than
reflecting clear-cut perspectives; and second, to contrast these playbooks
with the evidence of other dramatists' history plays – both in print and on
the stage.[11] The emphasis on commercial plays is sustained further to
reappraise modern critical accounts of history plays, which typically concentrate on those performed on public stages in front of paying audiences,
but also because publication patterns suggest that stationers developed
different strategies for commercial and non-commercial plays during the
late Elizabethan and Jacobean periods.[12] This book proposes that publication agents have actively defined and shaped the printed history play
through two interlinked agendas: strategies of selection (seen through print
contexts) and strategies of presentation (seen through print paratexts). By
choosing to invest in certain history plays, publication agents determined,
to a considerable degree, the survival of plays from the commercial stages,
and this selection process also suggests how stationers read the plays
alongside their wider output and the interests of the reading public.
Through the preparation of paratextual materials (such as title pages,
woodcut ornaments, contents pages, and addresses to readers), the

---

[11] For clarity, it is worth pointing out that I reserve the term 'playbook' exclusively for the book of the
play produced through the publication process, and not in application to any playscripts.

[12] I use the terms 'professional' and 'commercial' for plays performed by adult and boys' companies in
front of paying audiences, whereas I use 'non-professional' or 'non-commercial' for plays that were
written and staged at universities or Inns of Court, as well as closet plays, translations, and other
forms of entertainment, including pageants and masques. Because they emphasize the different
economies of staging plays for paying audiences and do not carry an additional evaluative
judgement, I favour the terms 'commercial' and 'non-commercial'.

publication process also shapes the presentation of plays as books, which both discloses and directs how history plays were used and categorized. In turn, these practices shed light on three kinds of readings: those of publication agents who oversaw the process; those of early modern readers who encountered history plays as books; and those of modern readers, who have been significantly influenced by some early uses (such as Shakespeare's Folio), but not others (such as the play catalogues issued by booksellers in the seventeenth century, including Edward Archer's 1656 list of 'all the Plaies that were ever printed', that sometimes included an assessment of genre).[13]

Through four chronological case studies, this book argues that the twinned acts of selection and presentation have led, in conjunction with Shakespeare's emerging cultural capital, to a narrow definition of the 'history play' that is not only detrimental for understanding Shakespeare's *oeuvre* but actually distorts the evidence of performance and print, which reveals that historical drama existed in a variety of forms and contexts. By concentrating on stationers' investment patterns, this book shows that history plays, alongside non-dramatic texts about the past, were a vital part of the period's historical culture. It demonstrates that stage and print patterns for history plays differed considerably, and that a thorough understanding of the publication process is necessary for determining what can – and cannot – be claimed about theatrical repertories. Despite the tendency of history-play studies to group together plays on the same historical past, this book argues that plays dramatizing different temporal and national histories were read together, a practice which should be reflected in our own critical approaches. To clarify the parameters and methodologies of this study, the Introduction first considers early modern ideas of history and history plays, and how the publication process contributes to this discourse. It then explores in more detail the print contexts and print paratexts that reveal how publication agents participate in and shape history as a genre.

Defining Histories: What's in a Name?

H: The plaies that they plaie in England, are nor right comedies.
T: Yet they doo nothing else but plaie euery daye.
H: Yea but they are neither right comedies, nor right tragedies.

---

[13] Archer's catalogue is appended to Philip Massinger, Thomas Middleton, and William Rowley's *The Old Law* (London, 1656; Wing M1048), a1r–b4v.

G: How would you name them then?

H: Representations of histories, without any decorum.

John Florio, *Florio's Second Fruits* (1591)[14]

Many history-play studies have concentrated on Shakespeare's English histories as if they define and largely constitute the genre, rather than reflecting the critical dominance of the 1623 Folio's design. Graham Holderness, for example, claims that accepting the Folio's division of plays and parameters for its histories presents 'few problems of a generic kind'.[15] The genre has been seen as synonymous with medieval English monarchical history in studies by Phyllis Rackin (1990), Benjamin Griffin (2001), and Ralf Hertel (2014). A terminological slipperiness can be witnessed in accounts that use 'history play' and 'English history play' interchangeably, which marginalizes – or indeed effaces – plays featuring non-English pasts.[16] This narrow definition and the influence of Shakespeare's Folio have also constructed a rise-and-fall trajectory for the genre – one that erases large chunks of theatre history and is too neatly linked to Shakespeare's *oeuvre* during the 1590s.[17] Such studies, as Kewes summarizes, have propagated 'the myth that there is a definable dramatic genre called the history play, which is distinct from both comedy and tragedy, which features the "English" past, and which reaches its artistic maturity with Shakespeare, swiftly declining thereafter'.[18] In *Stages of History*, for example, Rackin connects the (English) history play to a teleological narrative of historiographical development, suggesting that the genre died out when history became a clearly defined autonomous discipline by the early seventeenth century.[19] This approach overlooks enduring diversity in both dramatic and non-dramatic historical writing and closely follows the plays of Shakespeare, which move away from English history by the early Jacobean period. Ivo Kamps does not follow Rackin's Shakespearean emphasis, but similarly develops a rise-and-fall narrative that connects the history play with patterns in historiography, delaying the genre's

---

[14] *Florios Second Frvtes* (London, 1591; STC 11097), D4r.

[15] Holderness, *Shakespeare Recycled*, p. 1.

[16] Kewes, 'Elizabethan', pp. 170–93. See also Helgerson ('Shakespeare', p. 26), who argues that the cultural and critical emphasis on Shakespeare has resulted in 'a considerable narrowing in our understanding of the variety of perspectives on the English past – and thus on the English nation – that were available to Elizabethan theatregoers'.

[17] Accounts that offer rise-and-fall narratives include: Holderness, *Shakespeare Recycled*; Rackin, *Stages of History*; Ivo Kamps, *Historiography and Ideology in Stuart Drama* (Cambridge: Cambridge University Press, 1996); Benjamin Griffin, *Playing the Past: Approaches to English Historical Drama, 1385–1600* (Woodbridge, Suffolk: D. S. Brewer, 2001).

[18] Kewes, 'Elizabethan', p. 187.   [19] Rackin, *Stages of History*, pp. 21–32.

decline until the Stuart era. Kamps tends to dismiss non-dramatic historical sources as inferior to the history play: 'dramatists often show themselves to be better expositors of history than the historians; they show themselves to possess a clearer understanding of historiography's literary origins and its limitations as a knowledge-producing practice'.[20] This kind of approach, while rooted in discussions of historiography, reveals a relatively static reading of the connection between plays and their sources, depending on an assumption that plays are more sophisticated than other forms of historical writing and that there is some consensus about the purposes of history during the period, neither of which can be comfortably supported.[21]

As this study considers throughout, there is little evidence to suggest that Shakespeare's approach to history on stage neatly reflected the practices of other dramatists, that the strategies of the publication agents involved in the 1623 Folio offered representative ways of defining the genre, or that 'history' as a 'kind' of play was ever precisely or consistently defined. The term 'history', of course, applied to both dramatic and non-dramatic texts (that is, as Gérard Genette describes, to different 'modes of enunciation').[22] While tragedy and comedy also had non-dramatic traditions, they nevertheless had a classical heritage as dramatic categories and, in particular, 'tragedy', as Tamara Atkin discusses, seems to have been used on printed title pages by the mid-sixteenth century to invoke a 'direct or suggestive association with classical drama'.[23] Setting aside the issue of mode, 'history' carried a wide range of meanings, including, as the *OED* outlines, a sequence of past events – real or imaginary – such as those relating to the life of an individual, group of people, or nation; a branch of knowledge and enquiry into past events; and any account of such events.[24] 'History' is, as David Scott Kastan describes, a 'radically ambiguous' term

[20] Kamps, *Historiography*, p. 13.
[21] See also Holderness, *Shakespeare Recycled*; Pugliatti, *Shakespeare the Historian*. Irving Ribner's *The English History Play in the Age of Shakespeare*, rev. ed. (London: Methuen, 1965), first published in 1957, acknowledges the artificiality of a Shakespeare-centric evaluation of the history play and examines a much wider range of plays. However, Ribner's account is still driven by, in common with his contemporaries Tillyard and Campbell, an assumption that history has a clearly defined aim (to 'use the past for didactic purposes') and that plays about the past having 'little historical sense' or neglecting the 'legitimate purposes' of history must not be confused with the 'true history play', criteria which cannot be properly upheld or proposed (pp. 8, 25).
[22] Gérard Genette, *The Architext: An Introduction*, trans. Jane E. Lewin (Berkeley and Los Angeles: University of California Press, 1992), pp. 61–64.
[23] Tamara Atkin, *Reading Drama in Tudor England* (London: Routledge, 2018), pp. 33–35.
[24] See 'history, n.', *OED Online* (revised March 2021; accessed 12 April 2021).

that applies both to past events and to accounts of them.[25] It does not refer exclusively or self-evidently to those based on historical records or an accepted historical tradition (which is, however, the emphasis of this study), but also applies to entirely fictional events in a range of forms. The terms 'history' and 'story' were used interchangeably, and one of the dominant meanings of 'story' during the period was a narrative of events that were believed to have taken place in the past, an application that further limits the precision and usefulness of these terms in isolation.[26] For these reasons, understanding 'history' is a process of understanding how certain people have preferred to use and treat it. A discussion of historical drama involves both the modern critic's choice of how to define the genre and early modern forms of 'participation' – which, in this study, concentrate on the publication process and the way it continually reshapes the parameters and purposes of the history play through stationers' strategies of selection and presentation. Before addressing the print contexts and paratexts that reveal this negotiation, this section explores in more detail the semantic flexibility of history during the period and then clarifies this study's use of the term 'history play'.

Early modern discourses on genre – or, more accurately, on 'kinds' – confirm that history as a dramatic form did not have fixed parameters.[27] An interest in defining dramatic kinds is suggested by the extract from *Florio's Second Fruits* quoted above, but the exchange remains tantalizingly elusive. The characters in Florio's dialogue seem concerned with generic purity. Histories from the commercial stages are said to lack decorum: they are not part of a 'pure' or classical genre like comedy and tragedy, but no further indication of subject, style, or theme is suggested. Indeed, the dialogue does not make it clear whether 'history' is being used to refer to an account of the past or one of fictional events. In *A Survey of London* (1598), John Stow describes London's playhouses as offering 'Comedies, Tragedies, enterludes, and histories, both true and fayned', which attempts a generic distinction, but provides no firm sense of history's scope or expectations.[28] Stow seems to differentiate between plays that have a certain degree of historical veracity and those that are imagined or distorted, having a tenuous connection to a recognizable past. He nevertheless includes both forms within the category of 'history'.

---

[25] David Scott Kastan, *Shakespeare and the Shapes of Time* (Basingstoke: Palgrave Macmillan, 1982), p. 11.
[26] See 'story, n.', *OED Online* (revised March 2021; accessed 12 April 2021).
[27] See also Kewes, 'Elizabethan'; Janette Dillon, 'The Early Tudor History Play', in *English Historical Drama*, ed. Grant and Ravelhofer, pp. 32–57.
[28] John Stow, *A Survay of London* (London, 1598; STC 23341), F3r.

Similarly, Thomas Heywood includes mythological subjects that can be presented 'in the fashion of a History' as part of his *Apology for Actors* (written *c.*1608, published 1612). In contrast to Stow, Heywood constructs 'Hystories' as a theatrical genre with classical origins: 'I will begin with the antiquity of Acting Comedies, Tragedies, and Hystories.'[29] The genre seems to feature the worthy and memorable acts of individuals from the past, but further clarification proves difficult. Heywood separately discusses 'our domesticke hystories' (including *Edward III* and *Henry V*, B4r) and 'forreigne History' (involving 'the liues of Romans, Grecians, or others', F3v). He makes distinctions between histories of different national origins, but includes them all within the category of 'History'. For Heywood, the history play is not synonymous with English history. He aims instead to associate 'History' with as many profitable and laudable attributes as possible, which serves the *Apology*'s purpose of offering a defence of the theatre: 'there is neither Tragedy, History, Comedy, Morrall or Pastorall, from which an infinite vse cannot be gathered' (F4r). If any overarching consensus can be detected in the *Apology* it would be that the history play typically engages with some kind of recognizable past, whether native or foreign, true or feigned, recent or deriving from ancient or legendary history.

Plays from the period also directly explore ideas of dramatic genre. One of the most sustained examples appears in *A Warning for Fair Women*, which presents history as a character on stage.[30] This anonymous play from the Chamberlain's Men, written between 1596 and 1599 and published by William Aspley in 1599, dramatizes the murder of a London merchant, George Sanders, which took place in 1573, and includes an induction featuring 'Tragedie', 'Comedie', and 'Hystorie'.[31] Hystorie is presented with the attributes of a 'Drum and Ensigne', which suggests that the genre is dominated by battles, military subjects, and concerns of state. Tragedie is initially presented with a whip and a knife and identified with stories of revenge, murder, violence, and punishment, while Comedie favours material that is 'but slight and childish' (A2v). Grant and Ravelhofer suggest that the induction helps us to understand what contemporaries thought about these three dramatic kinds, but, to my mind, the distinctions are elided as the scene progresses and the personified

---

[29] Thomas Heywood, *An Apology for Actors* (London, 1612; STC 13309), B3r.
[30] See also Robert Wilson's *The Coblers Prophesie* (London, 1594; STC 25781), which features a scene (C1v–C3v) involving the classical muses Thalia (Comedy), Clio (History), and Melpomine (Tragedy).
[31] *A Warning for Faire Women* (London, 1599; STC 25089), A2r.

genres appear to overlap.[32] Descriptions of Tragedie merge with features
that had seemed to be unique to Hystorie: Tragedie also involves accounts
of monarchs and tyrants who strive 'to obtaine a crowne' (A2v). When
Tragedie is declared the victorious genre for the play, the summary of its
action recalls the concerns and attributes of Hystorie:

> My Sceane is London, natiue and your owne,
> I sigh to thinke, my subiect too well knowne,
> I am not faind: many now in this round,
> Once to behold me in sad teares were drownd.
>
> (A3r–v)

The subject matter of the play is 'not faind': it is based on a recognizable,
'too well knowne' historical past, and it blends the characteristics of
tragedy and history. The fact that the actors playing the parts of
Comedie, Hystorie, and Tragedie would have reappeared in other roles
within the main action could serve as a reminder, in performance, of the
interplay of different genres in one text and the impossibility of clear-
cut categories.

The participation that is part of defining, using, and negotiating history
as a dramatic form reflects the similar processes involved in approaching
history as a branch of knowledge and subject of enquiry about the past.
The history play transverses the categories of history and poetry that Philip
Sidney discusses in his *Defence of Poesy* (published in 1595, but written
during the early 1580s). The *Defence* proposes, in theory, clear distinctions
for history, philosophy, and poetry (which is 'subdiuided into sundry more
speciall denominations' and includes drama); but the treatise is informed,
as Blair Worden points out, by Sidney's agenda to defend poetry as the
superior form.[33] Poetry aims 'to teach and delight' (which echoes Horace's
Ars Poetica) and involves invention: it borrows 'nothing of what is, hath
bin, or shall be' (*Defence*, C2v). In contrast, history is 'so tied, not to what
should be, but to what is, to the particular truth of things' and is therefore
'lesse fruitfull' (D1r–v), while philosophy 'teacheth obscurely' (D2v). The
examples Sidney gives and the discussions he offers elsewhere, however,
demonstrate that these 'pure' genres or kinds are impossible in practice.
Sidney acknowledges that plays – which he largely divides into the two

---

[32] Grant and Ravelhofer, 'Introduction', in *English Historical Drama*, ed. Grant and Ravelhofer,
pp. 1–31 (pp. 12–15). See also Emma Whipday, *Shakespeare's Domestic Tragedies: Violence in the
Early Modern Home* (Cambridge: Cambridge University Press, 2019), pp. 14–15.

[33] Philip Sidney, *The Defence of Poesie* (London, 1595; STC 22535), C2v; Blair Worden, 'Historians
and Poets', *Huntington Library Quarterly*, 68:1–2 (2005), 71–93 (pp. 81–82).

classical genres of comedy and tragedy – sometimes dramatize the historical past, but claims that they are 'tied to the lawes of Poesie, and not of
Historie' (H4v). At the same time though, history – because of the
'clowdie knowledge of mankinde' (G1r) – cannot offer an accurate account
of the past, and so historiographers 'haue bene glad to borrow fashion and
perchance weight of the Poets' (B2v). It becomes difficult to distinguish
between poetry that draws on the past and history that uses the techniques
of poetry. '[R]yming and versing' (C3r), according to Sidney, are not the
defining features of poetry – indeed, history may be written in verse. For
Sidney, poetry is characterized by invention, and it is therefore an important part of many different kinds of writing, with one of its key purposes
being, as Kamps summarizes, 'to educate its readers and to spur them on to
noble action'.[34]

These aims, however, were also directly connected, by other writers, to
the purposes of history. The address 'A. B. To the Reader', prefacing Henry
Savile's translation of Tacitus (1591), argues that 'there is no learning so
proper for the direction of the life of man as Historie', as 'we are easlier
taught by example then by precept'.[35] History, according to the address, is
important because it profits readers, providing them with exempla to
imitate or avoid. George Puttenham's *Art of English Poesy* (1589) outlines
a similar purpose for history: he claims that historiographers use 'not the
matter so precisely to wish that al they wrote should be accounted true, for
that was not needefull nor expedient to the purpose, namely to be vsed
either for example or for pleasure'.[36] For Puttenham, written history brings
profit and pleasure to readers (and therefore overlaps with the features of
Sidney's poetry and the Horatian commonplace). It also does not need to
remain tied to records of the past, but can incorporate invention to further
its aims. John Hayward used the same defence when he came under
examination for *The First Part of the Life and Reign of King Henry IV*
(1599), claiming that it is 'lawfull for any historiographer to insert any
hystorie of former tyme into that hystorie he wright albeit no other
hystorian of that matter have meued the same'.[37] History-writing has a
complicated relationship to ideas of truth and invention. For writers such
as Savile, Puttenham, and Hayward, techniques of invention – including

---

[34] Kamps, *Historiography*, p. 82.

[35] Henry Savile and Tacitus, *The Ende of Nero and Beginning of Galba; Fower Bookes of the Histories of Cornelius Tacitvs; The Life of Agricola* (Oxford, 1591; STC 23642), ¶3r.

[36] George Puttenham, *The Arte of English Poesie* (London, 1589; STC 20519.5), F4v.

[37] See Margaret Dowling, 'Sir John Hayward's Troubles over his *Life of Henry IV*', *The Library*, 4th ser., 11:2 (1930), 212–24 (p. 216).

the addition of speeches as if they had taken place and the incorporation of large chunks of fictional writing (as in Savile's extended narrative that bridges the gap between the *Annals* and *Histories* of Tacitus) – could add to the truthful sentiment of an account, while departing from historical accuracy.[38]

Early modern readers may not have drawn sharp distinctions between historical drama and the writings of historians, including such varied authors as 'Holinshed', Savile, and Samuel Daniel. As Worden observes, many historians were also poets (including playwrights): Thomas Heywood wrote plays based on the reign of Elizabeth I (*1* and *2 If You Know Not Me, You Know Nobody*) in addition to a prose account on the same subject (*England's Elizabeth*), which recycles material from the plays.[39] Samuel Daniel wrote a classical history – *Philotas* – for the Children of the Queen's Revels, as well as a narrative poem on the Wars of the Roses (*The Civil Wars*) and a prose history beginning with the Saxons before the Conquest (*The Collection of the History of England*). A copy of Camden's *Britannia* contains, as D. R. Woolf identifies, marginalia by an early modern reader named John Thomas, who engaged in intertextual historical study, adding his own comments to Camden's text, as well as extracts from poetry, other histories, and other kinds of writing.[40] In Jonson's *The Devil Is an Ass*, Fitzdottrell claims that he is not 'cunning i'the Chronicle', but instead learns his history 'from the Play-bookes' because 'they are more authentique'.[41] Although Jonson satirizes this practice of reading history play*books* as accurate accounts of the past, his criticism suggests that it was relatively common. The fact that plays drama-tizing the past were sometimes referred to as 'histories', and not by the modern critical term 'history play', further encourages a reading that places them alongside non-dramatic histories.

While some modern critics have attempted to describe the period's dominant historiographical methods, typically outlining a progression from providential to humanist to antiquarian approaches to history, there is a danger in eliding forms of participation that endured but do not fit easily into a linear narrative of development.[42] Woolf's important

---

[38] Grant and Ravelhofer, 'Introduction' in *English Historical Drama*, pp. 2–3; Worden, 'Historians', p. 84.

[39] Worden, 'Historians', p. 72.

[40] D. R. Woolf, *Reading History in Early Modern England* (Cambridge: Cambridge University Press, 2000), p. 90. See also F. J. Levy, *Tudor Historical Thought* (San Marino, CA: The Huntington Library, 1967), which counts drama amongst historical forms of writing.

[41] Ben Jonson, *The Diuell is an Asse* (London, 1631; STC 14753.5), Q3v.

[42] See, for example, F. Smith Fussner's teleological account: *The Historical Revolution: English Historical Writing and Thought, 1580–1640* (New York: Columbia University Press, 1962).

monographs on historical thought have drawn attention to the experiences of a wide range of writers, readers, and, indeed, hearers of history, including playgoers, and an emerging critical trend is to be suspicious of master narratives.[43] Alex Davis opens his insightful study, *Renaissance Historical Fiction*, by acknowledging the importance of 'a historical tradition that is fractured and discontinuous rather than smoothly evolutionary'.[44] Even individual early modern historiographical treatises, such as Thomas Blundeville's *The True Order and Method of Writing and Reading Histories* (1574), offer contradictory views on the purposes and methodologies of history. Blundeville devotes much of his treatise to emphasizing causation, but then also claims that histories must affirm God's overarching plan and authority.[45] His treatise conflates a providential approach to history with a humanist drive, which leads to some conflicting statements: on the one hand, the purpose of writing and reading history is to understand why certain events took place, learn from them, and apply them to current times; but on the other hand, the treatise claims that the aim of history is to 'acknowledge the prouidence of God, wherby all things are gouerned and directed' (F2v). What my brief survey aims to show, in other words, is that there was no dominant method, purpose, or form for writing about history during the period – and history plays, for many of their audiences and readers, were a part of this fractured and varied discourse.

Modern genre theory offers some useful perspectives for approaching early modern texts. Already mentioned, Derrida describes genre as 'a sort of participation without belonging – a taking part in without being part of, without having membership in a set'.[46] More specifically, Rosalie Colie's and Alastair Fowler's work on Renaissance genre systems draws attention to the confusion and mutability of classification that dominates in the period, but also highlights the ubiquity of 'distinctive generic repertories' (Fowler) that offer 'a set of interpretations, of "frames" or "fixes" on the

---

Kamps offers a concise discussion of these three approaches in 'The Writing of History in Shakespeare's England', in *Companion to Shakespeare's Works*, ed. Dutton and Howard, pp. 4–25.

[43] D. R. Woolf, *The Idea of History in Early Stuart England* (Toronto: University of Toronto Press, 1990); *Reading History in Early Modern England* (2000); *The Social Circulation of the Past: English Historical Culture, 1500–1730* (Oxford: Oxford University Press, 2003). See also Arthur B. Ferguson, *Clio Unbound: Perception of the Social and Cultural Past in Renaissance England* (Durham, NC: Duke University Press, 1979).

[44] Alex Davis, *Renaissance Historical Fiction: Sidney, Deloney, Nashe* (Cambridge: D. S. Brewer, 2011), p. 19.

[45] Thomas Blundeville, *The true order and Methode of wryting and reading Hystories* (London, 1574; STC 3161), F2v–3r.

[46] Derrida, 'Genre', p. 59.

world' (Colie).[47] Genette carefully explores the conflation in genre theory between mode (as a linguistic category that specifies a means of enuncia- tion – 'pure narration/mixed narration/dramatic imitation') and genre (as a literary category that takes account of both thematic and formal ele- ments).[48] Indeed, ideas of history and historical drama are marked by an uncertain relationship between content and form. Parameters cannot be established only on the basis of means of enunciation: texts blend different modes (chronicle histories contain dramatic speeches, for example), and many efforts at categorizing reflect a partial assessment of formal and thematic features to serve a particular purpose. Genre is a lens for viewing: it focuses on certain aspects of a text and depends upon participation – not just of the writer, but of everyone who encounters a given text. Its negotiation is as active during the text's 'afterlife' as during the time of composition. All classifications and accounts of the history play, rather than being definitive, represent attempts at organizing, counting, and collecting according to different agendas. Indeed, Sidney shows what Derrida, Colie and others tell: his *Defence* is an example par excellence of participation informed by a clear agenda – in his case to elevate poetry above history and philosophy. Similarly, Florio's short dialogue on genre is part of a larger project. Taken as a whole, *Florio's Second Fruits* is a manual for learning Italian and developing colloquial conversation skills. Its main purpose is not the consolidation of dramatic categories, but rather the development of refined language skills and manners, which perhaps informs the emphasis on decorum in the dialogue's dismissal of 'histories'. As a final example, Francis Meres aims in *Palladis Tamia* (1598), a commonplace book and 'comparatiue discourse', to elevate English drama and compare it favourably to classical writers of comedy and tragedy.[49] It is this agenda that directs his classification of Shakespeare's *Richard II*, *Richard III*, *Henry IV* (no part specified), and *King John* as tragedies.[50] While *1 Henry IV* was printed in the same year as a 'history', Meres's assessment of genre depends on his overarching argument that Shakespeare is 'the best for Comedy and Tragedy' as Plautus and Seneca are 'among the

---

[47] Rosalie L. Colie, 'Genre-Systems and the Functions of Literature', in *The Resources of Kind: Genre-Theory in the Renaissance*, ed. Barbara K. Lewalski (Berkeley and Los Angeles: University of California Press, 1973), pp. 1–31 (pp. 8–9); Alastair Fowler, 'Genre and the Literary Canon', *New Literary History*, 11.1 (1979), 97–119 (p. 102).

[48] Genette, *Architext*, pp. 64–70.

[49] Francis Meres, *Palladis Tamia* (London, 1598; STC 17834), Nn7r.

[50] It is unclear whether Shakespeare had written *2 Henry IV* by the time of Meres's account. The fact that *Palladis Tamia* does not distinguish between the two parts could indicate that he had not, although Meres could be referring to both plays collectively.

Latines' (Oo2r). There is no room for an alternative lens or frame for viewing the plays.

While both Sidney and Derrida draw attention to the ways in which *texts* can be part of several genres or kinds, this study concentrates on *agents* of participation, because the individuals who collect, organize, and assess plays about the past are those who decide how a given text takes part. Their 'active participation', to quote Hans Robert Jauss, determines 'the historical life of a literary work'.[51] Rather than examining dramatists as the main makers of meaning, this study focuses on the agents involved in publication, as the playbooks they produce all make statements about genre – although these are rarely uniform across a large number of publications. For example, the classificatory labels that appear on title pages are one of the most prominent types of genre statement in play-books; yet these labels often lack clarity because the applications vary so widely. An eclectic range of plays are described as histories, which some-times carries the sense of an account of the past (*The Chronicle History of Henry V*, 1600), sometimes refers to the life of a central character (*The Famous History of the Life and Death of Captain Thomas Stukeley*, 1605), sometimes applies to a story of fictional events (*The History of the Trial of Chivalry*, 1605), and often blurs the boundaries between these meanings (which can be inferred from most of the above examples, as well as *The Honourable History of Friar Bacon and Friar Bungay*, 1594, a play that loosely follows the lives of historical individuals).[52] This terminological slipperiness does not mean that plays dramatizing the past could not be understood and described as a distinct category. Shakespeare's Folio is an example of using 'history' to refer to plays based on the lives of English monarchs. Similarly, as discussed in Chapter 2, Shakespeare's *1 Henry IV* (1598) is the first commercial playbook to be advertised as a 'history' with the unambiguous meaning of an account of the past. But the enduring malleability of genre labels suggests that they should not be one of the main ways of classifying and examining the history play. Even if a play or non-dramatic text is not described in print as a 'history', its account of the past was often a primary factor in shaping its use and reception. Most of Shakespeare's English histories were first published as 'tragedies'; however,

---

[51] Hans Robert Jauss, 'Literary History As a Challenge to Literary Theory', trans. Elizabeth Benzinger, *New Literary History*, 2:1 (1970), 7–37 (p. 8).
[52] Similarly, Griffin observes that, in the Elizabethan revels accounts after 1571, 'the word *history* is indiscriminately applied to any kind of dramatic show', as evidenced by the occasions on which the court recorder was clearly unaware of the title of a performed play and wrote only 'the history of' in the account book, leaving the remainder of the line blank (*Playing the Past*, p. 10).

as this book will argue, the fact that they dramatized the past informed their selection and printed presentation in important ways.

Somewhat surprisingly, the material conditions of textual production have been overlooked by history-play studies and no sustained account has examined history plays as books to be read – despite a prevailing interest in connecting history plays to works and patterns of historiography. In *Reading History in Early Modern England*, Woolf does concentrate on, as he puts it, the 'history of the history book *as* book', but plays do not feature centrally in his account.[53] History-play studies have tended to be dismissive of publication. While Benjamin Griffin observes that a significant number of history plays were printed between 1598 and 1613, which he sees as disclosing 'an unsuspected Jacobean passion for the histories', he claims that 'this consideration of the tastes of the play-reading public does not contradict the view that the history play was "obsolete" after about 1600; it merely reminds us that whatever becomes obsolete for the retailer thereby becomes valuable for the antique-shop'.[54] Griffin's focus is on performance patterns and theatre companies, which he describes here as the 'retailers' of history plays, while the actual booksellers are positioned as traders in antiques and obsolete goods. However, play*books* were not out-of-date commodities: if they were, it would have made little sense for publishers to invest in them.[55] Print offered a new medium and a new readerly audience, and history plays were often marketed for their 'currency', contemporaneity, and connection to non-dramatic texts. The interests of a play-reading public are integral for understanding these plays and their position within the wider historical culture of the period. Moreover, our access to the history plays that were performed on the early modern stages has been, as Marta Straznicky describes, 'decisively mediated' by publication and the fact that individuals working in the book trade chose to invest in them.[56]

At this stage, it is necessary to provide my own working definition of a history play, a key example of participation on my part. Drawing on early modern discourses about history and 'histories' outlined briefly above, I describe as a history play any dramatic text that engages with a recognizable historical past, regardless of whether this past is English/British or 'foreign', ancient or recent, closely following the evidence of primary

---

[53] Woolf, *Reading History*, pp. 1–5; see chs. 5 and 6.   [54] Griffin, *Playing the Past*, pp. 144–45.
[55] For archaism as a deliberate style and publishing strategy, see Lucy Munro, *Archaic Style in English Literature, 1590–1674* (Cambridge: Cambridge University Press, 2013).
[56] Marta Straznicky, 'Introduction: Plays, Books, and the Public Sphere', in *Book of the Play*, ed. Straznicky, pp. 1–20 (p. 4).

documents and records of a particular past or drawing significantly on legendary traditions. This definition is informed by Kewes's proposal: '[i]f we want to understand the place and uses of history in early modern drama, we should be willing to consider any play, irrespective of its formal shape or fictional element, which represents, or purports to represent, a historical past'.[57] Of course, what constitutes a historical past is open to debate, and the criteria suggested by this study are by no means definitive. I consider plays to be dramatizing a recognizable past if their characters or events are connected to a written or oral historical tradition and have at one time been thought to have existed or taken place. These broad parameters include plays that dramatize the legendary British past, as in *Locrine* (1595) and *King Lear* (1608); biblical history, as in *The Love of David and Fair Bathsheba* (1599); popular quasi-historical figures, including Robin Hood and his followers (who were included in accounts such as John Leland's *Itinerary* (written *c.*1540s)); and real people and events through an allegorical design, as in *The Whore of Babylon* (1607) and *A Game at Chess* (1625). Although it could be argued that all plays dramatize some sort of past, whether 'true or fayned', this study does *not* consider as a 'history' those plays which show few signs of being linked to an identifiable historical account. I do not discuss plays that are merely set *in* the past as histories, or those which evoke a specific location and time but are not otherwise associated with external sources or traditions that suggest the events were once regarded as part of a common past.[58] For example, Marlowe's *Jew of Malta*, which is set within the broad context of historical battles over Spanish and Ottoman control of the island (including the siege of Malta in 1565), is not counted, because the main characters and events are not clearly part of another oral or written account of the past.

There are particular advantages to the way this study loosely outlines the parameters of the genre. It avoids the problems associated with other attempts at classification: it does not privilege Shakespeare's English histories, nor does it suggest that history plays can be identified by their subject, style, patterns of conclusion, title-page descriptions, or ideology. Instead, it closely approximates the hybrid generic status of 'history' during the period and the fact that early modern writers and readers habitually made comparisons across a range of texts dealing with different historical pasts. It is, however, only a starting point. Genre becomes meaningful

---

[57] Kewes, 'Elizabethan', p. 188.

[58] This approach differs, therefore, from the scope of Davis's *Renaissance Historical Fiction* (2011), which defines historical fiction as anything set in the past (see pp. 1–39).

when specific statements are made about it. The examples given in this introduction testify to the fact that writers and readers make their own decisions about genre. My definition offers a broad framework that helps to recover how specific readers have understood history and historical drama. Each of my chapters explores how publication agents have chosen to define and use history – and makes a clear statement about their 'set of interpretations'.[59] My approach allows the evidence of early modern participation to emerge more vividly than if it were viewed through a narrow template that might overlook, for example, a reader's interest in legendary histories alongside Tudor histories (a case study featured in Chapter 3); but it does not use this openness to eschew genre definitions and specificity. My emphasis is on the prevalence of multiple perspectives that sometimes overlap, diverge, fracture, and contradict, and attest to the diversity of the period's historical culture.

Print Contexts: Strategies of Selection

The vast majority of early modern history plays that have survived have done so because they were printed. Our access to history plays is substantially determined by the publication process and the strategies of selection that have motivated stationers' investment in them.[60] This process not only unequivocally affects the survival of plays from the commercial stages, it also, as Zachary Lesser has shown, reveals readings of them.[61] The stationers who invested in plays *speculated* (one of Lesser's key terms) on their meanings for readers and how they respond to trends in the book market. Stationers also *specialized* (another of Lesser's core concepts) in certain kinds of texts, such as sermons, law books, plays, music books, schoolbooks, or news pamphlets – to name just a few (loosely defined) categories.[62] Richard Tottell, for example, specialized in law books; John

---

[59] Colie, 'Genre-Systems', p. 8.

[60] David McInnis and Matthew Steggle estimate that around 3,000 different plays were written and performed between 1567 and 1642 and, of these, approximately 543 are extant and 744 are 'identifiable as lost'. See McInnis and Steggle, 'Introduction: *Nothing* Will Come of Nothing? Or, What Can We Learn from Plays That Don't Exist?', in *Lost Plays in Shakespeare's England*. ed. David McInnis and Matthew Steggle (Basingstoke: Palgrave Macmillan, 2014), pp. 1–14 (p. 1).

[61] Zachary Lesser, *Renaissance Drama and the Politics of Publication: Readings in the English Book Trade* (Cambridge: Cambridge University Press, 2004), pp. 1–9.

[62] For his discussion of these two terms, see *Renaissance Drama*, ch. 1. They were used earlier by Peter Blayney in 'The Publication of Playbooks', in *A New History of Early English Drama*, ed. John D. Cox and David Scott Kastan (New York: Columbia University Press, 1997), pp. 383–422. For a short overview of specialization, see also Kirk Melnikoff, *Elizabethan Publishing and the Makings of Literary Culture* (Toronto: University of Toronto Press, 2018), pp. 70–76.

Day specialized in Protestant texts; and Matthew Law, during the early Jacobean period, specialized in texts by William Barlow. Publication involves an assessment of categories and belonging – which is one of the reasons why the actions of stationers provide an important point of entry for a study of the history play.[63] When stationers invest capital in a play, they make a decision about its meaning; they assess how it responds to their other publications and dominant specialisms; and they speculate how other readers will engage with it. These strategies of selection are not often visible in the playbooks themselves. But an analysis of patterns in the book trade and of stationers' published outputs helps to recover these strategies and reveal evidence of how 'real historical readers', rather than the ideal, implied readers of reader-response criticism, engaged with history plays.[64]

A pressing issue for this study is identifying which agents connected to the publication process controlled the transmission and preparation of plays from the stage as printed books. Ultimately, this question needs to be considered on a case-by-case basis, but a few general points can still be offered.[65] A play's dramatist(s) and/or the company that performed and owned the script sometimes collaborated in its publication and acted as overseers of the process. Ben Jonson regularly contributed signed paratexts to his playbooks – in, for example, *Sejanus* ('To the Readers', 1605) and *The Alchemist* (in his dedication to Lady Mary Wroth, 1612) – that announce his involvement. Shakespeare's First Folio contains a dedication and address from members of the King's Men – John Heminges and Henry Condell – that outline the company's role in providing 'True Originall Copies' for the collection (A1r). However, as Joseph Loewenstein and others have shown, these instances were more the exception than the norm, especially during the late sixteenth and early seventeenth centuries.[66] Most playbooks from the commercial stages do not indicate the direct involvement of dramatists or companies. For this reason, these agents do not occupy a central position in my study, which

---

[63] See also Farmer and Lesser, who describe 'categorizing books [as] an inherently critical exercise' (p. 22) in 'What Is Print Popularity? A Map of the Elizabethan Book Trade', in *The Elizabethan Top Ten: Defining Print Popularity in Early Modern England*, ed. Andy Kesson and Emma Smith (Farnham: Ashgate, 2013), pp. 19–54 (pp. 22–23).

[64] Jennifer Richards and Fred Schurink, 'The Textuality and Materiality of Reading in Early Modern England', *Huntington Library Quarterly*, 73:3 (2010), 345–61 (p. 346).

[65] For early Tudor drama, see Atkin (*Reading Drama*, p. 104), who argues that 'author–publisher–printer relationships resist systematic categorization; the arrangements between playwrights and stationers are likely to have varied from person to person, and might even have varied from text to text'.

[66] See Joseph Loewenstein, *Ben Jonson and Possessive Authorship* (Cambridge: Cambridge University Press, 2002), ch. 2.

is primarily concerned with the publication of history plays as printed books. Indeed, irrespective of whether dramatists and companies assisted in the process or stationers acted independently, publication remained a stationer-controlled enterprise. The Stationers' Company protected the activities of its members: only stationers could enter texts in the Register and hold the rights to them.[67] Even if dramatists (such as Jonson) or companies (such as the Chamberlain's Men) played a role in the publication of their plays, stationers were still responsible for the final decision on whether or not to invest in a play and how, in light of their knowledge of the book trade, to market it.

The significant influence stationers had over the publication of play-books has often been considered pejoratively or dismissively. New Bibliography aimed, in Fredson Bowers's phrase, to 'strip the veil of print' to access underlying 'authorial' playscripts, thereby relegating the role of stationers to mere transmitters of plays, who were often denigrated as unscrupulous and incompetent.[68] New Bibliographers, including W. W. Greg, R. B. McKerrow, and Alfred W. Pollard, tended to assert that stationers had an antagonistic relationship with dramatists and companies, and that they published stolen or reconstructed plays without the consent of their authors.[69] Thanks to the work of textual scholars over the past thirty years or so, these views have started to change. Rather than framing stationers as meddling, piratical, or underhand in their acquisition and transformation of texts, critics including D. F. McKenzie, Peter Blayney, Zachary Lesser, Alan Farmer, Sonia Massai, Lukas Erne, Marta Straznicky, Adam Hooks, Tamara Atkin, and Kirk Melnikoff have shown that the actions of stationers in the publication of drama were in line with the

---

[67] Blayney, 'Publication', pp. 390–99; Loewenstein, *Possessive Authorship*, ch. 1. For a history of the Stationers' Company and its practices, see Cyndia Susan Clegg, 'The Stationers' Company of London', in *The British Literary Book Trade, 1475–1700*, ed. James K. Bracken and Joel Silver, Dictionary of Literary Biography, vol. 170 (Detroit: Gale Research, 1996), pp. 275–91. See also Blayney, *The Stationers' Company and the Printers of London, 1501–1557*, 2 vols. (Cambridge: Cambridge University Press, 2013).

[68] Fredson Bowers, *On Editing Shakespeare and the Elizabethan Dramatists* (Philadelphia: University of Pennsylvania Library for the Philip H. and A. S. W. Rosenbach Foundation, 1955), p. 87.

[69] R. B. McKerrow, 'Booksellers, Printers, and the Stationers' Trade', in *Shakespeare's England: An Account of the Life and Manners of his Age*, 2 vols. (Oxford: Clarendon Press, 1916), II, pp. 212–39; Alfred W. Pollard, *Shakespeare's Fight with the Pirates and the Problems of the Transmission of His Text* (London: Alexander Moring, 1917); W. W. Greg, *Some Aspects and Problems of London Publishing between 1550 and 1650* (Oxford: Clarendon Press, 1956). For a dismissal of the players' alleged opposition to print, see Lukas Erne, *Shakespeare As Literary Dramatist*, 2nd ed. (Cambridge: Cambridge University Press, 2013), ch. 5.

normal operations of the book trade.[70] From a critical perspective, it is increasingly problematic to seek lost 'authorial' manuscripts and remove the mediation of the print process. Stationers are important collaborators in the construction of meaning: they speculate on how a text could be read (Lesser); they act as correctors and annotating readers who edit the text itself (Massai); and they create bibliographical and biographical identities for the dramatists they publish (Hooks). As this study explores, they also played a crucial role in assessing genre – an act that discloses their own readings of history plays and directs the readings of others.

Peter Blayney's seminal essay 'The Publication of Playbooks' helped to change the field by clarifying the different roles played by stationers in the publication process and the influence they had over the presentation of texts, which are important for me to summarize at the outset. 'Stationer' is an umbrella term that applies to those involved in book production or, more exclusively, to members of the Stationers' Company. As outlined by Blayney, the most influential agent is the publisher – a somewhat anachronistic term for the period, but which has recently featured prominently and productively within book history studies.[71] Stationers generally identified themselves as printers (who were responsible for producing the material texts) or booksellers (who were responsible for selling them). As Blayney observes, 'the early modern book trade had no separate word for what we now call a publisher', because 'publishing was not usually thought of as a profession'.[72] It is possible and, indeed, essential for modern critics to identify the stationer who, by investing, 'caused the text to be printed' and therefore acted as its publisher.[73] This identification is made possible by entries in the Stationers' Register (where the rights to titles are assigned to specific stationers) and/or by the texts' imprints (which provide publication details). For example, the 1597 edition (STC 22307) of *Richard II* claims that the play was 'Printed by Valentine Simmes for Andrew Wise',

---

[70] McKenzie, *Bibliography and the Sociology of Texts* (Cambridge: Cambridge University Press 1999); Blayney, 'Publication'; Lesser, *Renaissance Drama*; Farmer and Lesser, 'The Popularity of Playbooks Revisited', *Shakespeare Quarterly*, 56:1 (2005), 1–32; Massai, *Shakespeare and the Rise of the Editor* (Cambridge: Cambridge University Press, 2007); Erne, *Shakespeare and the Book Trade* (Cambridge: Cambridge University Press, 2013); Straznicky (ed.), *Shakespeare's Stationers: Studies in Cultural Bibliography* (Philadelphia: University of Pennsylvania Press, 2013); Hooks, *Selling Shakespeare: Biography, Bibliography, and the Book Trade* (Cambridge: Cambridge University Press, 2016); Atkin, *Reading Drama*; and Melnikoff, *Elizabethan Publishing*.

[71] See, for example, Hooks, *Selling Shakespeare*; Lesser, *Renaissance Drama*; Massai, *Rise of the Editor*; Melnikoff, *Elizabethan Publishing*.

[72] Blayney, 'Publication', p. 391.

[73] Laurie E. Maguire, 'The Craft of Printing (1600)', in *A Companion to Shakespeare*, ed. David Scott Kastan (Oxford: Blackwell, 1999), pp. 434–49 (p. 435).

which follows a common descriptive formula for imprints. It indicates that Simmes printed the text and Wise acted as the publisher, and is further corroborated by the Stationers' Register entry to Wise (dated 29 August 1597).[74] Wise was, by profession, a bookseller (he did not own a printing press) and, in addition to investing in the play, he stocked copies of *Richard II* for individual and wholesale purchase in his shop at the Sign of the Angel in Paul's Cross Churchyard. When booksellers or places of purchase are given in imprints, they usually indicate wholesale locations where copies of the edition could be purchased by other booksellers and individual readers. The same play could be traded and sold by booksellers throughout London, across the country, and further afield. The wholesale location was, nevertheless, the most important one for facilitating this exchange and was a permanent part of the book through the imprint.

In the case of *Richard II*, the *role* of the publisher was taken on by the wholesaler, Wise, rather than the printer, Simmes; but printers could act as publishers and, in theory, all three roles of printer, publisher, and bookseller could be undertaken by the same individual. These three key terms are more accurately function-specific, than agent-specific. The incorporation of the Stationers' Company in 1557 and the introduction of decrees that limited the number of master printers and new presses, however, pushed many printers into working for others as trade printers (meaning they did not invest capital in the texts themselves). By the end of the sixteenth century, the role of the publisher was most often taken on by booksellers, rather than printers – indeed, Melnikoff proposes the term 'bookselling publisher' to highlight their influence and ubiquity.[75] Printers still did act as publishers and some, including Thomas Creede and John Danter, switched between working as a printer-for-hire and a printer-publisher, a variation in their role that is indicated by imprints and entries in the Register. For example, the imprint in *Locrine* ('Printed by Thomas Creede', 1595; STC 21528) and corresponding Register entry suggest that Creede printed and published the play, whereas he acted as trade printer for *The First Part of the Contention Between the Two Famous Houses of York and Lancaster* ('Printed by Thomas Creed, for Thomas Millington', 1594; STC 26099).[76] Akihiro Yamada's monograph on Creede remains the most detailed study of his output to date, but it does not distinguish between

---

[74] SRO3977; Arber, III, p. 89.   [75] Melnikoff, *Elizabethan Publishing*, pp. 17–19.
[76] *Locrine* (STC 21528) is entered in the Register to Creede (SRO3644; Arber, II, p. 656), whereas *The First Part of the Contention* (STC 26099) is entered to Millington (SRO3582; Arber, II, p. 646).

Creede's work as a trade printer and as a printer-publisher.[77] In this study, I follow Lesser and others in suggesting that an understanding of stationers' selection strategies can most securely be reached when their *published* output is assessed (rather than their total output). The collaborative nature of the book trade and the networks that exist between printers and booksellers sometimes, however, make it difficult to untangle the roles performed by different individuals. The printers William and Isaac Jaggard (who occasionally acted as publishers) and bookseller Thomas Pavier worked together on the 1619 so-called Pavier Quartos (which I rename, in Chapter 4, the Jaggard–Pavier collection). It is not clear who took on the lead role in this venture, including who was the main investor and who directed the appearance of the playbooks. The concept of a publishing syndicate or collaborative network of exchange is a useful one when it is difficult to prise apart agency in the publication of plays.

Whether the role of the publisher was taken on by printers or booksellers, or was entangled within a network, stationers who invest in plays – or, indeed, in any text – are in the business of specializing in different 'kinds'. Although these specialisms were rarely declared through, for example, discursive paratexts, a contrastive analysis of publishers' outputs reveals them. An evaluation of bookseller Nathaniel Butter's extant output (discussed at length in Chapter 3) shows that he was a major publisher of topical pamphlets and newsbooks alongside history plays, and suggests that his investment in plays such as *King Lear* (1608) and *The Whore of Babylon* (1607) can – and should – be understood in relation to his non-dramatic output. For Butter, these are plays that engage with topical issues of church and state and blur the temporal distinctions between different 'pasts' in the service of contemporarily focused readings. Stationers' *strategies of selection*, as this study argues, not only determine the survival of many early modern texts but also help to reveal an evaluation of genre and a reading of the texts themselves.

Print Paratexts: Strategies of Presentation

Stationers not only chose which history plays to invest in, they also directed the plays' presentation as books and shaped their content. They oversaw the incorporation of print paratexts – one of the main textual sites in which readings of history plays can be witnessed. Genette brought the

---

[77] Akihiro Yamada, *Thomas Creede: Printer to Shakespeare and His Contemporaries* (Tokyo: Meisei University Press, 1994).

term 'paratext' into critical use, describing it as 'the means by which a text makes a book of itself and proposes itself as such to its readers, and more generally to the public'.[78] In this study, I primarily use the term to refer to the new print features that surround the main play and can include title pages, dedicatory epistles, addresses to readers, commendatory verses, actor and character lists, and contents pages (for collections). Because they carried the financial risk of the investment, publishers probably exerted the greatest influence on a text's presentation in print, including the *incorporation* of paratexts. A number of individuals may have participated in their *composition*, including the publisher, but also, in some cases, the play's dramatists, printers, and other writers. This section briefly considers some of these paratextual categories, the readings they offer, and the agency behind them.

Most readers first encountered history plays through their title pages, which were also used, as Tiffany Stern discusses, as advertisements that were pasted around the stalls, posts, and walls of a city.[79] Title pages needed to provide a snapshot of the texts they prefaced and, as satirized in Thomas Nashe's *Terrors of the Night* (1594), some early modern book browsers looked no further:

> [A] number of you there bee, who consider neither premisses nor conclusion, but piteouslie torment Title Pages on euerie poast; neuer reading farther of anie Booke, than Imprinted by Simeon such a signe, and yet with your dudgen iudgements will desperatelie presume to run vp to the hard hilts through the whole bulke of it.[80]

Rushed, inattentive reading did not stop book browsers from having opinions about certain texts, and the same goes for the agents who contributed to title pages, whose reading practices could vary between careful consideration of a play's content and quick 'position-takings', to adopt Pierre Bourdieu's phrase.[81] These key promotional materials often feature a main title, a short description of a few plot highlights or commentary, an ornament, and an imprint giving details of the stationers

---

[78] See Gérard Genette, 'Introduction to the Paratext', trans. Marie Maclean, *New Literary History*, 22:2 (1991), 261–72. Genette (pp. 263–64) also distinguishes between 'peritext' (the elements that surround the actual text in the same volume) and 'epitext' (the 'messages' that are situated outside the book, including relevant letters, correspondence, and interviews).

[79] Tiffany Stern, '"On each Wall and Corner Poast": Playbills, Title-pages, and Advertising in Early Modern London', *English Literary Renaissance*, 36:1 (2006), 57–89.

[80] Thomas Nashe, *The Terrors of the night* (London, 1594; STC 18379), A4r.

[81] Pierre Bourdieu, *The Field of Cultural Production: Essays on Art and Literature*, ed. Randal Johnson (Cambridge: Polity, 1993), p. 30.

involved in the edition. Some title pages also contain attributions to dramatists and to theatre companies and performance spaces. Many of these features have implications for understanding, categorizing, and reading history plays.

Most title pages include some kind of genre label, as in *The First Part of the Tragical Reign of Selimus* (1594) or *The Chronicle History of Perkin Warbeck* (1634). As mentioned already, these labels rarely offer consistent or precise statements about dramatic genres, but they sometimes encourage certain ways of reading the plays. For example, Peter Berek suggests that the label 'tragedy' is regularly (but not always) used during the sixteenth century to indicate the death of a character – historical or fictional – who behaves badly.[82] In Chapter 3, I propose that 'Chronicle History' is used during the early Jacobean period to promote the 'truth-fulness' of the play's subject, a pattern influenced by James I's interest in legendary British history. The plot descriptions or commentaries included on title pages also offer readings of the histories they contain; they are often, as Lesser proposes, the earliest examples of literary criticism for a play.[83] *The Valiant Welshman* (1615) has an extended title which describes it, approvingly, as 'The Trve Chronicle History of the life and valiant deedes, of Caradoc the Great, King of Cambria, now called Wales'.[84] The summary directs attention towards a monarchical figurehead, implying that the actions featured in this history are worthy of remembrance, celebration, and emulation.

Title pages sometimes include woodcut ornaments that carry interpretative significance for the history they preface. Creede's signature device showing the figure of Truth informs the reading of history plays from Queen Elizabeth's Men, a company that has become associated with the promotion of royalist and Protestant sympathies (discussed in detail in Chapter 1). As another example, the second edition of the anonymous play *Jack Straw* contains a striking woodcut (McKerrow #345) that displays publisher Thomas Pavier's initials and an image of a labourer with the inscription 'Thov shalt labor till thov retvrne to dvste' (see Figure 0.1).[85] While this woodcut is, as Hooks discusses, intended to be a paviour and thus recall Pavier's own name, I believe it takes on additional political

---

[82] Berek, 'Genres', p. 171.   [83] Lesser, *Renaissance Drama*, p. 8.
[84] Anon./'R.A.', *The Valiant Welshman* (London, 1615; STC 16), A2r.
[85] *The Life and death of Iacke Straw* (London, 1604; STC 23357), A1r. See Ronald B. McKerrow, *Printers' and Publishers' Devices in England and Scotland, 1485–1640* (London: Printed for the Bibliographical Society at the Chiswick Press, 1913), p. 134.

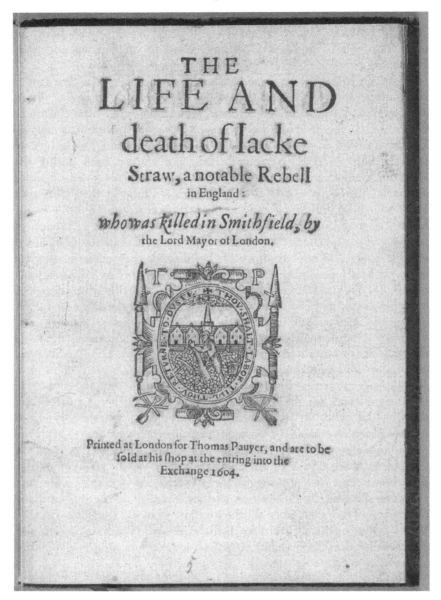

Figure 0.1   Title page from *Jack Straw* (Q2 1604; STC 23357).

significance in a history play about the Peasants' Revolt of 1381.[86] It recalls the plight of the workers, and the inscription seems to reflect directly on their hardships, prompting a reading that is sympathetic to their uprising against Richard II.[87]

The various attributions that appear on playbook title pages also have implications for the history play. By naming specific dramatists, companies, patrons, and stationers, playbooks associate these individuals and their reputations with the content of the history. Attributions to the Queen's Men in history playbooks published by Creede connect these plays to Elizabeth I and her authorizing influence as reigning monarch. The consistent appearance of Shakespeare's name on playbooks published by Andrew Wise in the late 1590s advances his print identity as a dramatist of English monarchical history (discussed in Chapter 2). Nathaniel Butter's prominent advertising of his own name and bookshop location in title-page imprints helps to establish his reputation as a well-known bookseller in Paul's Churchyard, which, in turn, could also direct the ways in which readers responded to his histories (discussed in Chapter 3).

Determining who was responsible for the different components of playbook title pages remains a matter of speculation and varies from play to play.[88] Title pages are a site of multiple agency and authorship. Stern suggests that dramatists and theatrical companies were involved in the preparation of title pages, arguing that these paratexts resemble the playbills that were used to advertise performances.[89] If playbills did shape title-page content, they would still need to be edited and updated to take proper advantage of the new medium in which plays were being presented. No title page would exactly reproduce the content of a playbill, which was designed to advertise a specific performance. Final decisions relating to title-page presentation were probably, therefore, the reserve of stationers. Farmer and Lesser take this position and clarify agency even further, claiming, as does Erne, that the 'responsibility for designing a book's title page typically fell to its publisher'.[90] Blayney has examined the connection between a rare example of an extant manuscript title page, prepared during

---

[86] Hooks, *Selling*, p. 118.

[87] See also Stephen Schillinger, 'Begging at the Gate: *Jack Straw* and the Acting Out of Popular Rebellion', *Medieval & Renaissance Drama in England*, 21 (2008), 87–127 (pp. 89–91).

[88] See also Helen Smith and Louise Wilson, 'Introduction', in *Renaissance Paratexts*, ed. Helen Smith and Louise Wilson (Cambridge: Cambridge University Press, 2011), pp. 1–14.

[89] Stern, 'Playbills', pp. 80–87.

[90] Alan B. Farmer and Zachary Lesser, 'Vile Arts: The Marketing of English Printed Drama, 1512–1660', *Research Opportunities in Renaissance Drama*, 39 (2000), 77–165 (p. 78). In *Literary Dramatist*, Erne claims that the title page is 'usually the publisher's rather than the writer's' (p. 60).

the publication of *Scala Coeli: Nineteen Sermons Concerning Prayer* (1611; STC 605), and the final printed version. Revealingly, the manuscript is in the hand of the text's publisher, Francis Burton, which intimates his agency in its design.[91] We should not, however, expect practices to be uniform for all stationers and I depart slightly from Blayney and other critics by suggesting that different agents – including trade printers – could have played important roles in the design of title pages. Ornaments, *mise en page*, and even some of the title-page descriptions may have been determined by the printer hired to manufacture the book. A quick comparison between two plays published by the same stationer but produced by different printing houses tends to reveal different design practices (see, for example, Wise's publications of *Richard II* (1597), printed by Valentine Simmes, and Q2 *Richard III* (1598), printed by Thomas Creede). These contributions could be significant and, in Chapter 2, I propose that the first appearance of Shakespeare's name on a playbook title page could have been the decision of a trade printer striving to distinguish between two history plays about similar subject matter.

Dedications, addresses to readers, and commendatory verses also reflect to some degree on a play's contents and offer a framework for reading it. Unlike title pages, many (but not all) of these paratexts were signed, making it possible to identify the individual responsible. One significant example of a publisher's paratext appears in Marlowe's *Tamburlaine* (1590), which features a dedication from stationer Richard Jones to the 'Gentlemen readers' who 'take pleasure in reading Histories'.[92] Not only is this, as far as I have identified, the first paratextual address ever to be affixed to a commercial playbook, it is also emphatic about the influential role taken on by a text's publisher in preparing the edition:

> I haue (purposely) omitted and left out some fond and friuolous Iestures, digressing (and in my poore opinion) far vnmeet for the matter, which I thought, might seeme more tedious vnto the wise, than any way els to be regarded, though (happily) they haue bene of some vaine conceited fondlings greatly gaped at, what times they were shewed vpon the stage (A2r).[93]

---

[91] Peter W. M. Blayney, *The Texts of 'King Lear' and Their Origins, Volume I: Nicholas Okes and the First Quarto* (Cambridge: Cambridge University Press, 1982), pp. 259–62. The manuscript is held in the Public Record Office (SP.14.48, art. 15).

[92] Christopher Marlowe, *Tamburlaine the Great* (London, 1590; STC 17425), A2r.

[93] In 1578, Jones published *1* and *2 Promos and Cassandra*, which also contain an address contributed by him. The theatrical origins of these plays are uncertain, so this playbook could offer an earlier example than *Tamburlaine*; but in either case, the precedent is established by Jones.

Jones (who acted as the printer, publisher, and bookseller for this edition) positions himself as an active reader and editor who has transformed Marlowe's plays as they were performed on stage and adapted them to suit a projected image of his reading public. The epistle, as Melnikoff explores, makes a sharp distinction between the stage and print versions of *Tamburlaine*.[94] Although Jones's claims of improvement cannot be securely confirmed or dismissed because no earlier version of the play is extant, his address implies that reading plays – especially those based on the past – is a serious and profitable activity for 'Gentlemen Readers'. His playbook also demonstrates the fluidity and hybridity of genre labels. *Tamburlaine* is loosely based on the fourteenth-century Turco-Mongol conqueror Timur or Tamerlane (1336–1405). Jones associates *Tamburlaine* with the 'Histories' enjoyed by 'Gentlemen Readers' in his preface (A2r), but the title page describes the plays as 'two Tragicall Discourses' (A1r) and the Stationers' Register entry on 14 August 1590 records them as 'the twooe commicall discourses of Tomberlein'.[95] As Tara L. Lyons proposes, the labels that appear in the playbook itself – 'Tragicall Discourses' and 'Histories' – could position the plays in the *de casibus* tradition where the central character's ambition is ultimately humbled and the history offered to readers for moral instruction.[96]

Interestingly, the first dramatist's paratext to reflect on 'history' as a genre appeared in 1606, years after the supposed heyday of the history play during the 1590s. *The Wonder of Women, or the Tragedy of Sophonisba* contains a signed address to the reader (see Figure 0.2) from John Marston that is alert to the distinctions between poetry and history explored by writers such as Sidney:

> Know, that I haue not labored in this poeme, to tie my selfe to relate any thing as an historian but to inlarge euery thing as a Poet, To transcribe Authors, quote authorities, and translate Latin prose orations into English bla[n]ck-verse, hath in this subiect beene the least aime of my studies.[97]

Marston seems anxious that readers might object to the 'invention' that is part of his classical history based on the Carthaginian princess Sophonisba.

---

[94] Kirk Melnikoff, 'Jones's Pen and Marlowe's Socks: Richard Jones, Print Culture, and the Beginnings of English Dramatic Literature', *Studies in Philology*, 102:2 (2005), 184–209 (p. 187).

[95] SRO3094; Arber, II, p. 558.

[96] Tara L. Lyons, 'Richard Jones, *Tamburlaine the Great*, and the Making (and Remaking) of a Serial Play Collection in the 1590s', in *Christopher Marlowe, Theatrical Commerce and the Book Trade*, ed. Kirk Melnikoff and Roslyn L. Knutson (Cambridge: Cambridge University Press, 2018), pp. 149–64.

[97] John Marston, *The Wonder of Women, or the Tragedie of Sophonisba* (London, 1606; STC 17488), A2r.

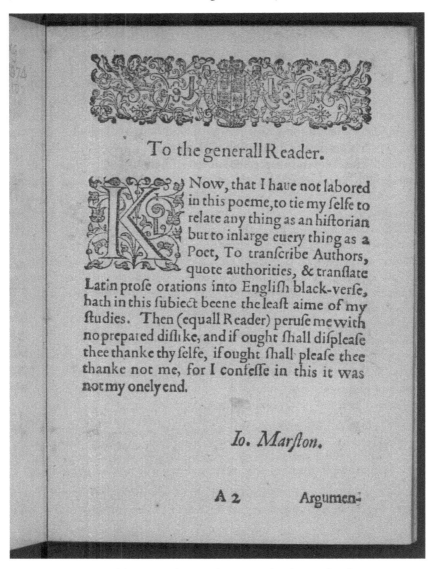

Figure 0.2   Address to readers in John Marston's *The Wonder of Women*
(1606; STC 17488), A2r.

According to his address, the role of the historian is to transcribe, translate, and quote authorities, rather than engage inventively with the events of the past – which instead marks out the terrain of a 'Poet'. Marston's concern about the truthfulness of his history echoes a similar refrain in the works of historians including John Hayward, quoted earlier, and Abraham Fleming (discussed in Chapter 1). Because this kind of paratextual statement was used so widely, it rather seems to underscore generic blurring and hybridity than establish clear distinctions between poets and historians. Instead, Marston uses Sidney's well-known – but primarily theoretical – divisions to advertise, in the form of an apology or defence, the superiority of his play (which 'inlarge[s] euery thing') over history (which ties down and limits).

The ways in which plays were bound together in stationers' shops – as planned and nonce collections – also make statements about genre and sometimes involve specially prepared paratexts. Shakespeare's First Folio and its contents page is perhaps the most influential example for modern criticism. Strikingly, this collection of commercial drama is the only one for the entire period to solidify history as a dramatic genre, which reveals how unrepresentative this publication venture actually is. In contrast, the contents page of Beaumont and Fletcher's 1647 Folio privileges the two classical genres, underscored further through the collection's title, *Comedies and Tragedies*. While they do not represent bound collections of plays, booksellers' catalogues – a number of which were published during the seventeenth century – advertise available stock, compile lists of the period's printed drama and other texts, and sometimes assign plays a generic category, usually indicated by a letter.[98] Edward Archer's 1656 catalogue (see Figure 0.3), for example, groups together Peele's *Edward I*, Marlowe's *Edward II*, the anonymous *Edward III*, and Heywood's *Edward IV* as tragedies ('T'), while Shakespeare's *1* and *2 Henry IV*, *Henry V*, *1–3 Henry VI*, and *Henry VIII* are histories ('H').[99] Characterized by idiosyncratic classifications, these catalogues highlight the mutability of genre labels to suit specific publishing agendas, which in this case might reflect the influence of Shakespeare's Folio classifications, as well as the plays' alphabetical ordering and proximity in the table. Together with other strategies of print presentation – involving title pages, discursive paratexts, and the preparation of collections – these materials contribute in important ways to the negotiation of the history play as a genre and reveal the central position of stationers in this construction.

Early Histories: The Example of *Gorboduc*

The strategies of selection and presentation outlined above did not emerge with the appearance of the first commercial plays in print, but developed

---

[98] For an account of publishers' catalogues, see Hooks, *Selling*, ch. 4.
[99] See *The Old Law* (M1048), a3r, a4r.

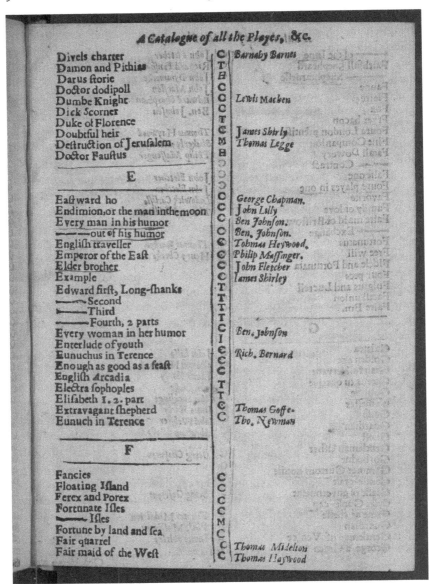

A Catalogue of all the Playes, &c.

Divels charter	C	Barnaby Barnes
Damon and Pithias	T	
Darus ftorie	H	
Doctor dodipoll	C	
Dumbe Knight	C	
Dick Scorner	C	Lewis Machen
Duke of Florence	T	
Doubtful heir	C	James Shirly
Deftruction of Jerufalem	M	Thomas Legge
Doctor Fauftus	H	

E

Eaftward ho	C	
Endimion, or the man in the moon	C	George Chapman.
Every man in his humor	C	John Lilly
————out of his humor	C	Ben Johnfon.
Englifh traveller	C	Ben, Johnfon.
Emperor of the Eaft	C	Tobmas Heywood,
Elder brother	C	Philip Maffinger.
Example	C	John Fletcher
Edward firft, Long-fhanks	T	James Shirley
————Second	T	
————Third	T	
————Fourth, 2 parts	T	
Every woman in her humor	C	Ben, Johnfon
Enterlude of youth	I	
Eunuchus in Terence	C	Rich, Bernard
Enough as good as a feaft	C	
Englifh Arcadia	C	
Electra fophoples	T	
Elifabeth 1. 2. part	T	Thomas Goffe.
Extravagant fhepherd	C	Tho. Newman
Eunuch in Terence	C	

F

Fancies	C	
Floating Ifland	C	
Ferex and Porex	C	
Fortunate Ifles	C	
————Ifles	M	
Fortune by land and fea	C	
Fair quarrel	C	Thomas Midelton
Fair maid of the Weft	C	Thomas Haywood

Figure 0.3   Page from Edward Archer's catalogue, appended to *The Old Law* (1656; Wing M1048), a3r.

through the publication of pre-playhouse and non-commercial plays. As Atkin proposes, 'well before the opening of London's commercial theatres' early printers of plays '[made] drama legible as a distinct category of text' – a process that has crucial implications for understanding how stationers shaped the history play as a print genre.[100] *Gorboduc*, an Inns of Court play written by Thomas Norton and Thomas Sackville, provides a useful opening example for this study. The play dramatizes the reign of the ancient British king Gorboduc and the disorder and destruction ensuing from his attempt to divide Britain between his two sons, Ferrex and Porrex. These events feature in Tudor chronicles (such as Holinshed), and although the historicity of these legendary pasts was challenged during the sixteenth century, they were still considered by many to be accurate accounts of early British history.[101] *Gorboduc* was first performed in the Inner Temple on Twelfth Night 1562 and at Whitehall on 18 January 1562 at Elizabeth I's command and was printed in three editions in the sixteenth century – 1565, *c.*1570, and 1590 – the second of which contains an address by its printer-publisher, John Day. This 1570 edition, which retitles the play *The Tragedy of Ferrex and Porrex*, is especially revealing for my purposes. It displays, as Atkin identifies, a dual interest in the play's status as a *performed* history (by advertising, on its title page, the royal audience it received) and as a *book* to be read, underlined through its paratextual materials.[102] These two, potentially competing, authorizing strategies would be variously taken up by later publishers of commercial plays. Day's edition reveals how he attempted to direct an understanding of the play, the history it offers, and its position as a book, particularly through his address to readers and by binding *Gorboduc* with a selection of non-dramatic texts.

This new paratext, 'The P[rinter] to the Reader' (A2r), is the very first address written by a stationer to appear in any English playbook (Jones's address in *Tamburlaine* is the first for a commercial play).[103] As Atkin identifies, discursive paratexts started to become common in playbooks

---

[100] Atkin, *Reading Drama*, p. 3.

[101] See Kim Gilchrist, *Staging Britain's Past: Pre-Roman Britain in Early Modern Drama* (London: Bloomsbury Arden, 2021).

[102] Atkin, *Reading Drama*, p. 94. The title page describes the play as 'the same [as] was shewed on stage before the Queenes Maiestie, about nine years past, *vz.* the xviij. [18] day of Ianuarie. 1561 by the gentlemen of the Inner Temple'. See Thomas Norton and Thomas Sackville, *The Tragidie of Ferrex and Porrex* (London, [1570]; STC 18685), A1r.

[103] When the heading 'The P. to the Reader' is encountered, the abbreviation should be expanded to 'printer', because the terminological distinction between printer and publisher had not yet stabilized. However, such addresses were usually written by the individual taking on the role of publisher, often distinct from the individual undertaking the printing (although not in the case of Day). See Maguire, 'Craft', p. 435.

after the publication of Jasper Heywood's translation of Seneca's *Troas* in 1559 and tended to mark out plays as either translations of classical or continental drama or as having connections with the Inns of Court or the universities – in other words, those with academic associations.[104] Day's address condemns the play's first edition, published in 1565 by 'W. G.' (William Griffith), and admonishes Griffith for procuring a copy of the text from some unscrupulous 'yongmans hand' and putting it forward in an 'excedingly corrupted' state. Day vividly compares the maligned printing of *Gorboduc* to the defiling of a 'faire maide', who is left 'beraryed and disfigured', unrecognizable to those who knew her previously (A2r). In this case, Day's accusations of textual piracy are a marketing strategy designed to promote the new edition: his text of the play does not differ significantly from Griffith's edition. Strikingly, Day does not refer to either dramatist on the title page of his edition, despite the prominence he affords to their authorizing function in the prefatory address and their central position on Griffith's title page, which even specifies the contributions made by Norton and Sackville.[105] It is, instead, Day's authority that is most conspicuous in his edition, the title page displaying his name in large type and all other authorizing references remaining vague, including the description that the play has been 'Seen and allowed &c' (A1r). As Douglas Brooks argues, Day's primary purpose is 'the re-embodiment and commodification of a playtext that had already been printed and marketed by someone else', an approach adopted by later publications, including Shakespeare's First Folio, which claims it was 'Published according to the True Originall Copies' and not the 'diuerse stolne, and surreptitious copies' that had appeared previously (1623; A1r, A3r).[106] Above all, Day's address draws attention to *his* agency in the publication process and his control over reader reception.

Day's wider output further clarifies how he read *Gorboduc* and highlights the new meanings a play could acquire throughout its reception history. While the first performances of the play were seen, by one playgoer, to reflect on Elizabeth I's marital prospects, the play's publication introduced new interpretive imperatives.[107] Day's edition appeared on the London bookstalls shortly after the Northern Rebellion of 1569, which

[104] Atkin, *Reading Drama*, pp. 8, 15.
[105] On the 1565 title page (STC 18684, A1r), Griffith specifies that 'three Actes were wrytten by Thomas Nortone, and the two laste by Thomas Sackuyle'.
[106] Douglas A. Brooks, *From Playhouse to Printing House: Drama and Authorship in Early Modern England* (Cambridge: Cambridge University Press, 2000), p. 35; see also pp. 27–37.
[107] An Elizabethan courtier, Robert Beale, saw the play as favouring Robert Dudley, earl of Leicester, as Elizabeth's suitor. See his testimony quoted in Greg Walker, *The Politics of Performance in Early Renaissance Drama* (Cambridge: Cambridge University Press, 1998), ch. 6 (pp. 210–11).

saw the uprising of disaffected Catholic earls in the north of England. An influential stationer, Day was a supporter of Reformation politics: he was the printer and co-editor of John Foxe's *Acts and Monuments* (1563, 1570, 1576, 1583); he was protected by William Cecil and Robert Dudley; and he was Thomas Norton's primary publisher.[108] Norton, in addition to his contributions to *Gorboduc*, was a pamphleteer of the Elizabethan government against the Northern Rebellion, and Day printed some of these treatises, which he compiled, alongside *Gorboduc*, in a nonce collection – that is, a group of independently printed texts bound together by a stationer. The general title page for *All Such Treatises As Have Lately Been Published By Thomas Norton* ([1570]) describes the collection as 'Seen and allowed according to the order of the Queenes Injunctions' and it contains two pamphlets directly opposing the Rebellion: 'To the Queenes Maiesties poore deceiued subiects of the Northe countrey drawen into rebellion by the Earles of Northumberland and Westmerland' and 'A warning against the dangerous practises of the Papistes, and specially the parteners of the late Rebellion'.[109] By binding *Gorboduc* in this nonce collection and preparing a general contents page (see Figure 0.4) that lists the play and the treatises with their extended, descriptive titles, Day encourages a contemporarily focused, religio-political reading of the play that is attentive to the dangers of a divided nation (as Gorboduc instigates).[110]

The play, following its 1565 edition, is described as a tragedy on the title page, in the argument, and on the contents page, but this label does not reveal any clear distinction between history and tragedy (or between history and poetry) – a point which attracted Sidney's criticism of *Gorboduc* in his *Defence*.[111] Rather, the use of 'tragedy' seems to emphasize its position as an admonitory play, which is also a theme of Day's paratextual address, urging readers to harbour and protect the previously violated text. By the mid-sixteenth century, this genre label frequently accompanied dramatic and non-dramatic texts that consider the story of a

---

[108] John N. King, 'John Day: Master Printer of the English Reformation', in *The Beginnings of English Protestantism*, ed. Peter Marshall and Alec Ryrie (Cambridge: Cambridge University Press, 2002), pp. 180–208.

[109] Thomas Norton, *All such treatises as haue been lately published by Thomas Norton* (London, [1570]; STC 18677), title page r–v. Publication date from STC.

[110] *All Such Treatises* is, in fact, the first printed collection containing a play to include a general list of contents (see Appendix), which is advertised on the title page: 'the titles whereof appeare in the next side'.

[111] Sidney praises *Gorboduc*, but claims that 'it is verie defective in the circumstances, which greeues mee, because it might not remaine as an exact moddell of all Tragidies' (H4r).

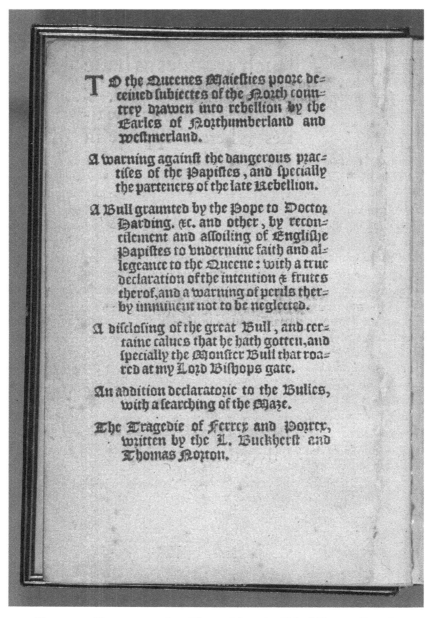

Figure 0.4   Contents page from Thomas Norton's *All Such Treatises* ([1570];
STC 18677).

fall and, as Berek proposes, it 'seems to be a mediating term in the process by which English readers come to see something that can be called English history as part of the same narrative as Continental history, biblical history, and the history of Greece and Rome'.[112] 'Tragedy' can be seen to authorize English/early British history in print. The collection's contents page spatially and thematically connects this approved history with topical political treatises to suggest that the volume as a whole is interested in the containment of rebellion.[113] All of these factors – the timing of Day's edition of *Gorboduc*, his reputation as a publisher, his contribution of a new prefatory address, and his inclusion of the play within a collection that promotes Elizabeth's authority – provide evidence of how he read this early British history and understood its connection to contemporary politics. As printed books, history plays could be used in analogous ways to political treatises and non-dramatic accounts of the past – and they could, as *Gorboduc* shows, authorize this use through advertising their performance auspices *and* their status as a book.

When commercial drama started to be published during the 1580s, very few playbooks contained discursive paratexts. Jones's practices in *Tamburlaine* (1590) were not representative, and most playbooks had limited prefatory material, often only a title page.[114] It was not until the late Jacobean and early Caroline period that playbooks from the commercial stages regularly included dedications, addresses to readers, and commendatory verses.[115] The publication history of pre-playhouse plays suggests that these materials became, during the late Elizabethan period, associated with non-commercial plays (specifically translations and those from the Inns of Court and universities) and that plays from the commercial theatres became legible in print by, as Atkin argues, underlining their status as *plays* – an issue that is explored in Chapter 1.[116] For this reason, understanding how stationers marketed, read, and shaped history plays from the commercial stages depends primarily on an assessment of strategies of selection (with reference to publishers' wider outputs) and the presentation of title pages as the main playbook paratext. The discursive

---

[112] Peter Berek, 'Tragedy and Title Pages: Nationalism, Protestantism, and Print', *Modern Philology*, 106:1 (2008), 1–24 (p. 7). See also David Bevington, 'Tragedy in Shakespeare's Career', in *The Cambridge Companion to Shakespearean Tragedy*, ed. Claire McEachern (Cambridge: Cambridge University Press, 2003), 50–68.

[113] See also Jaecheol Kim, 'The North–South Divide in *Gorboduc*: Fratricide Remembered', *Studies in Philology*, 111:4 (2014), 691–719 (pp. 699–701).

[114] Melnikoff, 'Jones's Pen', p. 189.   [115] See Conclusion, pp. 232–38.

[116] Atkin, *Reading Drama*, p. 69.

paratexts that Melnikoff examines in his recent study of dramatic and non-dramatic 'literary culture' or David Bergeron considers in his study on textual patronage are simply not available or representative for the majority of commercial playbooks published in the Elizabethan and Jacobean periods.[117] This absence does not, however, mean that stationers did not evaluate and respond to history as a dramatic genre, but that critics need to look elsewhere for the evidence.

Publishing the History Play in the Time of Shakespeare

This book consists of four main case studies spanning the Elizabethan and Jacobean periods, which overlap with Shakespeare's lifetime and the years, following his death, when the Folio was prepared and published. By concentrating on the conditions of textual production during the lifetime of the dramatist with whom the history play has been most closely associated, this book reveals how publication agents constructed and defined the genre and the implications of these strategies for modern criticism. It retains an interest in Shakespeare's *oeuvre*, because of the need, as Helen Smith proposes, to 'restore Shakespeare's early texts to the contexts of the bookstalls on which they first appeared', a process that clarifies the position of his 'histories' (broadly defined) and the plays of other dramatists within the period's historical culture.[118] In doing so, this book takes the case-study approach forward: it shows how individual examples of participation in genre-making are part of a diachronic discourse about history and its uses. Each case study has been selected on the basis of publication patterns, privileging those stationers who seem to specialize in history plays and non-dramatic historical texts. For this reason, stationers who publish only one or two history plays (such as Walter Burre, who invested in Jonson's *Catiline*, 1611) are not heavily featured. It is by concentrating on individuals who are clearly invested in ideas of history that ways of reading genre can be most fully explored.

One consequence of this approach is that, despite the broad parameters for 'history' that this study adopts, some types of history plays – including those based on classical and biblical pasts – do not take up a prominent place. Strikingly few biblical histories were published during the period:

---

[117] Melnikoff, *Elizabethan Publishing*; David M. Bergeron, *Textual Patronage in English Drama, 1570–1640* (Aldershot: Ashgate, 2006).

[118] Helen Smith, "'To London all'? Mapping Shakespeare in Print, 1593–1598', in *Shakespeare and Textual Studies*, ed. Margaret Jane Kidnie and Sonia Massai (Cambridge: Cambridge University Press, 2015), pp. 69–86 (p. 86).

George Peele's *The Love of David and Fair Bathsheba* (printed by Adam Islip in 1599) is one of a handful of examples, although they were clearly popular on stage.[119] Several influential classical histories were printed – such as Jonson's *Sejanus* (published in 1605 by Thomas Thorpe; first entered in the Register to Edward Blount) and Daniel's *Philotas* (published in 1605 by Blount and Simon Waterson). None of these stationers, however, invested regularly in history plays from the playhouses. Blount's involvement in Shakespeare's Folio is considered in Chapter 4; his collaboration with Waterson for *Philotas* and his edition of George Chapman's *Sir Giles Goosecap* (1606) are the only commercial plays he published prior to 1623. Blount and Waterson display an interest in non-commercial classical histories, such as Daniel's *Cleopatra* (1594, Waterson), Matthew Gwinne's *Nero* (1603, Blount), and William Alexander's *Monarchic Tragedies* (1604, Blount). It is possible, therefore, that some classical histories from the playhouses were seen as distinct from other histories – including those dramatizing English, ancient British, European, and recent pasts – and could be more easily marketed as prestigious publications, especially when they were written by individuals, such as Daniel, who were connected to important literary coteries. During the late Elizabethan and Jacobean periods, investment and print presentation practices seem to differ for commercial and non-commercial plays (especially those with 'academic' associations); and printed playhouse histories tend to feature biblical or classical pasts much less frequently than other kinds of historical subject matter, despite their prevalence on stage.[120] While classical histories appear prominently in non-commercial playbooks with elaborate, discursive paratexts, the printed history play from the playhouse tends, on balance, to favour English/British, European, Middle Eastern, and recent histories and, as will be shown, is often in conversation with a publisher's non-dramatic output.

Given the fact that the past was often used in 'politic' histories, such as Savile's *Tacitus* (1591), to comment on the present, it is not surprising that publishers were alert to the potential of their history plays for providing topical applications. For this reason, many of the discussions

---

[119] For biblical drama on the stage, see Annaliese Connolly, 'Peele's *David and Bethsabe:* Reconsidering Biblical Drama of the Long 1590s', *Early Modern Literary Studies*, Special Issue 16 (2007), 9.1–20.

[120] It may be worth observing that, of Shakespeare's plays, *Julius Caesar, Antony and Cleopatra*, and *Coriolanus* were not printed until the Folio (despite the fact that *Antony and Cleopatra* was entered in the Register to Blount in 1608 but not published), while one of the two issues of *Troilus and Cressida* in 1609 tried through its paratexts to sever its connection to the playhouse stages.

offered in this study will be politically focused – not because of an assumption that history plays are inherently so or that all individuals read them for their political cachet, but because publishers often seem to approach them in this way. Helgerson objects that 'the success the politic historians had in imposing their views has had a significant part in moving latter-day critics to accept a definition of the history play that puts a high premium on its political focus'.[121] It is therefore important to recognize that politic readings are not the only ones available for history plays – either for publishers or the wider book-buying public. In consequence, each chapter takes account of other factors that have informed a publisher's investment and that may have little to do with a detailed reading of a play's history and politics. The cultural cachet of a particular dramatist could be more important in the selection and presentation of a playbook; and the availability of playscripts also shapes investment patterns. Any playbook is a document that reflects a range of readings, strategies, and contexts. My emphasis on publishers' practices helps to avoid the critical problem of overstating the political force of a history play, as if it were the only measure of meaning.

Chapter 1 begins with printer-publisher Thomas Creede, who was the first stationer to invest significantly in history plays from the commercial stages. His playbooks feature diverse historical pasts, such as medieval English history in *The True Tragedy of Richard III* and *The Famous Victories of Henry V*, Scottish history in *James IV*, and Turkish history in *Selimus*. Because several of them contain attributions to Queen Elizabeth's Men, Creede's playbooks have been used by critics to expand and extrapolate patterns in the company's repertory. This chapter shows, however, that the enduring view of the Queen's Men as a company that promoted Protestant and Tudor sympathies is a consequence of the publication process and its strategies of selection and presentation. Creede's wider output demonstrates a sustained interest in history as a (true or invented) looking glass for readers that is not limited to plays from the Queen's Men. Not only is an analysis of publication strategies necessary for understanding the history play in print, it should also be a key component in assessing theatrical repertories and dramatic genre on the stage.

Chapter 2 continues to drive a wedge between history plays on the stage and in print at the end of the sixteenth century. It concentrates on publisher-bookseller Andrew Wise and his editions of *Richard II*, *Richard III*, and *1* and *2 Henry IV*, and argues that they constructed a print identity

---

[121] Helgerson, 'Shakespeare', p. 27.

for Shakespeare and the Chamberlain's Men as dramatizers of medieval English history. In contrast, performance records and the evidence of lost plays indicate that a wide range of historical subjects held sway on the playhouse stages. While Creede's interest in history as a model to emulate or avoid seems to have been independently maintained, Wise's investment may have arisen out of a publication network involving Shakespeare, the Chamberlain's Men, and their patron, George Carey, second Baron Hunsdon. This chapter draws attention to collaborative networks of exchange in the book trade that not only direct the selection of texts for publication, but also construct meaning. For Wise, the most useful kinds of history plays were those based on the lives of medieval English monarchs, because they responded to non-dramatic publications in the book market, appealed to the cachet and political interests of Shakespeare's patron, and could be applied to pressing concerns that dominated the end of Elizabeth's reign.

It is often claimed that the history play died out at the accession of James I in 1603; however, this is demonstrably not the case. New historical drama continued to be written, staged, and published. Chapter 3 concentrates on publisher-bookseller Nathaniel Butter, whose investment in dramatic and non-dramatic histories was directed by his interest in newsworthy texts that commented upon the religio-political issues dominating the beginning of James's reign. For Butter, history and news were two sides of the same coin; the temporal boundary between them was of minor consequence. This chapter offers a fresh perspective on early Jacobean historical drama, and explores the important, but neglected, parallels between plays that dramatize Tudor history – including Rowley's *When You See Me You Know Me*, Heywood's *1* and *2 If You Know Not Me, You Know Nobody*, and Dekker's *The Whore of Babylon* – and early British history, such as Shakespeare's *King Lear*. A detailed reading of these histories in light of Butter's wider output suggests that, for him, the plays reflect positively on James I's reign and the monarch's own use of legitimizing histories, but also register some dissenting views in relation to religious toleration and the extent of monarchical authority. This case study pushes, as far as possible, the evidence that can be recovered for one historical reader and uses it to draw attention to competing models and interpretations of history.

Chapter 4 examines collections of history plays to show that the ways in which plays are bound together make statements about genre and promote specific reading strategies. It proposes that the two earliest multi-play collections to prioritize histories from the commercial stages are the

Jaggard–Pavier collection in 1619 and Shakespeare's Folio in 1623. This chapter evaluates the principles of collection that underlie these publication ventures and how they participate in and construct 'history' as a dramatic genre. For both collections, the history play is mostly 'Shakespearean'. But, in contrast to the exclusivity and fixity suggested by the Folio, the Jaggard–Pavier collection promotes inclusivity and flexibility: it requires readers to draw their own connections between different types of historical pasts, including medieval English history and the legendary British past. The chapter ends by considering the impact of Shakespeare's Folio on subsequent publishing ventures and draws attention to the continuing malleability of genre reflected in booksellers' catalogues. Finally, the Conclusion briefly addresses some shifting patterns in Caroline playbook publication – the regular inclusion of discursive paratexts that directly announce play readings, and a split in the market between first and reprint editions – which have consequences for looking, both forwards and backwards, at the early modern history play.

Publishing the History Play in the Time of Shakespeare approaches historical drama through the strategies of its publishers, an emphasis that reveals what these plays meant to some of their earliest and most influential readers. History – as a subject of enquiry about the past – is substantially (although not exclusively) a history of reading, of engaging with and re-evaluating historical records, documents, and narratives. In a similar way, the early modern history play is a history of publishing interests and publishers' readings. It is not my aim to replace or uproot other critical methods for discussing history plays, but to offer a different perspective that draws on overlooked evidence to tell new stories of participation in the genre. As Hooks succinctly puts it, '[b]ook historians must engage in rigorous historical scholarship, but they should also derive compelling narratives from that research'.[122] Thus far, book history has tended to remain separate from the study of history plays, despite the fact that these plays – and, indeed, many of their sources – only survive because of print publication. In this study, I aim to show that applying the practices of book history to an evaluation of dramatic genre reveals compelling narratives that shed light on the period's historical culture and our access to it.

---

[122] Hooks, *Selling*, p. 33.

CHAPTER 1

'True' Histories
Thomas Creede's Looking Glasses and the Print Identity of Queen Elizabeth's Men

The first stationer to invest significantly in history plays from the commercial stages was printer-publisher Thomas Creede, whose strategies of selection and presentation for dramatic and non-dramatic texts reveal an interest in the past as a mirror or looking glass for the present. Prior to Creede, the only stationer to invest in more than one commercial history play was Richard Jones with Marlowe's *1* and *2 Tamburlaine* (1590) and Wilson's *Three Lords and Three Ladies of London* (1590), the latter allegorizing the defeat of the Spanish Armada in 1588. While Creede mostly worked as a trade printer for other stationers (printing Sidney's *Defence of Poesy* (1595) for William Ponsonby, for example), he also acted as a publisher, especially during the last decade of the sixteenth century. David Gants estimates that about two-thirds of Creede's output between 1593 and 1600 was self-published.[1] History plays were one of Creede's key investments during this period. In a short space of time between March and July 1594, Creede entered *A Looking Glass for London and England*, *The True Tragedy of Richard III*, *The Famous Victories of Henry V*, *Locrine*, and *The Scottish History of James IV* in the Stationers' Register, establishing his rights to plays that dramatize biblical, English, Scottish, and legendary British history.[2] In 1594, he published *A Looking Glass*, *The True Tragedy*, and *Selimus* (a Turkish history, which has no Stationers' Register entry), followed by *Locrine* in 1595, *The Famous Victories of Henry V* and *James IV* in 1598, and *Alphonsus, King of Aragon* (a pseudo-historical play) and *Clyomon and Clamydes* (an '*un*-history', as Lisa Hopkins describes, that evokes a chivalric past) in 1599, both without entries in the Register.[3]

---

[1] David L. Gants, 'Creede, Thomas (*b.* in or before 1554, *d.* 1616)', *ODNB*, online ed., September 2004, https://doi.org/10.1093/ref:odnb/6666 (accessed 16 September 2019), para. 2.

[2] During this time, Creede also entered *The Pedlar's Prophecy* and William Warner's translation of *Menaechmi*.

[3] Lisa Hopkins, 'The Danish Romance Play: *Fair Em, Sir Clyomon and Sir Clamydes*, and *Hoffman*', *Early Modern Literary Studies*, Special Issue 27 (2017), 1–17 (p. 2).

All of these playbooks have been connected at some point in their critical history to Queen Elizabeth's Men, which raises the possibility that Creede had a working relationship with the company and that he was interested in the kinds of histories that the Queen's Men had to offer. *The True Tragedy of Richard III, Selimus, The Famous Victories of Henry V,* and *Clyomon and Clamydes* are considered firmly a part of the company's repertory on the basis of external evidence, style, and Creede's title-page advertisements – all of these texts were 'playd by the Queenes Maiesties Players'.[4] *Locrine, James IV,* and *Alphonsus* have also been linked to the company, although the evidence is indeterminate. There are parallels in dramatic style and a link to Robert Greene (both *James IV* and *Alphonsus* carry attributions to Greene), but none of the playbooks contain company attributions and there is no conclusive evidence to support a connection.[5] Creede's investment in plays securely attached to the Queen's Men and his 1594 Stationers' Register entries have led some critics to propose that his other published playbooks must also have been part of the same repertory: G. M. Pinciss, for example, observes that 'no acted play entered or printed by Creede before 1600 is claimed on its title page for any company other than the Queen's', and, on the basis of Creede's involvement, he assigns many more plays to the company, including *A Looking Glass, James IV, Locrine, The Pedlar's Prophecy,* and *Alphonsus.*[6] While some of Pinciss's attributions may be correct, there are problems with this kind of reasoning: it does not necessarily follow that Creede's investment secures a company attribution, and the limitations of extant evidence make it unlikely that a firm conclusion will be reached. However, by looking at Creede as one of the first professional readers of history plays, this chapter offers an alternative perspective on the repertory of the Queen's Men. It uses the presentation of Creede's playbooks as evidence for how Creede read and marketed the plays, which establishes the coherence of his published output. One of the reasons why it is so tempting to attribute plays such as *Locrine* to the repertory of the Queen's Men is because of the consistency of Creede's wider investment patterns and paratextual practices.

---

[4] *The True Tragedie of Richard the third* (London, 1594; STC 21009), A2r. For evidence of the company's repertory, see Scott McMillin and Sally-Beth MacLean, *The Queen's Men and Their Plays* (Cambridge: Cambridge University Press, 1998), pp. 84–96.

[5] *James IV* is attributed to 'Robert Greene, Maister of Arts', whereas *Alphonsus* claims the play was 'Made by R. G.'

[6] G. M. Pinciss, 'Thomas Creede and the Repertory of the Queen's Men, 1583–1592', *Modern Philology,* 67:4 (1970), 321–30 (p. 322).

For Creede, the purpose of 'history' (broadly conceived) was to provide exemplary and counter-exemplary models for readers which could be used to further England's and Elizabeth I's interests. His history plays tend to promote patriotic sympathies through their selection and presentation as playbooks. They enlist different histories – from medieval English monarchical history in *The True Tragedy of Richard III* to Turkish history in *Selimus* – which are then framed through their paratexts to reflect positively on England's political present and future, in terms of both domestic stability and foreign conquest. This chapter argues that Creede's practices have shaped our understanding of the Queen's Men as a company that specialized in history plays. It first considers the critical reputation of the company, and then examines Creede's involvement as the main publisher of their plays. As outlined in the Introduction, early playbooks from the commercial stages infrequently contain the discursive paratexts that feature in other books. By profiling Creede's wider published output, his interest in 'histories' that provide looking glasses for Elizabethan England is revealed. His non-dramatic publications also highlight a tension between royalist sympathies and the promotion of a chivalric aristocratic elite that qualifies the histories' use as propagandistic or promotional materials for Elizabeth I. These overlooked texts can be used to examine the 'position-takings' of Creede's title-page paratexts in playbooks from the Queen's Men, which on the one hand seem to announce their connection to Elizabeth, but, when considered alongside his other publications, redirect this emphasis towards an aristocratic coterie – potentially those who could offer a sophisticated readership for the playbooks.[7] Looking beyond Creede's output, this chapter proposes that the history play occupied a pivotal position in the development of a market for commercial playbooks during the early 1590s and shows how these publications experimented with some – but not all – of the presentation strategies seen in pre-playhouse and non-commercial playbooks.

The Royal Histories of the Queen's Men

Recent studies of Queen Elizabeth's Men have tended to suggest that history plays – especially those that seem to promote a Protestant agenda and underline the authority of their patron Elizabeth I – were a prominent part of the company's repertory. In *The Queen's Men and Their Plays*, Scott McMillin and Sally-Beth MacLean claim that the 'most important kind of

---

[7] Bourdieu, *Field of Cultural Production*, p. 30.

play performed by the Queen's Men was the English history play', which the company established 'in the popular theatre before other companies took it up'.[8] This assessment concentrates on the company's extant repertory, which McMillin and MacLean limit to the nine plays that can be firmly linked to the company: *The Three Lords and Three Ladies of London* (which allegorizes English history), *The Troublesome Reign of King John* (English history), *Selimus* (Turkish history), *The True Tragedy of Richard III* (English history), *Friar Bacon and Friar Bungay* (English history), *The Old Wives' Tale*, *The Famous Victories of Henry V* (English history), *King Leir* (early British history), and *Clyomon and Clamydes* (which stages a fictional Danish past, nominally set during the reign of Alexander the Great).[9] Basing their analysis on the plays' style and subject matter, McMillin and MacLean argue that a significant proportion of the company's repertory dramatized English history and that, through the plays' combination of 'anti-Catholicism with a specifically Protestant style, "truth" and "plainness" intertwined', the repertory broadly supports a Protestant and royalist ideology.[10] Robert Dudley, earl of Leicester, and Sir Francis Walsingham were both involved in the formation of the company, and McMillin and MacLean adopt Conyers Read's description of them as key figures within 'an aggressively Protestant party' in the Privy Council.[11] In 1583, Walsingham instructed Edmund Tilney, Master of the Revels, to appoint the Queen's Men, an unusual development as the Revels office normally operated under the authority of the Lord Chamberlain.[12] The majority of the new 'all-star' troupe of actors was then provided by Leicester's Men. Because of these events, the company's court connections, and its touring networks, McMillin and MacLean propose that 'the Queen's Men were formed to spread Protestant and royalist propaganda through a divided realm and to close a breach within

---

[8] McMillin and MacLean, *Queen's Men*, pp. 33, 36.

[9] Ibid., pp. 88–89. Andrew Gurr offers a similar list of plays that can be firmly linked to the repertory of the Queen's Men: see Gurr, *The Shakespearian Playing Companies* (Oxford: Clarendon Press, 1996) pp. 210–11. As Martin Wiggins proposes, *Clyomon and Clamydes* may have been written during the 1570s, before the formation of the Queen's Men, but later inherited by the company; see Wiggins, II, p. 189 (No. 634).

[10] McMillin and MacLean, *Queen's Men*, p. 36.

[11] Conyers Read, 'Walsingham and Burghley in Queen Elizabeth's Privy Council', *English Historical Review*, 28:109 (1913), 34–58 (p. 41).

[12] Edmund Howes's additions to John Stow's *Annals* record that 'at the request of Sir Francis Walsingham, they [i.e. the company] were sworne the Queenes seruants, and were allowed wages, and liueries, as groomes of the chamber'. John Stow, *The Annales, or Generall Chronicle of England* (London, 1615; STC 23338), Mmm6r (p. 697).

radical Protestantism'.[13] Similarly, while Andrew Gurr's short account of the company tends to focus on the players and touring, he surmises from the extant repertory that 'moral and political conformism, even patriotism, shines out'.[14]

Other critics have questioned these assessments. Responding to McMillin and MacLean's study, Brian Walsh argues that 'the repertory of the Queen's Men can hardly be reduced to a coherent political or even theological agenda', and offers an important reminder that clear-cut ideological interpretations of the plays do not sufficiently attend to the performance context, which can encourage a range of perspectives.[15] Walsh suggests that political and religious complexities within the plays are activated by playing practices, such as doubling, and the performance settings, which limit the plays' ability to act as royalist propaganda. In her work on theatre companies and commerce, Roslyn Knutson challenges the assumption that companies, such as the Queen's Men, were pawns of their aristocratic or royal patrons and produced plays to support patrons' political and religious sympathies. Instead, Knutson demonstrates that playing companies operated as largely autonomous commercial ventures, staging plays on the basis of theatrical demand and audience taste, and argues that there is limited evidence to support the ongoing role of a meddling patron in the development of a company's repertory.[16] The assumption of a stable political identity for the Queen's Men is also suspect in the major edited collection on the company, *Locating the Queen's Men, 1583–1603* (2009), and most chapters prioritize a consideration of playing practices, performance conditions, and style over an assessment of the plays' ideology.[17] These have been profitable approaches; but studies thus far have not explored the possibility that the apparent unity of the company's extant texts, specifically their interest in history, could be a print phenomenon. Rather than assume that these patterns reflect performance repertories or are witness to the original political agenda of Leicester and Walsingham, this chapter draws attention to the interests of the plays'

[13] McMillin and MacLean, *Queen's Men*, p. 166.
[14] Gurr, *Shakespearian Playing Companies*, p. 211.
[15] Brian Walsh, *Shakespeare, the Queen's Men and the Elizabethan Performance of History* (Cambridge: Cambridge University Press, 2009), p. 31.
[16] Roslyn L. Knutson, *Playing Companies and Commerce in Shakespeare's Time* (Cambridge: Cambridge University Press, 2001). See also Knutson, 'What's So Special about 1594?', *Shakespeare Quarterly*, 61:4 (2010), 449–67 (p. 450).
[17] Helen Ostovich, Holger Schott Syme, and Andrew Griffin (eds.), *Locating the Queen's Men, 1583–1603: Material Practices and Conditions of Playing* (Farnham: Ashgate, 2009).

publishers and the influence of the printing process on the identity of the Queen's Men.

The printing process, for example, fixes some of the fluid and detachable features of the performed plays, such as their closing addresses or prayers to Elizabeth I, which tend to promote royalist sympathies. In the early Tudor period, it was common, as critics including Michael Hattaway and Tiffany Stern have explored, for plays to end with an epilogue prayer for the queen or sometimes for the Privy Council.[18] This practice was later adopted, on occasion, by the commercial theatres, and the appearance of these prayers in printed playbooks has been taken to indicate a court performance. Stern, however, offers a reappraisal of this view. The context of a concluding prayer sometimes indicates that the play was performed at court and that the epilogue was only relevant for that occasion, such as when the monarch is required to receive a gift from the actors. But, in other cases, it is possible that the concluding prayer was a regular feature of the play in performance and did not require the monarch's presence. As Stern outlines, the epilogue prayer could advertise the company's patron, bolster the authority of the play and players, and promote their repertory.[19]

A significant proportion of the plays from the Queen's Men contain a concluding prayer for Elizabeth – and, interestingly, most of these are part of plays that dramatize some kind of historical past, which seems to connect the queen with the use and staging of history. *The Three Lords and Three Ladies of London*, *Friar Bacon and Friar Bungay*, and *The True Tragedy of Richard III* all contain an address to Elizabeth I, and the context of each suggests that they were a regular feature in performance and were not designed for a specific occasion. The presentation of these addresses in the printed playbooks is also distinctive. The 'reusable' prayers that Stern discusses in plays such as *2 Henry IV* or *The Disobedient Child* (c.1570) are usually marked out as separate from the play by a heading or a stage direction that divides the play's action from the closing address. However, none of the plays from the Queen's Men contain a detachable epilogue. All of the prayers to Elizabeth are presented as part of the play itself.

---

[18] Michael Hattaway, 'Dating *As You Like It*, Epilogues and Prayers, and the Problems of "As the Dial Hand Tells O'er"', *Shakespeare Quarterly*, 60:2 (2009), 154–67; Tiffany Stern, 'Epilogues, Prayers after Plays, and Shakespeare's *2 Henry IV*', *Theatre Notebook*, 64:3 (2010), 122–29.

[19] Stern, 'Epilogues', p. 124. For patterns of prologue and epilogue inclusion in playbooks, see Sonia Massai and Heidi Craig, 'Rethinking Prologues and Epilogues on Page and Stage', in *Rethinking Theatrical Documents in Shakespeare's England*, ed. Tiffany Stern (London: Arden Shakespeare, 2020), pp. 91–110.

In the final scene of the anonymous *True Tragedy of Richard III*, for example, 'Eliza' (Elizabeth of York, consort of Henry VII), the 'Queene' (Elizabeth Woodville, consort of Edward IV), and a messenger address the audience directly and celebrate the 'ioyning of these Houses both in one' (I1v). They praise the Tudor line, giving laudatory accounts of Henry VII, Henry VIII, and Edward VI, who 'did restore the Gospell to his light', while rather tersely acknowledging the Catholic reign of 'a Mary' (meaning Mary I) and her marriage to 'Philip King of Spaine', who sent the Armada against England in 1588 (I1v–I2r). The play closes with the Queene offering a lengthy verse prayer for Elizabeth I, who is described as the 'lampe that keeps faire Englands light'. The prayer focuses on Elizabeth's position as a Protestant leader: it is through her faith that 'her country liues in peace', has 'put proud Antichrist to flight, | And bene the meanes that ciuill wars did cease' (I2r). The closing address extols the political stability brought by Elizabeth, even claiming that the Turk – the early modern period's religio-political scapegoat – 'admires to heare her gouernment . . . and hath sworne neuer to lift his hand, | To wrong the Princesse of this blessed land' (I2r). The fact that the play's address to the audience and prayer for Elizabeth are not separated – by heading or layout – from the rest of the text establishes their fixed position as the play's conclusion, while also reinforcing a teleological historical narrative that views the inauguration of the Tudor line as part of a divinely sanctioned process.

Similarly, the conclusion of Robert Greene's *Friar Bacon and Friar Bungay* offers a prognostication of Elizabeth's reign from the repentant Friar Bacon, who links Elizabeth with a legendary Trojan lineage:

> That here where Brute did build his Troynouant,
> From forth the royall garden of a King,
> Shall flowrish out, so rich and faire a bud,
> Whose brightnesse shall deface proude Phoebus flowre
> And ouer-shadow Albion with her leaues.
> Till then, Mars shall be maister of the field,
> But then the stormie threats of wars shall cease.[20]

For a comic play that is less reliant on chronicle sources than *The True Tragedy of Richard III* or *King Leir*, this allusion to legendary British history as a way of prefiguring the reign of Elizabeth is particularly striking and encourages a providential reading of history similar to *The True Tragedy*'s. In *Friar Bacon*, this sudden foreshadowing of Elizabeth's reign is

---

[20] Robert Greene, *The Honorable Historie of frier Bacon, and frier Bongay* (London, 1594; STC 12267), I1v–I2r.

assimilated within the main text and is followed by a concluding address from Henry III, which returns the audience to the events of the play. Walsh has described the play's praise of Elizabeth as a pessimistic elegy for the Tudor line (which was clearly drawing to a close), but its ebullient account of Elizabeth is fixed as a permanent part of the printed history.[21] As a material text, the playbook participates in the writing and circulation of history and offers an explicit reference – a printed monument – to a glorified role taken on by Elizabeth.

The inclusion of these concluding addresses or prayers to Elizabeth as a semi-regular feature of plays from the Queen's Men in performance – contained within the plot of the play, rather than as potentially detachable epilogues – emphasizes the company's connection to the queen and, implicitly, to her policies. The presentation of the playbooks, where the concluding addresses are not marked off as separate from the main play, adds to their propagandistic potential for readers by making these sections clear points of conclusion, rather than suggesting they could be detached, omitted, or replaced. As Kastan points out, 'our sense of the shape of a play . . . in large part emerges from our understanding of the way in which the drama begins and ends'.[22] Indeed, the fact that history plays from the Queen's Men often concluded in similar ways suggests an interpretative link between the different histories they dramatize: medieval English monarchical history (in *The True Tragedy*), loosely historical, citizen-based English history (in *Friar Bacon*), and Middle Eastern history (in *Selimus*) could be enlisted to serve Elizabeth and England and foster a patriotic collective identity for audiences and readers.

Ultimately, any understanding of the company's repertory depends on an analysis of printed playbooks and rests significantly on decisions stationers have made in the selection and presentation of plays. As with other theatre companies, the majority of plays performed by the Queen's Men were not printed and have not survived, disappearing without even leaving a record of their titles.[23] This paucity of evidence does not lead to an

---

[21] Brian Walsh, '"Deep Prescience": Succession and the Politics of Prophecy in *Friar Bacon and Friar Bungay*', *Medieval & Renaissance Drama in England*, 23 (2010), 63–85 (p. 71). Cf. David M. Bergeron, '"Bogus History" and Robert Greene's *Friar Bacon and Friar Bungay*', *Early Theatre*, 17:1 (2014), 93–112 (pp. 108–09).

[22] Kastan, *Shapes of Time*, p. 8.

[23] Lost plays associated with the company include 'Felix and Philomena', 'Five Plays in One', 'Phyllida and Corin', and 'Three Plays in One'; Gurr, *Shakespearian Playing Companies*, p. 211. See also the lists provided under 'Auspices' in the *Lost Plays Database*, ed. Roslyn L. Knutson, David McInnis, Matthew Steggle, and Misha Teramura (Washington, DC: Folger Shakespeare Library, 2018), www.lostplays.folger.edu.

interpretative impasse, but it necessitates some caution in terms of what can be claimed about the company. It may be problematic to assert confidently that the full performance repertory of the Queen's Men was composed mainly of history plays with a specific political design. It is possible, however, to discuss the unity of their printed representatives: the history play is the main genre of the Queen's Men *in print*. Of the nine plays that have secure attributions to the company, Creede invested in four of them (*True Tragedy, Selimus, Famous Victories*, and *Clyomon*); the other plays were published by Richard Jones (*Three Lords*, 1590), Sampson Clarke (*Troublesome Reign*, 1591), Edward White (*Friar Bacon*, 1594), Ralph Hancock and John Hardy (*The Old Wives' Tale*, 1595), and John Wright (*King Leir*, 1605). Creede was, therefore, the most significantly invested, and one of the main arguments of this chapter is that his practices helped to create a print identity for the Queen's Men that is too often conflated with their performance identity. A contrastive analysis of Creede's wider output suggests that the selection and presentation of his playbooks indicates his own publishing interests and reading of 'history', rather than providing a clear window onto the company's repertory and political sympathies.

Creede's Looking Glasses

Thomas Creede was made free of the Stationers' Company on 7 October 1578 and seems to have been a journeyman printer until 1593, when he opened his own printing house at the Sign of the Catherine Wheel near the Old Swan in Thames Street and entered his first titles in the Stationers' Register. From 1593 until the end of the sixteenth century, he made a consistent effort to publish texts independently, as well as acting as a trade printer for other stationers. Creede's early publications are dominated by playbooks and 1594 is a significant year for his acquisition of titles. With the exception of *Selimus* (1594), *Alphonsus, King of Aragon* (1599), and *Clyomon and Clamydes* (1599), which were published without entry in the Stationers' Register, Creede entered, in that year, all of the plays that he would eventually publish: *A Looking Glass for London and England* (entered 5 March 1594; published 1594); *The True Tragedy of Richard III* (entered 19 June 1594; published 1594); *The Pedlar's Prophecy* (entered 13 May 1594; published 1595); *Menaechmi* (entered 10 June 1594; published 1595); *Locrine* (entered 20 July 1594; published 1595); *The Famous Victories of Henry V* (entered 14 May 1594; published 1598); and *James IV* (entered 14 May 1594; published 1598). Creede therefore played an important role in the early publication of commercial plays. As Holger

Syme points out, only Edward White entered as many texts as Creede (seven altogether), only Cuthbert Burby published more playbooks (thirteen, compared to Creede's ten), and no stationer printed more plays between 1590 and 1604 (Creede printed twenty-six, compared to Edward Allde's twenty-two).[24]

A profile of Creede's non-dramatic publications from the 1590s suggests how he may have read these playbooks, which, with the exception of *Menaechmi* (a closet translation of Plautus), do not contain any discursive paratexts. Much of Creede's output during this time reveals an interest in 'histories' that offer looking glasses for readers and provide either a warning to avoid the misfortunes of those relayed in the texts or a spur for noble emulation. This use of history has parallels in a range of texts from the period, including *The Mirror for Magistrates*, which provides warnings to readers through its *de casibus* structure that outlines the fall of monarchs, aristocrats, and pretenders to power, and the exemplary 'politic' histories that became an important part of humanist historiography and were especially influential in England during the 1590s through Henry Savile's translations of Tacitus.[25] Creede's publications display an interest in fictional histories that can similarly be used as mirrors and applied to the present. The semantic flexibility of 'history' and the exemplary and counter-exemplary potential of both real and invented histories is reflected in the titles and discursive paratexts of his publications. Sometimes 'history' applies to an invented story and has much in common with Sidney's 'poetry'; other times 'history' is used specifically to mean an account of the past. For example, an English translation of Francisco López de Gómara's *Pleasant History of the Conquest of the West India, Now Called New Spain*, published by Creede in 1596, applies the term to an account of Spain's conquest of Mexico in 1521 led by Captain Hernán (or Hernando) Cortés. In other publications, such as Anthony Munday's translations of the *Palmerin* romances, 'history' applies to a story of chivalric deeds that do not advertise a clear connection to a documented past.[26] These histories

[24] Holger Schott Syme, 'Thomas Creede, William Barley, and the Venture of Printing Plays', in *Shakespeare's Stationers*, ed. Straznicky, pp. 28–46 (p. 28).

[25] See Jessica Winston, 'National History to Foreign Calamity: *A Mirror for Magistrates* and Early English Tragedy', in *Shakespeare's Histories and Counter-Histories*, ed. Dermot Cavanagh, Stuart Hampton-Reeves, and Stephen Longstaffe (Manchester: Manchester University Press, 2006), pp. 152–65; Paulina Kewes, 'Henry Savile's Tacitus and the Politics of Roman History in Late Elizabethan England', *Huntington Library Quarterly*, 74:4 (2011), 515–51.

[26] See also *The Honour of Chivalry*, an English translation of 'the most Famous Historie of the Magnanimous and Heroike Prince' Don Belianís of Greece. In this case, 'Historie' applies to a chivalric romance novel, originally written in Spanish by Jerónimo Fernández and translated into

are models to imitate, irrespective of whether the subject matter is invented or tied 'to the particular truth of things' (*Defence*, D1v).

A patriotic repurposing of a wide range of histories – often ones that were first printed in European languages and translated into English – takes place in Creede's paratexts. One address written by Creede and Valentine Simmes in their joint publication of *The Ancient History of the Destruction of Troy* (1597) sums up this overarching interest in profitable histories, which is witnessed throughout Creede's other publications, including his playbooks. This classic text was originally written in French by Raoul Lefèvre, translated into English and printed by William Caxton (as *The Recuyell of the Historyes of Troye*, 1473–74), and then updated by William Phiston for publication by Creede and Simmes. In this latest edition, the history's three books have separate title pages (although the pagination and register are continuous): Creede's name appears on the title-page imprints to Book 1 and Book 2, while Simmes's name appears in Book 3. The opening paratext – from 'The Printers to the curteous Reader, health and happinesse' – potentially indicates that both Creede and Simmes were involved in its composition.[27] The address's detailed account of the uses and definition of history succinctly sums up one of Creede's dominant publishing specialisms:

> [T]he reading of Annales, and Histories, most delighteth men of all ages, but especially yoong men, whose affections are quickly incensed, and their hearts set on fire with an emulation of whatsoeuer notable and valorous enterprises they shall heare or reade of: but most principally yoong Gentlemen and Noblemen, are by the viewing of memorable deeds and martiall prowesse so inflamed with an approbation of good and famous exployts ((x)iiir).[28]

Here, 'history' applies directly to accounts of the past, and its main purpose is to encourage 'Gentlemen and Noblemen' to emulate the deeds and conquests of the figures contained in the text – in this case, the

---

Italian by Oratio Rinaldi, but which could be used in the same way as 'true' histories. Jerónimo Fernández, *The Honour of Chivalrie*, trans. Oratio Rinaldi and 'L.A.' (London, 1598; STC 1804), A2r.

[27] Raoul Lefèvre, *The Auncient Historie of the destruction of Troy*, trans. William Caxton and William Phiston (London, 1597; STC 15379), (x)ivr. The agency of the stationers in the translation seems to be underscored through their claim to have 'caused' the 'sundry sentences so improperly Englished' in Caxton's earlier translation to 'bee made plainer English'.

[28] Syme also offers a profile of Creede's investments (in 'Thomas Creede', pp. 40–44), but concentrates on his business connection to Barley (which I discuss later) and an interest in 'big' books, like Munday's *Palmerin* romances. My discussion takes account of some of these texts, but I identify a core specialism in 'histories' that brings together pamphlet and large-scale formats.

'martiall prowesse' on display at Troy. Histories, the address explains, are 'committed to writing, and left to posteritie, in all ciuil Countries, to be as whetstones' ((x)iiiv). The other dominant sense of history is also introduced in the paratext: Creede and Simmes claim that 'to this purpose [i.e. noble emulation], not only true Histories haue always beene published, but many fictions of admirable and most straunge, yea of incredible things atchieued by industrious valour, and constancy in Louers' ((x)iiiv). Although the stationers rate more highly the 'true' accounts of the historical past (containing 'some poeticall paintings'; (x)iiiv), the purpose and subject matter of histories both true and feigned are strikingly similar and are connected to chivalric ideals of honour, conquest, and constancy. This edition of the Troy story, as A. E. B. Coldiron points out, reinforces 'a nostalgic, chivalric reading of empire(s)'.[29] The new address does not consider the catastrophic destruction of Troy, but concentrates on 'an approbation of good and famous exploits' ((x)iiiir) contained in the history. It also testifies to a late Elizabethan resurgence of interest in chivalric literature that was widespread and represented by works such as Spenser's *Faerie Queen* (1590; 1596), an interest that, as Melnikoff discusses in relation to Richard Jones, was not only martial in its emphasis, but was also 'inflected by humanist and pastoral models of courtesy'.[30] Indeed, the language of chivalry, as Helgerson outlines, also became 'the primary language of Elizabethan public display', making the appeal in Creede and Simmes's paratext a means of connecting the history with Elizabeth and a celebration of her court.[31]

The importance of history as a looking glass for the present is emphasized in an unsigned paratext 'To the Reader', which is part of *The Mutable and Wavering Estate of France, from the Year of our Lord 1460, Until the Year 1595* (1597; see Figure 1.1). This address was potentially written by Creede; it ends with the same salutation, 'Fare ye well', as the address in the Trojan history and makes similar points.[32] As described on its title page (and also repeated in the address), this anonymous history recounts the 'great Battailes of the French Nation, as well abroad with their

[29] A. E. B. Coldiron, *Printers without Borders: Translation and Textuality in the Renaissance* (Cambridge: Cambridge University Press, 2015), p. 60 (see also pp. 40–64).

[30] Melnikoff, 'Jones's Pen', p. 205. See also Arthur B. Ferguson, *The Chivalric Tradition in Renaissance England* (Washington, DC: Folger Shakespeare Library, 1986), pp. 66–107.

[31] Richard Helgerson, 'Tasso on Spenser: The Politics of Chivalric Romance', *Yearbook of English Studies*, 21 (1991), 153–67 (p. 160).

[32] Anon., *The Mutable and wauering estate of France, from the yeare of our Lord 1460, vntill the yeare 1595* (London, 1597; STC 11279), n.s.

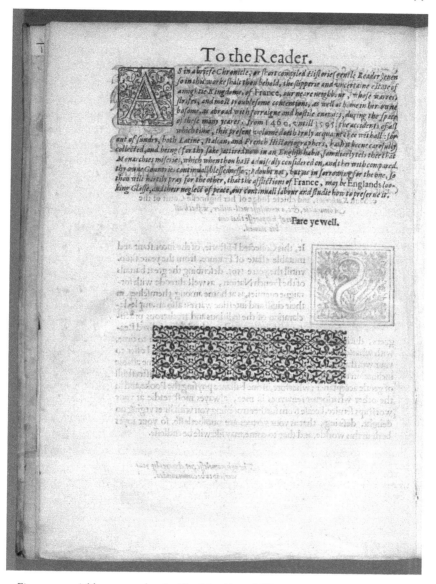

To the Reader.

AS in a briefe Chronicle, or short compiled Historie (gentle Reader) even so in this worke shalt thou behold, the slipperie and uncertaine estate of a mightie Kingdome, of France, our neare neighbour, whose warres, strifes, and most troublesome contentions, as well at home in her owne bosome, as abroad with forraigne and hostile enemies, during the space of these many yeares, from 1460, untill 1595, the accidents of all whichtime, this present volume doeth truly acquaint thee withall: for out of sundry, both Latine, Italian, and French Historiographers, hath it beene carefully collected, and being (for thy sake) attired new in an English habit, familiarly tels thee that Monarchies miseries, which when thou hast aduisedly considered on, and there with compared thy owne Countries continuall blessednesse; I doubt not, but as in sorrowing for the one, so thou wilt hartily pray for the other, that the afflictions of France, may be Englands looking Glasse, and their neglect of peace, our continuall labour and studie how to preserve it.

Fare ye well.

Figure 1.1 Address to readers in *The Mutable and Wavering Estate of France* (1597; STC 11279).

forraigne enemies, as at home among themselues, in their ciuill and intestine warres', which have been 'Collected out of sundry, both Latine, Italian, and French Historiographers' (t.p.). In this publication, 'history' applies specifically to events that have taken place and have a significant impact on a state's political stability. The address assumes an intimacy with English readers, encouraging them to apply the French 'Chronicle, or short compiled Historie' of 'our neare neighbour' to England, by comparing the state of France to 'thy own Countries continuall blessednesse'. It also, however, cautions readers to remember that 'the afflictions of France, may be Englands looking Glass, and their neglect of peace, our continuall labour and studie how to preserue it' (n.s.).[33] Histories, according to the claims in this paratext and Creede's wider output, should be mined for topical applications and used as models or warnings. The misfortunes of other countries are not just materials to aggrandize Elizabethan England, but also to make readers consider the speed with which political stability can be lost, particularly when individuals labour for themselves and not for their country's benefit, a point that is regularly emphasized in Creede's paratexts.[34]

This history reserves criticism for Spanish-Catholic influences, a reproval that is underscored through the title-page reference to the 'seditious and trecherous practises of that viperous brood of Hispaniolized Leaguers'; but Creede's other publications sometimes promote an international elite community that looks favourably on the conquests of European powers because of their potential as a spur for English readers. This way of reading has a direct parallel with humanist models of historiography and promotes, in Brian Lockey's phrase, 'trans-territorial values'.[35] For example, Creede's edition of *The Pleasant History of the Conquest of the West India, Now Called New Spain*, which was translated out of Spanish by Thomas Nicholas, contains a dedication to Walsingham (from the translator) that praises the actions of Captain Hernán Cortés who led the Spanish conquest: 'this delectable and worthie Historie' is 'a Mirrour and an excellent president, for all such as shall

---

[33] A similar emphasis on history as a looking glass for the present is witnessed in Creede's English translation of Jean de Serres's *Historical Collection of the Most Memorable Accidents and Tragicall Massacres of France, vnder the Raignes of Henry 2, Francis 2, Charles 9, Henry 3, Henry 4 now liuing* (London, 1598; STC 11275).

[34] See also Francisco López de Gómara, *The Pleasant Historie of the Conquest of the West India, now called new Spaine*, trans. Thomas Nicholas (London, 1596; STC 16808), a3v: 'euery true Cristian is born, not for his owne priuate wealth and pleasure' but for 'God' and 'prince'. For French history as a mirror for England, see Andrew M. Kirk, *The Mirror of Confusion: The Representation of French History in English Renaissance Drama*, new ed. (London and New York: Routledge, 2014), pp. 1–14.

[35] Brian C. Lockey, *Law and Empire in English Renaissance Literature* (Cambridge: Cambridge University Press, 2006), p. 95.

take in hand to gouerne new Discouerie; for here they shall behold, how Glory, Renowne, and perfit Felicitie, is not gotten but with great paines, trauaile, peril and daunger of life' (a2r–v). Although the Spanish conquest marked the beginning of that nation's colonization of the Americas, which might be seen to challenge England's power, the paratext, written especially for the English translation, presents Cortés as part of a chivalric elite that crosses state boundaries and traditional lines of division. The values of this international community of leaders are nevertheless redirected towards English projects in the dedication's final lines: it is to be hoped that 'within this happie Realme is nowe liuing a Gentleman, whose zeale of trauell and valiant beginning doth prognosticate great, maruellous, and happie successe' (a4r).

Creede's interest in the application of foreign and domestic histories for England's future benefit is underlined through his regular investment in works by Henry Roberts (*fl*.1585–1617), a patriot propagandist. Roberts pursued a naval career, although he may, as Helen Moore points out, have been a member of the Stationers' Company, and his works tend to commemorate English expeditions and conquests.[36] For example, *The Trumpet of Fame* (published by Creede in 1595) mourns the deaths of Sir Francis Drake and Sir John Hawkins, while also praising their colonial enterprises and 'what they have done against our foes'.[37] The poem offers a celebration of England and Elizabeth, predicts the nation's lasting fame, and ends with an acquisitive prayer that 'Phillips [i.e. Philip of Spain's] Regions may not be more stor[e]d, | with Pearle, Jewels, and the purest gold' than England's (B3r). Its potential for application is advertised on the title page and head title: the historical poem is offered as 'an encouragement to all Sailers and Souldiers that are minded to go in this worthie enterprise' (A2r, A3r). Similarly, Roberts's prose history, *Honour's Conquest* (1598), also celebrates adventures and victories over foreign forces, as described in its detailed title-page summary:

> the famous hystorie of Edward of Lancaster recounting his honourable trauailes to Ierusalem, his heroic adventures and honours, in sundrie countries gained: his resolutions, and attempts in armes. With the famous victories performed b[y] the knight, of the vnconquered castel, a gallant English knight, his admirable forces, and sundrie conquests obtained, with his passions and sucesse in loue: full of pleasant discourses and much varietie.[38]

[36] Helen Moore, 'Roberts [Robarts], Henry (fl. 1585–1617), author', *ODNB*, online ed., September 2004, https://doi.org/10.1093/ref:odnb/23753 (accessed 14 May 2020), para. 1.
[37] H[enry] R[oberts], *The Trvmpet of Fame* (London, 1595; STC 21088), A2r.
[38] H[enry] R[oberts], *Honours Conquest* (London, 1598; STC 21082), t.p.

This prose narrative recounts the earlier English history of Edmund of Lancaster, which is cast as a chivalric adventure, featuring foreign travels, successes in love, and martial victories that can help 'Gentlemen' readers to 'attaine true vertue' and 'an eternall reward of glorie'.[39] Creede published this history in the same year as his first edition of *The Famous Victories of Henry V* (discussed in the next section), a play that seems, at first glance, to share key parallels in subject, treatment, and presentation. Indeed, the plot summary in Roberts's text recalls the play's title through its description of a 'famous hystorie' and 'famous victories'. It is possible that Creede compiled the title-page blurb for *Honour's Conquest*, especially as the summary draws attention to the features that typically characterize his publications: an interest in battles, conquests, heroic and honourable adventures, and chivalric achievements.

In summary, a profile of Creede's non-dramatic publications, ranging from short pamphlets to longer prose accounts, reveals an interest in 'histories' that can be used by readers and applied to England's present and future.[40] Many of these texts were first written by European authors, before being translated (sometimes several times) into other languages and finally into English. Their histories are often of European states and figures; and they draw attention to an international chivalric elite that is invested in conquest. Their paratexts (sometimes contributed by Creede himself) position these histories as looking glasses for England and anticipate a future of military victories and political supremacy, which reflect the chivalric language and literature of the late Elizabethan period. These features introduce, however, two tensions. First, the forms and figures of chivalry could be, as Helgerson, Moore, and others have discussed, controversial; despite their importance for the Elizabethan court, they valorize

---

[39] See Roberts's address 'To the Courteous Reader'. A similar argument is also offered in Roberts's *Pheander: The Mayden Knight* (London, 1595; STC 21086), a chivalric romance dedicated to Captain Thomas Lee ('true professor, follower of Armes, and marshall discipline'; A3r). See also Lockey, *Law and Empire*, pp. 92–98.

[40] Creede also printed some texts on behalf of Elizabethan authorities. He published several editions of works by Ludwig Lavater, the Swiss Reformed theologian, including *Of Ghosts and Spirits* (London, 1596; STC 15321) and *Three Christian Sermons* (London, 1596; STC 15322). The latter was translated by William Barlow under the instruction of John Whitgift, Archbishop of Canterbury, and reflects on a period of prolonged famine and dearth in Switzerland, which, Creede's title page announces, is 'verie fit for this time of our Dearth' during the mid-1590s (A1r). In the book, Barlow's dedication to Whitgift explains that it was the Archbishop's idea 'that these Sermons of Lauatere shuld be vulgarly translated to the end that all sorts among vs, might in this time of Dearth, be directed to know both the proper cause and the right vse of this Iudgement' (A2r). Whitgift seems to have arranged the translation and its publication, and its paratextual materials recall Creede's own interest in providing instructive looking glasses for English readers.

and autonomize the chivalric knight as a militant aristocrat in a way that was politically charged and had the potential to disrupt the state.[41] As Moore describes, 'the identification of military leaders with chivalric heroes had reached its apotheosis in the person of Robert Devereux, the second Earl of Essex', whose challenges to monarchical authority ended in his execution in 1601.[42] Second, the promotion of chivalric ideals in Creede's publications emerges firmly through the paratextual materials, which offer explicit direction for how to read the histories. Some of the main texts are less optimistic or clear-cut than the paratexts. *The Ancient History of the Destruction of Troy* recounts the heroic deeds of its warriors, but the fall of Troy was also a threatening emblem of civic catastrophe – a reading that, while clearly implied through its main text, is not part of the history's paratexts. A hallmark of Creede's publications seems to be a clear paratextual framework that emphasizes the utility of the history and downplays its troublesome complexities, which is also a defining feature of his playbooks from the Queen's Men.

Creede's Print Brand for the Queen's Men

Creede's non-dramatic publications can be used to understand his investment in four playbooks from the Queen's Men that contain company attributions: *The True Tragedy of Richard III* (1594), *Selimus* (1594), *The Famous Victories of Henry V* (1598), and *Clyomon and Clamydes* (1599). As printed playbooks, they seem to announce Creede's agency in their selection and presentation – especially as he is the main publication agent involved, acting as both printer and publisher. Creede's acquisition of playscripts will be considered in more detail in the next section, but it does not appear that the plays' dramatists directly took part in the process. All of the plays were issued anonymously, which was common practice, but by advertising only the stationer and company, the playbooks seem to minimize the dramatist or at least imply that publication has been entrusted to these other agents. More tellingly, Creede published a number of plays that were, or have subsequently been, connected to Robert Greene, including *Selimus* (published anonymously, but attributed to the Queen's Men), *A Looking Glass* (advertised as by Greene and Lodge and performed by Lord Strange's Men), *James IV* (from an unspecified

---

[41] See, for example, Helgerson, 'Tasso', p. 159.
[42] Helen Moore, 'Jonson, Dekker, and the Discourse of Chivalry', *Medieval & Renaissance Drama in England* 12 (1999), 121–65 (p. 136).

company, but advertised as by Greene), and *Alphonsus, King of Aragon* (also from an unspecified company, but attributed to 'R.G.'). All of these were published after Greene's death in 1592, which clearly removes the dramatist's agency and prioritizes the stationer's.[43] Creede's playbooks tend to suggest either his sole agency in their publication or his role in a stationer–company network of exchange.

Holger Syme proposes, however, that Creede may have collaborated quite extensively during the 1590s with William Barley, who is listed as bookseller on the title-page imprints of several Creede publications, including *The True Tragedy of Richard III*, *Menaechmi*, *The Pedlar's Prophecy*, and *The Trumpet of Fame*.[44] Indeed, both Barley and Creede needed to collaborate with other stationers. Creede's printing house at the Sign of the Catherine Wheel was not a bookshop, meaning that he had to work with others in order to maximize profits; Barley's main shop on Gracechurch Street seems to have been a wholesale and retail location for a number of them. Barley was officially a member of the Drapers' Company, which prevented him from holding publication rights and entering texts in the Register (until he finally joined the Stationers' Company in 1606). He also had to collaborate, and Syme proposes a publishing syndicate with Barley providing financial backing to three printers: Creede, Abel Jeffes, and John Danter.[45] While it is possible that an exchange like this took place, the evidence of Creede's published output and paratexts suggests that, whatever arrangement may have existed with Barley, he retained control over text selection and presentation. The wider range of books on which Barley's name appears does not reveal a clear interest in history, nor does Creede become regularly involved in, for example, coney-catching pamphlets or music publications, the latter emerging as Barley's dominant specialism in the late 1590s.

Creede's playbooks from the Queen's Men share parallels in their title-page design and content, which help to construct a print identity for the

---

[43] Greene's authorship or co-authorship of *Selimus* has been proposed on the basis of stylistic analysis, the dramatist's connection to the Queen's Men, and the inclusion of six extracts from the play in *England's Parnassus* (1600), with an attribution to Greene. Many of the passages in *England's Parnassus* are misattributed, so the association with Greene cannot be taken as conclusive. See Donna N. Murphy, '*Locrine, Selimus*, Robert Greene, and Thomas Lodge', *Notes and Queries*, 56:4 (2009) 559–63; Darren Freebury-Jones, 'Determining Robert Greene's Dramatic Canon', *Style*, 54:4 (2020), 377–98.

[44] Syme, 'Thomas Creede', p. 30.

[45] Ibid., pp. 29–31. Syme calculates that, for the seven plays Creede entered in 1594, he 'must have spent over twenty pounds on authors' fees, licenses, and registration alone – and he maintained a similar rate of entrance for over five years' (p. 40). Syme suggests that it is unlikely – although not impossible – that Creede possessed these funds himself.

company and encourage a reading of their plays as profitable histories that promote England's and Elizabeth I's interests. One prominent title-page feature is Creede's signature woodcut ornament (McKerrow #299, see Figure 1.2), which appears on most of his published texts, as well as on many of the texts he printed for other stationers, such as the second edition of *Richard III* (1598, see Figure 2.3) for Andrew Wise and Sidney's *Defence* (1595). Because the design is so distinctive, it has the effect of creating a recognizable Creede brand. The woodcut features the personification of Truth as a naked woman being scourged by a hand descending from the clouds, with the initials 'TC' (Thomas Creede) and the inscription '*Viressit* [*sic*] *vulnere veritas*' ('Truth flourishes though wounded'). Yamada and McKerrow identify one other printer who used a similar design.[46] In 1589, Thomas Orwin printed Anne Dowriche's *The French History* (STC 7159) for Thomas Man, which shows the figure of Truth on both the title page and final page, alongside a verse interpretation. Orwin died in 1593 and, from that point, Creede seems to be the only London printer using this emblem on title pages. It is an apt woodcut for a stationer interested in histories that advertise their utility as 'true' models or warnings for readers, and appears in, for example *The Pleasant History of the Conquest of the West India*, *The Honour of Chivalry*, and *The Trumpet of Fame*. The woodcut carries added interpretative significance for plays that also contain an attribution to the Queen's Men. It implies that the plays from Elizabeth's company – and, by extension, Elizabeth herself – are invested in the discovery and promotion of truth.

Although these playbooks do not contain discursive paratexts, their title-page plot summaries put forward readings of the histories they contain and – similar to Creede's non-dramatic publications such as *The Ancient History of the Destruction of Troy* – they tend to downplay the complexities of their plots in favour of a patriotic reflection on Elizabethan England and an emphasis on using history to understand the present. For example, the anonymous *True Tragedy of Richard III*, which was one of Shakespeare's sources for the later *Richard III*, dramatizes the title character's usurpation of the English throne and his downfall. Tudor chroniclers and writers, including Vergil, More, Grafton, Hall, and Holinshed, frequently vilified Richard III, a practice that was at least partly in the service of the new royal dynasty established after his death at the Battle of Bosworth Field in 1485. Through its paratexts, this anonymous playbook encourages a reading in line with Tudor apologia. The title page

---

[46] Yamada, *Thomas Creede*, pp. 250–51. See also McKerrow, *Devices*, p. 117.

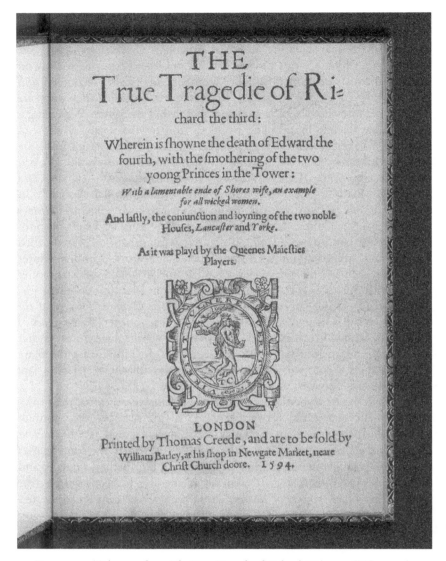

Figure 1.2   Title page from *The True Tragedy of Richard III* (1594; STC 21009).

(see Figure 1.2) draws attention to key narrative developments that promote a providential reading of history: the plot description appeals to a
sense of injustice at the 'smothering of the two yoong Princes in the
Tower' and anticipates the 'coniunction and ioyning of the two noble

Houses, Lancaster and Yorke' (A2r) with the marriage of Henry VII and Elizabeth of York. This phrasing echoes the title of Hall's chronicle, *The Union of the Two Noble and Illustre Families of Lancaster and York* (1548), a text that – at least on the surface – appears to engage in a project of Tudor mythologizing, although recent critics including Peter Herman have argued that Hall expresses an underlying scepticism about the Henrician court for which he was writing.[47] Similar to the laudatory title-page summary in Hall's Chronicle, which presents Henry VIII as the 'vndubitate flower and very heire of both the sayd Images', the play's paratexts position the text as a celebratory account of the inauguration and legitimation of the Tudor line.[48] The title page advertises the veracity of the play's treatment of history by drawing attention to the word 'True', which is presented in large type at the top of the page (A2r) and contained as part of the running title throughout the text. This epithet was not, however, featured in the Stationers' Register, which records the play as 'an enterlude intituled | The Tragedie of Richard the Third'.[49] Creede may have added this adjective to the printed playbook to complement his own ornament featuring 'Truth' and to further the reading of history suggested by the title-page description. McMillin and MacLean propose that plays from the Queen's Men frequently insist upon the truthfulness of their dramatizations and advocate a Protestant plainness in speech, but it is important to consider that this reading could, to a degree, be a product of the printed playbook and a publisher's marketing strategies.[50]

The seemingly straightforward interpretation implied by the paratextual materials is, however, complicated by a closer examination of the play. Walsh draws attention to the play's demystification of 'its own history-making by showing it to be the work of the players on stage'.[51] The induction involving the characters Truth and Poetry appears to suggest a Protestant desire 'for substantial truth and plain speech', but the role of Truth in the representation of history that follows is ambiguous.[52] Poetry asks 'will Truth be a Player' (A3r), and indeed, in light of theatrical doubling practices, both Truth and Poetry would have become players

---

[47] See Peter C. Herman, 'Henrician Historiography and the Voice of the People: The Cases of More and Hall', *Texas Studies in Literature and Language*, 39 (1997), 261–83; and 'Hall, Edward (1497–1547)', *ODNB*, online ed., November 2018, https://doi.org/10.1093/ref:odnb/11954 (accessed 16 September 2019).

[48] Edward Hall, *The Vnion of the two noble and illustrate famelies of Lancastre and Yorke* (London, 1548; STC 12721), ¶1r.

[49] SRO3636; Arber, II, p. 654.   [50] McMillin and MacLean, *Queen's Men*, p. 36.

[51] Walsh, *Shakespeare*, p. 101.   [52] McMillin and MacLean *Queen's Men*, p. 33.

in the main dramatization. The actors performing these roles would have reappeared in other parts, thus visually complicating the plainness and transparency of Truth and the play's depiction of a single and unchallenged history. It raises the possibility of multiple, endlessly qualified readings.[53]

When *The True Tragedy* is considered as a whole, it points to, as Walsh describes, the fallibility and '*belatedness* of historical narratives', and it complicates the Tudor apologia that other parts of the play seem to establish.[54] It recalls contemporary historiographical concerns about the inaccessibility of the past, such as those expressed by Abraham Fleming in his address 'To the Readers studious in histories', prefacing the second volume of Holinshed's *Chronicles* (second edition, 1587): 'it is a toile without head or taile euen for extraordinarie wits, to correct the accounts of former ages so many hundred years receiued, out of vncerteinties to raise certeinties, and to reconcile writers dissenting in opinion and report.'[55] Diverging, unreconcilable reports – and the character, Report – are a recurrent feature of the play. While also evoking the idea of a false account (later personified as Rumour in Shakespeare's *2 Henry IV*), Report allegorizes the historian through the character's search for the 'certain true report' (H3r) of the Battle of Bosworth; however, Report arrives after the battle, which suggests the writing of history is belated, flawed, and partial. In his account to Report, the Page frames Richard's death as a classical paradigm: 'Richard came to fielde mounted on horsback, with as high resolue as fierce Achillis mongst the sturdie Greekes ... to encounter worthie Richmond, [and he] would not yeeld, but with his losse of life he lost the field' (H3v). The Page – who, throughout the play, reflects on the inaccessibility of truth and often addresses the audience as a choric figure – rejuvenates Richard's reputation; and rather than offering a rigid moral judgement on the battle's outcome, provides a report that privileges neither Richard nor Richmond. While the play ostensibly remains a Protestant campaign for Tudor legitimacy, most notably through its overt political statements in the concluding prayer for Elizabeth and its explicit condemnation of Richard as 'a man ill shaped, crooked backed, lame armed' and 'tyrannous in authoritie' (A3v), the play also considers the

---

[53] See also Brian Walsh, 'Truth, Poetry, and Report in *The True Tragedy of Richard III*', in *Locating the Queen's Men*, ed. Ostovich et al., pp. 123–33.

[54] Walsh, *Shakespeare*, p. 88.

[55] Raphael Holinshed, *The First and second volumes of Chronicles* ... (London, 1587; STC 13569), II, title-page verso.

partiality of historical writing and, by implication, questions the truthfulness of its own representations.[56]

Of course, it is inevitable that the ways in which a play is marketed and makes a book of itself through its paratexts cannot capture the complexity of the full text. Title-page advertisements are, by necessity, selective: they sometimes feature just the title and at other times are supplemented with a few details from the plot. As Janette Dillon succinctly puts it, '[t]itle pages are devised in order to sell books, not to make precise scholarly statements about the texts they preface'.[57] We should not expect Creede's title pages to offer nuanced critical evaluations, but one of the reasons why his playbooks are particularly useful as a case study is owing to their consistent paratextual design. The playbooks' framing of history to appeal to the reigning monarch and England's political present can also be seen throughout many of Creede's non-dramatic publications that relay histories of battles, victories, and heroic exploits as models or warnings for their readers, an application that is often discussed explicitly in paratexts that tend to eschew the complexities of the main text.

The same pattern can be seen in *Selimus*, but in this case the subject matter of the play is drawn from Turkish history, which is used to reflect flatteringly on England. It is based on Selim I, who reigned from 1512 to 1520, and concentrates on events that took place between 1511 and 1513. The play's main sources are Thomas Newton's 1575 translation of Augustino Curione's *Sarracenicae Historiae libri III* (Basel, 1567) and Peter Ashton's 1546 translation of Paolo Giovio's *Comentarii della cose de Turchi* (Florence, 1531).[58] As a playbook, the new print paratexts of the 'most tyrannicall Tragedie and raigne of Selimus' (A3r) present the title character as the single source of unrest and corruption in the play, fashioning him as their religio-political target. The title-page plot summary describes in detail the immorality of this emperor of the Turks, including how he 'most vnnaturally raised warres against his owne father', 'caused him to be poysoned', and murdered 'his two brethren' (see Figure 1.3).[59]

---

[56] For a discussion of how the play in performance could have promoted affective, rather than reflective, responses in its audience, therefore encouraging an experience of 'royalist nationality', see Jennifer Roberts-Smith, '"What makes thou upon a stage?": Child Actors, Royalist Publicity, and the Space of the Nation in the Queen's Men's *True Tragedy of Richard the Third*', *Early Theatre*, 15:2 (2012), 192–205.

[57] Janette Dillon, 'Is There a Performance in This Text?', *Shakespeare Quarterly*, 45:1 (1994), 74–86 (p. 79).

[58] Daniel J. Vitkus, *Three Turk Plays from Early Modern England* (New York: Columbia University Press, 2000), p. 18.

[59] [Robert Greene]/Anon., *The First part of the Tragicall raigne of Selimus* (London, 1594; STC 12310a), A2r.

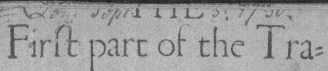

First part of the Tra-
gicall raigne of Selimus, sometime Empe-
rour of the Turkes, and grandfather to him
that now raigneth.

Wherein is showne how hee most vnnaturally
raised warres against his owne father *Baiazet*, and pre-
uailing therein, in the end caused him to
be poysoned;

Also with the murthering of his two brethren,
Corcut, and *Acomat*.

As it was playd by the Queenes Maiesties
Players.

LONDON
Printed by Thomas Creede, dwelling in Thames
streete at the signe of the Kathren wheele,
neare the olde Swanne.
1594.

Figure 1.3   Title page from *Selimus* (1594; STC 12310a).

This emphasis on a single, overreaching conqueror recalls Marlowe's *Tamburlaine* – a connection that is made even more explicit by its full title: 'The First part of the Tragicall raigne of Selimus'. No second part is extant or known to have been written, although the epilogue refers to the potential for a continuation, indicating the company's desire to capitalize on the successful Tamburlainean model from the Admiral's Men. However, *Selimus* rejects *Tamburlaine*'s amoral model: the play as a whole is aware, as Peter Berek observes, that 'the Tamburlainean conqueror posed ethical and dramaturgical problems' and its printed presentation strategies serve to condemn Selimus's actions.[60] The classification of this Turkish history as a 'tragedie' (in its head title) and 'tragical' (in its main and running title) furthers this judgement of the protagonist, as these genre labels were sometimes used, as Berek proposes, to indicate the 'death of one who behaves badly'.[61] Both *Selimus* and *The True Tragedy of Richard III* were published as 'tragedies' and feature villainous protagonists whose tyrannical actions are singled out in their paratexts. Significantly, *Selimus* does not actually dramatize the death of its central character, which adds to the sense that 'tragical' refers to a reading of his actions as immoral.

Selimus also contains a print prologue and epilogue that display the same evaluation: they denounce Selimus as 'a wicked soone' who pursues his 'wretched father with remorselesse spight' and 'kill[s] his friends in fight' (A2v). These materials likely have theatrical origins, but through their inclusion in the playbook the prologue and epilogue acquire a new interpretative fixity, which differs from their detachable and temporary status as performance parts. Indeed, they seem particularly suited to act as paratextual addresses in the printed book. The prologue describes how 'You shall behold him character in bloud, | The image of an vnplacable King' (A2v). The use of 'character' in this context implies that Selimus is characterized by his bloody conquests and betrayals and that he is symbolized by an image of blood; but it also connects him to a written history that both records and creates, 'character' and 'charactery' being terms for writing symbols and systems. As a fixed part of the playbook, the prologue characters Selimus as the 'vnplacable King' of this printed history. The fact that the epilogue is actually titled the 'Conclusion' (K3r) in the playbook furthers this idea that theatrical documents are being re-presented as printed documents that provide (textually) closed views on the play.

---

[60] Berek, '*Tamburlaine*'s Weak Sons: Imitation As Interpretation before 1593', *Renaissance Drama*, 13 (1982), 55–82 (p. 72).
[61] Berek, 'Genres', p. 171.

Together with Creede's signature woodcut on the title page, they also advertise the truthfulness of the play's account, describing it as 'a most lamentable historie | Which this last age acknowledgeth for true' (A2v). In the playbook, the conjunction of the terms 'history' and 'tragedy' (and their variants) offers a critical judgement on the play's dramatization of the past.

A closer look at *Selimus* reveals that the main play adopts a critical stance towards all of the Turkish leaders, while the playbook's paratexts concentrate on Selimus as the central villain and compress the play's sources of instability and corruption into a single figure. The paratexts gloss over the other power struggles, betrayals, and usurpations that take place, notably those involving Selimus's brother, Acomat, who is arguably even more tyrannical and extreme than Selimus, but who is represented on the title page with pathos as an unnaturally murdered brother. In fact, Selimus's dominance over the play, suggested by the title page and prologue, is belied by his absence from the drama between sigs. C4v and F4v (spanning about ten scenes and over 800 lines of dialogue). During this time, Acomat assumes the central dramatic position and enacts various atrocities that, as Berek observes, surpass Selimus's later brutality.[62] In a scene that possibly influenced Shakespeare's depiction of the blinding of Gloucester in *King Lear*, Acomat, with the assistance of Regan, blinds the loyal advisor Aga and cuts off both his hands, before sending him back to Bajazet.[63] The stage directions in the quarto edition specify that these actions be shown on stage and indicate the moments when Acomat 'Puls out [Aga's] eyes' and 'They [i.e. Acomat and Regan] cut of[f] his hands' (F2v–F3r). It is the most significant and sustained example of tyrannical action in the play and creates a striking disjunction with the title page's sympathy towards Acomat and his later fate.

Selimus's more moderate tactics to gain power are, in fact, derided by Acomat, whose sudden and insatiable desire for 'the crowne' (F2r) leads to civil destruction, including the murder of his nephews and the massacre of his subjects as part of an attempt to suppress all opposition:

> He [Selimus] should haue done as I meane to do,
> Fill all the confines, with fire, sword and blood.
> Burne vp the fields, and ouerthrow whole townes,
> And when he had endammaged that way,

---

[62] Ibid., pp. 73–74.
[63] Cf. Shakespeare, *True Chronicle Historie of the life and death of King Lear* (London, 1608; STC 22292), H1r–H2r. Berek, 'Weak Sons', p. 74.

> Then teare the old man peecemeale with my teeth,
> And colour my strong hands with his gore-blood
> . . .
> It is the greatest glorie of a king
> When, though his subjects hate his wicked deeds
> Yet are they forst to bear them all with praise.
>
> (F2r–v)

Acomat's switching of pronouns in this exclamation – from 'And when *he* had endammaged that way, | Then teare the old man peecemeale with *my* teeth' – marks the moment when Acomat's reflection on what Selimus should have enacted becomes an envenomed declaration of his own intended actions. Although Acomat claims that '[h]ate is peculiar to a princes state' (F2v), Selimus has the support of the people, as well as many of the main advisors, and he is recognized as a strong military leader. While he does eventually eliminate all opposition through orchestrating the deaths of his father and brothers, Selimus's actions are not presented in ways that surpass the visual impact and extremity of Acomat's, and what emerges is a state plagued by repeated power struggles between different factions. There is no overriding villain (as the paratextual materials seem to suggest) to contrast with a benign and effective alternative; instead, there are variations on a political model of domination and usurpation that arise from a state governed by the ineffective leader, Bajazet.

In common with many of Creede's non-dramatic publications, *Selimus*'s text and paratexts highlight the ways in which 'foreign' histories had wide application and could be used to reflect on contemporary political events at home. As Kewes discusses, the play evokes a familiar English landscape in the midst of the unfamiliar foreign setting and it is infused with English idioms, social descriptions, and place names (such as 'Holburne vp Tiburne', H4r), which recall late sixteenth-century London.[64] The scenes involving the play's clown, Bullithrumble, particularly encourage a connection (or conflation) with an English setting. Elizabethan clowns tended to be topical, and they frequently use contemporary colloquialisms and allude to current events.[65] Through its incorporation of anglicized characters and references, *Selimus*, as a history play, partly erases the distinction between past and present events and between native and foreign histories. The title page further announces the 'presentness' of the past by pointing out that Selimus is 'the grandfather to him that now raigneth', which encourages readers in England to look for the relevance of the events

---

[64] Kewes, 'Elizabethan', pp. 175–76. [65] See also Rackin, *Stages of History*, pp. 222–47.

presented in the play. Interest in Turkish history had been fuelled by the establishment of the 'Turkey Company' in 1581 (reorganized as the Levant Company in 1592), which regulated trade between England and the Levant and Ottoman Empire. Foreign trade was becoming more and more important, and as Daniel Vitkus describes, readers and theatregoers in England would have been 'increasingly aware of the power of the "Grand Seigneur" in Turkey'.[66] Accounts of Ottoman government, succession, and religion were not simply distant, detached histories (like the Troy stories) but pressingly current ones that could have a direct bearing on power dynamics in central Europe. Representations of these histories reflect an Anglocentric fascination with and desire to control the Ottoman past and present.[67]

Another way in which *Selimus* draws attention to its contemporaneity is through the scenes involving the poisoning of Bajazet, which are advertised on the title page. While the play was probably written and first performed by 1592 (especially if it is by Greene, who died that year), the fact that Selimus enlists the services of 'Abraham the Iew' (G3r–v) to murder his father would have prompted a topical reading in 1594. It would recall the accusations levelled against Elizabeth's physician, Roderigo Lopez, who was of Jewish heritage and had been executed in June 1594 for allegedly attempting to poison the queen.[68] Lopez's involvement and the details of the plot are uncertain, but the outcome of the trial was sealed once Robert Devereux, second earl of Essex, staked his reputation on the prosecution – partly because of a personal enmity against Lopez, his former physician, for revealing details of the earl's medical conditions, which 'did disparage his honour'.[69] The plot aroused extraordinary public interest in England, and spurred a series of pamphlets, including an official government account by William Cecil, who castigated Lopez as a treasonous rebel threatening the stability of the state.[70] As a book, therefore, *Selimus* acquired a new application – and one that is alert to the use of history for political

---

[66] Vitkus, *Three Turk Plays*, p. 43.

[67] For the use of the Ottoman Empire in the construction of European and English identities, see Ambereen Dadabhoy, 'Two Faced: The Problem of Othello's Visage', in *Othello: The State of Play*, ed. Lena Cowen Orlin (London: Arden Bloomsbury, 2014), pp. 121–47.

[68] Lopez's father had been baptized by force and, while outwardly conforming to the Anglican church, Lopez may have adhered to Judaism at home. Sir Edward Coke used Lopez's secret Judaism as a point of attack during his trial. See Kewes, 'Elizabethan', p. 176, and Edgar Samuel, 'Lopez [Lopes], Roderigo [Ruy, Roger] (*c.*1517–1594)', *ODNB*, online ed., January 2008, https://doi.org/10.1093/ref:odnb/17011 (accessed 16 September 2019), para. 1, 7.

[69] Samuel, 'Lopez', para. 6.

[70] William Cecil, *A Trve Report of Svndry Horrible Conspiracies* (London, 1594; STC 7603).

exempla. The overarching reading suggested by its paratexts demonstrates the appeal of simple, stereotyped historical verdicts and narratives. The paratexts compress the threat of corruption into the single figure of Selimus – who is both a hyperbolic Turkish antagonist and also a symbol of papal corruption, established through the allusion to Lopez, whose plot was supposedly at the behest of his Spanish contacts. Vitkus points out that some Protestant writers in England 'expressed a hope that the rival powers of pope and sultan would annihilate each other', and this kind of dual condemnation is witnessed in *Selimus*'s title page, alongside an anti-Semitic allusion.[71] The paratexts serve to reassure readers who are desirous of Anglocentric legitimacy, expansion, and control, while the play itself packages its concern about these foreign 'others' in a different way. Selimus ends the play in triumph, and the comeuppance suggested by the paratexts does not take place, at least in this part of the play, which marks a disjunction between the formal shape of its history and the clear didactic applications implied by the title page. The play is not as confident as its paratexts and displays a sweeping anxiety over Ottoman history and current events, including their ramifications for England's political and economic prosperity.

As a final example of a history playbook firmly connected to the repertory of the Queen's Men, *The Famous Victories of Henry V* creates a similar tension between text and paratext. It was performed by the company at some point between 1583 and 1587, making it one of their earliest extant plays.[72] Although it was entered in the Register on 14 May 1594, it was not published until 1598 and was therefore a relatively old play by the time it appeared in print. Indeed, *The Famous Victories* is sometimes described as the first English history play, and one that is representative of the company's repertory owing to its subject matter and the prominence of its clowning parts.[73] It features a monarch who was regularly invoked during the sixteenth century as an exemplum of military prowess in the service of national glory, in contrast to the villainous protagonists, Richard

---

[71] Vitkus, *Three Turk Plays*, p. 8.

[72] The dating of the play's early performances depends on an anecdote concerning Tarlton doubling the parts of Derick and the Lord Chief Justice, with William Knell as Henry V. As Knell was killed in a duel in June 1587 and Tarlton died in 1588, the play must have been performed at some point between the company's formation in 1583 and mid-1587. See *The Famous Victories of Henry the Fifth*, prep. Chiaki Hanabusa, Malone Society Publications, vol. 171 (Manchester: Manchester University Press for the Malone Society, 2007), pp. xx–xxii.

[73] Larry S. Champion, '"What Prerogatiues Meanes": Perspective and Political Ideology in *The Famous Victories of Henry V*', *South Atlantic Review*, 53:4 (1988), 1–19 (p. 1).

III and Selimus, from Creede's other playbooks.[74] The title page of *The Famous Victories* underscores this reading. After the main title, it singles out the depiction of the 'Honourable Battell of Agin-court' as the play's main feature – a wise marketing decision as the legacy of Henry V was so closely tied to this famous battle.[75] In the years following the defeat of the Spanish Armada, when hostilities with Spain continued and the threat of future armadas remained high, the playbook offers a reminder of one of England's most celebrated victories. Creede's regular ornament effectively labels the play a 'true' history and, together with the plot summary, encourages an optimistic reflection on England's political stability and ascendancy. As mentioned previously, it was published in the same year as Roberts's enthusiastic prose history, *Honour's Conquest*, that similarly praises England's 'famous victories'.

The play itself complicates this view, and instead of focusing on, as the paratexts suggest, 'Honourable' military exploits, it foregrounds Henry's transition from prince to monarch in social and political spheres that draw attention to his unflattering qualities, such as his ruthlessness. Indeed, the 'Battell of Agin-court', advertised so prominently on the title page, makes up a relatively small section of the play, the preparation, battle, and aftermath consisting of around 300 lines out of a total of approximately 1,720. Most of the play concentrates on colourful events from Henry's life, including his riotous youth and eventual succession to the English throne. Critics have described the play as a glorification of monarchy, suggesting that Henry emerges as an ideal prince at the point of his sudden repentance on his father's deathbed; but this reading has been partly influenced by a tendency to diminish the complexities of plays that are associated with Shakespearean equivalents (in this case, *1* and *2 Henry IV*, and *Henry V*).[76] Rather, the play's expansive scope, fast-paced action, and manipulation of its chronicle sources reveal a troubling representation of its central character. For example, unlike Shakespeare's *1 Henry IV*, *The Famous Victories* shows Henry as the instigator and ringleader of the robbery of his father's Receivers, an action that displays a disregard for public welfare and

---

[74] See Amy Lidster, 'Challenging Monarchical Legacies in *Edward III* and *Henry V*', *English: Journal of the English Association*, 68:261 (2019), 126–42.

[75] *The Famous Victories of Henry the fifth* (London, 1598; STC 13072), A1r.

[76] Tillyard (in *Shakespeare's History Plays*), Ribner (in *The English History Play*), and Madeleine Doran (in *Endeavours of Art: A Study of Form in Elizabethan Drama*) have stressed the play's patriotism and upholding of Henry V as a national hero.

which would have been especially apparent to the socially mixed early modern audiences.[77]

This disruptive presentation is highlighted in Henry's 'reformation' on his father's deathbed, which may be, as Larry Champion suggests, 'more politically expedient than genuine'.[78] In this scene, Henry enters wearing a 'cloake so full of needles', which he describes as 'a signe that I stand vpon thorns, til the Crowne be on my head' (C1v). He also carries a 'dagger in his hand' (C2v) in order to murder the king, a plan that is thwarted by his father's sudden awakening. While Henry's cloak recalls the morality play tradition and the symbolic robe that Mankind would wear and remove to signal his repentance, it does not indicate that Henry undergoes a genuine transformation.[79] Henry's repentance ensures his dying father's approval and is essentially motivated by personal gain. The representation of the heir apparent readying a dagger to murder the king constitutes a dangerous act of political subversion. Although the play is influenced by morality-play techniques, it reminds readers that Henry is not an everyman.

The events in France similarly challenge a clear-cut patriotic interpretation, showing that, as Karen Oberer describes, 'some of Henry's victories are not entirely worthy of being remembered in the chronicles'.[80] The play's subplot involving Derick and John Cobbler undermines the 'Honourable' claims of the title page. During the battle scenes, these characters – played by the company's clowns – exploit the casualties of war and scavenge the battlefield, removing shoes and valuables from both French and English soldiers (F4v–G1v). In contrast, the title-page paratexts recall the popular legacy of Henry V as it was invoked in Elizabethan military manuals, including Robert Barret's *Theory and Practice of Modern Wars*, published in the same year, which praises 'our noble Henry the fift at Agincourt' for showing 'constancy and true fortitude of mind in all perillous and daungerous successes' in the 'actions of warre'.[81] Creede's edition capitalizes on this reputation of Henry and encourages a reading of *The Famous Victories* as a jingoistic history that extols England's foreign conquests and military strength, despite the somewhat dishonourable actions that take place in the play and contrast with the paratextual values of his other publications, including *Honour's Conquest* and *The Ancient*

---

[77] Champion, '"What Prerogatiues Meanes"', pp. 2–4.   [78] Ibid., pp. 7–8.

[79] See Karen Oberer, 'Appropriations of the Popular Tradition in *The Famous Victories of Henry V* and *The Troublesome Raigne of King John*', in *Locating the Queen's Men*, ed. Ostovich et al., pp. 171–82 (p. 173).

[80] Ibid., p. 176.

[81] Robert Barret, *The Theorike and Practike of Moderne Warres* (London, 1598; STC 1500), Q1r.

History of the Destruction of Troy. Indeed, a contrastive analysis of the ideas typically explored in Creede's dramatic and non-dramatic paratexts seems to support a view of Henry as a kind of chivalric knight who takes part in 'Honourable' exploits – a reading that is qualified by the rather unchivalrous events featured in the main play.

As suggested by this brief survey, Creede's paratexts – sometimes written by him, sometimes contributed by others, but always overseen by him – tend to diminish the complexities of the main text in favour of advancing a simple, often didactic, reading that promotes the use of history for patriotic ends. In his playbooks, the authorizing figure of Elizabeth I, introduced through title-page attributions to the Queen's Men, enhances their potential as royalist histories that applaud the queen and the Tudor line. A play like *The Famous Victories* also draws attention to a chivalric culture that was widespread in Elizabethan literature and at court. On the one hand, this parallel secures an interpretative connection between Creede's published output and Elizabeth I; but, on the other hand, it also suggests an interest in aristocratic military exploits that could be controversial and challenge the authority of the monarch (which Henry's actions, as prince, initially do). Indeed, Creede's final playbook with a title-page attribution to the Queen's Men – *Clyomon and Clamydes* – clearly reflects the publisher's interest in the chivalric tradition and sheds light on the other playbooks' understanding of history. The title page describes the play as 'The Historie of the two valiant Knights, Syr Clyomon Knight of the Golden Sheeld, sonne to the King of Denmarke; And Clamydes the white Knight, sonne to the King of Suauia'.[82] Here, 'history' applies to a fictional story that is not otherwise connected to a written or oral historical narrative: as Lisa Hopkins discusses, there was no Danish king called Clyomon and, although the play features Alexander the Great as a character and is nominally set during his reign, it collapses distinctions between time and space by bringing this classical figure into a mythical setting.[83] *Clyomon* offers a tale of heroic adventures, a 'Glasse of glory shining bright', according to its prologue (A2v); but this is a publishing specialism that, across Creede's output, tends to unite real and fictional histories. In my working definition of the 'history play' outlined in the Introduction, I privilege plays that have a connection to an identifiable historical

---

[82] Anon./[George Peele?], *The Historie of the two valiant Knights, Syr Clyomon Knight of the Golden Sheeld, sonne to the King of Denmarke; And Clamydes the white Knight* (London, 1599; STC 5450a), A2r.

[83] Hopkins, 'Danish', pp. 2, 9.

tradition. Creede's practices, those of a real early modern reader, indicate how this boundary often breaks down. His understanding of 'history', true and feigned, centres on its ability to provide models or warnings for English readers, an application that sometimes introduces a slight tension between the autonomy of the monarch and the competing exploits of a noble elite.

Creede's investment in history and commercial drama has led critics, such as Pinciss, to attribute plays that have uncertain theatrical origins to the Queen's Men.[84] It is not my aim to evaluate the origins of Creede's other playbooks, most of which will remain a matter of speculation. What is interesting for my purposes is the fact that these playbooks draw attention to the consistency of Creede's publishing strategies. They all feature Creede's principal ornament showing 'Truth' and they dramatize a range of different histories that can be used for instruction and delight. *A Looking Glass for London and England*, which was in the repertory of Strange's Men by March 1592, presents its biblical history of Jonah and the sins of Nineveh in the eighth century BCE as a warning for Elizabethan London and England.[85] This admonitory potential is the exclusive emphasis of the playbook's title-page paratexts. Readers have to turn the page to discover the play's actual subject matter. *James IV* is labelled as a 'Scottish Historie', and the title page announces the play-book's interest in the past by advertising historical events that do not actually take place in the play (that is, that James IV was 'slaine at Flodden').[86] *Alphonsus* offers a pseudo-historical play set in Italy, Turkey, and the near East that personifies history through the inclusion of Clio as one of the characters. Similar to *Clyomon*, it seems to invest its fictional account with the signs and symbols of history through its emphasis on the utility of the past and its nominal setting at the time of the conquest of Naples in 1442.[87] Finally, *Locrine* features early British history that, according to the title page, is 'No lesse pleasant then profitable'.[88] It

---

[84] Pinciss, 'Repertory', pp. 321–30.

[85] Pinciss ('Repertory', p. 322) assigns *A Looking Glass* to the Queen's Men on the basis of Creede's involvement. Henslowe's *Diary* shows that the play was in the repertory of Strange's Men in March 1592, and Lawrence Manley and Sally-Beth MacLean argue convincingly that there is no clear reason to suppose it originated first with another company. See Manley and MacLean, *Lord Strange's Men and Their Plays* (New Haven and London: Yale University Press, 2014), pp. 101–03; R. A. Foakes (ed.), *Henslowe's Diary*, 2nd ed. (Cambridge: Cambridge University Press, 2002), pp. 16–17, 19.

[86] Robert Greene, *The Scottish Historie of Iames the fourth* (London, 1598; STC 12308), A2r.

[87] Robert Greene ('R.G.'), *The Comicall Historie of Alphonsus, King of Aragon* (London, 1599, STC 12233), A3v–A4v. Wiggins, II, pp. 381–85 (No. 788).

[88] Anon./'W.S.', *The Lamentable Tragedie of Locrine* (London, 1595, STC 21528), A2r.

suggests that the play's account of the 'warres of the Britaines, and Hunnes' (A2r) will be profitable for readers, and it echoes the paratextual agenda of Creede's other publications, such as *The True Tragedy*'s celebration of the Tudor line, *The Famous Victories*' commemoration of an 'Honourable' battle, and *The Trumpet of Fame*'s promotion of foreign exploration and acquisition. *Locrine*'s tumultuous events and civil wars – which are not advertised on the title page – introduce a disjunction with this triumphant paratextual reading.

While Creede had an interest in the Queen's Men, it was not an exclusive one. Other stationers (including Edward White) published plays from the company and Creede invested in plays from different playing troupes. Uncertain theatrical origins mean it is possible that half of Creede's playbooks were first performed by companies other than the Queen's Men.[89] Walsh suggests that the initial interest of the Queen's Men in history plays may have been 'driven by Ciceronian principles about the didactic powers of history', but 'the company's actual plays work to complicate the use of history to promote stable political messages'.[90] Creede's playbooks support a similar reading: their paratextual materials fashion a print brand for the Queen's Men as a company invested in the patriotic use of history, but the main plays are less clearly and consistently works of political propaganda. The fact that Creede's unattributed playbooks and non-dramatic texts also display the same interest in the application of 'histories' as contemporary exempla underpinned by an optimistic reflection on England's present and future securely establishes the Queen's Men playbooks as representative of *his* output, rather than the company's complete repertory.

For a few years during the 1590s, Creede emerges as an important printer-publisher in search of, as aptly suggested by his first play title in the Register, looking glasses for London and England. Although the paratexts in his dramatic and non-dramatic publications tend to overlook the complexities of the main texts, it does not follow that Creede was an unintelligent reader or that he was deliberately mispresenting texts. Publishers needed to choose a way to market their texts, and all reading – including, as this study argues, genre discussions – is motivated by an agenda. Indeed, holding a mirror up to nature is an act that suggests

---

[89] Of the roughly nine commercial plays that Creede published, the theatrical origins of *A Looking Glass*, *The Pedlar's Prophecy*, *Locrine*, *James IV*, and *Alphonsus* are uncertain or connected to other companies.

[90] Walsh, *Shakespeare*, p. 31.

partiality: to use history to reflect and instruct the present necessarily involves highlighting certain aspects and excluding others. It offers only a semblance of historical reality, and in Creede's case, his paratexts make a claim for the benefits of reading patriotically, of searching for models and warnings to assist late Elizabethan England.

Creede and the Emerging Market for Commercial Playbooks

All of Creede's Register entries for commercial plays took place in 1594 – and within a period of only a few months from March to July. He was not alone. In May 1594, Edward White also registered plays from the Queen's Men, and other stationers entered and published plays from different theatre companies at an unprecedented rate during the same year. In total, nineteen commercial plays were printed in 1594 – all of which were first editions with the exception of *The Spanish Tragedy* – and twenty-one were entered in the Register.[91] Although critics have debated the reasons for this 'bumper year', the prominence of history plays within the first major publication boom in commercial drama has not been recognized, which perhaps owes something to the enduring emphasis, in accounts of the genre, on Shakespeare's Folio histories, represented by just one of the 1594 plays – *The First Part of the Contention of the Two Famous Houses of York and Lancaster* (*2 Henry VI* in the Folio).[92] Moreover, only three of these plays are described as 'histories' on their title pages, a usage that, in the case

---

[91] The nineteen plays (with their Register dates, if entered) are: *The Spanish Tragedy* (6 October 1592 to Jeffes); *Edward II* (6 July 1593 to William Jones (2)); *Jack Straw* (23 October 1593 to Danter); *Orlando Furioso* (7 December 1593 to Danter); *A Knack to Know a Knave* (7 January 1594 to Richard Jones); *Titus Andronicus* (6 February 1594 to Danter); *A Looking Glass for London and England* (5 March 1594 to Creede); *The First Part of the Contention* (12 March 1594 to Millington); *The Taming of a Shrew* (2 May 1594 to Short); *Friar Bacon and Friar Bungay* (14 May 1594 to White); *The Wounds of Civil War* (24 May 1594 to Danter); *The Cobbler's Prophecy* (8 June 1594 to Burby); *Mother Bombie* (18 June 1594 to Burby); *The True Tragedy of Richard III* (19 June 1594 to Creede); *Dido, Queen of Carthage* (9 February 1596, transfer to Linley); *The Battle of Alcazar* (no entry); *Selimus* (no entry); *The Wars of Cyrus* (no entry); and *The Massacre at Paris* (no entry). The other plays entered in 1594 but not published that year are: *The Pedlar's Prophecy* (13 May to Creede, published 1595); *Locrine* (20 July to Creede, published 1595); *The Famous Victories of Henry V* (14 May to Creede, published 1598); *James IV* (14 May to Creede, published 1598); *David and Fair Bathsheba* (14 May to White, published 1599); *King Leir* (14 May to White, published 1605); *The Four Prentices of London* (19 June to Danter, published 1615); *The Jew of Malta* (14 May to Ling and Millington, published 1633); 'John of Gaunt' (14 May to White, lost); 'Robin Hood and Little John' (14 May to White, lost); and 'Heliogabalus' (19 June to Danter, lost).

[92] See Knutson, 'What's So Special about 1594?', pp. 449–67; and Holger Schott Syme, 'The Meaning of Success: Stories of 1594 and Its Aftermath', *Shakespeare Quarterly*, 61:4 (2010), 490–525.

of *Orlando Furioso* ('Historie') and *The Taming of a Shrew* ('Pleasant Conceited Historie'), mostly carries the meaning of a fictional story. Only *Friar Bacon and Friar Bungay* ('Honorable Historie') could convincingly be described as dramatizing the past through the connection of its title characters to the historical figures Roger Bacon and Thomas Bungay and the play's plot involving the future Edward I.[93] The limited and/or indeterminate use of 'history' as a label for plays that dramatize the past is in keeping with patterns on Creede's playbook title pages and for the period as a whole.[94] Creede specialized in accounts of the past that took dramatic and non-dramatic forms, but he favours the classically derived terms 'tragedy' and 'comedy' as genre labels for plays. Similarly, most of the other 1594 playbooks that feature an identifiable historical past are described as tragedies, or their broad thematic concerns about leadership, military conflict, and civil uprising are highlighted through terms such as 'battle', 'contention', 'massacre', 'reign', 'wars', and 'wounds'. In this section, I consider briefly the nature of this wider publication boom in history plays, arguing that it reveals an overlooked diversity in plays about the past, that it clarifies the emerging market for commercial playbooks, and that it was potentially a means of advertising the newly reopened theatres and developing a new platform for their plays as printed books.

The 1594 playbooks dramatize a wide range of histories, which qualifies one of the most quoted accounts of the period's theatrical offerings. In Thomas Nashe's *Pierce Penniless* (1592), the title character claims that the subject of plays 'for the most part' is 'borrowed out of our English Chronicles, wherein our forefathers valiant actes (that haue lyne long buried in rustie brasse and worme-eaten bookes) are reuiued'.[95] Nashe's text should not be taken too literally as an indicator of repertory patterns. His account of plays staged in London is part of the fictional narrator's supplication to the Devil and is contained within a section about the prevalence of sloth (one of the seven deadly sins) in sixteenth-century society. Plays are presented as an antidote to sloth, and Pierce's description is informed by his agenda to defend the theatres as a place of recreation and profitable instruction. Like Sidney's *Defence*, Nashe's prose narrative seems

---

[93] David Bergeron ('"Bogus"', pp. 93–112) also classifies the play as a 'history', carrying the meaning of an account of the past, and disagrees strongly with David Bevington's description of the play as 'bogus' history in *English Renaissance Drama: A Norton Anthology* (New York: Norton, 2002), p. 129.

[94] See Introduction, pp. 15, 25–31.

[95] Thomas Nashe, *Pierce Pennilesse his Supplication to the Diuell* (London, 1592; STC 18371), H2r.

to make a clear statement about theatrical patterns and kinds, but it is shaped by impulses other than a considered assessment of company repertories and is offered by a narrator who is far from reliable. Nashe may have underlined the significance of English history for other reasons too: Pierce goes on to recall the personation of 'braue Talbot' (H2r), which probably alludes to a production of *1 Henry VI* (as named in the Folio). Nashe likely contributed to this play, so the defence serves a promotional function as well.

The group of playbooks published in 1594 offers a better view of the historical pasts that appeared on stages in London and across the country than Nashe's account.[96] They feature classical history in *Dido, Queen of Carthage* and *The Wounds of Civil War* (which dramatizes the conflict between Marius and Sulla between *c.*88 and 87 BCE); biblical history in *A Looking Glass for London and England*; and relatively recent history in *The Battle of Alcazar* (dramatizing the historical battle from 1578) and *The Massacre at Paris* (dramatizing the St Bartholomew's Day massacre of 1572). Evidence from Henslowe's *Diary* indicates high performance takings and frequencies for some of these plays. Strange's Men performed *The Battle of Alcazar* (as 'mvlomvrco' and variants) fourteen times at the Rose theatre between February 1592 and January 1593, making it their third most frequently staged play, while *The Massacre at Paris* recorded the highest average receipts for the company.[97] Of course, the 1594 playbooks were written and first performed at different times and should not be seen to reflect, comprehensively and statically, repertory patterns from the early 1590s; but that does not alter the fact that they testify to the prominence of other histories in the public playhouses. Alongside Creede's biblical, English, and Turkish histories, they draw attention to the diversity of early modern historical culture on stage and in print. What remains particularly relevant about Nashe's discussion is its promotion of historical drama for the purposes of emulation – a factor that also informs Creede's investment and which ultimately serves to connect different histories rather than divide them.

By investing in these histories, publishers speculated that they would be of interest to readers, and the fact that some, like Creede, specialized in non-dramatic histories and topical news pamphlets implies an overlap – in

---

[96] See also Manley and MacLean, *Lord Strange's Men*, chs. 3 and 4, appendix B.
[97] It is uncertain if 'mvlomvcro' (meaning Muly Molocco) indicates Peele's *Battle of Alcazar*. Manley and MacLean argue that it does (ibid., pp. 75–78, 339); see also Wiggins, III, pp. 160–61 (No. 918).

theme and readership – between these materials. Thomas Millington, for example, published *The First Part of the Contention*, as well as short, politically invested texts such as *News from Brest* (1594) and *The Copy of a Letter Sent by the French King to the People of Artois and Hainault* (1595). The former is a pamphlet about Sir John Norris's successful attack, in 1594, on Fort Crozon outside Brest in Brittany, which was in aid of the Protestant Henri IV of France's efforts against the Catholic League and Spanish troops.[98] The latter is also concerned with the French Wars of Religion and features Henri IV's declaration of 'open warre against the king of Spaine and his adherents, and the causes him mouing therto'.[99] The staging of political debate, uprisings, and a French connection (through Margaret of Anjou) in *The First Part of the Contention* would therefore provide a fitting accompaniment to Millington's topical pamphlets. During the 1590s, playhouse plays 'began to establish a stable market' in print, as Andy Kesson and Emma Smith suggest, by ensuring they could be 'read well beyond the theatre by a wide readership as a means to connect with contemporary political and social debate'.[100] The first readers to make these connections were publishers, and the first site of exchange between non-dramatic texts and history playbooks was the bookstall.

Interestingly, Creede worked directly with Millington on *The First Part of the Contention*: he was hired as trade printer for the edition. The presentation of this playbook recalls the recognizable Creede brand discussed earlier.[101] The title page contains his signature woodcut of 'Truth', and its *mise en page* resembles those from his own publications, which offers a useful reminder of the influence that trade printers could have over the final design of playbooks. Millington entered the play in the Register on 12 March 1594 at a similar time to Creede's own entry, on 5 March, for *A Looking Glass for London and England*. These two playbooks link Creede to neighbouring booksellers who had premises close to theatrical venues. Barley's bookshop in Gracechurch Street, given in the title-page imprint of *A Looking Glass*, was in the immediate vicinity of Millington's shop under St Peter's Church, as well as two playing venues – the Cross

---

[98] Anon., *Newes from Brest* (London, 1594; STC 18654).
[99] Anon./Henri IV of France, *The Copie of a Letter sent by the French king* (London, 1595; STC 13119), A1r.
[100] Andy Kesson and Emma Smith, 'Introduction: Towards a Definition of Print Popularity', in *Elizabethan Top Ten*, ed. Kesson and Smith, pp. 1–15 (p. 6).
[101] See also Helen Smith, who writes of the 'Creede effect', because of his distinctive house style and its use within texts he published and those he printed for others. Smith, 'Mapping', p. 83.

Keys and Bell Inn, which were associated with the Queen's Men.[102] The geographical proximity of bookshops, theatrical venues, and Creede's dealings with both Barley and Millington could have shaped the stationers' investment and presentation strategies, contributed to the acquisition of playscripts, and encouraged trade from passing playgoers.

Because of their potential for contemporary application, history plays may have presented themselves as the most relevant thematic grouping for publishers, which offers a tentative explanation – dependent on playscript availability – for the dominance of historical subject matter in printed plays from this period. The acquisition of manuscripts must, however, be briefly addressed. As most of the 1594 plays (including Creede's) were entered in the Register between March and July, it appears as if a large number of plays from the commercial stages suddenly became available to stationers. For example, at almost the same time as Creede's entries, White received the rights on 14 May 1594 to *Friar Bacon and Friar Bungay* (published 1594) and *King Leir* (published 1605), both from the Queen's Men.[103] The fact that two London stationers, working independently, acquired a number of plays from the company suggests that members may have been actively offering their playscripts to stationers. One still-prevalent theory is that, because of prolonged theatre closures due to the plague, theatre companies released their playscripts to stationers as part of an effort to raise much-needed financial revenue. Recent scholars, including Erne, Knutson, and Syme, have substantially discredited this theory.[104] Playscripts (which were of considerably lower value than a company's other assets, such as costumes) would not have raised significant funds for the Queen's Men or for any theatre company.[105] The accompanying assumption that the sale of playscripts was a last resort for companies as their publication could limit performance takings is also untenable: the theatre and the book trade were two different environments and there is

---

[102] See, for example, the licence (28 November 1583) given to the Queen's Men to play at the Bull and Bell inns, in E. K. Chambers, *The Elizabethan Stage*, 4 vols. (Oxford: Clarendon Press, 1923), IV, p. 296; David Kathman, 'London Inns As Playing Venues for the Queen's Men', in *Locating the Queen's Men*, ed. Ostovich et al., pp. 65–76.

[103] In the same Register entry, dated 14 May 1594, White also entered Peele's *Love of David and Fair Bathsheba* (from an unknown company; published 1599) and the now-lost texts 'John of Gaunt' and 'Robin Hood and Little John', both of unknown origins and authorship. This batched entry shows White's name replacing Adam Islip for all five titles. See Arber, II, p. 649.

[104] Erne, *Literary Dramatist*, ch. 5; Knutson, 'The Repertory', in *New History of Early English Drama*, ed. Cox and Kastan, pp. 461–80; Knutson, 'What's So Special about 1594?', pp. 449–67; and Syme, 'Meaning', pp. 490–525.

[105] Blayney, 'Publication', pp. 394–96.

no clear evidence to indicate that the publication of plays curtailed their performance success.[106]

A narrative of company decline has also distorted the reasons for the release of playscripts from the Queen's Men, which has not only been seen as a consequence of theatre closures in London, but also of growing competition from other companies, specifically the Admiral's Men and the newly formed Chamberlain's Men.[107] There is not, however, any firm evidence that the Queen's Men were in decline in May 1594, when the majority of playscripts were entered in the Register.[108] During the 1593–94 Christmas court season, the Queen's Men provided (on 6 January) the only theatrical entertainment noted in the records.[109] In April, they performed at the Rose theatre with Sussex's Men, recording greater average takings per performance than the Admiral's Men would upon their establishment at the Rose later in the year.[110] When the Queen's Men started touring again in July 1594, the payments recorded in provincial accounts are consistent with earlier amounts and do not suggest a company struggling with financial difficulties.[111]

One useful and adaptable theory is that the publication of playbooks was intended as an advertisement for theatre companies and to anticipate the return of stable playing conditions.[112] In May 1594, playing resumed on a regular basis at the London theatres after periods of prolonged closure from mid-1592, owing to Privy Council orders and the plague.[113] Plays from the Admiral's Men and Pembroke's Men appeared on the bookstalls alongside those from the Queen's Men, possibly with an aim to generate interest in London's theatrical offerings. As it was common practice for the title pages of books to be pasted around London (on stalls, posts, and walls), the appearance of these playbooks – most of which contained attributions to their companies – could have worked alongside playbills

[106] Ibid., p. 386; Erne, *Literary Dramatist*, ch. 5.
[107] Gurr, for example, proposes that this 'duopoly' had severe repercussions for other companies, in *Shakespearian Playing Companies* (pp. 206–11).
[108] Knutson ('What's So Special about 1594?', pp. 449–67) and Syme ('Meaning', pp. 490–525) have challenged the view that other playing companies were floundering in the wake of the so-called duopoly, claiming it may well have been 'business as usual' (Knutson, p. 467). Syme offers a clear account of the development of Gurr's narrative and its problems – most notably, in the way in which it is increasingly stated as fact (see pp. 491–92).
[109] Chambers, *Elizabethan Stage*, IV, p. 108.   [110] See Syme, 'Meaning', p. 496.
[111] See McMillin and MacLean, *Queen's Men*, pp. 170–88.
[112] Blayney, 'Publication', pp. 386–87.
[113] Court documents and records in Henslowe's *Diary* suggest the London theatres were closed from 23 June to 28 December 1592, from 2 February to 26 December 1593, and from 7 February to 31 March 1594. Most (but not all) of these closures can be attributed to outbreaks of the plague. Foakes (ed.), *Henslowe's Diary*, pp. 19–21; Chambers, *Elizabethan Stage*, IV, pp. 313–14, 345–51.

to advertise the resumption of playing and add to the visual presence of theatre in the city. However, the fact that the plague often worsened in the summer months (as it did in 1593, one of the most devastating years) suggests that companies could not count on the long-term lifting of playing restrictions nor use the sale of playbooks to announce, with certainty, their return to venues in London.

The publication boom also reflects an emerging interest in a new medium for theatre – the play as a book. Jones's 1590 edition of *Tamburlaine* from the Admiral's Men may have been a turning point for the publication of playbooks. As discussed in the Introduction, Jones's unprecedented paratextual address announces the importance of commercial playbooks for 'Gentlemen Readers' (A2r) and he claims to have improved Marlowe's plays with the interests of his sophisticated readers in mind.[114] This repackaging of *Tamburlaine* was successful and Jones published another edition in 1593, just before the influx of Register entries in 1594. Although playscripts needed to be available in the first place, stationers carried the financial risk of the venture and had to choose to invest. The success of *Tamburlaine*, including its recent reprinted edition, could have prompted other stationers to publish plays from the commercial stages and experiment with this relatively new textual commodity.

Stationers adopted different marketing strategies, but one prominent approach for the 1594 playbooks – the inclusion of title-page attributions to gentlemanly writers and aristocratic patrons – potentially reveals the influence of non-commercial playbook practices and the ways in which they had already shaped drama as a textual category in print. As Atkin demonstrates, pre-playhouse plays with connections to the Inns of Court, the universities, or classical drama often announced their academic credentials through a range of title-page attributions and discursive paratexts.[115] While none of the 1594 playbooks contain paratextual addresses, a significant proportion name their dramatist(s) and give an indication of gentlemanly status or university education on the title page: *A Looking Glass for London and England* ('Made by Thomas Lodge Gentleman, and Robert Greene'), *The Wounds of Civil War* ('Written by Thomas Lodge Gent'), *The Massacre at Paris* ('Written by Christopher Marlow'), *Edward II* ('Written by Chri. Marlow Gent'), *Dido, Queen of Carthage* ('Written by Christopher Marlowe, and Thomas Nash. Gent'), *The Cobbler's Prophecy* ('Written by Robert Wilson. Gent'), and *Friar*

---

[114] For the significance of Jones's editions, see Melnikoff, 'Jones's Pen', pp. 184–209.
[115] Atkin, *Reading Drama*, pp. 120–33.

Bacon and Friar Bungay ('Made by Robert Greene, Maister of Arts').[116]
Many of these playbooks also specify the company that performed the
play, which, by extension, links aristocratic patrons with the text and serves
an additional authorizing function. These attributional innovations do not
represent a consistent design on the part of one publisher, as the playbooks
were issued by a number of different stationers, including Creede, Danter,
White, William Jones, Thomas Woodcock, and Cuthbert Burby. But they
do reveal that these stationers, none of whom invested significantly in non-
commercial drama, were adopting similar tactics to legitimize the status of
commercial plays as texts to be read.[117] These strategies did not, however,
establish a norm for playbook presentation, and detailed attributions like
these tend to disappear from commercial playbooks after 1594. It is not
until later in the period that playhouse plays start to resemble non-
commercial drama in their selection and presentation of paratexts.

   This chapter has shown that a contrastive analysis of performance
contexts and print patterns for history plays challenges two prevailing
assumptions about the Queen's Men: that they were in decline by
1594 and that their repertory was dominated by English history. First,
there is little evidence to prove that the Queen's Men were in financial
difficulty in May 1594, and Creede's entry of five play titles in the Register
between May and July (only two of which are securely attributed to the
company) does not support this assumption. The evidence of other
stationers' investments in this year also suggests a widespread interest in
(history) plays that is not dependent upon falling company fortunes.
Second, print and stage patterns should not be conflated. The reputation
of the Queen's Men as dramatizers of English history may be more
accurately a print identity. The example of Creede shows how his investment in history plays was likely contingent upon strategies of selection and
presentation for dramatic *and* non-dramatic texts. His playbooks enable
understanding, because they are one of our main points of access to the
repertory of the Queen's Men, but they also limit understanding, because
his choices are selective and speculative. One of the dominant critical views
of the Queen's Men – as a company designed to promote Protestant and

---

[116] Prior to these editions, no playbook from the commercial stages had contained unambiguous title-
page attributions to dramatists: previously, only *Three Ladies of London* (attributed to 'R.W.' on its
title page) in 1584 and *Edward I* (attributed to 'George Peele Maister of Artes in Oxenforde' on its
final page; L3v) in 1593 had referred to authorship.

[117] Of these stationers, only Creede (in *Menaechmi*, 1595) and Woodcock (in *Andria*, 1588) invested
in non-commercial drama.

royalist sympathies – owes much to the agendas and wider investments of the stationers who turned these plays into books.

Conclusions

As one of the first stationers to specialize in commercial plays that dramatize the past, Creede and his practices are key for understanding how history plays fit into the historical culture of the period and the book trade. Print paratexts tend to position his playbooks as profitable and truthful histories that could be used as looking glasses for the present. They sometimes advertise a link with important historiographical works (such as Hall's *Union* in *Richard III*) or contemporary events (such as the poisoning plot associated with Roderigo Lopez). They tend to offer readings that temper some of the histories' broader complexities and promote a patriotic ideological packaging that can be linked to the authorizing figure of Elizabeth I, especially when title pages contain attributions to the Queen's Men. Crucially for my purposes, Creede's playbooks, when considered alongside his wider output, draw attention to competing notions of 'history'. Although his texts tend to advertise their 'pastness' and seem to connote historicity, they variously draw on 'true' and fictional materials that are nevertheless united through a similar purpose: the provision of exemplary and counter-exemplary models for readers in England. Through Creede's investments, we can see how one early modern reader negotiated the unruly parameters and purposes of history.

CHAPTER 2

Authorizing Histories
Andrew Wise and Shakespeare's English History Plays

During the late 1590s and early 1600s, the plays which form the core of most critical studies of the history play were published in first and reprint single-text editions: *Richard II* (Q1 1597, Q2 1598, Q3 1598), *Richard III* (Q1 1597, Q2 1598, Q3 1602), *1 Henry IV* (Q1 1598, Q2 1598, Q3 1599), *2 Henry IV* (Q 1600), *Henry V* (Q1 1600, Q2 1602), *The First Part of the Contention of the Two Famous Houses of York and Lancaster* (Q2 1600), and *The True Tragedy of Richard Duke of York* (Q1 1600).[1] What is often overlooked is the fact that the majority of these editions were published by one stationer – Andrew Wise. Wise's investment in *Richard II*, *Richard III*, and *1* and *2 Henry IV* had, I argue, three important effects on the history play at the end of the sixteenth century. First, these editions advertised Shakespeare, through title-page attributions from 1598 onwards, as the period's most prominent dramatist of English monarchical history. Second, they inspired other stationers to invest in English histories by Shakespeare and other writers. And, most significantly for this study, they privileged medieval English history as a print identity for this dramatic genre – a branding that did not remain static, as the wider range of print histories discussed in Chapters 1 and 3 testifies, but which modern criticism tends to overlook. Directing Wise's publication of these plays was a complex interplay of different factors, which this chapter will consider one at a time, namely: the currency of medieval English monarchical history within the book trade; Wise's connection to George Carey, second Baron Hunsdon, Lord Chamberlain and patron of Shakespeare's company; and the growing marketability of Shakespeare's name, propelled by the success of his narrative poems, *Venus and Adonis* (1593) and *The Rape of Lucrece* (1594). Not all of these factors are connected to ideas and readings of 'history'; and it is crucial to recognize that discourses of genre

---

[1] *The True Tragedy of Richard Duke of York* was first printed as an octavo edition in 1595 and issued for the first time as a quarto in 1600 (hence Q1).

and, more broadly, our access to early modern drama are contingent upon sometimes disparate influences.

Building on my discussions in Chapter 1 which consider how the performance identity of the Queen's Men was mediated by publication, the first critical point for me to establish in this chapter is that Wise's editions were not representative of repertory patterns in the theatre. The final years of the sixteenth century have been described as the heyday of the history play, and Shakespeare's English histories have been seen as firmly establishing (and largely constituting) the genre.[2] Their apparent dominance is more precisely, however, a print development.[3] Not only does this pattern affect the early print reputation of the Chamberlain's Men, it also shapes Shakespeare's reputation and, through the cultural capital that Shakespeare has subsequently accrued, an understanding of history as a dramatic genre. It is essential, as both of my chapters emphasize, to examine this disjunction between stage and page patterns – and, indeed, to expect a discrepancy. As Holger Syme puts it, 'the most influential narratives of generic developments depend for their very elegance and power on the erasure of vast swathes of literary history'.[4] For the late Elizabethan history play, the success of the Wise editions contributed to this erasure. To recover a full understanding of the position of historical drama, it is essential for critics to acknowledge archival limitations, to work with evidence for 'lost' plays and, crucially, to evaluate the genre twice: on the stage and on the page.

Performance and payment records in Henslowe's *Diary* indicate that the commercial playhouses staged many histories featuring classical, biblical, ancient British, and recent pasts during the late 1590s – despite the fact that Henslowe only once uses the label 'history' to describe a play (for 'The French History of the Unfortunate General').[5] Although most of these plays are no longer extant, their titles frequently give an indication of their subject. Many refer to a historical figure or event, which can be cautiously used, as shown by the pioneering work of Roslyn Knutson, David McInnis, and Matthew Steggle, to consider the material they may have dramatized.[6] In addition to medieval English history, several historical

---

[2] See Introduction, pp. 1–8.   [3] See also Erne, *Book Trade*, ch. 1.
[4] Syme, 'Meaning of Success', pp. 522–24.
[5] Little is known about this play, including its subject, which Henslowe purchased for Worcester's Men at the Rose in January 1603. See 'French History of the Unfortunate General, The', *Lost Plays Database*; Foakes (ed.), *Henslowe's Diary*, p. 221 (F.118v–19v).
[6] See the *Lost Plays Database*; McInnis and Steggle (eds.), *Lost Plays in Shakespeare's England*; and Knutson, McInnis, and Steggle (eds.), *Loss and the Literary Culture of Shakespeare's Time* (Cham: Palgrave Macmillan, 2020).

clusters can be identified: early British history in, for example, the
'Conquest of Brute' (1598; F.49r–52v), 'Mulmutius Dunwallow' (1598;
F.50v), 'Uther Pendragon' (1597; F.26v–27r), and 'Ferrex and Porrex'
(1600; F.68r–69r); classical history in 'Julian the Apostate' (1596; F.15v),
'Phocasse' (1596; F.15v, 21v, 45v), and 'Catiline's Conspiracy' (1598;
F.49v); biblical history in 'Nebuchadnezzar' (1596; F.25v–26r),
'Jephthah' (1602; F.105v–106v), and 'Pontius Pilate' (1602; F.96r); and
recent history in the 'Civil Wars of France' (1598–99; F.50v–52v) and
'Sebastian King of Portugal' (1601; F.86v–87r) – to list only a few
examples.[7] Early British history seems to have proved popular with theatregoers.[8] 'Vortigern' (F.22v–26r, 95r) – probably based on events from
the life of a fifth-century CE British ruler featured in Geoffrey of
Monmouth's *Historia Regum Britanniae* – recorded twelve performances
between 1596 and 1597; and 'Chinon of England' (F.14r–15v, 21v, 25r) –
involving characters from the time of King Arthur – received fourteen
performances in 1596. At the opposite end of the temporal spectrum,
relatively recent history was also staged regularly and sometimes prompted
sequels.[9] 'The Civil Wars of France' (performed in four parts – including
the 'First Introduction' – between 1598 and 1599) clearly dramatized
the much-discussed religious wars of France. It likely featured the
St Bartholomew's Day massacre of 1572 and the series may have included
events as recent as the Edict of Nantes in April 1598. Similarly, Chettle
and Dekker's 'Sebastian King of Portugal' (1601) probably capitalized on
the frequent reports of Sebastian I's escape from the Battle of Alcácer
Quibir (also known as the Battle of Three Kings), at which he disappeared,
and presumably died, in 1578. John Chamberlain's letters often make
reference to these reports of Sebastian's survival and his reappearance in
various European locations, some of which were contemporary with the
time of the play's entry in Henslowe's records.[10]

---

[7] For all lost plays, the folio numbers refer to their location in Henslowe's manuscript accounts,
which can be cross-referenced in Greg's and Foakes's editions of the *Diary*, as well as through the
Henslowe-Alleyn Digitisation Project, https://henslowe-alleyn.org.uk. While outside the scope of this
chapter, further details about the historical subjects of these plays are available through the *Lost Plays
Database* (by title) and Wiggins's *Catalogue*.

[8] See also Misha Teramura, 'Brute Parts: From Troy to Britain at the Rose, 1596–1600', in *Lost Plays
in Shakespeare's England*, ed. McInnis and Steggle, pp. 127–47.

[9] For the interest of the Chamberlain's Men in current events, see Roslyn L. Knutson, 'Filling Fare:
The Appetite for Current Issues and Traditional Forms in the Repertory of the Chamberlain's
Men', *Medieval & Renaissance Drama in England*, 15 (2003), 57–76.

[10] Norman Egbert McClure (ed.), *The Letters of John Chamberlain*, 2 vols. (Philadelphia: American
Philosophical Society, 1939), I, pp. 48–50, 62–65, 69–71, 73–76, 106–107, 111–14.

Although I have divided these lost history plays into different categories on the basis of their broad historical subjects, their inclusion as part of Henslowe's repertories emphasizes the connections between them. For example, between 1600 and 1602, Henslowe's records provide details for several plays based on biblical history, including 'Judas', 'Joshua', 'Jephthah', 'Tobias', and 'Samson' (F.69v, 95r–v, 105v–108r) – all of which, on the basis of their titles, featured a central role for an Old Testament patriarch or warrior. Annaliese Connolly connects these plays to the opening of the Fortune Theatre in 1600 and Edward Alleyn's return to the stage, and suggests that they would have recalled the parts – especially Tamburlaine – with which Alleyn was associated.[11] John H. Astington agrees: '[t]here seems to be little doubt that Alleyn would have played the title role in all these, and they may have been written with him in mind, in that Samson is a kind of Hercules, and Joshua a kind of Tamburlaine'.[12] Staging practices, such as typecasting, pulled together different historical subjects and established interpretative parallels between them. Similarly, early British histories, such as the 'Conquest of Brute' (which refers to the legendary Trojan founder of Britain), probably responded to theatrical demand for martial plays featuring a Tamburlainean conqueror, as Misha Teramura proposes.[13] In this case, these character types could encourage playgoers to draw comparisons between different pasts. Another lost play from this period – 'Hannibal and Scipio' (1601, F.31v, 71r) – most likely dramatized events from the Second Punic War and featured a Tamburlainean leader in the figure of Hannibal, adding a classical history to this mixture of plays united through casting practices and audience interest in particular kinds of roles and narratives. One of the central arguments of this book is that printed plays featuring different historical pasts were read alongside each other and that maintaining rigid period distinctions is not necessarily productive as patterns in a publisher's output and the wider book market often reveal how these pasts were in dialogue. Connections between historical pasts were also established in the theatre, although it may be the case that staging practices exerted more influence on these trans-territorial and trans-temporal interpretations than patterns in the book trade.

---

[11] Connolly, 'Reconsidering Biblical Drama', para. 18. See also Paul Whitefield White, '"Histories out of the scriptures": Biblical Drama in the Repertory of the Admiral's Men, 1594–1603', in *Loss and the Literary Culture*, ed. Knutson et al., pp. 191–214.

[12] John H. Astington, 'Playing the Man: Acting at the Red Bull and Fortune', *Early Theatre*, 9.2 (2006), 130–43 (p. 133).

[13] Teramura, 'Brute Parts', pp. 131–33.

The histories performed on stage during the final years of the Elizabethan period were largely unrepresented in printed playbooks, which, led by the Wise quartos, favour English monarchical history. None of the plays listed above were published. While Henslowe's ownership of the playscripts controlled, in the first instance, stationers' access to them, publishers' investment strategies were also a factor. For example, between 1596 and 1603, stationers did not, on the basis of extant playbooks, invest in any early British history plays, despite their success on the stage. It could be that playhouses favoured these legendary histories because of the connections that many shareholders, dramatists, and actors had to city livery companies, which celebrated London's roots in Troynovant ('new Troy') in their narratives of origin.[14] These historical pasts may have had less currency – in terms of marketability and topicality – in the book trade during the late 1590s, a pattern that would change on the accession of James I. The Stuart monarch utilized 'Britain's' originary narratives as part of his own mythologizing strategies, which promoted the publication and circulation of ancient British histories (discussed at length in Chapter 3).

In contrast, during the late 1590s, the market for history favours events from the lives of medieval English monarchs. To give a rough indication of numbers, between 1595 and 1599, forty-two editions of plays from the commercial theatres appeared in print. Of these, fifteen prioritize, through their content and printed titles, medieval English monarchical history.[15] The majority of these English history playbooks (eight) are Wise's and he would go on to publish another two editions between 1600 and 1602, the year of his last publications. Of course, this five-year snapshot of print patterns is an arbitrary window; different year selections would yield different results. Caution is necessary in quantifying history plays, but it is nevertheless revealing to compare with patterns for the previous five years. Between 1590 and 1594, thirty-four editions of commercial playbooks were published, and only five dramatize the medieval English monarchical past.[16] As considered in Chapter 1, history playbooks at this time represent a range of historical pasts. Rather than simply indicating

---

[14] See Tracey Hill, *Anthony Munday and Civic Culture* (Manchester: Manchester University Press, 2004).
[15] These fifteen editions are: *The True Tragedy of Richard Duke of York* (1595), *Edward III* (1596 and 1599), *Richard II* (1597, 1598 ×2), *Richard III* (1597, 1598), *1 Henry IV* (1598 ×2, 1599) *Edward II* (1598), *The Famous Victories of Henry V* (1598), *Edward I* (1599), and *1 and 2 Edward IV* (1599).
[16] These five editions are: *1 and 2 Troublesome Reign of King John* (1591), *Edward I* (1593), *The First Part of the Contention* (1594), *The True Tragedy of Richard III* (1594), and *Edward II* (1594).

variation in playscript availability, the peak in medieval English history in the second half of the decade is led by reprints, which are closely connected to market demand. Of the fifteen playbook editions, eight are reprints, while *The Famous Victories of Henry V* (1598) is a first edition of a title that Creede had entered in the Register years before, meaning that its publication was not determined by new playscript availability, but by the stationer's decision to invest in it *at that time.*[17]

Irrespective of how the market statistics for English histories are calculated, the fact that modern criticism tends to use Shakespeare's English histories to define the history play as a genre is problematic. This assumption dangerously conflates stage and print patterns, ignores the evidence for other historical pasts that were a vital part of theatrical repertories, and overlooks the interplay of agents and influences that control the transmission of plays in print. The singularity and success of Wise's editions allow me to make a more emphatic point than I do in my discussion of Creede's histories. In Chapter 1, I propose that the evidence of playbooks has directed the critical reputation of the Queen's Men, when, in fact, the notion of history suggested by these texts might be indicative of Creede's interests. In this chapter, I also consider how Wise's strategies of print selection and presentation shaped the reputation of the Chamberlain's Men (especially at the end of the sixteenth century), but I push this further by showing how publication also affects the reputation of a dramatist *and* of a theatrical genre. Wise's investment in Shakespeare's English histories has been, rather unproductively, a catalyst for thinking of Shakespeare as *the* dramatist of England's national past and for defining the history play as a genre about the lives of English monarchs – an assessment that neglects evidence of performance repertories and publication patterns, both before and after the Wise quartos.

Wise is a somewhat unusual candidate for exerting such a strong influence on the history play in print. He was not a major publisher. After completing his apprenticeship under Thomas Bradshaw in Cambridge, he established his bookshop at the Sign of the Angel in Paul's Cross Churchyard in *c.*1593, where he published and sold books until 1603, at which point he disappears from historical records.[18] His career did not last for very long, nor did he publish a large number of texts – about twenty-four distinct editions in total.[19] Beyond Shakespeare's

---

[17] Creede entered this title in the Register on 14 May 1594.
[18] Hooks, *Selling*, p. 72; STC, III, p. 185.
[19] Erne, *Literary Dramatist*, p. 112. For a list of Wise's published output, see Massai, *Editor*, pp. 96–97.

plays, Wise does not display a sustained interest in history, unlike other stationers considered in this study, including Creede and Butter. While his other publications, such as the sermons of Thomas Playfere and Thomas Nashe's religious lament *Christ's Tears over Jerusalem*, incorporate biblical histories and figures, they do not prioritize their historical subjects in the same way. Wise offers an important case study because of the interplay of factors that shaped his investment and which resists a single narrative – a condition that is especially useful for assessing the publication of Shakespeare's history plays, which, because of their subsequent cultural capital, tend to promote the erasure that Syme discusses in relation to genre. By being alert to these influences and the position of Shakespeare's plays in the book market, we can recognize that their publication and success with readers was contingent and responsive, rather than predetermined.

This chapter argues that Wise read Shakespeare's history plays as traversing a boundary between private and public exchange that could be capitalized on in print: they dramatize the medieval English history that was proving so marketable and 'current' within the book trade at that time, but they also reveal a connection to George Carey, patron of Shakespeare's company and Wise's other published writers – Nashe and Playfere.[20] By featuring the first title-page attributions to the Chamberlain's Men, Wise's editions promote an interpretative link to the Carey family, which could 'authorize' specific readings of the plays in line with the family's military and political reputation. These circumstances might seem to indicate a private exchange between Wise and Carey, but, as this chapter argues, it was more likely a public, commercial one shaped by a private exchange between company and stationer. Important work by Lukas Erne, Adam Hooks, Tara L. Lyons, and Sonia Massai has variously emphasized Wise's connection to Shakespeare and the Chamberlain's Men (Erne), Wise's connection to Carey as a patron (Massai), or Wise's own agency in the publication of Shakespeare (Hooks and Lyons).[21] This chapter draws on, but also departs from, these critical approaches. Rather than emphasizing a single publishing strategy or narrative, this chapter argues that the print

---

[20] Massai, *Editor*, ch. 3; and Massai, 'Shakespeare, Text and Paratext', *Shakespeare Survey* 62 (2009), 1–11 (p. 6).

[21] Erne, *Literary Dramatist*, ch. 3, and *Book Trade*, pp. 161–64; Adam G. Hooks, 'Wise Ventures: Shakespeare and Thomas Playfere at the Sign of the Angel', in *Shakespeare's Stationers*, ed. Straznicky, pp. 47–62, and *Selling Shakespeare*, ch. 2; Tara L. Lyons, 'Serials, Spinoffs, and Histories: Selling "Shakespeare" in Collection before the Folio', *Philological Quarterly*, 91:2 (2012), 185–220 (pp. 189–93), and Massai, *Editor*, ch. 3.

presentation and prominence of Shakespeare's English history plays at the end of the sixteenth century was contingent on three main factors, which will be addressed separately: the book trade's interest in English monarchical history and its application to Elizabethan politics; the connection of Wise to Shakespeare's company and to Carey's patronized writers, which can be seen as a flexible model of textual patronage that eschews a direct link between patron and stationer; and the growing marketability of Shakespeare's name. The result is an assessment of Shakespeare's histories that reveals the intersection of multiple agendas: it draws attention to the book trade as a collaborative system of exchange that frustrates efforts at singularizing agency. This approach enhances our understanding of history plays not just because it highlights the partial print record that is left of them, but also because it reveals different ways of reading history, which can involve 'politic' applications to pressing state issues, as well as locally inflected political interpretations, and those that do not place significant weight on the histories' political force.

Wise Histories

The shape of the reading market at the end of the sixteenth century may have persuaded Wise, in the first instance, to invest in Shakespeare's monarchical histories and then to issue reprints in quick succession. These plays appeared in bookshops at a time when medieval English history was playing an important role in commentary on Elizabethan political concerns, especially in relation to the succession, the role of royal councillors, and the dangers of civil war. Although manuscripts of Shakespeare's plays had to become available to Wise in the first place (an issue that is examined in the next section), he still maintained a considerable degree of independent agency in choosing to invest and reinvest in these histories. The latter process is, as Farmer and Lesser outline, a key indicator of consumer demand and a publisher's recognition of it.[22] This section considers how patterns and geographies in the book trade directed Wise's strategies of selection and his investment in a series of plays that dramatize civil and successional conflicts from the reigns of medieval English monarchs. It argues that Shakespeare's histories played an important and dynamic role in textual and politic exchanges between dramatic and non-dramatic publications and between the different editions of these texts. This section suggests that Wise's strategies of print presentation

---

[22] Farmer and Lesser, 'Playbooks', pp. 5–6.

enhanced this exchange: his title pages usually draw attention to the plays' historical events and figures, and the preparation of printer's copy suggests an interest in historicity and topical political application.

Histories of medieval English monarchs proliferated in a number of relatively short publications during the 1590s and seem to have acquired a new, pressing currency. While Tudor chronicles, such as those by Holinshed, Grafton, and Stow, feature accounts of medieval monarchs (and borrow from earlier historians, including More and Vergil), these histories are contained within expansive texts that cover vast periods of time and do not therefore privilege a particular reign. A few influential texts offer a narrower scope – such as Hall's *Chronicle* on the reigns of Henry IV to Henry VIII and *The Mirror for Magistrates*, which, in its 1559 edition, covers the fall of rulers and other prominent figures from the reigns of Richard II to Edward IV. In both, multiple figures, reigns, and events compete for readers' attention, a polyphony of voices that, in the *Mirror*, is furthered by its history of extensive revisions and expansions by different contributors between 1559 and 1610.[23] At the time of their first publication, these histories do not, however, seem to have prompted shorter, narrowly focused texts, such as plays, to use the Wars of the Roses as subject matter. Jessica Winston shows that the *Mirror*'s interest in the downfall of figures of authority was taken up by dramatists, but that they passed over the English subject matter in favour of classical, early British, and world histories.[24] It was not until later in the Elizabethan period that the reigns of medieval monarchs take centre stage within pamphlets, political treatises, and short histories, which are particularly useful as a barometer for understanding shifting patterns in historical and political thought.[25] At this time, the medieval English past is used to offer politic histories that can be applied – most often as counter-exemplary warnings – to national issues of succession and monarchical authority. As Worden points out, 'politic history stood back from narrative to reflect upon it', although a separation (in purpose and form) between historical narrative and the political application of history cannot be clearly drawn.[26]

---

[23] For the most detailed study of the *Mirror*'s revisions and rewritings, see Harriet Archer, *Unperfect Histories: The Mirror for Magistrates, 1559–1610* (Oxford: Oxford University Press, 2017).

[24] Winston, 'National History', pp. 152–56.

[25] For this shift in the market for histories, see also Jean-Christophe Mayer, 'The Decline of the Chronicle and Shakespeare's History Plays', *Shakespeare Survey 63* (2010), 12–23.

[26] Worden, 'Historians', p. 79. Although the precise targets are unclear, the Bishops' Ban of 1599 forbade the publication of new 'English histories' without approval from members of the Privy Council. See Adam Hansen, 'Writing, London, and the Bishops' Ban of 1599', *The London Journal*, 43:2 (2018), 102–19 (p. 103).

Nevertheless, these shorter, focused histories – as distinct from expansive chronicles and antiquarian studies – often promote specific ways of reading that direct their users towards immediate political reflection and the drawing of parallels with the present.

One of the most notorious new histories was Hayward's *First Part of the Life and Reign of King Henry IV* (1599), which, despite the emphasis suggested by its title, focuses on Richard II's reign and deposition, ending after just the first year of Henry IV's rule. It examines the secular causes and consequences of Richard II's overthrow, considering whether it is justified to remove an unfit monarch and examining the limits of royal authority and the damaging influence of corrupt advisors.[27] Hayward's *Henry IV* follows very similar material to Shakespeare's *Richard II*, published by Wise in three single-text editions between 1597 and 1598; and it may be the case, as F. J. Levy suggests, that Hayward was influenced by the play, a possibility that draws attention to the exchange between dramatic and non-dramatic histories that this chapter explores in further detail.[28] Hayward directly instructs readers to apply his history to Elizabethan England. In a paratextual address, 'A. P . to the Reader' (modelled on the preface in Savile's translation of Tacitus), he outlines the purpose of historical writing: to 'set foorth vnto us, not onely precepts, but liuely patterns, both for priuate directions and for affayres of state' (A3r).[29] History, as the address explicitly sets out, should be mined for examples that can be applied to the instruction – especially the political instruction – of the present. The address concentrates on the virtues of classical Roman and Greek exempla, which are then redirected towards the use of English history in the main text. Hayward's provocative parallels between Richard II and Elizabeth I, and between Henry Bolingbroke and Robert Devereux, second earl of Essex, assist in the application of his medieval history. Although comparisons between Richard and Elizabeth had been offered as early as 1580, Hayward makes this resemblance pressingly urgent, by emphasizing concerns over unworthy royal favourites and other issues that

---

[27] Levy, for example, describes it as 'the first realization in England of a history in which the causes of events were seen in terms of the interrelationship of politics and character rather than in terms of the working out of God's providence'. See F. J. Levy, 'Hayward, Daniel, and the Beginnings of Politic History in England', *Huntington Library Quarterly*, 50:1 (1987), 1–34 (pp. 2–3).

[28] Ibid., pp. 16–19.

[29] John Hayward, *The First Part of the Life and raigne of King Henrie the IIII* (London, 1599; STC 12995), A3r. In Savile's Tacitus (1591; STC 23642), an address, 'A. B. To the Reader', outlines the benefits of reading histories: they are 'so proper for the direction of the life of man' (¶3r) as they teach by example and provide models for political action. Savile's translation was reprinted in 1598.

dominated both reigns and through the inclusion of a dedication to Essex, which may have been added at the advice of his publisher, John Wolfe.[30] It is a paratext that insists upon a topical reflection, bringing the history into the late Elizabethan present.[31] Indeed, it became invested with even more 'currency' in the aftermath of Essex's disastrous 1599 campaign in Ireland, when the second edition of Hayward's book was burned and the writer was imprisoned and interrogated by Attorney General Edward Coke and the Lord Chief Justice Sir John Popham about the seditious applications of his history.[32]

In the years leading up to Hayward's *Henry IV*, a number of other publications feature medieval English history, although they do not always announce their politic potential as emphatically as Hayward's later text. During the 1590s, narrative poetry – such as Samuel Daniel's *Civil Wars* (first printed as four books in 1595), Michael Drayton's *Mortimeriados: The Lamentable Civil Wars of Edward II and the Barons* (1596; later revised and published as *The Barons' Wars* in 1603), and the anonymous *First Book of the Preservation of King Henry VII* (1599) – displays a similar interest in English monarchs and the problems of civil war. And an increasing number of political treatises, incurring varying degrees of censorship, approach the question of Elizabeth's successor directly and make use of monarchs such as Richard II and Henry IV as part of their discussions, confirming, as Worden summarizes, that political and historical thought often coincide.[33] Prominent examples on opposing sides of a confessional divide include the Jesuit Robert Persons's *Conference About the Next Succession to the Crown of England* (written in 1593; published in Antwerp in 1595) and the Puritan Peter Wentworth's *Pithy Exhortation to Her Majesty for Establishing Her Successor to the Crown* (written in c.1587,

---

[30] In a manuscript from 1580, Henry Howard urged Elizabeth I to marry the Duke of Anjou as 'there will not lack a Henry Bolingbroke presumptuously to undertake the usurpation of the royal dignity'; R. Malcolm Smuts, 'States, Monarchs, and Dynastic Transitions: The Political Thought of John Hayward', in *Doubtful and Dangerous: The Question of Succession in Late Elizabethan England*, ed. Susan Doran and Paulina Kewes (Manchester: Manchester University Press, 2014), pp. 276–94 (p. 278); Levy, 'Hayward', p. 16.

[31] See, for example, state accounts of Essex's trial that refer to Hayward's book: 'It was remembered there was a book of Henry IV, with many things to make those times like these, and himself [i.e. Essex] like Henry IV, which he countenanced, whilst pretending to disapprove it' (18 February 1601); *Calendar of State Papers, Domestic: Elizabeth: 1598–1601*, ed. Mary Anne Everett Green (London: Longman, 1869), p. 584.

[32] For the text's complicated history of suppression, see Alexandra Gajda, 'The Earl of Essex and "Politic History"', in *Essex: The Cultural Impact of an Elizabethan Courtier*, ed. Annaliese Connolly and Lisa Hopkins (Manchester: Manchester University Press, 2013), pp. 237–59 (p. 254, n. 21).

[33] Worden, 'Historians', p. 72.

published in 1598), which feature accounts of Edward II, Edward III, Richard II, Henry IV, and Henry VI.[34]

Of particular significance is Persons's *Conference*, published under the name of 'Doleman', which created 'a minor sensation in England' as it draws on the reigns of medieval monarchs to conclude that birthright is 'not sufficient to be admitted to a crowne' and that the question of Elizabeth's successor is 'extreme[ly] doubtful as touching the best right'.[35] The *Conference* strongly attacks the absolutist doctrine of Pierre de Belloy, undercuts James VI of Scotland's claim to the English throne, and recommends the title of Isabella, the Spanish Infanta (although, as Victor Houliston discusses, it 'stops short of endorsing hers as the strongest claim').[36] What is significant for my purposes is the treatise's provocative use of medieval English *exempla*, particularly a detailed evaluation of Richard II's reign. Persons first claims that, 'by reason', an unfit king 'may and hath and ought to be [deposed], when vrgent occasions are offred' (V4r) and then asserts that 'king Richards gouerment was intolerable and he worthy of deposition', owing to the 'euil counsel of his fauorites', 'the peruerting of al lawes', and 'the ioyning with his mynions for opressing the nobility' (V5v–6r). The text features a controversial dedication to Essex, which brought political difficulties to the earl and was likely intended to discredit his standing with James VI, with whom he was in regular contact.[37] Rooting the treatise within the Elizabethan court, the dedication to Essex claims that 'no man is in more high and eminent place or dignitie at this day', and, most controversially, that he has the 'high liking of the people', meaning that 'no man [is] like to haue a greater part or sway in deciding of this great affaire' (*2v–*3r). The text's significance lies beyond the issue of succession because of its interests in 'the proper limits to the authority of monarchs' and competing sources of power.[38] Both its dedicatory paratext and the use of English *exempla* emphasize this broader, destabilizing point.

---

[34] For a contrastive analysis of these treatises and others, see Paulina Kewes, 'The Puritan, the Jesuit and the Jacobean Succession', in *Doubtful and Dangerous*, ed. Doran and Kewes, pp. 47–70.

[35] Victor Houliston, 'Persons [Parsons], Robert (1546–1610)', *ODNB*, online ed., September 2004, https://doi.org/10.1093/ref:odnb/21474 (accessed 16 September 2019), para. 18. [Robert Persons]/ 'R. Doleman', *A Conference About the Next Svccession to the Crowne of Ingland* (N [i.e. Antwerp], 1594 [1595]; STC 19398), *1v.

[36] For the political thought of Persons's treatise, see Victor Houliston, 'The Hare and the Drum: Robert Persons's writings on the English Succession, 1593–6', *Renaissance Studies*, 14:2 (2000), 235–50 (p. 239).

[37] Houliston, 'The Hare and the Drum', p. 240.

[38] Blair Worden, 'Afterword', in *Doubtful and Dangerous*, ed. Doran and Kewes, pp. 295–303 (p. 298).

It is important to situate Wise's editions within this context and consider how Shakespeare's histories interacted with these non-dramatic texts on the bookstalls and in the collections and *Sammelbände* of readers. While history-play studies have regularly shown how Shakespeare's plays display a clear interest in the historiographical and political debates of their time of composition, the fact that this connection is enhanced by the plays' publication and introduces new and vibrant textual exchanges is often overlooked. It is not only the first edition of a text that is significant, but its history of subsequent editions.[39] Often, the publication of playbooks (and indeed of any text) does not involve just one moment of selection, but multiple moments. The collective market for first and reprint editions during the late 1590s indicates consumer demand for politically reflexive medieval histories and provides a narrative of this demand. Wise's first editions and reprints were circulated at the same time as Persons's *Conference*, Daniel's *Civil Wars*, Drayton's *Mortimeriados*, and Hayward's *Henry IV*, and evidence from the book trade suggests a two-way exchange between some of these texts and Shakespeare's plays, as well as details about their wider cultural–political use. If Augustine Phillips's claim in 1601 that the 'play of Kyng Rychard' was 'so old and so long out of vse' on stage is to be believed (and not merely reflect his strategy under Privy Council examination for the company's role in the Essex rising), it may have been the prominence of Wise's printed editions that recommended the play to Essex's followers who arranged the performance on 7 February 1601, the eve of their uprising.[40] By this time, Wise had issued three editions of *Richard II* in quick succession, and it was becoming one of the most quoted of Shakespeare's plays in commonplace books and miscellanies, such as *Belvedere* (1600).[41] It is not my intention to suggest that all

---

[39] See also Amy Lidster, '"With much labour out of scattered papers": The Caroline Reprints of Thomas Heywood's *1* and *2 If You Know Not Me You Know Nobody*', *Renaissance Drama*, 49:2 (2021), 205–28.

[40] National Archives: State Papers Domestic, Elizabeth I; SP 12/278, fols. 85r–86v. See 'Examination of Augustine Phillips', *Shakespeare Documented*, convened by Folger Shakespeare Library (created 2016) https://shakespearedocumented.folger.edu (accessed 16 April 2021). Worden argues that the play was instead a dramatization of Hayward's history ('Which Play Was Performed at the Globe Theatre on 7 February 1601?', *London Review of Books*, 25:13 (10 July 2003)). This seems unlikely: as Paul E. J. Hammer has shown, if a play had been based on Hayward's book, this point would surely have been recorded somewhere in the extensive state documents covering the events. See Hammer, 'Shakespeare's *Richard II*, the Play of 7 February 1601, and the Essex Rising', *Shakespeare Quarterly*, 59:1 (2008), 1–35 (pp. 20–25).

[41] In *Belvedere*, *Richard II* is Shakespeare's most quoted play (with forty-nine quotations); *Richard III* and *Romeo and Juliet* are in joint second place, with fourteen quotations each. See Lukas Erne and Devani Singh (eds.), *Bel-vedére or The Garden of the Muses: An Early Modern Printed Commonplace Book* (Cambridge: Cambridge University Press, 2020), p. 348. See also Amy Lidster, 'At the Sign of

histories about the medieval past were read in the same way; but, as Worden succinctly puts it, texts differing in form, style, agenda, and the use and analysis of sources often have 'purposes of persuasion cutting across them'.[42] One of the key points I wish to emphasize is that, during the 1590s, the range of publications about the origins and conclusions of the Wars of the Roses reveals a widespread interest in the application of these histories to the Elizabethan present that is not restricted to elite circles, but is part of a commercial book trade that involves an expanding readership invested in politic interpretations.

Wise's publishing strategies capitalize on the potential of Shakespeare's plays as printed histories that could be read and used alongside other non-dramatic histories on the bookstalls. His investment in four plays about the Wars of the Roses initiated the print serialization of Shakespeare's English histories, which enhances the connection between these plays and other publications, such as Daniel's *Civil Wars*. Lyons's work on collections has shown that Wise's single-text editions resemble a proto-collection of plays.[43] Critics often describe Shakespeare's Folio Histories as forming two tetralogies – one featuring *Richard II*, *1* and *2 Henry IV*, and *Henry V*, and the other consisting of *1–3 Henry VI* and *Richard III* – which are bookended by *King John* and *Henry VIII*.[44] Wise's editions offer what could be described as a compressed tetralogy. Two of the plays are directly linked as part of a sequence: the main, head, and running title of 'The second part of Henry the fourth' establishes the play's position next to 'The Historie of Henry the fourth'.[45] As a group, the four plays have a good claim to be the first series of Shakespearean histories that could be purchased from a stationer. Although Millington published *The First Part of the Contention* in 1594 and *The True Tragedy of Richard Duke of York* in 1595, these editions were not in the same format. They were printed as a quarto and octavo, respectively, making them less suitable for binding together. In contrast, Wise's editions offered readers the first tetralogy, in quarto format, on the Wars of the Roses that concentrates on some key political turning points, beginning with the Wars' historical origins – the deposition of Richard II – and concluding with the accession of Henry VII

---

the Angel: The Influence of Andrew Wise on Shakespeare in Print', *Shakespeare Survey 71* (2018), 242–54 (pp. 252–53).

[42] Worden, 'Afterword', p. 297.   [43] Lyons, 'Serials', pp. 189–93.

[44] For the two tetralogies and the processes of theatrical serialization, see Nicholas Grene, *Shakespeare's Serial History Plays* (Cambridge: Cambridge University Press, 2002).

[45] Shakespeare, *The History of Henrie the Fovrth* (London, 1598; STC 22280), A2r; and *The Second part of Henrie the fourth* (London, 1600; STC 22288), A2r.

in *Richard III*. One of the oft-cited features of history plays is their supposed 'open-endedness': history, by its very nature, does not have an ending.[46] Written histories nevertheless do provide some kind of artificially imposed narrative of closure. They offer, to repurpose Thomas Browne's phrase, a 'Parenthesis in Eternity', and they differ significantly in the extent to which resolution is achieved and advertised.[47] *The First Part of the Contention*, ending in the midst of conflict, has a much greater sense of open-endedness than *Captain Thomas Stukeley* or *Macbeth*, which resolve their main action and end with explicit statements underscoring that resolution. However, the ways in which these histories are used and combined – as part of performance repertories and as printed books – can alter the dynamics of their individual endings. Wise's printed editions create a sequence that emphasizes the continuation of successional conflict and concerns over monarchical authority in common with, for example, the genealogies of Persons's *Conference*.

One particularly significant example of a serialized medieval history that was involved in a two-way exchange with Shakespeare's plays is Daniel's *Civil Wars*. Modelled on Lucan's *Pharsalia* and offering an English epic poem in *ottava rima*, *The Civil Wars* focuses on the conflicts between the 'houses of Lancaster and Yorke', using events from the reigns of Richard II to Edward IV (in its later continuations) to reflect on the Elizabethan present.[48] As critics including Levy, Alzada Tipton, and Gillian Wright have explored, Daniel incorporates different approaches to historiography, sometimes advancing providential claims that celebrate political stability through the Tudor line and sometimes concentrating on ideas of secular causation that are much more sceptical.[49] Above all, Daniel's verse history highlights the horrors and destruction of civil conflict which 'wast[e] so much [on] warre without a foe' (B1v), and its regular references to events and individuals from the 1590s seem to suggest, as Daniel later observed in his 1609 dedication to the Countess of Pembroke, that the final years of Elizabeth's reign marked a renewed threat of civil conflict, 'a time which was not so well secur'd of the future'.[50] During this period of political and

[46] See G. K. Hunter, 'Truth and Art in History Plays', *Shakespeare Survey 42* (1990), 15–24 (p. 20).
[47] Thomas Browne, *Christian Morals* (London, 1716), p. 124.
[48] Daniel, *The First Fowre Bookes of the ciuile warres* (London, 1595; STC 6244), t.p.
[49] Levy, 'Hayward'; Alzada Tipton, 'Caught between "Virtue" and "Memorie": Providential and Political Historiography in Samuel Daniel's *The Civil Wars*', *Huntington Library Quarterly*, 61:3/4 (1998), 325–41; Gillian Wright, 'The Politics of Revision in Samuel Daniel's *The Civil Wars*', *English Literary Renaissance*, 38:3 (2008), 461–82.
[50] Daniel, *The Civile Wares* (London, 1609; STC 6245), A2v.

successional anxiety, Simon Waterson published Daniel's *First Four Books of the Civil Wars* (1595) and its impact was, according to John Pitcher, 'felt throughout the literary scene at once'.[51] It is likely that Shakespeare himself drew on these books for *Richard II* 'within weeks of the poem going on sale', which was probably in November 1595.[52] In turn, some of Daniel's revisions to later editions – such as the representation of the Battle of Shrewsbury in his 1609 expansion – were probably influenced by Shakespeare's English histories, published by Wise.[53] Indeed, Daniel's dedication to the Countess of Pembroke emphasizes the theatrical quality of his history: he gives orations, or speeches, to the characters, and he invokes the *theatrum mundi* metaphor to reinforce his claim about the truthfulness of his account: 'all these great actions are openly presented on the Stage of the World' (A3r, 1609). Particularly on paper stages, the Wars of the Roses offered material for politic readings that was part of a non-linear web of exchanges between different texts and between different publishers.

Informing this exchange was the physical geography of the book trade in St Paul's Churchyard. Thanks to the work of Peter Blayney, this area can be explored and mapped in detail. Waterson's shop at the Sign of the Crown (act. 1589–1634) was just a few hundred metres away from Wise's premises at the Sign of the Angel (act. 1593–1602) in Paul's Cross, the north-east corner of the churchyard (see Figure 2.1).[54] At the same time as Wise invested in first and reprint editions of Shakespeare's histories, Waterson issued multiple editions of Daniel's *Civil Wars*, meaning that two serialized histories of the Wars of the Roses were published at neighbouring bookshops in Paul's Cross.[55] In fact, the ensuing success of Wise's histories (with nine editions by 1600) may have motivated the expansions to *The Civil Wars*. After the *First Four Books* in 1595 and the publication of a fifth book in an undated edition (bound as an attachment to the four books and included as part of *The Poetical Essays of Samuel Daniel* in 1599), Waterson asked Daniel in about 1600 to continue the

[51] John Pitcher, 'Daniel, Samuel (1562/3–1619)', *ODNB*, online edn, September 2004, https://doi .org/10.1093/ref:odnb/7120 [accessed 16 September 2019], para. 7.
[52] Ibid. [53] See Wright, 'Politics', p. 467.
[54] Peter W. M. Blayney, *The Bookshops in Paul's Cross Churchyard*, Occasional Papers of the Bibliographical Society, No. 5 (London: Bibliographical Society, 1990).
[55] These appeared in the following order: the *First Four Books* in 1595; Q1 *Richard II* and Q1 *Richard III* in 1597; Q2 and Q3 *Richard II*, Q2 *Richard III*, Q1 and Q2 *1 Henry IV* in 1598; *The Poetical Essays of Samuel Daniel* (which contains reissues of the first five books of *The Civil Wars*) and Q3 *1 Henry IV* in 1599; Q1 *2 Henry IV* in 1600; *The Works of Samuel Daniel* (containing six books of *The Civil Wars*) in 1601; and Q3 *Richard III* in 1602.

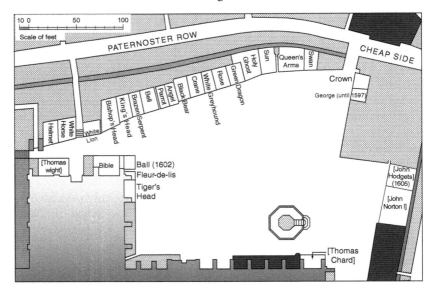

Figure 2.1   Map of Paul's Cross Churchyard (*c.*1600).

series.[56] A sixth book was then added to a new edition of *The Civil Wars* that appeared as part of *The Works of Samuel Daniel* in 1601. Waterson was clearly aware of the reading public's interest in these monarchs and the country's civil wars, which was perhaps compacted by the geography of the book trade and the investments of nearby stationers. While Daniel's *Civil Wars* is often considered a source for Shakespeare, what has not been explored is the possibility that the publication of Daniel's and Shakespeare's histories in multiple 'parts' was spurred on by the success of the two ventures.[57] It represents a kind of indirect collaboration between stationers as they respond to each other's practices and relay that exchange to their authors. This serialization may also carry interpretative significance. Some of Shakespeare's plays and individual books of *The Civil Wars* end on a note of uncertainty or pessimism: *Richard II* concludes with Bolingbroke's admission of guilty remorse and Book 2 of *The Civil Wars* abruptly shifts from a celebration of worthy Elizabethans to a reminder that 'we must now returne againe to bloud' (M4r, 1595). The publication

[56] Pitcher, 'Daniel', para. 11.
[57] Geoffrey Bullough, *Narrative and Dramatic Sources of Shakespeare*, 8 vols. (London: Routledge and Kegan Paul, 1957–75), IV (1962), pp. 254–56.

history of these texts compounds their formal and thematic lack of closure. New instalments and editions of the Wars of the Roses reinscribe these histories with a political and textual scepticism of resolution.

Another key feature of Wise's Shakespearean editions is a title-page emphasis on their historicity, which furthers their connection to other types of printed history.[58] The title pages contain plot descriptions that draw attention to the plays' engagement with historical events and expand the titles recorded in Stationers' Register entries. *Richard III* dramatizes the monarch's 'treacherous Plots against his brother Clarence: the pittiefull murther of his innocent nephewes: his tyrannicall vsurpation: with the whole course of his detested life and most deserued death', which is, in contrast, succinctly and impartially described in the Register as 'The tragedie of kinge Richard the Third with the death of the duke of Clarence'.[59] The title page offers a clear reading of the play through its emphatic condemnation of Richard III's actions, which tempers the theatrical vitality of the character on the stage. In *2 Henry IV* (published jointly by Wise and William Aspley), the title page emphasizes historical events and sequences: the play not only dramatizes events from the reign of Henry IV, but also continues 'to his death, and [the] coronation of Henrie the fift' (A1r). Neither of these two events are mentioned in the lengthy title recorded in the Stationers' Register, which even includes an attribution to Shakespeare and is the first appearance of his name in the Register.[60] The reference to Henry V on the playbook title page not only capitalizes on Shakespeare's new play about this monarch (performed in 1599 and also printed in 1600), it crucially reinforces the seriality of Wise's venture and the way in which the print presentation and packaging of these histories helps to position them as part of an ongoing politic discourse about the Wars of the Roses. As a group, they offer a continuous historical narrative that provides different points of entry for examining the Elizabethan succession question and the threat of renewed civil war.

The printed presentation of *1 Henry IV* provides another important example. The main title is given as 'THE HISTORY OF HENRIE THE FOVRTH', and the largest type is used for the play's classification as a

---

[58] I am indebted here to Lyons's application of the term 'historicity' in her work on playbook collections. See 'Serials', p. 209.

[59] Shakespeare, *The Tragedy of King Richard the third* (London, 1597; STC 22314), A1r. See SRO3997; Arber, III, p. 93.

[60] *2 Henry IV* was entered to Wise and Aspley on 23 August 1600; the full description reads: 'the second parte of the history of kinge henry the iiijth with the humours of Sir John Fallstaff: Wrytten by master Shakespere.' SRO4341; Arber, III, p. 170.

history – indeed, *the* history of the king (see Figure 2.2). It is one of the first uses of the term 'history' on a playbook originating from the commercial stages to signify, unambiguously, an account of the historical past. As discussed in Chapter 1, earlier uses mostly apply to a fictional narrative, as in *A Pleasant Conceited History Called The Taming of a Shrew* (1594) and *The History of Orlando Furioso* (1594). Wise's title page also refers to 'the battell at Shrewsburie, betweene the King and Lord Henry Percy, surnamed Henrie Hotspure of the North' (A1r), which again recalls events and figures that appear in the non-dramatic histories that were being published at the same time, such as Daniel's *Civil Wars*. Hotspur and the rebellion of 'The Percies' feature prominently in the third book of *The Civil Wars* and are also mentioned in the separate argument that prefaces the book (N1r).[61] Moreover, none of the extant title pages for *1 Henry IV* acknowledge the text's performance origins. I believe, as discussed in the next section, that this omission could be a result of the Oldcastle debacle and a desire to keep the Chamberlain's Men off the title page. Company attributions feature on all of Wise's other playbooks, marking this text as unusual. It nevertheless has the effect of closely aligning the playbook with non-dramatic printed histories and, interestingly, it would have borne something of a resemblance to Hayward's *Henry IV*, once the latter text appeared on the bookstalls in 1599.

A recurrent question in this book is who was responsible for the design and content of title pages, paratexts that had such a key role in advertising playbooks and shaping readers' experiences of them. With Wise, as with other publishers who invested in commercial plays, it is reasonable to suppose that he must have had the final say.[62] It is possible that some title-page phrasing was, as Stern argues, inherited from playbills, while the design of title pages may have been shaped by the printers Wise hired – including Valentine Simmes, Peter Short, and Thomas Creede.[63] An interesting case is provided by Creede, who printed Wise's second and third editions of *Richard III* in 1598 and 1602. The second edition of *Richard III* reproduces the title-page description from the first edition printed by Simmes and Short, but Creede's printing house has changed the *mise en page* (see Figure 2.3). The layout of the lines on the page brings to mind Creede's own playbooks (especially his edition of *The True Tragedy of Richard III*; see Figure 1.2), as does the inclusion of his familiar device showing the figure of Truth. This new title page for Shakespeare's

[61] For the account of the Percys' rebellion, see Q4r–R4r.   [62] Farmer and Lesser, 'Vile Arts', p. 78.
[63] Stern, 'Playbills', pp. 57–89.

THE
HISTORY OF
HENRIE THE
FOVRTH;

With the battell at Shrewsburie,
betweene the King and Lord
Henry Percy, furnamed
Henrie Hotfpur of
the North.

Collated
&
Perfect.
D. 1827.

With the humorous conceits of Sir
Iohn Falftalffe.

First Edition.

AT LONDON,
Printed by *P. S.* for *Andrew Wife*, dwelling
in Paules Churchyard, at the figne of
the Angell. 1598.

Figure 2.2   Title page from *1 Henry IV* (Q2 1598; STC 22280).

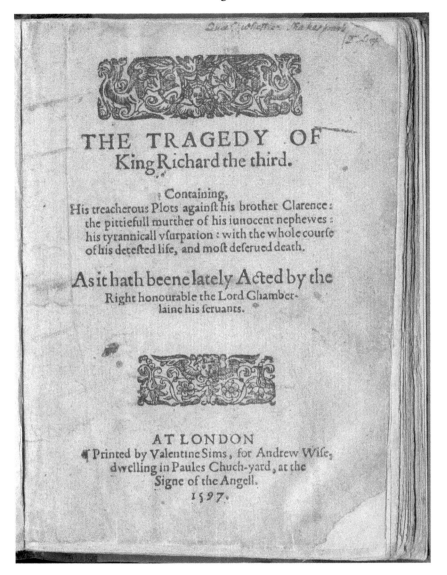

Figure 2.3 Title pages from *Richard III*, Q1 1597 (STC 22314) and Q2 1598 (STC 22315).

THE
TRAGEDIE
of King Richard
the third.

Conteining his treacherous Plots againſt his
brother *Clarence*: the pitiful murther of his innocent
Nephewes: his tyrannicall vſurpation: with
the whole courſe of his deteſted life, and moſt
deſerued death.

*As it hath beene lately Acted by the Right honourable
the Lord Chamberlaine his ſeruants.*

By William Shake-ſpeare.

LONDON
Printed by Thomas Creede, for Andrew Wiſe,
dwelling in Paules Church-yard, at the ſigne
of the Angell. 1 5 9 8.

ſecond Edition.

Figure 2.3 *(cont.)*

Richard III might even engender confusion between the two plays based on the life of the same monarch and covering similar events – were it not for the new title-page attribution to Shakespeare that appears in Wise's edition. I believe, as discussed later in the chapter, that the introduction of title-page attributions to Shakespeare was partly owing to the success of his narrative poems, but it could also reveal an effort to distinguish between two plays about the life of Richard III. As soon as Creede, the publisher of the earlier play, acted as trade printer for the second edition of the later play, an unprecedented title-page attribution to Shakespeare was included.[64] Creede could have suggested this addition, particularly as he sometimes placed prominent attributions to dramatists in his own publications, such as *A Looking Glass for London and England*. Although publishers were the main overseers of the production process, it should not be assumed that every decision relating to playbook design was taken by them. The evidence from print paratexts suggests a model of collaborative agency. Indeed, Short and Simmes were both printers for Daniel's *Civil Wars*, indicating that Wise's and Waterson's bookshops were sites of exchange involving similar networks of print professionals, who may also have exerted some influence on the preparation of playbooks.

This idea of uncertain and collaborative agency leads to my final point about the presentation of Wise's playbooks: the preparation of printer's copy seems to indicate an interest in the plays' historicity and political application. As Massai has shown, publication agents acted as annotators or editors of texts, and Wise may have taken on this role for his playbooks, although other agents, including Shakespeare, cannot be ruled out.[65] In *Richard III*, for example, the speeches of Richard and Richmond to their armies (5.4 and 5.5 in modern editions) are prefaced with the italicized headings 'His oration to his souldiers' and 'His Oration to his army', respectively (see Q1 M1v, M2v). The term 'oration' is particularly unusual as part of a stage direction and seems to be an explanatory note for readers rather than a direction for stage action.[66] These descriptions could have been added as part of the publication process. They recall the orations of historical characters that featured in works such as More's *Richard III*, Holinshed's *Chronicles*, *The Mirror for Magistrates*, Daniel's *Civil Wars*

---

[64] Shakespeare's name first appeared on playbook title pages in 1598 for Q2 *Richard II*, Q2 *Richard III*, and Q1 *Love's Labour's Lost*. It is unclear which was the first.

[65] Massai, *Editor*, pp. 102–105.

[66] See also John Jowett's discussion of the orations and their stage directions, which he describes as 'literary in quality'. William Shakespeare, *The Tragedy of King Richard III*, ed. John Jowett (Oxford: Oxford University Press, 2000), pp. 384–85.

and, later, Hayward's *Henry IV*.[67] Passages of direct (and invented) speech from historical figures were a common, although not uncontentious, feature of printed histories. The headings and typographical separation seen in Shakespeare's *Richard III* can also be witnessed in earlier works. English translations of Thucydides use this device and, as Grant and Ravelhofer point out, separate the orations from the narratives through page breaks and titles like 'The Oration of the Corcyriens bifore the counsayle of the Athenyans'.[68] As part of Wise's edition, this print feature proposes a connection between the history play and 'non-dramatic' histories. It draws attention to the mixed forms of enunciation that appear in histories that are not exclusively plays and include narration and direct speech. These techniques and their typographical presentation encourage readers to make comparisons across a range of printed histories.

The two variant textual states of *2 Henry IV* (QA and QB) also suggest that publication agents made decisions about the preparation of history plays in ways that affected and responded to the text's dialectic with its sources and political contexts. Of particular significance is an extra scene in QB that is absent from QA (3.1 in F and modern editions).[69] The provenance of the scene is uncertain, but Jowett and Taylor suggest that the scene was contained on a separate manuscript leaf (possibly 'Shakespeare's addition to his own foul papers'), which was accidentally omitted in the first printing.[70] Whatever its precise origins, it is clearly a later addition to the playbook and one which publication agents made a considerable effort to include. An examination of the texts reveals that QA was set and printed first and that E3 and E4 were reset with two new leaves (E5 and E6, containing the extra scene), which were then stitched in with E1 and E2 from the first issue.[71] At the time of *2 Henry IV*'s entry in the Register (23 August 1600) and publication, the political climate in England was particularly tense. Essex had returned in disgrace from his failed campaign in Ireland, undergone a trial for insubordination, and had only recently been granted his liberty on 26 August, after his confinement in

---

[67] For Daniel's defence of this technique and its classical origins, see *Civil Wars* (1609), A2v. The use of this device was one of the criticisms levelled against Hayward's *Henry IV* when the author was imprisoned and interrogated about the text's seditious intent. See Levy, 'Hayward', pp. 18–19.

[68] Grant and Ravelhofer, 'Introduction', in *English Historical Drama*, p. 3.

[69] The additional scene appears from E3v to E5r in *The Second part of Henrie the fourth* (London, 1600; STC 22288a).

[70] John Jowett and Gary Taylor, 'The Three Texts of *2 Henry IV*', *Studies in Bibliography*, 40 (1987), 31–50 (pp. 33–34, 38). Their examination of the cancel's watermarks and Simmes's type and titles demonstrates that the additional scene was probably printed and added in late 1600.

[71] Ibid., pp. 31–34. The numbers of surviving copies of Q1 (ten copies of QA and eleven of QB) reveal that both versions of the play were sold and circulated.

York House and Essex House. The nature of the additional scene in QB is largely political: it shows Henry IV reflecting on his usurpation of the crown, one of the most pressing points of discussion in texts about the origins of the Wars of the Roses, including Hayward's *Henry IV*. In Shakespeare's scene, Henry presents himself as reluctant in his accession '[b]ut that necessitie so bowed the state, | That I and greatnesse were compeled to kisse' (E4v). This argument that the well-being of the state can justify extreme measures was a key feature of Persons's *Conference*, and Essex himself made a similar remark in a letter to James VI of Scotland, following his trial in 1600: Essex saw himself as 'summoned of all sides to stop the malice, the wickednes and madnes [and] to releeve my poore cuntry that grones under hir burthen', claiming that his 'reason, honour and conscience' commanded him 'to be active'.[72] The scene's repeated references to necessity compelling unexpected action and the difficulty of controlling subjects' loyalties have immediate parallels with Elizabethan political debate, Essex's own situation, and the accusations levelled against him.[73] Its indirectness and the fact that it eschews a clear allusion probably protected it from censorship.[74] Because the stationers involved in the play's publication, Simmes as printer and Wise as publisher, went to some lengths to include the material, it may be that the scene's very currency – the fact that it engages with matters of intense political interest without being explicit or overtly contentious – motivated their efforts.

The scene's attractiveness was also perhaps owing to its representation of a sleep-deprived Henry IV that has its origins in a similar portrait in the third book of Daniel's *Civil Wars* (see R4r–S3r).[75] Shakespeare's portrayal draws very little on his sources in Holinshed, Hall, Stow, and *The Famous Victories of Henry V*.[76] Daniel, however, presents a lengthy account of the king's unceasing worries about the stability of his realm, which led to a sleepless, restless condition:

> For ô no peace could euer so release
> His intricate turmoiles, and sorrowes deepe,
> But that his cares kept waking all his life
> Continue on till death conclude the strife.
>
> (R4v)

---

[72] BL Add. MS 31022 (R), fol.107r–108r. For extracts from this letter, see Hammer, 'Essex Rising', pp. 10–11.

[73] Hammer, 'Essex Rising', pp. 4–10.

[74] René Weis suggests that the shorter version of 3.1 is the result of self-censorship on the part of the Chamberlain's Men, who were concerned about the passage's potential for offence. One of the problems with this theory is that the shorter version was clearly printed first. See *Henry IV, Part 2*, ed. René Weis (Oxford: Oxford University Press, 1997), pp. 78–99.

[75] See also Jowett and Taylor, 'Three Texts', pp. 35–36.   [76] Bullough, *Narrative*, IV, pp. 254–56.

Not only, therefore, did Daniel's *Civil Wars* inform Shakespeare's addition to the play, it may also have spurred on the stationers' efforts to include the accidentally omitted scene, which reinforces the textual exchange taking place between the two publishing houses. Indeed, shortly before the publication of *2 Henry IV*, the first five books of *The Civil Wars*, containing this material as well as a direct approbation of Essex, had been reissued as part of *The Poetical Essays of Samuel Daniel* in 1599. Daniel's representation of Henry and the politic potential of the history may have been fresh in the stationers' minds. Significantly, in the 1601 edition of *The Works of Samuel Daniel*, these two stanzas praising 'worthy Essex' and celebrating his valour as 'The Mercury of peace, the Mars of warre' (M3r, stanzas 126–27) were removed as part of Daniel's ongoing revision of the poem. By this time, it was likely in response to the increasingly hostile political environment which made direct and approving references to the earl unadvisable.[77]

The influence of politically alert publication agents as compilers and editors of texts offers an explanation for one of the most unresolved textual issues relating to Wise's editions: the problem of the deposition or 'Parliament Sceane' in *Richard II*.[78] This scene did not appear in any of Wise's editions and was first published by Matthew Law in 1608 (Q4). It could be a later addition to the play, meaning that censorship was not involved (as Leeds Barroll and David Bergeron have suggested) or, as Janet Clare, Cyndia Clegg, Paul Hammer, Jean-Christophe Mayer and others have argued, it may have been part of the original play and censored either by the Master of the Revels or the company (in the case of self-censorship) prior to performance, or by ecclesiastical agents prior to publication.[79] If a form of censorship was involved, the wholesale excision of a scene typically indicates a decision made during the publication process, rather than the work of a theatrical or authorial agent. Although the Stationers' Register does not actually reveal that the play was authorized prior to publication (not in itself an uncommon practice), Clegg proposes that an ecclesiastical

---

[77] Even in private correspondence, direct references to Essex were avoided. A letter (dated 20 February 1600) from John Harington to Anthony Standen refers to Essex in strikingly oblique terms: 'You wonder I write nothing of *one:* - believe me I hear nothing; but *he* is where he was, and I think must be, till these great businesses be concluded.' Norman Egbert McClure (ed.), *The Letters and Epigrams of Sir John Harington; Together with The Prayse of Private Life* (Philadelphia: University of Pennsylvania Press, 1930), p. 80.

[78] *The Tragedie of King Richard the Second* (London, 1608; STC 22311), A1r.

[79] For a summary of these positions, see Cyndia Susan Clegg, '"By the choise and inuitation of al the realme": *Richard II* and Elizabethan Press Censorship', *Shakespeare Quarterly*, 48:4 (1997), 432–48 (pp. 432–34).

representative, such as the Bishop of London, requested the removal of this scene.[80] Clegg offers a compelling account of how the scene encourages a dialectic with Persons's *Conference*.[81] It presents Parliament as an agent of deposition through the figure of Northumberland, who requests that Richard publicly read out a list of the commons' complaints:

> No more, but that you read
> These accusations, and these greeuous crimes,
> Committed by your person, and your followers,
> Against the State and profit of this Land,
> That by confessing them, the soules of men
> May deeme that you are worthily deposde.
>
> (H2v)

The scene stages a power negotiation between Richard and his nobles, acting transparently (as they claim) on behalf of Parliament and the needs of the people, and requiring Richard 'in common view' to resign his title, so they can 'proceed without suspition' (H1v). In contrast to Holinshed's account, where, as Clegg identifies, Parliament is presented as '*consenting to Richard's abdication*', Shakespeare's dramatization shows the commons summoning the king to his deposition.[82] The Q4 scene seems to echo Persons's notorious claim that 'the king was deposed by act of parlament and himselfe conuinced of his vnworthy gouerment, and brought to confesse that he was worthely depriued' (*Conference*, V7r). Because Wise's publication strategies and his indirect 'exchange' with Waterson suggest he was attentive to the contemporaneity of the Wars of the Roses and how these histories were used in other texts, an alternative possibility is that he (potentially in collaboration with his printer, Simmes) was responsible for its removal.[83] As the scene recalls the radical claims of Persons's treatise and Elizabethan resistance theories, the stationers may have decided to censor it as a precautionary measure, whilst, at a similar time, continuing to encourage politic readings through indirect representations, such as the added scene in *2 Henry IV*.

Wise's editions are particularly significant for my purposes because they demonstrate that the publication and presentation of history plays were

[80] SRO3977; Arber, III, p. 89.
[81] Clegg, '"By the choise"', pp. 432–48. See also Jean-Christophe Mayer, 'The "Parliament Sceane" in Shakespeare's *King Richard II*', *XVII–XVIII: Bulletin de la société d'études anglo-américaines des XVIIe et XVIIIe siècles*, 59 (2004), 27–42.
[82] Clegg, '"By the choise"', pp. 443–44.
[83] See also John Jowett and Gary Taylor, 'Sprinklings of Authority: The Folio Text of *Richard II*', *Studies in Bibliography*, 38 (1985), 151–200 (pp. 195–200).

responsive to patterns in the book trade – ones which can even be geographically mapped – and to wider political contexts. These key factors also directed the responses of other print professionals and readers. For example, a *Sammelband* held by Lambeth Palace Library (1600.22) contains one of Wise's playbooks bound together with a selection of topical, non-dramatic texts in the following order: *Thameseidos* (published by Waterson), *England's Hope Against Irish Hate* (Thomas Heyes), *The King's Declaration* (John Flasket), *Album, seu nigrum amicorum* (Wise), *An Italian's Dead Body, Stuck with English Flowers* (Wise), and *2 Henry IV* (Wise and Aspley). The texts were compiled, as Jeffrey Todd Knight identifies, by the archiepiscopal library at Lambeth Palace, which bound shorter publications by year – a practice that seems to have been influenced by Matthew Parker's collecting practices.[84] The arrangement was therefore determined by a shared year of publication: 1600. Nevertheless, the choice of which texts to feature in this yearbook approach to collection still carries interpretative weight. This *Sammelband* gathers texts that were united through physical spaces and political subjects. All of them were published by stationers based in Paul's Cross (see Figure 2.1) – and several contain the signatures of their publishers, including Wise's on the end of the flyleaf of *2 Henry IV*. As a group, they seem to underscore the political and newsworthy issues dominating the end of Elizabeth's reign. Edward Wilkinson's *Thameseidos*, published by Waterson, offers a panegyric to Elizabeth I that celebrates her reign and the political stability brought about by this 'womanish Empire'.[85] *England's Hope Against Irish Hate*, published by Heyes at the Green Dragon, is a political poem about the Nine Years War that is intensely anti-Irish and praises Essex for having once brought 'the snowtes of these rebellious Swine, | Within their Confines'.[86] Next door to Wise's bookshop, at the Sign of the Black Bear, Flasket published *The King's Declaration and Ordinance Containing the Cause of His War*, which contains Henri IV of France's declaration of war against the Duke of Savoy, '[a]ccording to the copie printed at Paris'.[87] In addition to *2 Henry IV*, the *Sammelband* is rounded out by Wise's two collections of funeral elegies – one in English (*An Italian's Dead Body,*

[84] Jeffrey Todd Knight, 'Making Shakespeare's Books: Assembly and Intertextuality in the Archives', *Shakespeare Quarterly*, 60:3 (2009), 304–40 (pp. 321–23).

[85] [Edward Wilkinson], *E.W. His Thameseidos* (London, 1600; STC 25642), D2r.

[86] Anon./'J. G. E.', *Englands Hope, Against Irish Hate* (London, 1600; STC 7434.7), D1v. Its authorship is sometimes attributed to Anthony Nixon.

[87] Henri IV, King of France, *The Kings Declaration and Ordinance, Containing the Cause of His Warre* (London, 1600; STC 13121), A1r.

Stuck with English Flowers, STC 19154.3) and one in Latin (*Album, seu nigrum amicorum*, STC 19154). They were prepared by Theophilus Field (brother of the actor and playwright, Nathan Field) on the death of Sir Horatio Palavicino (*c*.1540–1600), a merchant and diplomat who fought in Elizabeth's wars and worked as an intelligencer for the English government.[88] As the episcopal library did not generally prioritize literary texts, some of these publications, including Shakespeare's *2 Henry IV*, are unusual inclusions, potentially prompted by the cross-genre exchange of politically invested texts that drove stationers' investments, such as Wise's, in the first place.[89] Indeed, this topical *Sammelband* – featuring texts that were bound together materially, temporally, and geographically – encourages, as Knight proposes, a reading of *2 Henry IV* that is attentive to the play's interest in succession and territorial control above the theatrical vitality of Falstaff and his Eastcheap companions.[90] While Wise's publications do not necessarily offer a clear application to the times through their paratexts – they take part in a debate, without making a precise statement about it – the orthodox emphasis of this volume promotes and is perhaps witness to a reading of the play's political plot that emphatically condemns the rebellious lords and Falstaff's anarchic potential.

Wise's successful editions also prompted other stationers to invest (or reinvest) in medieval English history plays. In 1600, Busby and Millington published the first edition of *Henry V*, while Millington issued his second editions of *The First Part of the Contention* and *The True Tragedy of Richard Duke of York*, therefore making up a three-part series in quarto format that would complement (and expand) the tetralogy published by Wise. Other stationers invested in similar histories: in 1598, Creede finally published the first edition of *The Famous Victories of Henry V*, a title he had entered in the Register in 1594 but had not printed. In 1599, John Oxonbridge invested in Heywood's two-part history play, *Edward IV*, issuing the plays as a collection from his bookshop at the Sign of the Parrot, only a few doors away from Wise's premises in Paul's Cross.[91] By the end of the Elizabethan period, the market for history plays was dominated by those featuring the medieval English monarchical past, a print identity that was directed by Wise's publishing strategies and the editions' success with readers. These patterns did not, however, reflect the position of the history

---

[88] Ian W. Archer, 'Palavicino, Sir Horatio (*c*.1540–1600)', *ODNB*, online edn, January 2008, https://doi.org/10.1093/ref:odnb/21153 (accessed 16 September 2019).
[89] Knight, 'Making', p. 321.   [90] Ibid., pp. 322–23.
[91] Second editions of *Edward I* (William White) and *Edward III* (Cuthbert Burby) were also published in 1599.

play on stage, nor did they remain static. Rather, this print identity characterized the market for only a few years, spurred on by the currency of the Wars of the Roses in a range of 'non-dramatic' texts and political treatises that also encouraged comparative, serialized readings, both within and across different editions.

Wise Networks

Looking beyond Shakespeare's plays, Wise's interest in history is not sustained to the same extent throughout the rest of his output, which suggests that other selection strategies may also be at play. The majority of his published output involves the work of writers – most centrally, Shakespeare, Nashe, and Playfere – who were, as Massai identifies, patronized by George Carey, second Baron Hunsdon.[92] Wise's publications announce their connection to the Carey family through dedications in Nashe's and Playfere's works and through the first ever title-page attributions to the Chamberlain's Men in Shakespeare's playbooks. Wise therefore consistently invests in Carey as a textual patron. This striking specialism could indicate that he had a private link to the Careys and was involved in publishing their patronized writers. I do not, however, believe that the extant evidence supports a direct connection between Wise and Carey. Instead, I would like to propose that a flexible patronage model involving different kinds of private and public exchanges drove Wise's output. I believe that Wise's connection to Carey was a public, textual one within the commercial book trade that may have been facilitated by personal contact with Carey's writers. In this section, I build on David Bergeron's work on the coexistence and interplay of commerce and patronage in printed texts.[93] While Bergeron concentrates on paratextual dedications and addresses, these print features do not appear in Wise's playbooks, and my evidence derives instead from the publisher's overall output, discursive paratexts in non-dramatic publications, stationers' records, and playbook title pages. Erne's work on these editions devalues Wise's agency and argues that Shakespeare and the Chamberlain's Men sought out the publication of their plays.[94] While dramatist and company may have collaborated, I believe that Wise is a key mover in the process and that his history of investment in Nashe and Playfere and his location in Paul's Cross informed his presentation strategies, which make

---

[92] Massai, 'Shakespeare', p. 6.   [93] Bergeron, *Textual Patronage*, pp. 1–21 (esp. pp. 11–18).
[94] Erne, *Literary Dramatist*, ch. 3.

commercial use of a link to Carey and, in later editions, to 'Shakespeare' as part of title-page attributions. As printed texts, Shakespeare's history plays can not only be situated within the dynamic book trade in English monarchical history that encompassed a wide range of publications and political sympathies, but also within a textual patronage network involving a smaller, coterie group of writers. Rather than diminishing the significance of the plays' historical subjects, this network encourages competing notions and applications of history that are attentive to the authorizing role and political reputation of the Carey family, and offers a narrower interpretative framework for directing readings.

Wise's focus on Carey's writers came about through chance, strategy, and book trade connections, which can be clarified by examining the publication contexts of their work. Nashe's *Christ's Tears Over Jerusalem* (1593) is the first text to be associated with Wise and he is identified in the imprint as its bookseller. A connection with printer James Roberts determined his involvement in this edition, and it is the only text of Nashe's with which Wise is linked. That Nashe was under the direct patronage of the Careys is shown by surviving letters and dedications, including the address to Elizabeth Carey (George's wife) in *Christ's Tears*, which claims that his 'choisest studies' were directed to 'the eternizing of the heroycall familie of the Careys'.[95] In a letter to his wife, dated 13 November 1593, Carey disburses a financial reward for Nashe's dedication to Elizabeth and claims that the writer 'shall not finde my purs shutt to relieue him out of prison there presently in great missery, malicied for writinge against the londoners'.[96] Indeed, Carey welcomed Nashe as a guest at Carisbrooke Castle, Isle of Wight, following the writer's release from prison, a mark of support and hospitality that Nashe alludes to in *Have With You to Saffron-Walden* (1596).[97]

It is unlikely that Wise sought a link with Nashe or Carey in the publication of *Christ's Tears*; instead, his involvement was shaped by, as Erne has identified, events and individuals within the book trade.[98] *Christ's Tears* was entered in the Stationers' Register to Alice Charlewood (widow of John Charlewood) on 8 September 1593.[99] When she married James Roberts later that year, all of her publishing rights passed to him. The title

95 Thomas Nashe, *Christs Teares Over Ierusalem* (London, 1593; STC 18366), *2v.
96 Berkeley Muniments General Series Letters Bundle 4; reproduced in facsimile and transcribed in Katherine Duncan-Jones, '*Christs Tears*, Nashe's "Forsaken Extremities"', *Review of English Studies*, 49:194 (1998), 167–80 (pp. 170–75).
97 Thomas Nashe, *Haue with you to Saffron-walden* (London, 1596; STC 18369), P1v.
98 Erne, *Book Trade*, p. 162.   99 SRO3509; Arber, II, p. 635.

page of *Christ's Tears* (1593) indicates that it was 'Printed by Iames Roberts, and are to be solde by Andrewe Wise, at his shop in Paules Churchyard' (*1r), while the 1594 reissue claims that it was 'Printed for Andrew Wise'.[100] It is therefore slightly unclear as to whether Roberts or Wise was the main investor in the text and acted as its publisher, but regardless, Wise's involvement came about through a business relationship with Roberts, who held the rights to Nashe's text because of his recent marriage.

Wise was the only publisher of Playfere's sermons until 1603, which seems to suggest that he had a direct connection with the preacher. Playfere exclusively dedicates his sermons (printed between 1596 and 1603) to either George or Elizabeth Carey, and the nature of the dedications reveals measurable support from the Carey family. In *The Pathway to Perfection* (1596), for example, he credits his university education to the Careys, claiming that by George's 'munificence and bountie my studies haue been hitherto continued'.[101] The relationship between Playfere and Wise, however, was – at least at the beginning – notably hostile. In 1595, Wise published two different but closely related editions of the sermon that Playfere preached at St Mary Spital in Easter week 1595 as *A Most Excellent and Heavenly Sermon* (STC 20014 and STC 20014.3).[102] These editions were not overseen by Playfere and he objected, claiming they were printed from reported texts that had been written down by someone listening to the sermon.[103] This practice was relatively common and was a means of preserving spoken sermons. As Stern shows, 'preachers did not write entire texts before preaching, but spoke from notes of their own; the published "bad" texts were the most complete records available of what had been preached'.[104] Some individuals, including Playfere, nevertheless disapproved of this process of transmission and the 'mangled' texts that resulted.[105]

Although Wise was fined by the Stationers' Company for publishing this sermon 'without aucthoritie' (meaning ecclesiastical allowance), he

---

[100] Thomas Nashe, *Christs Teares Over Iervsalem* (London, 1594; STC 18367), *2r.

[101] Thomas Playfere, *The Pathway to Perfection* (London, 1596; STC 20020), A3r.

[102] Arnold Hunt, *The Art of Hearing: English Preachers and Their Audiences, 1590–1640* (Cambridge: Cambridge University Press, 2010), p. 145. As Hunt proposes, they were likely prepared from two different shorthand texts. Another edition STC 20014.5 also appeared in 1595.

[103] See Thomas Playfere, *The Meane in Movrning* (London, 1596; STC 20015), A2r–4r.

[104] Tiffany Stern, 'Sermons, Plays, and Note-Takers: *Hamlet* Q1 as a "Noted" Text', *Shakespeare Survey 66* (2013), 1–23 (p. 7). See also Mary Morrissey, *Politics and the Paul's Cross Sermons, 1558–1642* (Oxford: Oxford University Press, 2011), ch. 2.

[105] Playfere, *Meane*, A2r.

held the rights to it, and Playfere was obliged to work with him to produce
the authorized version, which was published in 1596 as *The Mean in
Mourning*.[106] In a dedicatory address to the 'Lady Elizabeth Carey, wife to
the thrise-noble, Sir George Carey, Knight Marshall', Playfere describes
how 'this sermon hath been twise printed already without my procure-
ment' (A2r) and that he has 'played the surgeon' (A3r) to redress the faults
in the text. A contrastive analysis of Wise's earlier editions and the
authorized edition shows that Playfere's most extensive revisions relate to
the style, presentation, and annotation of the text. Playfere adds elaborate
printed marginalia in English, Latin, Greek, and Hebrew, and includes
references and digressions that were not part of the spoken text, as he
acknowledges in his dedication.[107] Playfere's sermons offer an interesting
case study of an author evaluating the merits of publication within a book
trade in which stationers held the rights to procure and register texts. The
fact that Wise also published Playfere's *Pathway to Perfection* in 1596
(which was issued together with *The Mean in Mourning*) suggests some
degree of cooperation between the preacher and stationer, because Playfere
did not need to use Wise as a publisher for another sermon. Hooks
proposes that the stationer's initial investment in Playfere was motivated
by Nashe's approbation of the preacher and his sweet, 'mellifluous' style –
a term that would also be used to describe Shakespeare.[108] It may be the
case that stylistic interests prompted Wise's first investments, before an
interplay of further factors – such as the marketability of English history –
propelled later investments. As Hooks observes, 'Playfere's case is instructive, since it so clearly demonstrates how the trade connections and
cultural awareness of a stationer could alter an author's career, proving
his viability as a published author, and hence showing him the possibilities
afforded by print'.[109] It draws attention to the role of print professionals in
shaping writers' outputs, considered earlier in this chapter with Waterson
and Daniel, and implies that Wise's interests, rather than Playfere's or
Carey's, drove the *initial* investment.

---

[106] W. W. Greg and E. Boswell (eds.), *Records of the Court of the Stationers' Company: 1576–1602*
(London: Bibliographical Society, 1930), p. 51. See also Arber, II, pp. 823, 827. Wise was fined
forty shillings on 28 June 1595 'for master Playfordes sermon'.

[107] Playfere claims that although the reader 'haue all heere which he heard then, yet hee heard not all
then, which he hath heere' (A3v). See, for example, F8r–G1r for Playfere's multilingual marginal
annotations. See also Hunt (*The Art of Hearing*, p. 160) for Playfere's 1596 addition about the
response of his audience.

[108] See Hooks, 'Wise', pp. 50–55, and *Selling*, ch. 2.   [109] Hooks, *Selling*, p. 70.

George Carey became patron of Shakespeare's company in July 1596, following the death of his father, Henry Carey, and it is through this connection that Shakespeare can be seen as one of Carey's patronized writers. Shortly after this, Wise started to invest in plays by Shakespeare, publishing ten editions between 1597 and 1600, more than any other stationer. He did not publish plays by other dramatists, and most of his editions contain attributions to the Chamberlain's Men. Even Creede's specialism in histories from the Queen's Men is not as exclusive. Cuthbert Burby published a range of texts comparable to that of Wise, including sermons, plays, and news pamphlets; but he did not concentrate on works connected to one patron or plays performed by one company or written by one dramatist.[110] Wise's specialism suggests that he may have had a direct connection with Carey's company that motivated his investment in Shakespeare's English histories and, later, his edition of *Much Ado About Nothing* (1600) which, despite its wartime setting, departs from the historical emphasis of the other playbooks. Because his involvement in texts by Nashe and Playfere came about by circumstance, book-trade associations, and/or a proactive acquisition of manuscripts, it is unlikely that Wise had a personal connection with Carey himself, in the manner of the stationer/patron networks that existed between, for example, John Wolfe and George Goring, or between Christopher Barker and Francis Walsingham.[111] However, Wise surely would have been aware, while he was investing in Shakespeare's histories, that all of his publications to date could be linked to Carey. He may have sought out a connection to the Chamberlain's Men or, when an opportunity came along to publish plays from Carey's company, he seized it.

This connection between Wise and Carey can be reclarified as one that was public and textual, rather than private and measurable, and that was facilitated through a cooperative and potentially collaborative relationship between Wise and the Chamberlain's Men that directed the plays' dissemination in print. While I disagree with Erne's downplaying of Wise's

---

[110] Burby published *Love's Labour's Lost* (1598) and *Romeo and Juliet* (1599, second edition) from the Chamberlain's Men, as well as *George a Greene* (1599) from Sussex's Men, and *Mother Bombie* (1594 and 1598) from the Children of Paul's.

[111] For example, Goring, an Elizabethan courtier and diplomat, provided Wolfe with a letter of support on 18 October 1582 following his difficulties with the Stationers' Company and prosecution for challenging printing privileges. The Register records Thomas Norton's response to Goring on 23 October 1582, when he requests that 'you must oppose your self as aduersarie Either to Wolf your man, or to your mistresse the Quene and to all her maiesties seruantes' (Arber, II, pp. 773–76). In addition to acting as the queen's printer, Barker was patronized by Walsingham and marked his texts with a tiger's head from Walsingham's crest.

agency in their publication, his proposition that James Roberts assisted in acquiring playscripts and initiating a connection with the company is plausible.[112] The two stationers had previously worked together on the publication of *Christ's Tears* in 1593 and Roberts held the exclusive rights to publish playbills (which he had also inherited through his marriage to Alice Charlewood). This monopoly over playbill publication meant that Roberts was in regular contact with theatre companies, which could have spurred on the publication of their plays as books.[113] Indeed, when comparing Wise's editions with those of other stationers who published Shakespeare's plays between 1594 and 1603, the relative quality of Wise's texts becomes apparent. *Romeo and Juliet* (printed in 1597 by John Danter and Edward Allde), *Henry V* (published in 1600 by Thomas Millington and John Busby), and *The Merry Wives of Windsor* (published in 1602 by Arthur Johnson) differ considerably from Wise's editions in terms of the quality of the texts they preserve, leading to stronger claims for memorial reconstruction, particularly in *The Merry Wives of Windsor*.[114] Of all the stationers investing in Shakespeare's plays at this time, Wise produced some of the least textually problematic playbooks – ones which are routinely classified as 'good' quartos and used as the copy texts for modern editions.[115] A professional relationship possibly existed between the Chamberlain's Men and Wise, who was, propelled by circumstance or by strategy, fashioning himself as the main publisher for writers patronized by George Carey.

A staying entry recorded in the Stationers' Register on 4 August 1600 might be seen as complicating the claim of a cooperative exchange between Wise and the Chamberlain's Men. It indicates that the printing of 'As you like yt', 'Henry the ffift', 'Euery man in his humor', and 'The commedie of muche A doo about nothinge', all plays from the Chamberlain's Men, are 'to be staied' (that is, stopped).[116] This attempt

---

[112] Erne, *Literary Dramatist*, pp. 111–12.

[113] The rights to playbills were held successively by four printer-publishers between 1587 and 1642: John Charlewood (until 1593), Roberts (until c.1606 to 1615), William and Isaac Jaggard (until 1627), and Thomas and Richard Cotes (until 1642).

[114] Laurie E. Maguire, *Shakespearean Suspect Texts: The 'Bad' Quartos and Their Contexts* (Cambridge: Cambridge University Press, 1996), pp. 257–58, 285–86, 301–302.

[115] Wise's publication of *Richard III* (Q1 1597) provides the only possible exception, but recent reappraisals have stressed the high quality of this edition and its underlying manuscript. See *Richard III*, ed. Jowett, pp. 110–27; *King Richard III*, ed. James R. Siemon (London: Arden Shakespeare, 2009), pp. 417–60.

[116] Worshipful Company of Stationers and Newspaper Makers, Liber C, flyleaf; facsimile and transcription available on *Shakespeare Documented* (accessed 7 April 2021). See also Arber, III, p. 37.

at publication control could be an effort to prevent stationers from printing the company's plays and, at this time, Wise was probably interested in one of them – *Much Ado About Nothing* – which he would later publish with Aspley. However, it is unclear, as Joseph Loewenstein points out, whether the entry was intended to prevent the publication of these plays or to forestall them temporarily until certain conditions were met.[117] Following the staying order, *Henry V*, *Every Man In His Humour*, and *Much Ado* were almost immediately entered in the Register and published between 1600 and 1601.[118] The lack of evidence for any negative repercussions suggests that whatever preconditions were required by the staying order were quickly and satisfactorily met.[119] Indeed, the order implies a growing interest in the publication of plays from the Chamberlain's Men, possibly instigated by the success of Wise's earlier editions of *Richard II*, *Richard III*, and *1 Henry IV*. Rather than restricting Wise's activities, the order may indicate that the Chamberlain's Men were trying to allocate the publication rights for their plays to specific stationers approved by the company.

One effect of Wise's editions is their creation of a print identity for Shakespeare and his company as dramatizers of medieval English monarchical history. In 1597, *Richard II* and *Richard III* became the first playbooks to contain title-page attributions to 'the right Honourable the Lorde Chamberlaine his Seruants', having been entered in the Register shortly after Carey was invested with the chamberlainship on 14 April 1597.[120] Clarifying the agency behind this attribution and the extent to which Shakespeare and the Chamberlain's Men were involved in the publication process remains a matter of speculation, but two points are worth considering. First, none of Shakespeare's plays display any clear evidence of their dramatist's direct involvement in publication. Although Erne has argued at length for Shakespeare and the company's interest in publication, even he acknowledges that Shakespeare's paratextual silence seems to indicate that the dramatist 'entrusted [the plays] to the care of his publishers and readers', a point which underlines Wise's

---

[117] Loewenstein, *Possessive Authorship*, pp. 42–44.

[118] The plays were entered between 14 and 23 August 1600. Only *As You Like It* remained in manuscript until the 1623 Folio.

[119] See Loewenstein (*Possessive Authorship*, pp. 35–49) for a clear account of other staying entries and efforts at publication control.

[120] See *The Tragedie of King Richard the second* (London, 1597; STC 22307), A1r, which was entered in the Register on 29 August 1597. The first edition of *Romeo and Juliet* was also published in 1597 (STC 22322); but its attribution to the 'L. of Hundson his Seruants' suggests that it was printed before Carey was invested with the chamberlainship.

agency.[121] Second, through an investment in Shakespeare's plays, Wise added another writer patronized by George Carey to his published output, a connection that could have prompted him to include company attributions. Before 1600, the only other playbooks to name the Chamberlain's Men were *A Warning for Fair Women* (1599) – another history play – and the second edition of *Romeo and Juliet* (1599).[122] For the first few years of the company's print history, they were primarily dramatizers of medieval English history written by Shakespeare.

Although title-page references to playing companies were not unusual, Wise's attributions are significant because they united all of his publications under the cachet of a single aristocratic patron and because this print emphasis could 'authorize' specific readings of the histories – by Carey's own circle and by the wider public – that were attentive to the political interests and reputation of the Carey family. During Elizabeth's reign, the Careys were closely involved in governing the area around the Scottish border, known as the Marches, maintaining working but authoritative relations with the Scots, and carefully prioritizing the issue of succession. Henry Carey was appointed governor of Berwick in 1568, worked in the borders at a time of political instability and sensitivity, and played a prominent role in the suppression of the Northern Rebellion in 1569, which was an attempt by Catholic nobles to depose Elizabeth on behalf of Mary, Queen of Scots.[123] Similarly, George Carey served on important committees concerning the fate of Mary, Queen of Scots, the regulation of the Scottish borders, and the aftermath of the Northern Rebellion, and was knighted for his military service at Berwick on 11 May 1570. The range of dedications accrued by the Careys from writers who were not, as far as extant evidence suggests, under their direct patronage reinforces the family's political and military activities. Dedications appear in, for example, Humfrey Barwick's *A Brief Discourse Concerning the Force and Effect of All Manual Weapons of Fire* (c.1592, dedicated to Henry Carey), Thomas Churchyard's *A Pleasant Discourse of Court and Wars* (1596, dedicated to George Carey), Marin Barleti's *The History of George Castriot, Surnamed Scanderbeg, King of Albania*

---

[121] Erne, *Book Trade*, pp. 128–29.
[122] When Burby's edition of *Love's Labour's Lost* was published in 1598, it advertised a royal performance ('As it was presented before her Highnes this last Christmas'; STC 22294, A1r), rather than a connection to the Chamberlain's Men.
[123] Wallace T. MacCaffrey, 'Carey, Henry, first Baron Hunsdon (1526–1596)', *ODNB*, online ed., September 2014, https://doi.org/10.1093/ref:odnb/4649 (accessed 16 September 2019), para. 5, 22.

(1596, dedicated to George Carey), Giles Fletcher's *The Policy of the Turkish Empire* (1597, dedicated to George Carey), and William Warner's *Albion's England* (1586, 1589, 1592, 1596/97, and 1602, dedicated to Henry Carey and, later, George Carey).[124] The Careys seem to have been associated with the books that Sidney singled out for assisting in 'the trade of our lives' – that is, those concerning politics and 'souldiery' that either 'profess the arte' or recount the 'historyes' which show 'what hath bene done'.[125]

Wise's investment in Shakespeare's history plays seems alert to the reputation of the company's patron – especially in light of the issues addressed in these plays, such as the numerous rebellions that took place in the reigns of Richard II, Henry IV, and Richard III; the political instabilities arising from powerful court factions; and the debates surrounding succession. In *1 Henry IV*, the events of the rebellion, chiefly staged in the north and west of England, had a recent parallel in the Northern Rebellion of 1569, when Henry Carey commanded Elizabeth's forces and his family worked to restore control of the border area. Shakespeare may have deliberately heightened the parallels in his dramatization: as David Bevington observes, Henry IV's account of civil uprising recalls the *Homily Against Disobedience and Wilful Rebellion* ([1570]), which was incorporated into *The Second Tome of Homilies* (1571) immediately after the Northern Rebellion and was required to be read regularly in churches.[126] Henry IV describes how insurrectionists 'face the garment of rebellion | With some fine colour that may please ... fickle changlings and poore discontents' who 'gape and rub the elbow at the newes | Of hurly burly innouation' (Q2 I2v). It echoes the *Homily*'s concern with the ways in which popular rebellion 'pretende[s] sundrie causes', such as 'the redresse of the common wealth', and makes 'a great shewe of holy meaning ... ensigns, and banners, whiche are acceptable vnto the rude ignoraunt common people, great multitudes of whom by suche falsee pretenses and shewes they do deceaue'.[127] Wise's playbooks could encourage readers – including the Careys and their circle, as well as the wider public who were aware of the family's political interests – to link

---

[124] For dedications to both Careys, see the fourth edition (STC 25082) of 1596/97: A2r–v for Henry; P1v for George. Further editions were issued in the Jacobean and Caroline periods.

[125] Letter from Sidney to Edward Denny on 22 May 1580. See *The Correspondence of Sir Philip Sidney*, ed. Roger Kuin, 2 vols. (Oxford: Oxford University Press, 2012), II, pp. 980–85 (p. 982).

[126] Shakespeare, *Henry IV Part I*, ed. David Bevington (Oxford: Oxford University Press, 1987), p. 263.

[127] *An Homilie Against Disobedience and Wylfull Rebellion* (London, 1570; STC 13680), F4r–v.

these histories with the instances of rebellion and unrest that had taken place earlier in Elizabeth's reign and which achieved resolution through the efforts of the Carey family. They could offer readings that shore up the political influence and acumen of the Careys, who, through their close connection to the Scottish monarchy (cautiously) supported James VI's succession to the English throne.[128] On a more limited scale than the broader reading approaches outlined in the first section of this chapter, Wise's playbooks could prompt some readers to see these histories and their contemporaneity as authorized by Carey as Lord Chamberlain.

The Oldcastle-Falstaff controversy provides a final example of how Wise's playbooks were attentive to the interests of the Carey family and the impact that contemporary allusions could have on the interpretation of histories (and their historicity). This episode is rendered a permanent part of *1* and *2 Henry IV* through Wise's printed editions and in a way that pacifies but also courts attention. On stage, Shakespeare's original use of the name 'Oldcastle' for Falstaff had attracted opposition from the Cobham family, who traced their lineage to the Lollard leader, Sir John Oldcastle, martyred in 1417 during the reign of Henry V.[129] Shakespeare's theatrically vivacious knight is, of course, the most conspicuous 'unhistorical' addition to the source materials. Even Shakespeare, as Bergeron points out, associates the word 'counterfeit' with him.[130] But the fact that Shakespeare assigned him the name of a real individual, together with the opposition it attracted, had the effect of historicizing and contemporizing the fictional character. It becomes difficult to separate Shakespeare's character from the Cobham family's ancestor and the real controversy the naming provoked in the Elizabethan period. There is, as James Marino

---

[128] George's brother, Robert Carey, described their closeness to James VI, claiming that when the king 'had a matter of great importance to acquaint his sister the Queene of England withall', he would not trust anyone but 'my father [Henry], or some of his children'. Robert Carey, *Memoirs of the Life of Robert Cary, Baron of Leppington, and Earl of Monmouth; Written by Himself* (London: R. and J. Dodsley, 1759), p. 69.

[129] The reasons for Shakespeare's original choice, the timing of the play's first performance, and the connection of the controversy to the tenure of William Brooke, Baron Cobham, as Lord Chamberlain (between August 1596 and March 1597) are matters of continuing debate. For a careful assessment, see James M. Gibson, 'Shakespeare and the Cobham Controversy: The Oldcastle/Falstaff and Brooke/Broome Revisions', *Medieval & Renaissance Drama in England*, 25 (2012), 94–132. See also the account of the antiquarian Richard James in 1625: British Library, Add. MS 33785, fol. 2r; available in facsimile and transcription through *Shakespeare Documented* (accessed 7 April 2021).

[130] Bergeron, 'Bogus', p. 97.

describes, a 'durable entanglement' of Falstaff/Oldcastle within and out-side the text, which historicizes the play's most fictional element.[131]

Wise's editions, on the one hand, seem sensitive to the demands of correction and censorship and the political difficulty that could have been experienced by the Carey family. For performance in the playhouse, the name 'Sir John Falstaff' was used as a replacement, which is also reflected in Wise's printed editions. Traces of 'Oldcastle' remain in both *1* and *2 Henry IV* through speech prefixes and stage directions, in addition to Hal's reference to Falstaff as 'my old lad of the castle' (Q2 *1 Henry IV*, A4r). Privately, the Carey family seem to have enjoyed the original naming and used it as a shorthand for the play as a whole. A letter from Rowland Whyte to Sir Robert Sidney in March 1600 indicates that George Carey entertained an ambassador by having his players act 'Sir John Old Castell, to his great Contentment'.[132] Rather than indicating Drayton, Hathaway, Munday, and Wilson's *1 Sir John Oldcastle*, which was performed by the Admiral's Men as a response to Shakespeare's play and was not owned by Carey's company, this title probably refers to *1 Henry IV* and testifies to the ongoing 'double identification' of Falstaff and Oldcastle.[133] Some sensitivity about the debacle is suggested, however, by the fact that none of Wise's extant editions of *1 Henry IV* contain title-page attributions to the Chamberlain's Men. Q1 survives in only one sheet, its title page no longer extant, while Q2's title page (1598) refrains from mentioning those involved in the offence: Shakespeare and George Carey's company. Q3 (1599) adds a new title-page reference to Shakespeare as a corrector. Unlike Wise's other editions that, from 1598 onwards, contain the attribution 'By William Shakespeare', Q3 claims that the play has been 'Newly corrected by W. Shakes-peare'.[134] In contrast to the assertive claims of authorship on the other Wise quartos, Q3's attribution empha-sizes the play's 'corrected' state.[135]

On the other hand, some features of the printed editions encourage a recollection of the debacle. All extant title pages advertise 'the humorous conceits of Sir Iohn Falstalffe' (Q2 *1 Henry IV*, A1r) in their plot descrip-tions, which draws attention to this extratextual character and associates

---

[131] James J. Marino, *Owning William Shakespeare: The King's Men and Their Intellectual Property* (Philadelphia: University of Pennsylvania Press, 2011), pp. 123–24.

[132] E. K. Chambers, *William Shakespeare: A Study of Facts and Problems*, 2 vols. (Oxford: Clarendon Press, 1930), II, p. 322.

[133] Marino, *Owning*, p. 122.

[134] *The History of Henrie the Fovrth* (London, 1599; STC 22281), A1r.

[135] See also Lidster, 'At the Sign of the Angel', p. 249.

him with firmly 'historical' figures, such as Hotspur and Henry IV (see Figure 2.2). Bevington describes the publication of the play as an act of 'goodwill' to assist in 'setting the record straight' on the Oldcastle-Falstaff controversy, but the editions do not suggest a clear conciliatory effort.[136] *1* and *2 Henry IV* remind readers of the dispute through references to Falstaff on the title pages of both parts and in the epilogue to part 2, which claims that 'Olde-castle died Martyre, and this [i.e. Falstaff] is not the man' (L1v). Reintroducing and emphasizing the link between Oldcastle and Falstaff at the end of the play is hardly the most effective or unambiguous placatory gesture. The epilogue's inclusion also makes it a permanent feature of the printed playbook, which is distinct from its theatrical status as a detachable document.[137] Wise's editions seem to display a tension between offering suitably censored texts and eliciting the very parallels elided through censorship – ones that had been enjoyed by the Careys and by the plays' audiences. By preserving some traces of the Falstaff-Oldcastle controversy, the playbooks inscribe their unhistorical character with continuing contemporaneity and historicity.

In summary, I believe that Wise's initial investment in Shakespeare's plays was directed by a complex interplay of agents and influences that reflect private and public exchanges between Wise and the Chamberlain's Men, Wise and Carey, and Wise and other stationers connected through geographies and investment patterns within the book trade. Wise was influenced not only by the prominence and utility of medieval English history in non-dramatic publications, but, as discussed in this section, by a connection to Carey's patronized writers. Owing to the limitations of extant evidence, it is not possible to determine the precise nature of this patronage network involving Wise, Shakespeare, the Chamberlain's Men, and George Carey. It likely featured transactions of a private and measurable kind (such as a direct interaction between Carey and the company, and between Wise and the company), as well as public and commercial interactions (through, for example, the use of title-page attributions to Carey's company) that could authorize different readings of the plays. For the history play, Wise's editions demonstrate that strategies of selection and presentation could be informed by multiple, collaborative networks, and they draw attention to the different readerships that could be imagined

---

[136] *1 Henry IV*, ed. Bevington, pp. 87, 90.

[137] The fact that a version of the Epilogue is also included in the 1623 Folio text underscores its position as a fixed point of conclusion for the play that recalls Oldcastle in its final lines. For epilogues as detachable documents, see Tiffany Stern, *Documents of Performance in Early Modern England* (Cambridge: Cambridge University Press, 2009), ch. 4.

by a history play's publisher – ranging from those who concentrated on politic applications, to those who were influenced by the authorizing power of patrons, and those who were invested in the theatrical vitality of specific characters.

Wise Attributions and Conclusions

In 1598, Shakespeare's name first appeared – unambiguously – on the title pages of playbooks in Wise's second editions of *Richard II* and *Richard III* and Burby's first (extant) edition of *Love's Labour's Lost*.[138] Burby's practices, which I have discussed at length elsewhere, do not reveal a sustained interest in Shakespearean attribution: his edition of *Romeo and Juliet* in 1599 does not include Shakespeare's name, and the full attribution in *Love's Labour's Lost* reads 'Newly corrected and augmented | By W. Shakespere' (A1r), which aligns the dramatist with the processes of correction and expansion, rather than initial authorship.[139] Wise, on the other hand, consistently invested in 'Shakespeare' from 1598 onwards.[140] I believe the introduction of Shakespeare's name on playbook title pages was contingent upon the responsive and collaborative nature of the book trade and that it was instigated by Wise's editions. It is also a development that has consequences for the history play as a genre. This chapter concludes with three points about these Shakespearean attributions that shed light on Wise's strategies and how they shaped the print identity of the history play at the end of the sixteenth century.

First, the title-page attributions in Wise's editions established Shakespeare as the most prominent named dramatist of English monarchical history in print at the end of the Elizabethan period. They differ from the history plays published by other stationers during the late 1590s, most of which were issued anonymously. *The Famous Victories of Henry V* (published in 1598 by Creede) and Thomas Heywood's *1* and *2 Edward IV* (published in 1599 by Oxonbridge) do not contain any indication of authorship. Of course, the strategies of anonymous editions and the factors

---

[138] There may have been an earlier edition of *Love's Labour's Lost* in 1597, of which no copies survive. A printed edition is referred to in a manuscript catalogue from the Viscount Conway with a date of 1597. See Andrew Murphy, *Shakespeare in Print: A History and Chronology of Shakespeare Publishing* (Cambridge: Cambridge University Press, 2003), p. 461.

[139] Burby's only other playbook to contain an attribution to a dramatist is *The Cobbler's Prophecy* (to 'Robert Wilson, Gent.'). See Lidster, 'At the Sign of the Angel', p. 248.

[140] Attributions to Shakespeare (including his identification as a corrector) appear in *Richard II* Q2 (1598) and Q3 (1598), *Richard III* Q2 (1598) and Q3 (1602), *1 Henry IV* Q3 (1599), *2 Henry IV* Q1 (1600), and *Much Ado About Nothing* Q1 (1600).

that direct their presentation cannot be easily generalized – but, for my purposes, what is especially relevant is the consequence of this anonymity in relation to ideas of genre and the history play. As discussed in the introduction to this chapter, the fifteen playbooks of English monarchical history published between 1595 and 1599 are – with the two exceptions of Marlowe's *Edward II* and Peele's *Edward I* – either attributed to Shakespeare or anonymous editions.[141] At the end of the sixteenth century, Shakespeare's name is the one most consistently connected to the dramatization of England's medieval monarchical past.

Second, the evidence of Wise's playbooks suggests that publication agents, rather than theatrical ones, were responsible for the introduction of Shakespeare's name on title pages, a development that underscores their influence in preparing the editions, already explored in this chapter in relation to plot summaries, company attributions, and the preparation of copy. Wise's first editions of *Richard II* and *Richard III* in 1597 do not contain attributions to Shakespeare, which implies that the marketability of his name was not immediately apparent and that, if the dramatist and/or the Chamberlain's Men were involved in publication, it was not part of their initial design to create a print identity for 'Shakespeare'. The 1598 attribution – 'By William Shakespeare' – is a striking development (see Figure 2.3). As Erne points out, 'it is precisely the replacement of an anonymous edition by an authored one that is unusual'.[142] The publication of reprints tended to be more narrowly controlled by stationers than first editions, which depended on the acquisition of a manuscript and involved some kind of exchange with individuals outside of the book trade. It is therefore likely that a publication agent, such as Wise, took the decision to include Shakespeare's name on later editions. Wise was also involved in the first appearance of Shakespeare's name in the Stationers' Register, as part of his and Aspley's combined entry, on 23 August 1600, for *2 Henry IV* and *Much Ado About Nothing*.[143] Together these two developments mark a shift in the status and importance of Shakespeare as a printed dramatist.[144] They also reinforce my argument that Wise's *initial* design had not been to invest in 'Shakespeare', but rather English monarchical history and Carey as patron of the 'Chamberlain's Men'.

Third, the decision to include Shakespeare's name on playbook title pages was contingent upon developments, networks, and geographical

---

[141] Both Marlowe's and Peele's plays contain references to their authorship.
[142] Erne, *Literary Dramatist*, p. 82.   [143] See note 60 above.
[144] See also Hooks, *Selling*, pp. 66–68; Erne, *Literary Dramatist*, p. 87.

proximity in the book trade – sources of influence that also shaped Wise's interest in medieval English history and the ways in which his editions seem responsive to, for example, Daniel's *Civil Wars*, published by Waterson. It is unclear whether *Richard II* or *Richard III* appeared first with a Shakespeare attribution in 1598; in the case of the latter, Creede's role as trade printer for this edition and publisher of *The True Tragedy of Richard III* may have determined the new attribution. The investment of Wise's neighbouring stationers in Shakespeare's narrative poems – *Venus and Adonis* and *The Rape of Lucrece* – also added to the marketability of Shakespeare's name, a related factor that may have influenced title-page design. I have discussed this connection in detail elsewhere; but, in brief, these poems contain signed dedications by Shakespeare to his patron, Henry Wriothesley, third earl of Southampton, and they were the only printed texts associated with Shakespeare as named author before 1598.[145] Both poems proved exceptionally popular with readers, judging by their numerous subsequent reprints, and most of these were published and offered for wholesale by stationers at the Sign of the White Greyhound, just three doors away from Wise's shop in Paul's Cross (see Figure 2.1).[146] The success and strategies of the narrative poems, which would have been especially visible to Wise, perhaps directed the stationer's exclusive concentration on Shakespeare's plays and the inclusion of attributions to him from 1598. In turn, the success of Wise's editions may lie behind the title-page attribution 'By W. Shakespeare' that appeared, in 1599, on the second edition of *The Passionate Pilgrim*, an octavo collection of poems published by William Jaggard and sold by William Leake at the White Greyhound.[147] Until this time, Shakespeare's name had only featured on the title pages of his printed *playbooks*. *The Passionate Pilgrim* became the first non-dramatic text attributed to Shakespeare on its title page, and this sequence of events reveals another textual 'exchange' taking place between the bookselling publishers in Paul's Cross.

Largely owing to the success of Wise's editions, Shakespeare emerged, at the end of the sixteenth century, as the most attributed commercial dramatist in print – and one of the most quoted.[148] Miscellanies published under the auspices of John Bodenham – *Belvedere, or The Garden of the*

[145] Lidster, 'At the Sign of the Angel', pp. 250–51. See also Adam Hooks, 'Shakespeare at the White Greyhound', *Shakespeare Survey 64* (2011), 260–75; and Smith, 'Mapping', pp. 69–86.
[146] Blayney, *Bookshops*, p. 76.
[147] *The Passionate Pilgrime* (London, 1599; STC 22342), A2r. No copies of the title page for the first edition (STC 22341.5) are extant. Of the twenty poems in the volume, only five can be attributed to Shakespeare (numbers 1, 2, 3, 5, and 16).
[148] Shakespeare had nine playbook attributions by 1600, whereas Robert Greene, the second most attributed, had five. I am counting the attribution to 'R. G.' in *Alphonsus* (1599). See also Lukas Erne, 'The Popularity of Shakespeare in Print', *Shakespeare Survey 62* (2009), 12–29 (pp. 26–27).

Muses (1600) and *England's Parnassus* (1600) – tended to favour extracts from Wise's editions.[149] One reader, William Scott, includes passages from *Richard II* alongside classical and contemporary English exempla in his manuscript treatise on poetics, *The Model of Poesy* (*c.*1599). This elevation of vernacular commercial drama was, as Gavin Alexander notes, unprecedented and testifies to the growing status of Shakespeare in print.[150] The editions' success, presentation strategies, and interest in history may also have shaped readers' collecting practices. As discussed, *2 Henry IV* ended up in a *Sammelband* with politically invested pamphlets and poetry. Indicated by a manuscript list of plays (from *c.*1609–10), the histories first published by Wise also feature prominently in the personal collections of Sir John Harington (*bap.* 1560, *d.* 1612). The first volume of his *Sammelband* collection contains Shakespeare's 'Henry the fourth: 1', 'Henry the fourth: 2', and 'Richard the 3rd', arranged in the historical order of their monarchs, rather than their order of composition or publication.[151] Indeed, these plays were carefully guarded by their next publisher, Matthew Law, who inherited the rights from Wise in 1603.[152] The 1623 Folio syndicate had some difficulty securing Law's permission to include these plays in the collection, which, if not obtained, would have significantly altered the balance of the Folio.[153]

   Wise's editions are therefore particularly important for understanding the early modern history play in print, but not necessarily for the reasons that are usually suggested. These plays are not simply documents back to stage: they should not be used as evidence for the dominance of medieval English history in the London theatres, which instead staged a diverse range of historical pasts. More accurately, they highlight the ways in which print and stage patterns could *differ* and they underscore my overarching argument in this book that a critical understanding of repertories, dramatists' outputs, and genres needs to consider the possibility of a disjunction between the theatre and the book trade. The promotion of medieval English history in Wise's editions complements patterns in the book trade, which in turn reveals how commercial plays – repositioned as books – were

---

[149] See Lidster, 'At the Sign of the Angel', pp. 252–53; and Zachary Lesser and Peter Stallybrass, 'The First Literary *Hamlet* and the Commonplacing of Professional Plays', *Shakespeare Quarterly*, 59:4 (2008), 371–420 (p. 395).

[150] [William Scott, *The Modell of Poesye*], BL Add MS 81083, fols.12r, 26r, 39r; facsimile and transcription available on *Shakespeare Documented* (accessed 7 April 2021); Gavin Alexander (ed.), *William Scott, The Model of Poesy* (Cambridge: Cambridge University Press, 2013), p. lxi.

[151] BL Add MS 27632, fol. 43.   [152] SRO4718; Arber, III, p. 239.

[153] See Chapter 4, pp. 210–11.

part of the market in historical texts, rather than being 'obsolete' goods sold in the 'antique-shop'.[154] These editions also draw attention to the influence of physical spaces and proximity in the book trade, as Wise's investment may have been motivated by the practices of neighbouring stationers in Paul's Cross, an issue that is also explored in the next chapter. Nevertheless, caution is necessary. Wise's editions demonstrate how multiple factors shape the publication of history plays and ideas of dramatic genre – and it is important not to overstate the significance of one strategy, despite its narrative appeal. Wise likely read Shakespeare's histories in different ways. They spoke to the contemporaneity of medieval English history at the end of the sixteenth century, but they were also marketable (and perhaps available) because of the authorizing agents associated with them: George Carey, as patron of the Chamberlain's Men and Wise's other published writers, and Shakespeare. The 'aftermarket' of print publication is a site where multiple agents, transactions, and readings are in play, and this participation is crucial for understanding why certain plays survive, what influenced their presentation in print, and how these histories were – and continue to be – received by readers.

---

[154] Griffin, *Playing*, pp. 144–45.

CHAPTER 3

United Histories
Nathaniel Butter and his Newsworthy Playbooks

Critical interest in bookseller Nathaniel Butter as a publisher of history plays has been limited, despite his investment in a range of 'pasts' from the legendary British chronicle history of *King Lear* (1608) to the recent Tudor history of *When You See Me You Know Me* (1605). From his business location at the Sign of the Pied Bull in St Paul's Churchyard, Butter started to specialize, during the early Jacobean period, in the publication of histories and news pamphlets. For Butter, news – as an account of the recent past – was similar in terms of purpose, style, and strategies to accounts of older pasts, such as the Tudor and ancient histories dramatized in his playbooks. He did not draw a clear distinction between history and news, and his practices break down the temporal divisions between different history plays. Because Butter is so invested in ideas of 'history', it is possible to use his output to develop a detailed profile of an early modern reader – one whose selection of texts with Protestant and union preoccupations offers a distinctive perspective on history plays and introduces a slight tension with James I's own political and religious policies.

The evidence of Butter's practices and wider output as a news publisher suggests that he was interested in the timeliness and newsworthy quality of texts, which, for Creede and Wise, was a contributing but not exclusive factor. In this chapter, I argue that Butter's investment in history plays was determined by their ability to engage with issues of religious and political unification (and division), pressing concerns that dominated the early Jacobean period. Unlike Creede and Wise, Butter's non-dramatic publications (such as *The Devil of the Vault*) reveal a clear partisan alignment: he concentrates on texts that promote Protestant sympathies and an international Protestant cause, the anti-Catholicism of his publications intensifying in the aftermath of the Gunpowder Plot. This emphasis informed Butter's selection of plays such as Samuel Rowley's *When You See Me You Know Me* (1605), Thomas Heywood's *If You Know Not Me, You Know Nobody* (Part 1: 1605; Part 2: 1606), and Thomas Dekker's *The Whore of*

Babylon (1607), all of which offer loosely historical accounts of Tudor monarchs, reshaped to promote an assertive Protestant agenda. Similarly, Butter's interest in *King Lear* (1608) was likely determined by the play's application to James I's plans for the union of England and Scotland, which is also reflected in his non-dramatic publications, including John Davies of Hereford's *Bien Venu* (1606). For Butter, the history play is a genre that engages with the past in order to reflect on contemporary religio-political issues which, in the context of the early Jacobean period, meant plays that explore how (historical and ongoing) disputes between Catholics and Protestants compromised the nation's stability or feature (historical and ongoing) debates about the union of nations. While his wider output often seems sympathetic to royal policy, it sometimes differs. When explored through his own reading strategies, Butter's history play-books sometimes promote a political perspective on specific points of Jacobean debate that is more assertive and militant than James's own agenda.

Of all the stationers considered in this book, Butter has perhaps the strongest claim for individual agency in the publication of history plays. In contrast to Creede, who invested repeatedly in plays from the Queen's Men, or Wise, who likely had a direct connection to the Chamberlain's Men, Butter does not seem to have been associated with a particular company or patron. Although his publication of first editions implies some contact with the theatres in order to acquire playscripts, he does not specialize in plays from one company. This chapter argues that Butter is at the centre of a stationer-driven publication network. His non-dramatic texts indicate that a considerable amount of editorial work was involved in selecting, reshaping, and analysing them for prospective readers, practices that need to be considered alongside Butter's history plays because they help us to understand how these plays may have been prepared for publication, how they were marketed, and how they define and use 'history'. The consistency of Butter's output facilitates a detailed literary critical analysis of these plays through the eyes and strategies of one of their earliest readers.

This case study on Butter's early Jacobean output also offers an important corrective to the still-prevalent critical narrative that the history play declined in popularity at the accession of James I. As outlined in the Introduction, this theory depends on a definition of the history play as synonymous with medieval English monarchical history – a definition that is closely linked to Shakespeare's *oeuvre* and the fact that he stopped writing these kinds of histories after *Henry V*. Rackin proposes that this abandonment of historical subject matter was a consequence of developments in historiography: that history had emerged as 'an autonomous discipline with its own purposes and methods, clearly distinct from myth and literature'.[1] However, there is no evidence to support the view that, for example, humanist and providential approaches to history were completely replaced by sound antiquarian research based on the examination of records and artefacts. As Kamps summarizes, while we can 'discern the seeds of modern historiography in the early seventeenth century', it is clear that 'nothing like a uniform approach either to the nature or to the purpose of history-writing had emerged'.[2] New developments in historiography do not infiltrate and uproot theatrical practices or the full spectrum of historical writing, especially not immediately.

Tensions between different approaches to history continued to be felt even within the same text. In his revised edition of *A Survey of London* (1603), Stow suggests that gathering and evaluating evidence should be the basis for writing the history of London, and claims in the dedicatory epistle that he has 'attempted the discouery of London' by examining 'sundry antiquities' and conducting a 'search of Records'.[3] Stow immediately qualifies this approach in the text's opening section, where he addresses Geoffrey of Monmouth's twelfth-century *Historia Regum Britanniae*, which traces the foundation of London to 'Troian progenie' (B1r), namely Brutus, the great-grandson of Aeneas. This narrative had been challenged throughout the sixteenth century, beginning with Polydore Vergil's *Anglica historia* (first published in 1534). In the expanded second edition, Stow assesses this tradition and acknowledges, via a quotation from Livy, the importance of these narratives of origin that can perform an integral function in the creation and transmission of a city's (or nation's) past:

> But herein as Liuie the most famous Hystoriographer of the Romans writeth[:] Antiquitie is pardonable, and hath an especiall priuiledge, by interlacing diuine matters with humane, to make the first foundations of Cities more honourable, more sacred, and as it were of greater maiestie.[4]

With this new addition to the 1603 text (which, as will be seen, closely connects to James I's interest in ancient British history), Stow's *Survey* draws attention to the overlaps and tensions that exist between different

---

[1] Rackin, *Stages of History*, p. 19.   [2] Kamps, *Historiography*, pp. 12, 29.
[3] John Stow, *A Svrvay of London* (London, 1603; STC 23343), A2v.
[4] Ibid., B1r. This second edition advertises the text's expansion on its title page: 'Since by the same Author [i.e. Stow] increased, with diuers rare notes of Antiquity, and published in the yeare 1603' (A1r).

historiographical methods. In practice, if not also in theory, the distinctions are blurred between models that prioritize the evaluation of evidence and those that prioritize the construction of historical narratives to serve a particular purpose or use (such as providing exempla for the present).

On the Jacobean stage, the 'force of ever-liuing Historie' continued to thrive.[5] Although medieval English history does not appear to have been as prominent – on stage or in print – as it was during the late Elizabethan period, other historical pasts came to the fore, including Tudor history and legendary British history, the latter promoted by the new Stuart monarch. Butter was one of the major publishers of these histories, issuing them alongside 'news' pamphlets that engaged with ongoing religio-political concerns. As this chapter argues, the plays' migration into a print medium where dramatic and non-dramatic histories overlap materially, thematically, and geographically promotes an interpretative exchange between the histories they represent.

This chapter has four parts: first, it considers Butter's investment in news publications to show that, for Butter, history and news were two sides of the same coin and to provide evidence of the processes of composition and compilation that took place in Butter's bookshop, which reveals his 'hands on' approach in publishing these texts. The chapter then concentrates on the two dominant strands that can be identified in Butter's publications: an interest in polemical Protestant texts and in topical histories that relate to Jacobean politics. These strands unite not only Butter's output, but also history plays dramatizing such widely separated pasts (in terms of time and availability of evidence) as the recent Tudor dynasty (discussed first) and Britain's legendary monarchs (discussed second). Finally, this chapter builds on my earlier discussions about the geography of the book trade and the role it may have played in connecting different histories. Butter's bookshop near St Austin's Gate was part of a gathering place for trading in news – but also for publishing, during the early Jacobean period, history plays by Shakespeare and other dramatists. This spatial unity raises the possibility that areas of St Paul's (and the London book trade more widely) could become associated with particular stationers and types of publication, links that have implications for history-play survival, print presentation, and reception.

---

[5] Barnabe Barnes, *The Divils Charter* (London, 1607; STC 1466), A4v.

'True Paules bred': Butter's Networks at the Sign of the Pied Bull

Nathaniel Butter was born into the book trade: his father (Thomas Butter, active 1576–90), mother (Joan Butter, later Newbery, active 1590–1617), and stepfather (John Newbery, active 1594–1603) were stationers and they all owned bookshops in and around St Paul's Churchyard.[6] He was, as Jonson alludes to in *The Staple of News*, 'True Paules bred'.[7] After serving his apprenticeship, Butter was admitted to the Stationers' Company on 20 February 1604 and, until his death in 1664, his publications were marked by an interest in topical matters of church and state. By the end of the Jacobean period, Butter had acquired a popular reputation as a publisher of news, and he became the target of satirical attacks by writers including Jonson and Abraham Holland. The latter's 'Continued Inquisition Against Paper-Persecutors' capitalizes on the humorous potential of the stationer's last name, by describing London's walls as 'Butter'd with weekely Newes compos'd in Pauls, | By some Decaied Captaine'.[8] Similarly, Jonson's *Staple of News* targets Jacobean newsmakers, including Butter, presenting them as unscrupulous publishers and 'decay'd Stationer[s]', who know 'Newes well, can sort and ranke 'hem ... And for a need can make 'hem' (Bb1v). Both Holland and Jonson criticize Butter for his methods of publishing news, including a proclivity to shape and produce (both materially and creatively) accounts of current events.[9]

A brief consideration of Butter's late Jacobean practices and reputation can be cautiously used to shed light on his early playbooks and non-dramatic texts, which are the focus of this chapter. Beginning in 1621–22, and in regular partnership with Nicholas Bourne from 1624, Butter was among the first serial news publishers in England. His reports mainly covered events from the Thirty Years War – a conflict which involved many European states and encompassed a range of political issues and shifting alliances, but which was frequently simplified (especially by continental and British newsbooks) in stark binary terms as a war fought

---

[6] STC, III, pp. 33–35, 123–24. See also S. A. Baron, 'Butter, Nathaniel (*bap.* 1583, *d.* 1664)', *ODNB*, online ed., January 2008, https://doi.org/10.1093/ref:odnb/4224 (accessed 17 April 2021).

[7] Ben Jonson, *The Staple of Newes* (London, 1631; STC 14753.5), Bb1v.

[8] Abraham Holland ('A. H.'), 'A Continved Inqvisition against Paper-Persecutors', in John Davies of Hereford ('I. D.'), *A Scovrge for Paper-Persecutors* (London, 1625; STC 6340), A3v–A4r. 'A. H.' is sometimes identified with Abraham Hartwell.

[9] For an excellent reading of the context of news publication explored in Jonson's play, see Alan B. Farmer, 'Play-Reading, News-Reading, and Ben Jonson's *The Staple of News*', in *The Book of the Play*, ed. Straznicky, pp. 127–58.

along Protestant–Catholic divisions.[10] Butter's newsbooks sometimes claim that they are 'not partiall' to any side, but this defence is a marketing strategy to advertise the truthfulness of the reports, which were, as Jonson's *Staple of News* exemplifies, under regular attack.[11] For the most part, Butter's newsbooks display strongly Protestant sympathies.[12] Some even feature the coat of arms of Frederick V, the Elector Palatine (and James I's son-in-law), who was the Protestant figurehead in the conflict.[13] This visual identifier of the Protestant cause, which typically takes up the full page on the verso of the title leaf, announces the news venture's partisan alignment. In other cases, their sympathies are advertised through title-page summaries: 'the lamentable losse of the City of Heidlebergh, after many braue repulses given to the Enemie; and the names of some princi-pall Leaders, as were slaine in defence of the towne'.[14] This siege in 1622 was led by the Imperial–Spanish army (the Catholic 'Enemie'), and involved the death of the Protestant English commander Sir Gerard Herbert. Far from being neutral and objective, Butter's newsbooks – through their labelling of contemporary figures, arrangement of reports, and inclusion of partisan visual identifiers – offer accounts of the conflict that are invested in the Protestant cause and display a clear interest in the fate of the country's forces abroad.

Butter's newsbooks also feature, through paratextual addresses, a strong editorial voice that discusses their construction and directs readers' inter-pretation. These paratexts are the hallmark of English newsbooks. As Folke Dahl observes, one of the main differences between English and European newsbooks was the large number of 'editorial notices' that appear in the former and which establish an intimacy between the editor/publisher and the reader.[15] They are usually unsigned, so it is not often clear who wrote them. The process of news publication, as Jayne Boys has shown, could involve a network of different individuals who variously sourced, trans-lated, compiled, and edited the materials.[16] Identifying the author of

---

[10] See Folke Dahl, *A Bibliography of English Corantos and Periodical Newsbooks, 1620–1642* (London: Bibliographical Society, 1952), pp. 18–27; Jayne E. E. Boys, *London's News Press and the Thirty Years War* (Woodbridge, Suffolk: Boydell, 2011).

[11] See, for example, *A Continuation of More Newes from the Palatinate [13 June 1622]* (London, 1622; STC 18507.51A), ¶4r.

[12] For Butter's religio-political sympathies and investment in newsbooks during the late Jacobean and Caroline periods, see Farmer, 'Play-Reading', pp. 134–51.

[13] See *The certaine Newes of this present Weeke [23 August 1622]* (London, 1622; STC 18507.72), A2v. Also see STC 18507.75 (4 September 1622); STC 18507.77 (14 September 1622); and STC 18507.79 (25 September 1622).

[14] *Newes From Most Parts of Christendome [25 September 1622]* (London, 1622; STC 18507.79), t.p.

[15] Dahl, *Bibliography*, pp. 20–21.   [16] See Boys, *London's News Press*, esp. chs. 5 and 6.

unsigned paratextual notices remains a matter of speculation. It may be significant to note, however, that in 1622, before his partnership with Bourne was firmly established, Butter published a number of newsbooks independently, and they share a similar paratextual voice. In one of them, a plan for news publication is set out:

> If any Gentleman or other accustomed to buy the Weekely Relations of Newes, be desirous to continue the same, let them know that the Writer or Transcriber rather of this Newes, hath published two former Newes ... all which doe carrie a like title, with the Armes of the King of Bohemia on the other side of the title page, and haue dependance one vpon another: which manner of writing and printing, he doth purpose to continue weekely by Gods assistance from the best and most certaine Intelligence.[17]

Although some caution is necessary as the terms may not have been used with precision, the address connects the 'Writer or Transcriber' of the newsbook to the individual who has undertaken its publication – which, taken literally, would indicate that Butter was the transcriber and editor of the newsbook and possibly the author of the paratext. Interestingly, the address also establishes the coat of arms of Frederick V as a kind of visual brand for the series and invests Frederick with the title – King of Bohemia – that he had been forced to relinquish in 1620 after the Catholic victory at the Battle of White Mountain. The address therefore connects Butter to the composition of the pamphlet and to a Protestant print identity that announces its support for Frederick's (much contested) claim over the Bohemian throne. It suggests Butter was an active agent involved in constructing and positioning newsbooks – processes that also took place in the publication of his history plays.

Another newsbook published independently by Butter explicitly aligns news and history writing through a prominent (and unsigned) address 'To the Reader'. The pamphlet is described on its title page as *A Continuation of More News from the Palatinate* and it claims to offer an accurate account of the conflict that will 'stay the vncertaine reports of partiall newes-mongers, who tell euery thing as themselues would haue it'.[18] To achieve (and advertise) its purpose, the paratext invokes a model of history writing: it aims to 'keepe nere to the Lawes of Historie, to guesse at the reasons of the actions by the most apparent presumptions, and to set downe the true names and distances of places' (¶4r). For my purposes, the address is particularly significant because it claims that the principles,

---

[17] *Newes [23 August 1622]* (STC 18507.72), C4r.
[18] *More Newes [13 June 1622]* (STC 18507.51A), ¶3v.

features, and utility of written news and history are similar – a point that is crucial for understanding Butter's wider output (including his history plays) and for recognizing the formal and temporal fluidity of 'history' during the period, which is often overlooked when teleological narratives of historiographical development are favoured. As Woolf proposes more broadly, early modern individuals saw the present as 'only an existential instant, an ephemeral joint between a dead past and an unborn future', through most of the period 'recognizing no "present" beyond that instant'.[19] 'News' already belonged to the past, albeit a recent one – or in other words, as Cymbal from Jonson's *Staple of News* declares, 'when Newes is printed, | It leaues Sir to be Newes' (Bb1r).

A strong paratextual voice and a conflation of news and history – both as records of the past – can be detected in Butter's earliest publications, which perhaps indicates the root of his later specialism in serial newsbooks. In his discussion of Butter's publication strategies during the Caroline period, Farmer argues that 'the politics of play-reading and news-reading were intimately connected during the reign of Charles I'.[20] With Butter, this exchange can already be seen in his earliest publications. Leona Rostenberg calculates that, between 1602 and 1622, Butter published about 200 books, 'of which 41 per cent may be regarded as news-tracts'.[21] One of his early pamphlets, *News From Lough Foyle in Ireland* (1608), connects news writing with the work of historians and uses this link to assess the merits of stage plays. It argues that accounts of events that have actually taken place 'ought much more to moue vs to commiseration' than tragedies on the stage, 'whereof the matter is many times vntrue, and but inuented'.[22] The pamphlet – which reports a recent uprising in Ireland – recalls Sidney's *Defence*, where invention is prized above adherence to historical records, but reverses that judgement: readers should be more affected by accounts of the past, whether recent or distant. The author of the pamphlet is unknown, but the style, titling, length, and anti-Catholicism of the text parallel Butter's later newsbooks. Butter – or someone who worked for him at the Sign of the Pied Bull – may have

---

[19] Daniel Woolf, 'News, History and the Construction of the Present in Early Modern England', in *The Politics of Information in Early Modern Europe*, ed. Brendan Dooley and Sabrina A. Baron (Abingdon: Routledge, 2001), pp. 80–118 (pp. 82–84).

[20] Farmer, 'Play-Reading', p. 130.

[21] Leona Rostenberg, 'Nathaniel Butter and Nicholas Bourne, First "Masters of the Staple"', *The Library*, 5th ser., 12:1 (1957), 23–33 (p. 25).

[22] *News from Lough-foyle in Ireland* (London, 1608; STC 18784), C1v–C2r.

been responsible for its composition and/or compilation. Indeed, it might shed light on Butter's consistent investment in plays that feature historical pasts, rather than those that 'moue vs to commiseration' through invented stories. Of the plays he published from the commercial stages, only *The London Prodigal* (1605), *The Trial of Chivalry* (1605), *The Fleer* (1610, second edition), and *2 The Honest Whore* (1630) do not dramatize material from a historical past.[23]

Other early publications reveal Butter's interest in newsworthy texts and draw attention to vibrant networks of textual exchange at his bookshop, the existence of which have consequences for his acquisition of history plays and their presentation in print. For example, *Sir Thomas Smith's Voyage and Entertainment in Russia* (1605) contains an unsigned address 'To the Reader' that, judging by its content, was written by an individual closely connected to – and perhaps residing in – Paul's Churchyard (see Figure 3.1). The address claims that 'hearers' of Smith's Russian travels have 'way-laid the Newes' in order to 'scrap[e] together many percels of this Rushian commoditie', which has resulted in 'false reports' delivered in 'Paules Church-yard'.[24] To remedy this, the writer of the address has taken 'the truth from the mouths of diuers gentlemen that went in the Iourney, and hauing som good notes bestowed vpon me in writing, wrought them into this body'. The writer continues: 'I have done this without consent either of Sir Tho[mas] himselfe, or of those gentlemen my friends that deliuered it vnto me' (A2r). It is therefore the author of the address, rather than Smith (*c.*1558–1625), who has prepared the entire account. As discussed, Butter's popular reputation was directly linked to the location of his bookshop in Paul's Churchyard. His identity was blurred or conflated with the area: the walls were 'Butter'd' and 'Batter[ed]' with him.[25] Similarly, the author of the paratext seems to be a part of the Churchyard, or at least is a regular presence there. This unattributed, unsigned voice may be Butter's. Regardless of the author's precise identity, the pamphlet and the paratextual account of its construction draw attention to recurring features in Butter's published output: an investment in newsworthy texts that seem to announce their connection to the Churchyard through

---

[23] Although its events are entirely fictional, *The Trial of Chivalry* presents its subject as a pseudo-history, or, as Gillian Woods succinctly puts it, the play seems to 'connote historicity' and is 'self-conscious in its sense of "pastness"'. See Gillian Woods, 'The Contexts of *The Trial of Chivalry*', *Notes & Queries*, 54:3 (2007), 313–18 (pp. 317–18).

[24] *Sir Thomas Smithes Voiage and Entertainment in Rushia* (London, 1605; STC 22869), A2r.

[25] Holland, 'Inqvisition', A3v–A4r.

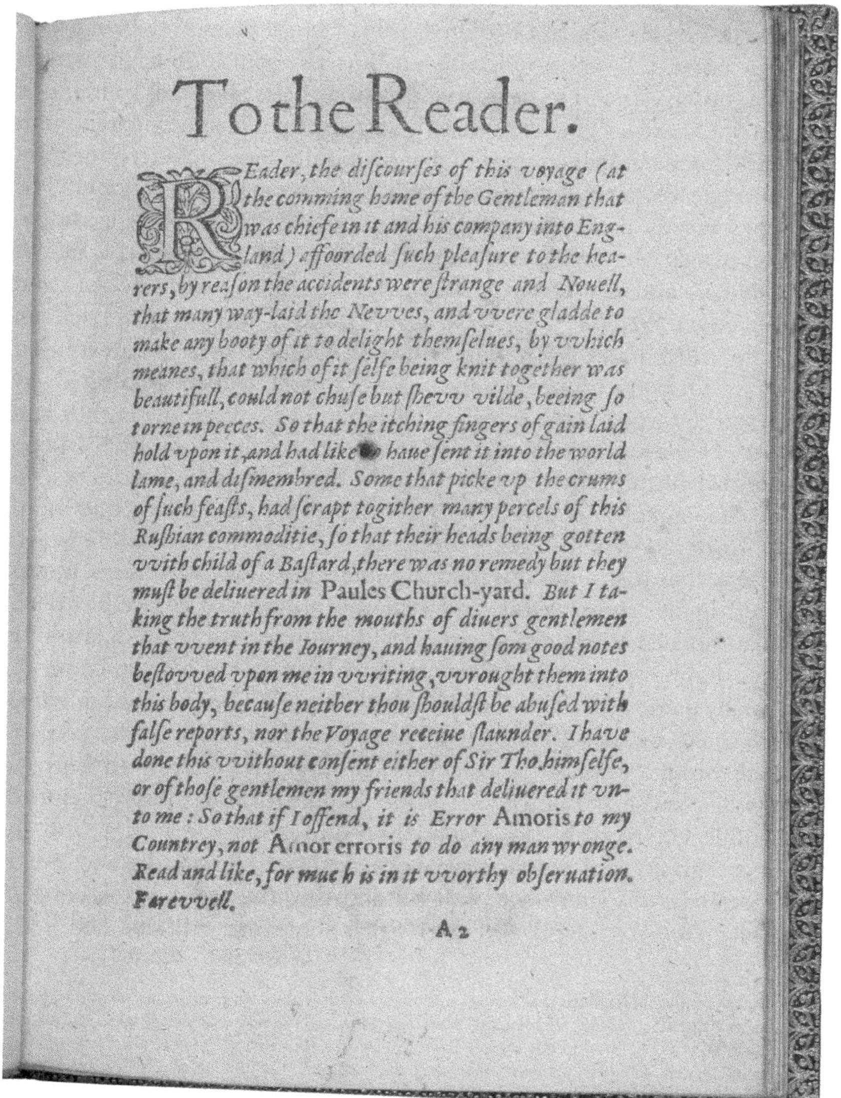

To the Reader.

Eader, the difcourfes of this voyage (at
the comming home of the Gentleman that
was chiefe in it and his company into England) affoorded fuch pleafure to the hearers, by reafon the accidents were ftrange and Nouell,
that many way-laid the Nevves, and vvere gladde to
make any booty of it to delight themfelues, by vvhich
meanes, that which of it felfe being knit together was
beautifull, could not chufe but fhevv vilde, beeing fo
torne in peces. So that the itching fingers of gain laid
hold vpon it, and had like to haue fent it into the world
lame, and difmembred. Some that picke vp the crums
of fuch feafts, had fcrapt togither many percels of this
Ruffian commoditie, fo that their heads being gotten
vvith child of a Baftard, there was no remedy but they
muft be deliuered in Paules Church-yard. But I taking the truth from the mouths of diuers gentlemen
that vvent in the Iourney, and hauing fom good notes
beftovved vpon me in vvriting, vvrought them into
this body, becaufe neither thou fhouldft be abufed with
falfe reports, nor the Voyage receiue flaunder. I haue
done this vvithout confent either of Sir Tho. himfelfe,
or of thofe gentlemen my friends that deliuered it vnto me: So that if I offend, it is Error Amoris to my
Countrey, not Amor erroris to do any man wronge.
Read and like, for much is in it vvorthy obferuation.
Farevvell.

A 2

Figure 3.1   Address in *Sir Thomas Smith's Voyage* (1605; STC 22869), A2r.

networks of influence and exchange and to negotiate ideas of 'truth' and accuracy, issues that are also explored in his history plays.[26]

At this point, it is worth reflecting on Butter's acquisition of playscripts and what his investment in news and history suggests about his sourcing of commercial drama. The fact that Butter's playbooks originated with different theatre companies implies that he did not have a close connection with a single company (as Creede and Wise seem to have done). His playbooks mostly derive from the three royally patronized adult companies: the King's Men (*King Lear*), Prince Henry's Men (*When You See Me You Know Me* and *The Whore of Babylon*), and Queen Anne's Men (*1* and *2 If You Know Not Me, You Know Nobody* and *The Rape of Lucrece*, on which he collaborated with John Busby). The authorial paratexts that appear in Dekker's dramatic and non-dramatic works (published by Butter and discussed later) reveal a collaboration between the author and stationer. However, Heywood's response to the publication of his plays suggests that Butter acquired scripts for the two parts of *If You Know Not Me* 'by Stenography' and that he put them 'in print, scarce one word true'.[27] In his address to readers prefacing *The Rape of Lucrece*, Heywood claims that he agreed to this play's publication only to ensure it was presented in its 'natiue habit' and that the printing of his earlier plays was unauthorized.[28] Heywood criticizes those responsible for corrupting his plays that have 'vnknown to me, and without any of my direction . . . accidentally come into the Printers handes' (A2r). While he does not name any stationers or identify which of his plays have been, as he sees it, mangled through publication, Heywood is probably referring to Butter's editions of *1* and *2 If You Know Not Me*. Unlike his other plays, they had been published recently (in 1605, 1606 and 1608 for Part 1 and in 1606 for Part 2) and would have been fresh in Heywood's and other readers' minds.[29] A later stage prologue added to the eighth quarto of *1 If You Know Not Me* (1639) also asserts that the earlier editions had been

[26] For Butter's early publications that feature paratextual commentary supplied by publication agents, see Jérôme Bignon, *A Briefe, Bvt An Effectuall Treatise of the Election of Popes*, English translation (London, 1605; STC 3058), Dr2; Daniel Tilenus, *Positions Lately Held by the L. Du Perron, Bishop of Eureux, against the sufficiency and perfection of the Scriptures* (London, 1606; STC 24071), A2r–A4r; Charlotte Brabantina, *The Conuersion of a most Noble Lady of France In Iune last past* (London, 1608; STC 11262), A2r–v.

[27] Thomas Heywood, *If you know not mee, You know no body* (London, 1639; STC 13335), A2r. See also Lidster, 'Caroline Reprints', 205–28.

[28] Thomas Heywood, *The Rape of Lvcrece* (London, 1608; STC 13360), A2r.

[29] The only other plays connected to Heywood that had previously been published were *1* and *2 Edward IV* (1599), *How a Man May Choose a Good Wife from a Bad* (1602), and *A Woman Killed With Kindness* (1607).

sourced from someone who 'drew | The Plot' (A2r) during the play's performance.[30] The accusations imply that Butter did not have a working relationship with Heywood and that he sought out these texts through interlocutors.

There is, of course, a strong possibility that Heywood's objections are formulaic claims that express reluctance towards publication as part of a *humilitas* topos and do not indicate genuine criticism.[31] Given that Butter was responsible for the supposedly maligned editions of *If You Know Not Me*, it is puzzling that Heywood would work with him on the 'authorized' *Rape of Lucrece*, unless there was some degree of cooperation between the dramatist and stationer. Moreover, Heywood continued to employ this kind of critical preface in his later texts, which David Bergeron sees as reflecting his 'struggle to position himself as a writer associated with the theatre'.[32] Between 1631 and 1638, for example, Heywood supplied paratexts to seven first-edition commercial plays, which suggests he was actively pursuing print publication, but yet, in these addresses, adopts a sceptical attitude towards its merits.[33] In the address 'To the Reader' prefacing *The English Traveller* (1633), Heywood declares that 'it neuer was any great ambition in me, to bee in this kind Voluminously read', which, in the context of overseeing seven playbook editions in quick succession, seems to be somewhat disingenuous or at least does not accurately reflect his ongoing evaluation of the benefits of playbook publication.[34]

On the other hand, however – given the strength of Heywood's early objections and the considerable lapse of time between these first editions and the later publication boom of his plays during the 1630s – a reasonable hypothesis is that Butter acquired *1* and *2 If You Know Not Me* through non-authorial agents. His bookshop at the Sign of the Pied Bull was certainly well connected to networks of domestic and international exchange. The fact that Butter and Busby jointly entered *Lucrece* in the

---

[30] Maguire argues that there is 'insufficient evidence to confirm a case for MR' (i.e. memorial reconstruction). Instead, the outer leaves of the manuscript may have been damaged and required rewriting, which could have prompted Heywood's criticism. *Suspect Texts*, pp. 261–63.

[31] See also Massai, *Editor*, pp. 165–70.

[32] Bergeron, *Textual Patronage*, p. 159. See also Loewenstein, *Possessive Authorship*, ch. 3.

[33] The seven professional plays are: *1* and *2 The Fair Maid of the West* (1631), *1* and *2 The Iron Age* (1632), *The English Traveller* (1633), *A Maidenhead Well Lost* (1634), and *Love's Mistress* (1636).

[34] Thomas Heywood, *The English Traueller* (London, 1633; STC 13315), A3r. For Heywood's aborted collection, see Benedict Scott Robinson, 'Thomas Heywood and the Cultural Politics of Play Collections', *Studies in English Literature, 1500–1900*, 42:2 (2002), 361–80.

Register and that Butter is unnamed on the title page of the first two
editions (1608 and 1609) could be a result of Heywood's criticism. Only
Busby's initials appear in the imprints, while Butter's bookshop is given as
the wholesale location – that is, until Q3 (1614), when Butter becomes the
sole publisher. I do not wish, however, to resurrect New Bibliography's
theories about rogue stationers. It must be emphasized that Butter's
practices reflect the normal workings of the book trade. Dramatists could
not enter plays in the Stationers' Register and hold publication rights to
them. Heywood's early and vocal interest in the publication of his plays is
more the exception.

Whatever the precise nature of the relationship between Butter and
Heywood, what is useful for my purposes is the fact that Butter's output
and the paratexts contributed by him or concerning his involvement
emphasize the central role of publication agents in sourcing and compiling
texts. Because none of Butter's playbooks contain stationer-authored,
discursive paratexts – an absence that also characterizes Creede's and
Wise's editions – an evaluation of his non-dramatic publications is crucial
for understanding the strategies of selection and presentation that shaped
his history plays. As shown in this section, Butter's output reveals a
distinctive interest in history and news (and the fluid boundary between
them) that was made possible by networks of agents connected to his
bookshop and by processes of translation, composition, and commentary.
Butter's imprints consistently and prominently give his name and usually
his bookshop location, helping to establish a popular reputation for the
stationer that was so connected to his shop at St Austin's Gate. Situating
Butter's history plays within this wider context helps us to see that similar
processes of gathering, positioning, and editing may have taken place
during the plays' transmission from stage to page and to understand how
Butter read and applied these dramatizations of the past.

Publishing Protestant History Plays

During the early years of James I's reign, several plays based on the lives of
Tudor monarchs were written and performed, including Rowley's *When
You See Me You Know Me*, Heywood's *1* and *2 If You Know Not Me, You
Know Nobody*, Dekker's *The Whore of Babylon*, and Dekker and Webster's
Famous History of Sir Thomas Wyatt. These plays draw on John Foxe's *Acts
and Monuments* (first published in 1563 and reprinted with revisions in
1570, 1576, and 1583), which positions events and individuals from
(mostly English) history within an apocalyptic narrative of Protestant

persecution under the tyranny of Catholicism.[35] Little critical attention has been paid to Butter's role as the publisher of Rowley's, Heywood's, and Dekker's plays. Judith Doolin Spikes describes them as 'Elect Nation' plays invested in England's providential deliverance from the influence of the Roman Catholic Church, but does not discuss the plays' shared publisher.[36] While Teresa Grant does identify the connection, as well as Butter's 'fascination with anti-Catholic propaganda', the plays' publication is not the main focus of her discussion.[37] Alan Farmer's interest in the politics of Butter's playbooks is an exception, but his published work concentrates on their Caroline reprints.[38] As this section shows, an evaluation of Butter's involvement helps to clarify why these plays were selected for publication in the early Jacobean period, how their 'history' was understood, and what they meant to one of their first readers – a bookseller who specialized in newsworthy texts that advertised a Protestant agenda in the interests of national and international political stability.

In the absence of stationers' paratexts in the playbooks, Butter's firmly anti-Catholic strategies are clarified through his non-dramatic output, outlined in the previous section in relation to his newsbooks and underscored by his earliest publications, which I briefly consider here. According to the STC, the first text – or, more accurately, paratext – to display Butter's name is the cancel title page for Thomas Bell's *Downfall of Popery* (1604; STC 1818.5). Bell was a Roman Catholic priest turned Protestant polemicist, who was employed – first by Elizabeth's government and then by James's – as an informer and writer of virulently anti-Catholic tracts.[39] As part of a dedication to James, *The Downfall of Popery* condemns the Catholic Church, reserving especial criticism for Jesuits and seminary priests, who 'by treacherous practices and most bloodie complots, haue long sought for the vtter ruine and conquest of noble England'.[40] The emphasis is on the political repercussions of their influence, as 'disposing of

[35] For the plays' use of Foxe, see Mark Bayer, 'Staging Foxe at the Fortune and the Red Bull', *Renaissance and Reformation*, 27:1 (2003), 61–94.

[36] Judith Doolin Spikes, 'The Jacobean History Play and the Myth of the Elect Nation', *Renaissance Drama*, 8 (1977), 117–49. Spikes offers John Bale's *King Johan* (written in the 1530s) as an early exemplar of this subgenre, which she sees as ending in the late Jacobean period with *The Duchess of Suffolk* and *A Game at Chess*.

[37] Teresa Grant, 'History in the Making: The Case of Samuel Rowley's *When You See Me You Know Me* (1604/5)', in *English Historical Drama*, ed. Grant and Ravelhofer, pp. 125–57 (p. 143).

[38] Farmer, 'Play-Reading', pp. 127–58.

[39] Alexandra Walsham, 'Bell [*alias* Burton], Thomas (*b. c.*1551, *d.* in or after 1610)', *ODNB*, online ed.. January 2008, https://doi.org/10.1093/ref:odnb/2026 (accessed 8 April 2020).

[40] Thomas Bell, *The Downefall of Poperie* (London, 1604; STC 1818.5), *iiv.

scepters, with other matters of like qualitie, are their chiefe studies' (A1r).
The text was entered in the Stationers' Register to Arthur Johnson, whose
name appears on the original title page (STC 1818).[41] The degree to which
Butter invested in the edition is unclear, but he probably oversaw the
preparation of the cancel title page, which features his name as sole
publisher and links him with the work of a government propagandist
who fashioned religious controversy in starkly political terms. A similar
religio-political emphasis can be seen in Butter's edition of *The True Copy
of Two Letters ... Wherein the Principal Points in Controversy with the
Papists, are Learnedly and Fully Confuted* (1605), written originally in
French by the reformer Daniel Tilenus and translated into English by
'D. D. S.' The text contains a dedication to James I (by 'D. D. S.') that
asks the monarch to pursue with severity apostates who have renounced
their Protestant faith. It sets out the dangers to church and state of travel to
Spain and Italy, 'places most dangerous for practising of treasons', where
one would find 'Antichristian Vipers, with whose venome being once
stung, hard was it to find such medicine, for the cure of so dangerous a
disease'.[42] Through the new dedication, Butter's English edition repurposes the French text for use by readers in Britain and, specifically, by
James I as an imagined reader and patron who lends authority and
currency to the translation. Butter's penchant for translated European
works – seen also in an English edition of Jérôme Bignon's *Traite sommaire
de l'élection du pape*, which he retitled in one issue as *Anti-Christ's Pride to
Saint Peter's Chair* (1605) – suggests that, from the beginning of his career,
Butter had access to networks of exchange and translation that centred
upon religio-political texts that could be used to condemn Catholic
influence.[43]

   This pattern becomes pronounced after the exposure of the Gunpowder
Plot in 1605, as popular anti-Catholic and anti-Spanish sentiment
increased in virility.[44] Published by Butter, a verse narrative of the

[41] Johnson entered the title on 19 March 1604 (SRO4786; Arber, III, p. 254). The printing was
   undertaken by Adam Islip.
[42] Daniel Tilenus, *The True Copy of two Letters ... Wherein the principall poynts in controuersie with the
   Papists, are learnedly and fully confuted* (London, 1605; STC 24072), A2v. Tilenus would become a
   Pelagian at the Synod of Dort, but in 1605 he was, in Grant's phrase, 'simply a robust anti-Catholic
   writer' (Grant, 'History', p. 153).
[43] Butter published an English translation of Bignon's tract under three titles: *The True Maner of
   Electing of Popes* (STC 3057.7); *A Briefe, Bvt An Effectuall Treatise of the Election of Popes* (STC
   3058); and *Anti-Christs Pride to Saint Peters chaire* (not in the STC; a copy of this issue is held at
   Longleat House).
[44] See also Butter's edition of Henoch Clapham, *Errour on the Left Hand* (London, 1608; STC 5342),
   which offers a series of anti-Catholic dialogues, one of which describes the 'Vault gunpowder, that

attempted treason – *The Devil of the Vault* (1606) – concentrates blame on 'these bloud-bathed Romish Wolues' whose 'strict Religion grounded false, | on proud rebellion stands'.[45] It reserves particular venom for 'Tygrish blood-sworne Iesuites, | Spanized Brittish slaues', and displays an anxiety about European Catholic powers – especially Spain – and the political destruction that has been narrowly avoided (A4v). A similar targeting of Jesuits can be seen in Butter's edition of *The Jesuits' Play at Lyons* (1607). This short pamphlet consists of an eyewitness account of a play performed by a group of Jesuits in 'August last past' that resulted in, as the title page advertises, the providential 'destruction of the Actors'.[46] The author – identified on the title page by the initials 'R. S.' – could have been responsible for an unsigned address 'To the Reader' which offers a commentary on the text's usefulness, but this paratext closely recalls and summarizes Butter's publishing strategies. It describes how religion and politics are intimately connected, and it specifies that religious concerns are often used to disguise (and justify) political agendas. It claims that readers 'shall find by this discourse, that Religion is made the Target to defend Treason: Ambition, the Originall, and confusion the end', and that the text is 'sent vnto thee as a warning peece shot off, to admonish thee that thou fall not into the presumption into which these Iesuites and their Disciples run headlong' (A3r). The text has a clear aim to condemn Catholic, and, specifically, Jesuit, influences, highlighting the dangers they pose to religious and secular matters. As the narrator claims, the publication of these events is necessary for the good of the country – '*Nassimur pro patria*' (A4v). This angle characterizes Butter's output: most of the short, topical pamphlets in which he specialized position their anti-Catholic propaganda in relation to political consequences.

At this stage, it is important to clarify the anti-Catholicism of Butter's output, his position as a 'Protestant' publisher, and how these points relate to early Jacobean religious debate, specifically James's policy of toleration that aimed to unite Protestant and Catholic conformists. When he succeeded to the English throne, James favoured a policy of moderation,

---

should haue blowne vp the Parliament-house in Westminster, together with all the heads of the Country' (B1v).

[45] Anon./'I. H.', *The Divell of the Vault* (London, 1606; STC 12568), D2v; A4v. The text's attribution is sometimes expanded to John Heath, although the identification is doubtful. See N. D. F. Pearce and Christopher Burlinson, 'Heath, John (*b. c.*1585), epigrammatist', *ODNB*, online ed., September 2004, https://doi.org/10.1093/ref:odnb/12838 (accessed 9 April 2020), para. 2.

[46] Anon./'R. S.', *The Iesuites play at Lyons in France* (London, 1607; STC 21513.5), A2r.

opposing Catholicism only when it was synonymous with political disloy-
alty. He condemned Jesuits and seminary priests, issuing proclamations
that commanded them to leave Britain, but also opposed assertive efforts
for puritan reform (or innovation) that might disturb the status quo and
challenge his authority.[47] Butter's publications suggest slightly different
sympathies: they tap into a popular anti-Catholicism that seems to have
been widespread even amongst a moderate majority. Although Jesuits and
seminary priests are often the main targets, his publications do not extend
a tolerant attitude towards lay Catholics in England. In 1607, for example,
Butter published an unauthorized account of Edward Coke's speech at the
Norwich Assizes (*The Lord Coke His Speech and Charge*), which was
written by Robert Pricket and was suppressed the day after its appearance
on the bookstalls. According to Coke's accusations, Pricket's account was
completely inaccurate.[48] It used Coke's speech as an occasion to put
forward anti-Catholic polemic under his name, and asserted that, 'if in
great Brittaine, there were no Papists, this Monarchy should be as free
from treason as any Nation in the world', a claim that seems to disavow the
merits of toleration.[49]

Butter's interest in Protestant history and news is hard to define narrowly and precisely in terms of doctrinal distinctions. In line with James's
policies, Butter's output does not suggest clear sympathies for Protestant
non-conformists and radical 'puritan' reform to the Anglican Church.
Indeed, in 1609, he published a defence of conformist ministers that was
dedicated to Richard Bancroft, Archbishop of Canterbury, and Thomas
Ravis, Bishop of London.[50] However, some of his publications – such as
the Tudor history plays – do seem to favour an element of Protestant
reform, particularly through the figure of Prince Henry, James's son and
heir. As Isabel Karremann explores, these histories draw on a prevailing
nostalgia for Tudor monarchs, celebrating (and exaggerating) their
Protestant victories in a way that could be seen as predictive or hopeful
of continued reform during James's reign, or as implicitly critical of his

---

[47] James's views were communicated to the reading public through proclamations, printed addresses
to Parliament, and his own political writings (including the *Apology for the Oath of Allegiance*). See
Kenneth Fincham and Peter Lake, 'The Ecclesiastical Policy of King James I', *Journal of British
Studies*, 24:2 (1985), 169–207.

[48] See the complaint in Edward Coke, *La Sept Part Des Reports Sr. Edw. Coke* (London, 1608; STC
5511), A5v–A6r. Also see John Chamberlain's letter to Dudley Carleton on 13 February 1607 in
McClure (ed.), *Chamberlain*, I, p. 243.

[49] Robert Pricket, *The Lord Coke His Speech and Charge* (London, 1607; STC 5492), F2v.

[50] John Freeman, *The Apologie for the Conformable Ministers of England For their Subscription to the
present Church Government* (London, 1609; STC 11366.5), A2r–A3r.

emerging policy of religious toleration and his self-fashioning as a peace-maker – *Rex Pacificus*.[51] As might be expected from a publisher who was not himself engaged in theological debate, the parameters of Butter's brand of Protestantism are rather vague, but they probably reflect the views and sympathies of his customers, as well as the transnational networks of exchange at his bookshop. Most of Butter's texts are not invested in doctrinal definitions and concentrate instead on the political consequences attendant on religious disunity – not only on a domestic, but also a European stage. In *The Devil of the Vault*, for example, the threat posed by Catholicism has an international flavour: the verse narrative shows that similar Popish plots threatening 'state affaires' have taken place in Germany and France when the 'Papists through large Europe ranged | the Protestants to sley' (B4r–C1r). By specializing in texts that tend to eschew precise theological points and promote a reformed church in broad brush strokes, Butter advances a politicized, international Protestantism that is distinct from both James's moderate policies and from domestic debates about reform to the Anglican Church, relating to issues such as the use of ceremonies and the English Book of Common Prayer.

These points help to clarify Butter's investment in the Tudor history plays and how he read them. For Butter, they offer short, topical histories that target Catholicism, whilst remaining doctrinally vague, and they use history to trumpet the political and secular victories of their Protestant monarchs in ways that are contemporarily defined. The parameters of reform are sketchily outlined: the plays seem to champion key signs and symbols of a Protestant Reformation – the English Bible, Tudor figure-heads, printed texts as agents of reform – but are less invested in the specifics of Jacobean theological debate. David Loewenstein and Michael Witmore argue that early modern plays register a 'wide range of religious beliefs, practices, and confessional positions' and the Protestant/Catholic binary is something of a fallacy.[52] We should not expect these Tudor histories to offer homogeneous religious perspectives, but concentrating on Butter helps us to clarify the experience of one early modern reader, whose involvement may have directed the readings of others. The rest of this section discusses important interpretative paratexts from the printed play-books that were overseen by Butter, before showing how these history

---

[51] Isabel Karremann, 'A Passion for the Past: The Politics of Nostalgia on the Early Jacobean Stage', in *Passions and Subjectivity in Early Modern Culture*, ed. Brian Cummings and Freya Sierhuis (Farnham: Ashgate, 2013), pp. 149–64.

[52] David Loewenstein and Michael Witmore (eds.), *Shakespeare and Early Modern Religion* (Cambridge: Cambridge University Press, 2015), p. 3.

plays can be used, in turn, to clarify the 'truthfulness' of Butter's non-dramatic histories.

Butter's edition of *When You See Me You Know Me* emphasizes the play's historicity, as well as its connection with the Jacobean present, which is advanced through the figure of Prince Henry, James I's eldest son. The play's first edition in 1605 establishes a direct connection between the Tudor monarch Edward VI and Prince Henry by offering the following title-page description:

> When you see me, | You know me. | Or the famous Chronicle Historie | of king Henry the eight, with the | birth and vertuous life of Edward | **Prince of Wales.** | As it was played by the high and mightie **Prince** | **of Wales his seruants.** | By Samvell Rowley, **seruant** | **to the Prince.**[53]

The playbook adopts the same title 'Prince of Wales' to refer to two different individuals: the first use applies to Edward VI, who is one of the play's main characters, and the second (and third, in a shortened form) indicates Prince Henry, the playing company's patron. The description seems to conflate their identities. Grant argues that *When You See Me* is 'a tributary play for [Prince] Henry', and her important scholarship has explored how 'much of the play was deliberately angled towards the company's patron'.[54] The printed presentation of the playbook further crystallizes this alignment. It is unclear how Butter acquired Rowley's play and if the dramatist was involved in its publication and title-page design.[55] Given the processes of compiling, annotating, and translating that took place through Butter's bookshop, it is possible that a publication agent was responsible for the title-page summary. At the very least, Butter, as publisher, would have endorsed its design. The Stationers' Register entry to Butter on 12 February 1605 is a provisional one, requiring Butter to 'gett good alowance for the enterlude of King Henry the 8th ... and then procure the wardens handes to yt'.[56] This caution in the licence unlikely indicates Rowley's objection or confirms his lack of involvement in the edition: authorial permission was not required for publication. But the entry is revealing for its description of the play as an 'enterlude' about Henry VIII. In contrast, the playbook's title page emphasizes the role of Edward VI (through its three conflated invocations); defines the play as a

---

[53] Samuel Rowley, *When you see me, You know me* (London, 1605; STC 21417), A1r (emphasis mine).

[54] Grant, 'History', pp. 132, 145.

[55] The playbook seems to have been printed from authorial foul papers. See Wiggins, V, p. 145 (No. 1441).

[56] SRO4942; Arber, III, p. 283.

'famous Chronicle History', which invests it with the status of a written history that connotes accuracy and adherence to records; and advertises a connection to a Jacobean figurehead, Prince Henry.

For the most part, *When You See Me You Know Me* dramatizes events from the reign of Henry VIII, but in a loosely historical style, telescoping time, including unhistorical episodes, and unambiguously condemning Catholic influences. The printed title page also draws attention to the 'birth and vertuous life' (A1r) of Edward VI, who is shown in the play as an ideal Protestant prince. In a crucial scene, Edward reads from letters penned by his two sisters, the future Mary I and Elizabeth I, and assesses their relative merits: Mary is superstitious and has been 'blinded … with foolish herisies' by her Catholic tutors, Bonner and Gardiner, whereas Elizabeth shuns 'Idolatrie' and 'of Prince Edwards loue hast greatest part' (I1r).[57] The scene capitalizes on the broad targets of anti-Catholicism – the use of ceremonies, superstition, the mediation of scripture by priests – and celebrates the importance of the English Bible (*sola scriptura*) and independent critical reflection, which is channelled through Prince Edward, who is described as the 'hope that England hath' (H2r). This characterization recalls the role assigned by early Protestant reformers to the historical Edward VI: his reign (1547–53) was marked by the pursuit of a more active reformist agenda than that of his father, Henry VIII; and, following Edward's early death in 1553 at the age of fifteen, he was repeatedly invoked as an incipient hero of Protestantism.[58]

During the early Jacobean period, Prince Henry was fashioned in a similar way to Edward VI. His court attracted noblemen who looked to the prince to undertake a comparable role to his Tudor predecessor, particularly because they were dissatisfied with James's policy of religious toleration and the Treaty of London (1604), which established peace with Spain, Europe's most powerful Catholic nation.[59] Rowley's play makes clear the parallel between the two princes, even alluding to Prince Henry as a new Protestant hope: when Henry VIII asks Queen Jane (Seymour) to

---

[57] See also Brian Walsh's discussion of the influence of morality play tropes on this scene, in *Unsettled Toleration: Religious Difference on the Shakespearean Stage* (Oxford: Oxford University Press, 2016), p. 149.

[58] Dale Hoak, 'Edward VI (1537–1553)', *ODNB*, online ed., May 2014, https://doi.org/10.1093/ref:odnb/8522 (accessed 16 September 2019), paras. 34–39.

[59] Grant, 'History', pp. 133–36; Susan E. Krantz, 'Thomas Dekker's Political Commentary in *The Whore of Babylon*', *Studies in English Literature, 1500–1900*, 35:2 (1995), 271–91 (pp. 274–80); Roy Strong, *Henry Prince of Wales and England's Lost Renaissance* (New York: Thames and Hudson, 1986).

'Be but the Mother to a Prince of Wales | Ad a ninth Henrie to the English Crowne' (B1r), the choice of name evokes Prince Henry's position as a future Henry IX, rather than the birth of Edward VI in 1537. This phrasing and the connection between Prince Henry and his reformist Tudor predecessors can be found in other texts from the period. The title page of John Harington's posthumously published *Brief View of the State of the Church of England* (1653) claims that it was written '[f]or the private use of Prince Henry, upon occasion of that Proverb, *Henry the eighth pull'd down Monks and their Cells. | Henry the ninth should pull down Bishops and their Bells.*'[60] This jingle, as Susan Krantz observes, seems to have been popular during the Jacobean period and clarifies Prince Henry's reputation: it connects Henry to progressive reformist measures in opposition to the status quo preserved through James and the episcopacy.[61]

One of Butter's own texts seems to further this reputation of Prince Henry. In 1608, Butter published the third edition of Henoch Clapham's *Brief of the Bible's History*, containing a new dedication to the prince. Clapham's text was first printed in Edinburgh in 1596 (STC 5332) with a dedication to Thomas Mylot. In 1603, a new edition published in England by John Newbery replaced Mylot with Prince Henry as dedicatee. Written by Clapham, the dedication concentrates on the fate of the book – 'this Litle-one thus stepping out, as a Iornay-man to work' – including its search for a patron to whom the author 'might Dedicate it worthily'.[62] When Butter published the third edition, Clapham supplied a new dedication to Henry that emphasizes his role as a Protestant prince. It concludes by hoping that 'no lesse good may bee deriued in due times from you to the publique good of great Britaine, then sometime did befall Iudea from yong Iosiah'.[63] This comparison is a telling one: Josiah, the sixteenth King of Judah (*c.*640–609 BCE), was renowned for religious reform, including the compilation of Hebrew scriptures and the destruction of altars and pagan images. Josiah's reforms (discussed in 2 Kings 22–23 and 2 Chronicles 34–35) centre around the importance of the written word and the devaluation of religious iconography, and therefore suggest a connection with the Protestant reformist agendas that were, for example, brought to the Hampton Court Conference in 1604, but were,

---

[60] John Harington, *A Briefe View of the State of the Church of England* (London, 1653; Wing H770), A1r. A variant title page from the same year omits this description.
[61] Krantz, 'Political Commentary', p. 276.
[62] Henoch Clapham, *A Briefe of the Bibles Historie* (London, 1603; STC 5333), A2v.
[63] Henoch Clapham, *A Briefe of the Bibles History* (London, 1608; STC 5334), A2v.

for many on the Protestant left, unsatisfactorily resolved.[64] The new dedication in Butter's edition optimistically casts Prince Henry in Josiah's role.

However, the fact that Butter's edition of *When You See Me* predates many of these texts that negotiated Prince Henry's image somewhat tempers the Jacobean reformist drive of this history. Grant suggests that Rowley's play represents an early attempt at shaping the prince's popular reputation, casting Henry in a reformist role from a position of 'relative ignorance of his interests and preferred self-representation'.[65] Butter's printed edition certainly strengthens the connection between Henry and the play's Edward VI, the title page blurring their identities and appointing Henry as a Protestant figurehead.[66] But the timing of the edition suggests that, at this stage, an invocation of Prince Henry was not tied to notions of episcopal change, and it qualifies the history's reformist sympathies, which are broadly conceived. The play advances progressive ideas that tend to collect around symbols of Protestantism – including Edward VI and the English Bible – but do not map on to early Jacobean theological debates in a single way.

The printed presentation of Heywood's *1* and *2 If You Know Not Me, You Know Nobody* is similarly invested in establishing the plays' broad Protestant sympathies and historicity, but displays a stronger emphasis on their political import than Rowley's playbook. As discussed earlier, Heywood's objection to the publication of his plays was probably directed towards these editions, which, unlike Butter's other playbooks, appear without an authorial attribution on the title pages. Given Heywood's apparent lack of involvement, Butter, acting independently as publisher, would have overseen their design. The two parts dramatize events from the life of Elizabeth I. Part 1 recounts her difficulties, including her imprisonment, under the rule of her Catholic sister, Mary I, and Part 2 concentrates on events from Elizabeth's reign, including assassination plots and the building of the Royal Exchange.[67] The playbooks underscore their position as Tudor histories with a monarchical focus: neither part makes any reference to the texts' status as plays or includes a company attribution.

---

[64] For a summary of these agendas, see Roger Lockyer, *The Early Stuarts: A Political History of England, 1603–1642*, 2nd ed. (London: Longman, 1999), ch. 3.

[65] Grant, 'History', p. 132.   [66] Cf. Spikes, 'Elect Nation', pp. 127–30.

[67] Teresa Grant, 'Drama Queen: Staging Elizabeth in *If You Know Not Me You Know Nobody*' in *The Myth of Elizabeth*, ed. Susan Doran and Thomas S. Freeman (Basingstoke: Palgrave Macmillan, 2003), pp. 120–42 (pp. 130–33); Astrid Stilma, 'Angels, Demons, and Political Action in Two Early Jacobean History Plays', *Critical Survey*, 23:2 (2011), 9–25 (p. 23).

The title pages are dominated by a large woodcut ornament of Elizabeth, who features in both parts – although she has a much shorter role in Part 2. An alternative title – 'The troubles of Queene Elizabeth' – appears alongside the first title in Part 1 and as a separate cancel title page for Part 2 (STC 13336.5), which describes the play as 'The Second Part of Queene Elizabeths troubles'.[68] The plays are therefore presented, on the basis of their title pages, as accounts of the late queen's reign, and in a way that partly obscures (or at least does not advertise) their performance origins. The woodcuts also highlight a secular reading of their providentially inflected histories. Gina Di Salvo offers an insightful analysis of Heywood's plays as casting Elizabeth in the role of a virgin martyr saint and recovering hagiography for Protestantism.[69] Butter's woodcut of Elizabeth refocuses her role as a Protestant icon within a political dimension (see Figure 3.2). She is shown in her monarchical regalia, invested with the symbols of monarchical power – the orb and the sceptre. The former bears a cross and emphasizes her position as a Christian monarch and God's representative, but together with the sceptre, they reinvest the play's Protestant hagiography with an image of secular rule.

The political import of Protestant unity is also highlighted through the title-page descriptions. Part 2, for example, outlines key historical events from the play, including 'Doctor Paries treasons: The building of the Royall Exchange, and the famous Victorie in 1588' (STC 13336.5).[70] This plot summary refers to William Parry's attempted assassination of Elizabeth; the defeat of the Spanish Armada; and Thomas Gresham's founding of the Royal Exchange, which, in the context of the play, emerges as a symbol of 'extra-civic' nation building that counters the threat of Catholic powers (via Parry and the Armada).[71] The title page focuses attention on the play's central moments of Catholic deception and Protestant victory that have political, military, and economic dimensions. The play's historical events and individuals are part of a providential account of Protestant triumphalism, and the title-page paratexts direct this emphasis towards secular concerns, rather than doctrinal ones.

---

[68] See *If you know not me, you know no bodie* (London, 1605; STC 13328), A2r; *The Second Part of If you know not me, you know no bodie* (London, 1606; STC 13336, STC 13336.5). The first issue of Part 2 does not contain the woodcut of Elizabeth.

[69] Gina M. Di Salvo, '"A Virgine and a Martyr both": The Turn to Hagiography in Heywood's Reformation History Play', *Renaissance and Reformation*, 41:4 (2018), 133–67.

[70] The first issue (STC 13336) does not refer to Parry's treason.

[71] See Andrew Griffin, 'Thomas Heywood and London Exceptionalism', *Studies in Philology*, 110:1 (2013), 85–114 (p. 85).

If you knovv not me,
You know no bodie:
Or,
The troubles of Queene ELIZABETH.

AT LONDON,
Printed for Nathaniel Butter. 1605.

Figure 3.2　Title page from *1 If You Know Not Me, You Know Nobody* (Q1 1605; STC 13328).

Butter may not have worked with Rowley or Heywood in the publication of their plays, but it seems he collaborated with Dekker in preparing *The Whore of Babylon* for readers and shaping the play's presentation of history. Butter published a number of Dekker's non-dramatic texts during the early Jacobean period, which suggests they had a working relationship, especially as most of these contain authorial paratexts that intimate Dekker's involvement in the process.[72] Rather than announcing a connection to a historical past (as Rowley's and Heywood's plays do), the title page of *The Whore of Babylon* seems most invested in an anti-Catholic discourse, emphasized by its title, attribution to 'the Princes Seruants' (which connects the play to a Protestant figurehead), and its use of red lettering. With the exception of one variant which contains only black letters, the lines on the title page alternate between red and black, the former being the colour associated with the Book of Revelation's Whore of Babylon, whom Reformation writers had started to identify with the Catholic Church.[73] Indeed, the main play is virulently anti-Catholic: it offers an apocalyptic religious allegory that stages the triumph of Protestantism (through the figure of Titania, the Faerie Queen) over the Roman Catholic Church (represented by the Empress of Babylon)[74] It draws not only on Foxe, but also Spenser's *Faerie Queene* (1590; 1596), and its hyperbolic anti-Catholicism recalls Butter's other post–Gunpowder Plot publications, such as *The Devil of the Vault* and *The Jesuits' Play at Lyons*.

Paratexts within the playbook do, however, draw attention to its interweaving historical allegory and instruct readers how to understand and apply its history. Covering similar historical ground to Heywood's plays, *The Whore of Babylon* allegorizes Elizabeth I's reign and the various assassination attempts on her life, including those of William Parry (as Paridel), Edmund Campion (as Campeius), and Roderigo Lopez (as Ropus), and concludes with the defeat of the Spanish Armada. The 'Lectori' tells readers that the play presents the 'Heroical vertues of our late Queene[;] And (on the contrary part) the inueterate malice, Treasons, Machinations, Vnderminings and continual blody stratagems of that Purple whore of Roome, to the taking away of our Princes liues, and vtter

---

[72] Butter also published Dekker's *Seuen deadly Sinnes of London* (1606; STC 6522), *Iests to make you Merie* (1607; STC 6541), *Belman of London* (1608; STC 6481), *Worke for Armorours* (1609; STC 6536), and *Foure Birds of Noahs Arke* (1609; STC 6499).

[73] Thomas Dekker, *The Whore of Babylon* (London, 1607; STC 6532), A1r. Butter's edition of Dekker's *Seven Deadly Sins* also featured a title page in red and black. On the Whore of Babylon, see Victoria Brownlee, 'Imagining the Enemy: Protestant Readings of the Whore of Babylon in Early Modern England, c.1580–1625', in *Biblical Women in Early Modern Literary Culture, 1550–1700*, ed. Victoria Brownlee and Laura Gallagher (Manchester: Manchester University Press, 2015), pp. 213–33.

[74] For the play's apocalypticism, see Gretchen E. Minton, 'Apocalyptic Tragicomedy for a Jacobean Audience: Dekker's *Whore of Babylon* and Shakespeare's *Cymbeline*', *Renaissance and Reformation*, 36:1 (2013), 129–52.

extirpation of their Kingdomes' (A2r). Although the paratext is unsigned, it is written from the perspective of the dramatist. It outlines Dekker's intention for 'this Drammaticall Poem' and describes the play's (unfavourable) reception on the stage, for which the actors are blamed, being 'Instruments . . . for the most part out of tune' (A2v). Dekker repurposes his theatrical failure and remarkets it for a different audience and in a different medium. This re-presentation also serves to make the historical allegory and its purpose more direct. The threat of Catholicism is specifically connected to political instability and treason, such as the taking of monarchs' lives and the destruction of their kingdoms.[75] The address's sharp antithesis between the 'Heroical vertues' of Protestant monarchs and the 'malice, Treasons, Machinations' of Catholic powers eschews any measured distinctions between the plays' antagonists.

An interest in the political dimensions of this apocalyptic rewriting of history is furthered by the character list and marginalia, which make the historical allusions explicit and a permanent part of the printed text.[76] The 'Drammatis persone' indicates that 'our late Queene Elizabeth' is represented by Titania and that 'Rome' is figured through the Empress of Babylon (A2v). Titania's predecessors are indicated in printed marginal notes: Elfiline is 'Hen. 7' and Oberon is 'Hen. 8' (see Figure 3.3), and the three kings attempting Titania's overthrow originate from Spain, France, and Rome (B4v–C2r). Dekker's history, as Victoria Brownlee explores, is attentive to the secular dimensions of religious conflict and their application to Jacobean politics.[77] Its presentation as a playbook, overseen by Dekker and Butter, emphasizes this aspect. James I, for example, is alluded to as a 'second Phoenix . . . of larger wing, | Of stronger talent, of more dreadfull beake' that 'may shake all Babilon' (F2v). What was left implicit on the stage is made explicit through the playbook's marginal identification of 'K. Iames' (F2v) as this second phoenix around whom further hope of Protestant success gathers. This section of the play is regularly used to evaluate Dekker's attitude towards James and his policies of moderation and toleration.[78] The hyperbolic description of James's assertiveness may offer implicit criticism rather than praise. The play provides different possibilities for interpretation, but its presentation as a playbook emphasizes the political dimensions of Protestant–Catholic conflict that link the

---

[75] Krantz, 'Political Commentary', pp. 272.

[76] See Bayer, 'Staging', p. 83 for an annotator who made even more explicit identifications in marginalia throughout the text.

[77] Brownlee, 'Imagining', pp. 223–27; see also Minton, 'Apocalyptic', pp. 139–42.

[78] See Minton, 'Apocalyptic', pp. 137–38.

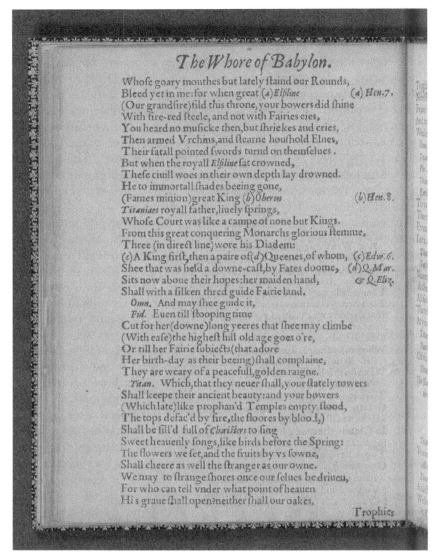

Figure 3.3 Printed marginalia in *The Whore of Babylon* (1607; STC 6532), B4v.

potential for monarchical criticism with a concern for state stability and preservation, especially in the aftermath of the Gunpowder Plot. Alongside Butter's other publications, *The Whore of Babylon* directs its religious and historical allegory towards the unity of the political nation, which lessens

its investment in doctrinal differences (and perhaps highlights their destabilizing potential, as James was also at pains to do); but it does not
necessarily align its unified Protestant state with the policies of the
Jacobean monarch, whose passivity could also be a source of political
instability.

A contrastive analysis of Butter's output suggests that he read his
providential Tudor histories as contemporarily focused plays that were
invested in the political future of the Jacobean state with limited interest in
the specifics of doctrinal definition and reform – an emphasis that also
helps to clarify the relationship of his histories and news publications to
ideas of 'truth' and accuracy. While Butter's news pamphlets sometimes
feature paratexts that assure readers of the accuracy of the histories they
contain, this defence should not be taken to indicate impartiality. They are
not committed to the representation of historical fact – a point that can be
parsed further by considering the 'Lectori' in Dekker's *Whore of Babylon*:

> And whereas I may, (by some more curious in censure, then sound in
> iudgement) be Critically taxed, that I falsifie the account of time, and set
> not down Occurrents, according to their true succession, let such (that are
> so nice of stomach) know that I write as a Poet, not as a Historian, and that
> these two doe not liue under one law' (A2r–v).

Dekker draws a distinction between two kinds of 'truth': rather than
dramatizing events in their 'true succession' (that is, with adherence to
historical records), he follows Sidney's example in the *Defence* and writes
'as a Poet, not as a Historian'.[79] Dekker separates plays about the past from
other written histories that prioritize historical accuracy, a perspective that
is also adopted by Marston in his address prefacing *The Wonder of Women*
(1606).[80] Dekker's and Marston's distinctions are, however, more theoretical (and defensive) than practical. While *The Whore of Babylon* certainly
does 'falsifie the account of time' by manipulating its Tudor history, it has
a clear interest in promoting a universal truth in the service of Protestant
policies. The prominence of 'Truth' in the Prologue and opening dumb
show make this point clear: Elizabeth is presented as a Protestant leader
who 'wakens Truth' (A3r) – the final word of the Prologue – which is
then followed by a dumb show that describes how, during the reign of
Mary I, Truth was discarded and dressed 'in sad abiliments' (A3v). The
play's investment in a Protestant truth is most effectively served by

---

[79] See Grant, 'History', p. 138.   [80] See Introduction, pp. 29–31.

departing from the 'truth' of historical records. This exchange of historical accuracy for a truthful sentiment is an argument often shared by historical writing from the period, including not only providential histories like Foxe's *Acts and Monuments*, but also secular ones, such as Hayward's *Life and Reign of King Henry IV* and the example from Stow's *Survey of London*, which opened this chapter. Butter's output suggests the same evaluation: claims for truthful representations are a vital component of his history plays and news reports, but rather than indicating historical accuracy, they offer a 'truthful sentiment' that corresponds to how the texts use and manipulate their histories to advance a broad brand of Protestantism that flattens doctrinal distinctions and prioritizes vivid anti-Catholicism in the interests of political unity.

Butter, *King Lear*, and Histories of Unity and Division

Butter's investment in texts that could be used to reflect on political issues current at the time of their publication suggests a reason for his interest in *King Lear* in 1608. At first glance, Butter's involvement in this edition might seem to depart from the publishing strategies outlined in the previous two sections. *King Lear* does not promote a Protestant agenda and, rather than dramatizing recent Tudor history, it draws on the ancient British past. Indeed, Butter acquired the rights to Shakespeare's play and a sermon by John Pelling at the same time, and as Blayney has shown through an analysis of Nicholas Okes's printing house, he sent *A Sermon of the Providence of God* (1607; STC 19567) to press immediately, while *King Lear* was put aside to, as Arnold Hunt describes, 'wait its turn in the queue'.[81] Although this sermon was the only one of Pelling's to achieve a printed edition, Butter perhaps thought that its religious subject and newsworthy quality – it was preached on 25 October 1607 – resonated more strongly with his publishing interests than Shakespeare's play. Nevertheless, the fluid history/news divide that characterizes Butter's publications also applies to Shakespeare's *King Lear*, which clarifies his investment in the play. The opening scene announces its application to the heated debates concerning the Jacobean union of England and Scotland, and Butter possibly acquired this ancient history because of its new

---

[81] Butter entered Pelling's sermon on 18 November 1607 and Shakespeare's play on 26 November 1607. See Blayney, *The Texts of 'King Lear'*, p. 81; Hunt, 'Art of Hearing', p. 163.

currency. This section first discusses the contemporaneity of legendary British history spurred on by James I's union project and then considers how Butter's early Jacobean publications invest in a debate that dominated political thought: as one commentator remarked in 1604, 'there is nothing more in the mouthes of men then discoursing the Union of England and Scotland'.[82] While dramatizing a distant history, Shakespeare's play in the bookshop of a news publisher who specialized in topical matters of church and state encourages a reading alert to the repercussions of Jacobean division. By examining Butter's wider output, an overlooked interpretative link emerges between *King Lear* and the Tudor histories, where patterns of division find their redress in a unified Protestant state.

When James I succeeded to the English throne in 1603, England and Scotland became united under the same reigning monarch, while remaining separate political and economic nations.[83] James was, however, keen to make provision for statutory unification, which involved legal reforms, the naturalization of the *post-nati*, and the adoption of a new Royal Style.[84] James made his first public comment on the 'union of the two Realmes' through a royal proclamation on 19 May 1603, expressing his desire that 'with all conuenient diligence' the 'happy Union should be perfected'.[85] An accession medal was also produced in 1603, naming James as the 'emperor of the whole island of Britain', and the new one-pound coin (called 'the Unite') identified James as 'King of Great Britain'.[86] His plans, however, proved controversial and dominated political debates between 1604 and 1608 – when *King Lear* was published.[87] James felt Parliament's opposition to union infringed on his royal prerogative and he antagonized the Houses further by resorting to a proclamation to announce his new

---

[82] BL Stowe MS 158, fol. 34; quoted in Bruce R. Galloway and Brian P. Levack (eds.), *The Jacobean Union: Six Tracts of 1604* (Edinburgh: Clark Constable, 1985), p. xxviii.

[83] Material from this section appears in my chapter 'Publishing *King Lear* (1608) at the Sign of the Pied Bull', in *Old St Paul's and Culture*, ed. Shanyn Altman and Jonathan Buckner (London: Palgrave Macmillan, 2021), pp. 293–318.

[84] For the union debate, see Bruce Galloway, *The Union of England and Scotland 1603–1608* (Edinburgh: John Donald, 1986); Jenny Wormald, 'The Creation of Britain: Multiple Kingdoms or Core and Colonies?', *Transactions of the Royal Historical Society*, 2 (1992), 175–94; Glen Burgess, Rowland Wymer and Jason Lawrence (eds.), *The Accession of James I: Historical and Cultural Consequences* (Basingstoke: Palgrave Macmillan, 2006).

[85] James I, 'By the King [19 May 1603]' (London, 1603; STC 8314), 1 page.

[86] See James Shapiro, *1606: William Shakespeare and the Year of 'Lear'* (London: Faber, 2015), pp. 40–41.

[87] Andrew Hadfield, *Shakespeare, Spenser, and the Matter of Britain* (Basingstoke: Palgrave Macmillan, 2004), pp. 1–6.

Royal Style, which was a major source of contention in the debates.[88]
On 20 October 1604, James declared that he would 'discontinue the
diuided names of England and Scotland' and would assume 'by Our
absolute power' the 'Name and Stile of King of Great Brittaine, France,
and Ireland'.[89]

James's promotion of 'Britain' as the preferred collective name for the
countries over which he reigned was not a new styling. It is recorded in
Geoffrey of Monmouth's *Historia Regum Britanniae* (and subsequent
medieval and Tudor chronicles) as the earliest name for the whole island.
Holinshed begins his history of England in the second volume of the
Chronicles by stating that 'this our country ... hath most generallie and of
longest continuance beene knowne among all nations by the name of
Britaine'.[90] To promote his agenda, James drew on these ancient British
histories, which provided a precedent for union through the reigns of
monarchs such as Brutus, Leir, and Lud.[91] In his speeches to Parliament
(which were also published and made available to the public), James
claimed that he 'came from the loines of your ancient Kings' and that
the union of the houses of York and Lancaster was 'nothing comparable to
the Vnion of two ancient and famous Kingdoms, which is ... annexed to
my Person'.[92] Although the historicity of these accounts of Britain's pre-
Christian past, which traced the nation's heritage back to its Trojan
founder, Brutus, was being progressively challenged during the sixteenth
and seventeenth centuries, the question of their veracity was not crucial for
their application to the union debates, which aimed instead, as Philip
Schwyzer observes, to encourage people to 'start thinking of themselves as
Britons'.[93]

These accounts of ancient British history also provided a warning: both
Brutus and Leir divided their united kingdoms amongst their successors,

[88] James outlined his ideas of prerogative in *The Trve Lawe of free Monarchies* (Edinburgh: 1598: STC
14409), which was reprinted in England in 1603 (STC 14410).
[89] James I, 'By the King [20 October 1604]' (London, 1604; STC 8361), pp. 2–3.
[90] Holinshed (1587), II, A1r (beginning 'The First Booke of the historie of England').
[91] David Bergeron suggests that James was inspired by the civic pageant in 1604 that was staged to
mark his accession and which took place four days before his first speech to Parliament. See
Bergeron, 'King James's Civic Pageant and Parliamentary Speech in March 1604', *Albion*, 34:2
(2002), 213–31; Tristan Marshall, *Theatre and Empire: Great Britain on the London Stages under
James VI and I* (Manchester: Manchester University Press, 2000), ch. 1.
[92] James I, *His Maiesties Speech to Both the Houses of Parliament* [31 March 1607] (London, 1607;
STC 14395), D2v; *The Kings Maiesties Speech* [19 March 1604] (London, 1604; STC 14390), A4v.
The latter was James's first speech to Parliament and was printed in four editions in 1604.
[93] Philip Schwyzer, 'The Jacobean Union Controversy and *King Lear*', in *Accession of James I*, ed.
Burgess et al., pp. 34–47 (p. 35).

actions that led to disorder and civil war. When James's *Basilikon Doron* was published in England in 1603, it contained several important additions to the original 1599 edition, which had been published in Edinburgh by Robert Waldegrave when Elizabeth I was still queen of England. In both editions (which are dedicated to Prince Henry and profess to be for the instruction 'of a Prince in all the points of his calling'), James warns against dividing a kingdom, as it will 'leaue the seede of diuision and discord among your posteritie'.[94] The 1603 edition adds a specific reference to early British history by continuing the line: 'as befel to this Ile[,] by the diuision and assignement therof, to the three sonnes of Brutus[:] Locrine, Albanact, and Camber' (H2r).[95] James's revision stresses the importance of a united England and Scotland, which, as he declared in his first address to Parliament on 19 March 1604, he saw as being 'confirmed in me'.[96]

The connection between ancient British history and the union debate is also reflected in a considerable number of early Jacobean performances and publications.[97] George Owen Harry's officially sanctioned *Genealogy of the High and Mighty Monarch, James* (1604) constructs the lineal descent of James from Noah and Brutus, while also outlining the Stuarts' Welsh connections through Cadwallader (the 'last King of the Brittish bloud') and Owen Tudor (grandfather of Henry VII).[98] It aims to reinforce James's monarchical claim to the whole island of Britain, which is outlined in detail through the text's extended title-page summary. The anonymous and pro-union 'Treatise about the Union of England and Scotland' (written *c.*1604) claims that the renewal of 'the ancient appellation either of Albion or of Great Brittanie to the whole iland' would be 'no small band to knit together the two peoples'.[99] In this case, ancient precedents and histories provide not merely a model for the Jacobean state but are also an active means of binding England and Scotland together and ensuring their amity. Royal entertainments designed by Jonson, Middleton, and Dekker

[94] James I, *Basilikon Doron* (London, 1603; STC 14353), 4r, H2r. In the 1599 edition (STC 14348), these lines appear on A4r and O2r.
[95] Cf. 1599 edition (STC 14348), O2r.   [96] *Speech* [19 March 1604], A4v.
[97] See also Marshall's account in *Theatre and Empire*, ch. 2; Leah S. Marcus, *Puzzling Shakespeare: Local Reading and Its Discontents* (Berkeley: University of California Press, 1988), ch. 3; and Lisa Hopkins, *Drama and the Succession to the Crown, 1561–1633* (Farnham: Ashgate, 2011).
[98] George Owen Harry, *The Genealogy of the High and Mighty Monarch, James* (London, 1604; STC 12872), (a)1r.
[99] Galloway and Levack (eds.), *The Jacobean Union*, p. 61. The treatise survives in one manuscript copy held by Trinity College, Cambridge (R5.15, No. 10).

to celebrate James's ceremonial entry into London also used these legendary histories, describing Britain as 'so rich an Empyre' that 'Contaynes foure Kingdomes': 'By *Brute* diuided, but by you alone, | All are againe vnited and made *One*'.[100] And, as critics including Gordon McMullan have discussed, plays from the commercial theatres – such as *Nobody and Somebody* – similarly explored this line of descent.[101] Performed by Queen Anne's Men and published by John Trundle in about 1606, the anonymous *Nobody and Somebody* dramatizes the legendary histories of two British kings, Archigallo and Elidure: it involves the deposition of Archigallo by his nobility and the reluctant accession of Elidure, who is crowned king three times, in response to changing political alliances. For my purposes, it is significant that all of the ancient British history plays that were published during the height of the union debates contain the same title-page label: 'True Chronicle History'. As an adjective or noun, 'chronicle' was rarely used on playbook title pages: it appeared on only nine first editions spanning 1593 to 1634.[102] At the same time as the reigns of early British monarchs were being featured in royal entertainments, parliamentary addresses, treatises, and genealogies, three playbooks – the anonymous *King Leir* (1605), *Nobody and Somebody* (c.1606), and Shakespeare's *King Lear* (1608) – incorporate the expanded phrase 'true chronicle history' as part of their titles.[103] By doing so, the playbooks seem to advertise the 'truthfulness' of their legendary British pasts, their claim blurring a distinction between ideas of historical veracity

---

[100] Thomas Dekker [and Thomas Middleton], *The Magnificent Entertainment* (London, 1604; STC 6510), I1r. See also Stephen Harrison, [Thomas Dekker, and John Webster], *The Archs of Trivmph* (London, 1604; STC 12863); Ben Jonson, *King James his Royall and Magnificent Entertainment* (London, 1604; STC 14756); and Anthony Munday, *The Trivmphs of re-vnited Britania* (London, 1605; STC 18279). The latter was part of the Lord Mayor's Show in 1605, which was not performed for James, but it celebrates the king as 'our second Brute' (B2r). See also Hill, *Anthony Munday* and *Pageantry and Power: A Cultural History of the Early Modern Lord Mayor's Show 1585–1639* (Manchester: Manchester University Press, 2011).

[101] See the appendices which outline lost and extant early British history plays between 1560 and 1625 in Gordon McMullan, 'The Colonization of Early Britain on the Jacobean Stage', in *Reading the Medieval in Early Modern England*, ed. Gordon McMullan and David Matthews (Cambridge: Cambridge University Press, 2007), pp. 119–40 (pp. 138–40). See also Paul Frazer, 'Shakespeare's Northern Blood: Transfusing *Gorboduc* into *Macbeth* and *Cymbeline*', in *Shakespeare in the North: Place, Politics and Performance in England and Scotland*, ed. Adam Hansen (Edinburgh: Edinburgh University Press, 2021), pp. 41–59.

[102] These nine editions are: *Edward I* (1593), *Henry V* (1600), *Thomas Lord Cromwell* (1602), *When You See Me* (1605), *King Leir* (1605), *Nobody and Somebody* [1606], *King Lear* (1608), *The Valiant Welshman* (1615), and *Perkin Warbeck* (1634).

[103] *Nobody and Somebody* is undated but, given its entry in the Register on 12 March 1606, the play probably reached the bookstalls later in the same year. See also Gilchrist, *Staging Britain's Past*, ch. 3.

and true sentiment. They underscore the 'currency' – in terms of timeliness and marketability – of this history in early Jacobean Britain.

Aside from *King Lear,* Butter invested in other texts that responded to the ongoing union debates.[104] In 1606, for example, he published John Davies of Hereford's *Bien Venu,* which is a celebration of King Christian IV of Denmark's visit to England in July 1606. However, its language and allusions suggest an additional application: England and Scotland's union. Davies's *ottava rima* poem claims to memorialize the 'union' of James and Christian, effected through Queen Anne (James's royal consort and the Danish king's sister), but it is clearly intended to evoke the connection between England and Scotland and their conjunction under James's rule:

> O VNION! that enclaspest in thyne armes,
> All that in Heau'n and Earth is great, or good,
> (Thou Heau'nly Harbour from all earthly harmes)
> Thou Damm, that straist the Streames of humane bloud)
> What humane Heart but (maugre Hatreds Charms)
> Will not desire thee, as the Angells food?
> Sith through thy powr thou makst mans powr so strong
> As not to offer, much lesse suffer wrong.[105]

This extended passage does not refer directly to Britain and Denmark, a pattern which recurs throughout the poem. Davies celebrates the benefits of 'one vnited Might' that provides shelter from 'all earthly harmes' using non-specific language that could be applied to different contexts (C4r). Adding to the impression that Davies intends to recall England and Scotland's union, the poem draws attention to Britain's united past and James's position as a new leader who restores and solidifies this unity:

> Thou Royall Seat of farre renowned Kings,
> (Britaines great Monarks, Kings of great Britaine,
> Whose name from LVD, thy much inlarger Springs).
>
> (B3v)

King Lud was a legendary pre-Roman monarch, who was described in chronicle accounts as having refortified London.[106] Davies's poem consistently appropriates the material and rhetoric of pro-union accounts, such as *The Joyful and Blessed Reuniting* [c.1605], which celebrates the 'ancient name

---

[104] See also Robert Pricket's *Lord Coke His Speech and Charge* (1607), which celebrates 'vertuous King Iames' as 'the Emperiall Maiesty of great Brittaines Monarchy' (G1r) and the pamphlets of Anthony Nixon (such as STC 18594 and STC 18596), which regularly engage with ideas of twinned nations.
[105] John Davies of Hereford, *Bien Venu* (London, 1606; STC 6329), A4r.   [106] Stow, *Svrvay,* B1r.

of great Brittaine'.[107] Indeed, Davies, a poet and writing master, had connections to the Jacobean court. He worked as a handwriting instructor for Prince Henry, as well as aristocratic families, including the Percys, the Herberts, and the Pembrokes, a connection that may have informed his treatment of the royal visit and its clear application to the union of England and Scotland.[108]

Butter's publication of *Bien Venu*, which was entered in the Stationers' Register on 29 July 1606, capitalizes on the newsworthy quality of both the royal visit and the union debates. The title page presents the text as: 'Bien Venv. | Great Britaines | Welcome to Hir Greate | Friendes, and Deere Brethren | The Danes' (A1r). The largest type is used for 'Great Britaines', while 'The Danes' appears in the smallest type, which seems to emphasize Britain's central position in the two unions evoked by the poem. Henry Roberts's account of the royal visit, published by William Welby in the same year, offers a useful contrast to Butter's publication and its emphasis. *England's Farewell to Christian the Fourth* (1606) is nowhere concerned with the rhetoric of union. Indeed, Robert's account explicitly presents the royal visit as a meeting between *England* and Denmark, exclusively referring to James as the 'King of England' (A4r).[109] His earlier texts published by Creede are characterized by their celebration of specifically English worthies, a national imagining that Roberts continues in the Jacobean period and which elides or erases the positions of Scotland and Wales that featured in other accounts, such as those published by Butter.[110]

Within the context of Butter's wider output, his interest in *King Lear* is clear: Shakespeare's play draws on the early British histories that were so prominent following James I's succession, but, in contrast to a text like *Bien Venu*, features an account of disintegration, rather than unification. The opening lines of the play launch readers into the midst of a political debate and immediately introduce the issue of kingdom division:

> KENT[:] I thought the King had more affected the Duke of Albany then Cornwell.
>
> GLOST[:] It did all waies seeme so to vs, but now in the diuision of the kingdomes, it appeares not which of the Dukes he values most, for equalities are so weighed, that curiositie in neither, can make choise of eithers moytie (B1r).

[107] [John Thornborough] 'John Bristoll', *The Ioiefvll and Blessed Revniting* (Oxford: [c.1605]; STC 24036), ¶1r.

[108] P. J. Finkelpearl, 'Davies, John (1564/5–1618)', *ODNB*, online ed., September 2004, https://doi.org/10.1093/ref:odnb/7244 (accessed 16 September 2019), para. 2.

[109] Henry Roberts, *Englands Farewell to Christian the fourth* (London, 1606; STC 21079), A4r.

[110] See Chapter 1, pp. 57–58.

The play's first audiences and readers would probably have recognized a connection between this discussion of division and the Jacobean union debates that made use of ancient British history as both a precedent for union and a warning against division. Indeed, images of division dominate the play. Lear's first action when he appears on stage is to request a map to help illustrate his plan to allocate each of his daughters a section of Britain:

> Mean time we will expresse our darker purposes,
> The map there; know we have diuided
> In three, our kingdome, and tis our first intent,
> To shake all cares and busines of our state,
> Confirming them on yonger yeares.
>
> (B1v)

Accompanying Lear's voluntary divesting of his monarchical power, the map is, as John Gillies observes, a 'signal of national decay rather than the celebration of national mystique'.[111] As revealed through the rest of the play's action, the map's boundaries and newly applied lines of division fragment the kingdom, rather than reflecting the triumphalism that can be witnessed in contemporary maps, such as Christopher Saxton's *Atlas of the Counties of England and Wales* (1579).

While the play explores the destruction accompanying various types of division, it does not offer a clear perspective on kingdom division and how it relates to Jacobean politics. As Schwyzer summarizes, 'the play is so cagey and ambiguous on the union question that it admits of flatly contradictory readings'.[112] *King Lear* can be read as a unionist work: it opens with the dukes of Albany and Cornwall, which suggests an immediate connection to James I's court. These titles had been assigned to his two heirs: Prince Charles was created duke of Albany (which was associated with Scotland) at his baptism in 1600, and Prince Henry was created duke of Cornwall in 1603. Through the prominence of these titles, Shakespeare draws attention to questions of *Jacobean* rule, and in Butter's 1608 edition Albany is given the play's final lines, which the Folio assigns to Edgar. While it is outside the purposes of this chapter to engage with the provenance of Q1, the allocation of these lines to Albany firmly situates the playbook within contemporary union debates. As Richard Dutton observes in his cautiously pro-union reading, these lines

---

[111] John Gillies, 'The Scene of Cartography in *King Lear*', in *Literature, Mapping, and the Politics of Space in Early Modern Britain*, ed. Andrew Gordon and Bernhard Klein (Cambridge: Cambridge University Press, 2001), pp. 109–37 (p. 111).
[112] Schwyzer, 'Jacobean Union', p. 39.

could be seen to position Albany – an individual with Scottish ties – as the reunited nation's next ruler, thus prefiguring James and his sons.[113] However, the conclusion is far from reassuring, and Shakespeare's departure from the historical narrative would have been apparent to Jacobean audiences and readers, not solely because of the play's unexpected tragic ending, but also for its effective negation of James's genealogy.[114] As Schwyzer explores in an anti-unionist reading, the chronicle tradition reveals that neither Albany nor Edgar inherit the kingdom. Instead, the monarchical line continues through Cordelia and her nephews Cunedagius and Marganus.[115] Shakespeare's rewriting of this history allies Jacobean attempts at promoting an illustrious line of descent with the fragmentation and division that inhere throughout the play. *King Lear* can be read as disrupting the traditional narrative of succession that was central in Jacobean unionist accounts and negating their triumphalism.

However, by focusing on Butter's investment in *King Lear*, it is possible to clarify what this play meant for one of its first (and most important) readers. When Butter's early Jacobean publications are considered collectively, they tend to support unionist readings. *King Lear* demonstrates the dangers of a divided kingdom; *Bien Venu* celebrates the security and 'Heavnly Habour' provided by 'one vnited Might' (A4r); and Pricket's *The Lord Coke His Speech and Charge* champions the absolute sovereignty of James: 'he is ouer vs the Lords anointed . . . Vnto his Highnesse then let our liues submission bend' (C1v). The title page of *King Lear* also prominently advertises the play's performance in front of James on St Stephen's Night (26 December). Although references to royal performances on playbook title pages were a common promotional strategy, this case is significant, as it links the play's (timely) dramatization of legendary British history with James's court and his implicit approval. The phrasing on the title page seems to announce the newsworthy quality of the royal performance: *King Lear* was 'played before the Kings Maiestie at Whitehall vpon S. Stephans night' (A4r). As Blayney observes, this description is ambiguous and its lack of specificity encourages readers to suppose that the performance happened on 26 December 1607, just before the play reached the bookstalls; but it actually took place one year earlier in 1606.[116] Through its paratexts, *King Lear*'s ancient chronicle history advertises a

---

[113] Richard Dutton, '*King Lear, The Triumphs of Reunited Britannia* and "The Matter of Britain"', *Literature and History*, 12:2 (1986), 139–51 (pp. 146–47).
[114] See also Hadfield, *Matter of Britain*, pp. 151–68.   [115] Schwyzer, 'Jacobean Union', pp. 39–43.
[116] Blayney, *Texts of 'King Lear'*, p. 83.

close and current connection with the Jacobean court, which, by extension, could be read as offering implicit support for James's policies.

The two dominant concerns of Butter's early Jacobean publications –
the union debate and an international Protestant agenda – are brought
together in a number of his texts and shed further light on his reading of
King Lear and the Tudor histories. For example, ideas and rhetoric of
union feature in Heywood's *1 If You Know Not Me, You Know Nobody*;
but, in this case, the play explores the wrong kind of union – one with a
Catholic imperialist nation. Heywood's dialogue is alert to the possibility
for contemporary application when it describes Philip II of Spain and
Mary I of England as newly united rulers through their marriage, made
most explicit when Philip proclaims their 'new vnited Stile':

> PHIL: Now Spaine and England two populous Kingdomes,
> That haue a long time been oppos'd
> In Hostile emulation, shalbe at one:
> This shalbe Spanish England, ours English Spaine.
>
> QUEE: Harke the redoubling ecchoes of the people,
> How it proclaymes their loues; and welcome to this Vnion.
>
> (B3r)

While the repetition of 'vnited' and 'Vnion' echoes the political buzzwords of
the early Jacobean period, the joining of Spain and England, as audiences and
readers would have recognized, was not fortuitous. This alliance was short-
lived; and, contrary to the aims of English Protestants, it formally reinstated
the Catholic faith. At the time of the play's performance and publication,
James had established peace with Spain through the Treaty of London
(1604). The events of the play seem to point to the dangers of this union,
anticipated, for example, in the quarrel between two minor characters, an
Englishman and a Spaniard, that ends with the Englishman's death (E1v).
Looking beyond Heywood's play, none of Butter's other publications have
anything positive to say about Protestant–Catholic unions. In the dedication
to James added to the English translation of Tilenus's *True Copy of Two Letters*
(1605), the translator (D. D. S.) goes so far as to recommend travel restrictions
to Spain and Italy because of a fear of Catholic corruption (A2r–A3r).

These two strands of Butter's output complemented each other: a
united and politically stable nation would be better able to handle international threats and the religio-political power of the Catholic Church. In
The Devil of the Vault, the danger of the Catholic plot is expressly
presented in terms of its consequences for Britain as a united nation under
James: 'Papists at once would haue consum'd | **Brittaines** King, Prince,
and Peeres' (B3v, my emphasis). Similarly, Pricket uses (and celebrates)

James's adopted Royal Syle when describing the threat of treason posed by
Catholics in Britain, outlining a sharp division between the state of union
idealized through James and his unionist propaganda and the destabilizing
potential of religious division (*Lord Coke*, F2v). *King Lear* is, in contrast,
theologically plural, despite its allusions to Samuel Harsnett's *Declaration
of Egregious Popish Impostures* (1603).[117] Butter may have read the play as
offering, through its dramatization of destruction ensuing from division, a
topical narrative that reinforces the political advantages of a united Britain
against international political powers. Moreover, Butter's emphasis on a
united Britain clarifies his Protestant interests. Rather than drawing attention to theological distinctions in the Protestant church, Butter's publishing strategies could be seen as unifying nations such as Scotland and
England that had very different doctrinal practices and structures, in the
service of an outward-looking, secularized Protestantism.

This emphasis also helps to clarify the relationship of Butter's output to
the policies and propaganda of the Jacobean court. While Butter's publications advance Protestant sympathies, the aims of James's union project,
and the ancient histories prioritized by the monarch, Butter cannot be
comfortably described as a 'royalist' publisher. His texts are most closely
aligned with the Jacobean court when circumstances (such as the aftermath
of the Gunpowder Plot) pushed James into being critical of Catholic
influence.[118] Some of his publications reveal a more assertive stance than
James was prepared to take. The translator's dedication to James in
Tilenus's *True Copy of Two Letters* seems anxious to cajole the monarch
into decisive action against Catholics in England, which differs from
James's policy of toleration. Butter's late Jacobean newsbooks are even less
supportive of James's pacifist policies, especially following the outbreak of
the Thirty Years War. In 1620, for example, Butter published a pamphlet
describing Ferdinand II, Holy Roman Emperor and the new Habsburg
King of Bohemia, as 'a Bastard, borne of more then an Illegittimate, yea of
an execrable Mariage': both Butter and his printer, William Stansby, were
imprisoned.[119] Between 1628 and 1641, Butter also seems to have had a
direct connection with Joseph Hall, Bishop of Exeter, who favoured

---

[117] *King Lear*, ed. R. A. Foakes (London: Arden Shakespeare, 1997), pp. 102–4.
[118] See, for example, James's *Triplici nodo, triplex cuneus, or An Apology for the Oath of Allegiance*
(1607, STC 14400; reprinted in 1609 (STC 14401) with an attribution to the king), which was
published in response to criticism of his 1606 Oath of Allegiance required of English Catholics.
[119] *A Plaine Demonstration of the Vnlawful Svccession of the Now Emperovr Ferdinand the Second* ('the
Hage' [i.e. London], 1620; STC 10814), ¶3v. See also Cyndia Susan Clegg, *Press Censorship in
Jacobean England* (Cambridge: Cambridge University Press, 2001), pp. 184–85.

intervention in the Palatinate and a united Protestantism in the face of Catholic political threats. Butter was, as Peter McCullough identifies, the exclusive publisher of Hall's religious works during this time and stood surety for eight clerical appointments in the diocese of Exeter.[120] For Butter, then, 'history' – broadly conceived, encompassing recent and ancient pasts, and displaying Protestant sympathies – might be his dominant publishing specialism, but it is not, contrary to first appearances, a history controlled and authorized by the monarch.

Selling Histories at St Austin's Gate

The final part of this chapter considers the physical geography of the book trade as a place for interpretative exchange and indirect collaboration, and applies these ideas to the histories offered for wholesale at St Austin's Gate. As discussed, Butter's bookshop can be seen as a crossroads for exchange: texts in English and European languages passed in and out of his shop, as did a range of publication agents, including translators, printers, authors, scribes, and correctors. A bustling, chaotic environment is evoked by Jonson's satirical representation in *The Staple of News*. Butter's selection of texts and their printed presentation depended on the publication networks that centred around his bookshop at the Sign of the Pied Bull – and, to a considerable degree, his publications defined the area. Between 1605 and 1629, the only other stationer working in Butter's corner of Paul's Churchyard's was Matthew Law, meaning that St Austin's Gate was largely characterized by the offerings of these two bookshops.[121] There is no evidence that Butter and Law actively collaborated on the publication of any texts; but as Wise and Waterson (discussed in Chapter 2) probably responded to each other's publications, so too did Butter and Law. This exchange represents a kind of indirect collaboration – and it is one in which history plays, non-dramatic histories, and topical religious texts occupy an important position.

Both stationers display an interest in history plays – and, in Law's case, specifically Shakespeare's histories to the extent that this area of Paul's Churchyard was a new central point for Shakespearean publication during the early Jacobean period. Between 1603 and 1608, six editions of plays advertising their connection to Shakespeare – *1 Henry IV* (1604, 1608),

[120] Peter McCullough, 'Print, Publication, and Religious Politics in Caroline England', *The Historical Journal*, 51:2 (2008), 285–313 (p. 295).
[121] STC, III, pp. 103, 246.

Richard III (1605), *The London Prodigal* (1605), *Richard II* (1608), and *King Lear* (1608) – were published at St Austin's Gate (when only three other 'Shakespearean' editions were published elsewhere).[122] At the Sign of the Fox, Law produced reprints of Shakespeare's most successful English histories – *Richard II* (Q4 1608, Q5 1615), *Richard III* (Q4 1605, Q5 1612, Q6 1622, Q7 1629) and *1 Henry IV* (Q4 1604, Q5 1608, Q6 1613, Q7 1622) – after acquiring the rights from Wise on 25 June 1603.[123] Although Law published first editions of non-dramatic texts, his dramatic output from 1604 to 1629 (which marks the end of his publishing career) consists entirely of reprinted editions.[124] Unlike Butter, Law did not need to acquire playscripts. Acting independently of the King's Men and their leading dramatist, he invested in already-proven playbooks and published new editions during key moments of political unrest or transition, suggesting that, similar to Butter, he 'read' history plays in light of their contemporaneity. Law's reprinted editions of *Richard III* (1613) and *1 Henry IV* (1613), for example, were likely prompted by Prince Henry's death in 1612, which led to a resurgence in concerns about succession and government, issues that are central in both of these plays. At the same time, Butter issued new editions of *When You See Me You Know Me* (1613) and *1 If You Know Not Me, You Know Nobody* (1613), which, in this context, seem to respond to the loss of Henry as a Protestant figurehead and reflect critically on James's pacifism and religious toleration. The simultaneous publication of Butter's and Law's reprinted histories strongly implies that both stationers were attentive to each other's publications, as well as the political context that propelled readers' interests in monarchical histories that engage with successional and Protestant concerns – both linked through the figure of Prince Henry, who had been James's heir and a symbol for Protestant reform.

Butter's investment in 'Shakespeare' as a marketing strategy may have been influenced by Law's output. All of Law's editions follow Wise's playbook precedents and contain prominent title-page attributions to Shakespeare. In 1605, Butter published *The London Prodigal*, the plot of which shares similarities with the inverted 'prodigal father' subplot in *King Lear*. Its title page contains an attribution to 'William Shakespeare', which

[122] The only other play by Shakespeare to be printed between 1603 and 1608 was *Hamlet* (Q1 1603; Q2 1604), published and sold by Nicholas Ling (and John Trundle for Q1). Thomas Pavier published *A Yorkshire Tragedy* in 1608 with an attribution to 'W. Shakespeare'.

[123] SRO4718; Arber, III, p. 239.

[124] After publishing two first editions at the beginning of his career, Yarington's *Two Lamentable Tragedies* (1601) and Heywood's *How a Man May Choose a Good Wife from a Bad* (1602), Law specialized in reprints of commercial plays.

is generally regarded as false, although *The London Prodigal* was added to Shakespeare's Third Folio in 1664 and was included in the Fourth Folio of 1685, Nicholas Rowe's 1709-11 collected edition, and in later single-text and collected editions through to the nineteenth century.[125] Whether or not Butter believed the play was by Shakespeare, the playbook makes a clear effort to advertise his authorship and establishes a link with Law's Shakespearean editions, two of which – *1 Henry IV* (Q4 1604) and *Richard III* (Q4 1605) – had been published by this point. Moreover, Butter's edition of *King Lear* contains the most emphatic promotion of Shakespeare's authorship of any early quarto, the first line on the title page indicating (in large type) that the book is by 'Master William Shakspeare' and contains 'HIS | True Chronicle Historie of the life and | death of King LEAR and his three | Daughters' (see Figure 3.4).[126] Of course, this emphasis on Shakespeare's authorship, even ownership, of the play is motivated by the need to distinguish Butter's edition from the anonymous *King Leir*, which was published in 1605 by John Wright near Newgate Market and featured a similar title-page description: 'The True Chronicle History of King LEIR, and his three daughters, Gonorill, Ragan, and Cordella'.[127] Butter's edition indicates its connection (in terms of subject matter) to the earlier anonymous play, but seems to declare its superiority through the prominent advertisement of Shakespeare's authorship. Law's neighbouring editions may have partly directed this attribution. It is significant to note that six of the nine Shakespearean playbooks published between 1603 and 1608 advertise the same local habitation and a name: they feature attributions to Shakespeare and title-page imprints that connect the playbooks to the south-east corner of Paul's Churchyard.

Aside from Butter's and Law's shared interest in history plays and Shakespearean attribution, another significant point of overlap is their investment in texts that engage with pressing political and religious concerns from the early Jacobean period. Butter prioritized newsworthy texts that advance anti-Catholic views in the service of a politically inflected Protestantism. His publications tend to offer support for James's rule and policies, but that was a secondary factor. In contrast, Law's output is closely tied to the Jacobean court, demonstrated especially by the fact that,

---

[125] On the apocryphal plays, see Peter Kirwan, *Shakespeare and the Idea of Apocrypha: Negotiating the Boundaries of the Dramatic Canon* (Cambridge: Cambridge University Press, 2015), ch. 1.

[126] Zachary Lesser and Peter Stallybrass, 'Shakespeare between Pamphlet and Book, 1608–1619', in *Shakespeare and Textual Studies*, ed. Margaret Jane Kidnie and Sonia Massai (Cambridge: Cambridge University Press, 2015), pp. 105–33 (pp. 105–9).

[127] Anon., *The True Chronicle History of King Leir* (London, 1605; STC 15343), A1r.

M. William Shak-fpeare:

HIS
True Chronicle Hiftorie of the life and
death of King L E A R and his three
Daughters.

With the vnfortunate life of Edgar, *fonne*
and heire to the Earle of Glofter, and his
fullen and affumed humor of
To M of Bedlam :

As it was played before the Kings Maieftie at Whitehall vpon
S. Stephans *night in Chriftmas Hollidayes.*

By his Maiefties feruants playing vfually at the Gloabe
on the Bancke-fide.

LONDON,
Printed for *Nathaniel Butter,* and are to be fold at his fhop in *Pauls*
Church-yard at the figne of the Pide Bull neere
S^t. *Auftins* Gate. 1 6 o 8

Figure 3.4   Title page from *King Lear* (Q1 1608; STC 22292).

between 1601 and 1609, he was the exclusive publisher of William Barlow (Bishop of Lincoln from 1608). Barlow was a leading churchman involved in state politics and the authorization of texts for publication: as chaplain to Whitgift, he approved *Richard III* for publication in 1597 and he was commissioned as a government propagandist to write the official account of the Essex rising (*A Sermon Preached at Paul's Cross*, 1601; STC 1454).[128] During James's reign, Barlow continued to promote the views of the reigning monarch. He worked to bolster the king's reputation after the exposure of the Gunpowder Plot in 1605 (in, for example, *The Sermon Preached at Paul's Cross, the Tenth day of November, Being the Next Sunday After the Discovery of this Late Horrible Treason*, 1606; STC 1455) and in response to Robert Persons with his *Answer to a Catholic Englishman* (1609; STC 1446).[129] He was also commissioned to produce the official account of the Hampton Court Conference of 1604 (as *The Sum and Substance of the Conference*), which was criticized for making James side exclusively with the bishops and assigned James the famous line, 'No Bishop, no King'.[130] As Law's early output is mostly characterized by Barlow's commissioned works of Jacobean propaganda and Shakespeare's histories, this narrow publishing specialism informs a reading of the plays and an understanding of how they were viewed by their publisher. Farmer has discussed how John Norton's Caroline investment in these same Shakespearean histories – which he inherited from Law – promotes a 'royalist' reading.[131] A similar point can be made for Law's editions. For Butter, 'history' was not necessarily allied to the monarch, despite the stationer's exclusive involvement in monarchical histories; but for Law, it was. At the Sign of the Fox, Shakespeare's histories exist alongside state-sponsored Jacobean propaganda to promote the authority of the monarch.

Law's investment in the fourth quarto of *Richard II* (1608), a playbook that is rarely considered in the context of its Jacobean publication, provides a revealing example. In this edition, which consists of two issues with variant title pages, the 'Parliament Sceane and the deposing of King Richard' is printed for the first time and advertised on the title page of one issue (STC 22311; see Figure 3.5). The provenance of the Q4 scene is a complex issue: critics are divided over whether it was censored during

[128] SRO3997; Arber, III, p. 93.
[129] C. S. Knighton, 'Barlow, William (*d.* 1613)', *ODNB*, online ed., January 2008, https://doi.org/10 .1093/ref:odnb/1443 (accessed 13 June 2020), paras. 5–6.
[130] *The Svmme and Svbstance of the Conference* (London, 1604; STC 1456), F2v.
[131] Alan Farmer, 'John Norton and the Politics of Shakespeare's History Plays in Caroline England', in *Shakespeare's Stationers*, ed. Straznicky, pp. 147–76 (esp. pp. 170–74).

Figure 3.5 Title page from *Richard II* (Q4 1608; STC 22311).

Elizabeth's reign or represents a later addition to the play.[132] By whatever means Law acquired the new scene and inserted it within his text, what is especially interesting – but mostly overlooked – is the way in which this scene resonates with Jacobean political concerns and Law's output. As discussed in Chapter 2, the scene explores the role and power of Parliament, and it first appeared in print at a time when James was engaged in increasingly heated debates about the issue of union and Parliament's right to be an agent of monarchical opposition. James explicitly outlined his views on the responsibilities of the king and Parliament and, in his 1607 address, suggested the impropriety of the Houses' resistance:

> Every honest man desireth a perfect Vnion ... If after your so long talke of Vnion in all this long Session of Parliament, yee rise without agreeing vpon any particular; what will the neighbour Princes iudge, whose eyes are all fixed vpon the conclusion of this Action, but that the King is refused in his desire, whereby the Nation should be taxed, and the King disgraced?[133]

Significantly, the title page of Law's playbook describes the addition as 'the Parliament Sceane'. On a Jacobean publication, this designation has much more application to the union disputes in Parliament that challenged James's authority, than to a recollection of Elizabethan successional issues – which tends to be the emphasis of most critical discussion. Law may have been responsible for naming it the 'Parliament' scene, and his contribution to government propaganda through an investment in Barlow's works also suggests a way of reading this scene and the play as a whole: Parliament's resistance to Richard and its work as an organ of monarchical deposition is emphatically condemned. *Richard II*, with its new addition, offers a vivid account of the divesting and division of monarchical authority with disastrous consequences. In contrast, Butter's editions register more tension in their connection to James I. The proximity of the two stationers fuelled their investments and, for readers, potentially activated an interpretative connection between publications offered for retail and wholesale purchase at St Austin's Gate, which is further enhanced through imprints that created new geographies of material texts.

Conclusions

While history-play studies tend either to ignore the Jacobean period or claim that the genre died out by the time of James's reign, performance

---

[132] See Chapter 2, pp. 111–112. [133] *Speech* [31 March 1607], C2v.

and print patterns reveal that this narrative of decline is not accurate. Impelled by the change in monarch and the new political issues and mythologies that came to the fore, different kinds of histories became prominent on stage and in print. Butter's output offers a revealing case study. As a publisher, he consistently invested in news and history and his practices suggest that he was at the centre of a stationer-driven publication network that shaped and read the history play in ways that are almost diametrically opposed to the usual critical narrative. His dramatic and non-dramatic publications blur the boundary between news and history, showing them to have similar uses and highlighting the artificiality of rigid temporal distinctions. His output suggests how plays dramatizing ancient British history and recent Tudor history could be linked together through an interest and investment in topical texts that promote a politicized Protestant agenda. Despite the increasing importance of antiquarian principles for some early Jacobean historians, Butter resolutely uses and reads history in providential terms, with an eye to secular concerns of state. His publishing strategies reveal critically overlooked ways of reading history plays: they highlight connections between the 'chronicle histories' *When You See Me You Know Me* and *King Lear* that achieved a new currency at the beginning of James's reign, and between *If You Know Not Me* and *King Lear*, both invested in ideas of union squared through its political dimensions and application to Jacobean England. Butter's ways of reading were informed by the physical geography of the London book trade: his bookshop at the Sign of the Pied Bull in St Paul's Churchyard was at the centre of a gathering place for acquiring news, engaging in political and religious discussion, and publishing Shakespeare.

One of the central arguments of this book is that publishers are key participants in directing ideas, parameters, and experiences of genre. They are historical readers, who determine the presentation of history plays in ways that also affect how other readers – both early modern and modern – approach these plays. Butter's editions and his reputation within the book trade have been largely overlooked by modern criticism. Our access to these plays has, however, been mediated by Butter's interest in them and an understanding of his publishing strategies helps us to situate these plays in their early modern context. The experiences of early modern readers and book buyers may have been shaped by Butter's role as publisher – a point that also tends to be overlooked. Butter acquired a popular reputation in St Paul's Churchyard as a bookseller of newsworthy texts. All of his independently published playbooks prominently advertise his name on their title-page imprints, usually alongside his bookshop location. Although not all publishers' imprints carry interpretative currency, Butter's possibly did. He became part of the material texts, and his publication 'brand' – one that favoured topical matters of church and state with broadly conceived Protestant sympathies – may have profoundly directed the interpretations of other readers.

CHAPTER 4

Collecting Histories
The Jaggard–Pavier Collection (1619) and Shakespeare's First Folio (1623)

This chapter concentrates on history plays in collection because the act of gathering and publishing texts as a bound group involves an assessment of 'kinds', makes a statement about genre, and promotes an interpretative, intertextual exchange across the plays. My previous chapters have examined processes of print selection and presentation for single-text history plays, showing how publishers' reading strategies and their understanding of 'history' can be accessed through an assessment of their wider output. Except as they mingled on the bookstalls and in the *Sammelbände* of readers (such as John Harington), these playbooks were not materially found or bound together. In contrast, collections issued by stationers offer specific parameters for comparative readings, which are often directed by collective paratexts, such as general title pages and contents pages. For history plays, these practices of collection construct overarching historical narratives and they sometimes indicate which histories were most valued, as stationers select and privilege certain pasts above others.

This chapter argues that, beyond two-part plays, the first collections of commercial drama to prioritize 'history' as part of their design were the planned collection of ten plays published in 1619, which I call the Jaggard–Pavier collection, and Shakespeare's First Folio in 1623.[1] While my discussion highlights the collections' overlap in agency, author, and play selection, I also emphasize the distinctiveness of their two approaches to history as a dramatic genre. The Jaggard–Pavier collection draws attention to the flexibility, fluidity, and inclusivity of history. It incorporates monarchical histories alongside citizen and legendary histories, and resembles *Sammelbände* in its material construction, encouraging readers to

---

[1] This group of ten plays published in 1619 is usually labelled the 'Pavier quartos', after publisher Thomas Pavier and their format. Recent critics, including James Marino (*Owning*, p. 111) and Adam Hooks (*Selling*, pp. 119–20), have referred to them by their printer, William Jaggard. I expand on the reasons for my designation later in the chapter.

participate not only in the arrangement of texts but in their construction of genre. Shakespeare's First Folio, in contrast, singularizes and solidifies its 'Histories'. It proposes a dramatic category that is based exclusively on English monarchical history from the medieval and Tudor periods. This chapter argues that focusing on history plays in collection helps us to understand the different ways in which history could be defined, ordered, and interpreted and to complicate the ongoing use of Shakespeare's Folio as a touchstone for the early modern history play. While my previous chapters have mainly considered individual publishers, this chapter draws attention to evidence of collaborative (and indeterminate) agency in the collections' design, and shows how members of a publishing syndicate might even advance competing notions of history – in relation to, for example, ideas of timelessness and timeliness. It highlights the multiple readings of publication agents, which, in turn, open up the potential for a wide range of responses from book buyers.

Defining what is meant by a 'collection' of plays is a task fraught with difficulty. In his monumental *Bibliography of the English Printed Drama to the Restoration*, Greg admitted that distinguishing between single editions and collections 'caused more trouble than any other point of procedure', and he ultimately 'let convenience rather than logic' govern the process.[2] Greg orders his list of collections by author and when he doubts a collection's status, he incorporates it, by default, into his main chronological list of single-text editions. For Greg, collections tend to be sizable, reaching a considerable number of pages, and two-part play collections are not counted.[3] While crucially departing from Greg's gathering of play paratexts printed in collection alongside single-text editions of the same play, Berger and Massai's *Paratexts in English Printed Drama to 1642* broadly follows Greg's identification of collections and also arranges them by author.[4] The list provided by Kewes ('Collected Editions of Plays, 1604–1720') in *Authorship and Appropriation* similarly excludes two-part plays, whilst further narrowing the parameters of collections by omitting translations of classical and continental plays, nonce collections,

---

[2] Greg, IV, p. xxviii.

[3] Greg incorporates plays that 'bore some close relation to one another' in the chronological list of single-text editions (ibid.).

[4] Thomas L. Berger and Sonia Massai (eds.), with Tania Demetriou, *Paratexts in English Printed Drama to 1642*, 2 vols. (Cambridge: Cambridge University Press, 2014), I, p. xvii; II, pp. 955–59.

and those 'which are primarily non-dramatic (even if they contain plays)'.[5]

In contrast, I follow the criteria adopted by Farmer and Lesser's *Database of Early English Playbooks* where any book that contains more than one text, at least one of which is a play, counts as a dramatic collection.[6] This inclusive definition incorporates large multi-play collections, two-part play collections, and those which feature a single play alongside non-dramatic texts. It is important for me to consider two-part plays (such as *Tamburlaine*) as a collection: despite their shared characters and continuous storyline, they are nevertheless separate plays that were performed on different days in the theatre. The fact that Millington inititally published *The First Part of the Contention* and *The True Tragedy of Richard Duke of York* as single-text editions in different formats (quarto and octavo) demonstrates that it was not inevitable that multi-part plays would be issued and read together. Although readers may have collected these plays themselves, publishers did not combine them until *The Whole Contention* in 1619. While there is a clear difference in design between multi-part play collections that continue the same narrative and collections, especially expansive ones such as Jonson's and Shakespeare's folios, that unite plays on different subjects, they are both still 'collections'; and the former is useful for understanding the origins of larger collections. Similarly, collections that include a single play alongside non-dramatic texts do not privilege drama in the same way as, for example, Edward Blount's edition of Lyly's *Six Court Comedies* (1632); but they suggest how plays were read alongside non-dramatic texts, promote specific interpretations of the included items, and shed light on the development of exclusively dramatic collections.

A similar starting point is also favoured by Lyons in her work on play collections, although I do exclude single-text editions that could be connected in terms of seriality and/or related content, but that never materialized as collections bound by stationers.[7] Lyons pushes the concept of a collection to its extreme and shows how texts that were not strictly issued together may have been marketed as a 'serial collection' – an example being John Lyly's plays (*Endymion*, *Galatea*, and *Midas*) that were published as individual quarto editions between 1591 and 1592, and united through a

---

[5] Paulina Kewes, *Authorship and Appropriation: Writing for the Stage in England, 1660–1710* (Oxford: Clarendon Press, 1998), pp. 236–46.

[6] 'Types of Records', *DEEP*, http://deep.sas.upenn.edu/using_deep.html (accessed 9 April 2021).

[7] Lyons, 'Serials', pp. 185–220; Lyons, 'English Printed Drama in Collection before Jonson and Shakespeare', unpublished PhD thesis, University of Illinois (2011), ch. 1.

collected Stationers' Register entry on 4 October 1591.[8] Lyons's approach is vital for understanding the flexibility of collections and the processes of book-buying and reading that informed planned collections. I am interested, however, in texts that actually left publishers' hands as a bound group. My previous chapters consider how publishers' specialisms construct 'conceptual' collections of history plays (such as Wise's medieval histories or Butter's Protestant histories), despite being sold as single-text editions. The development of bibliographically identifiable history-play collections, the focus of this chapter, is significant as they materially define the genre in relation to a number of specific texts and direct the experience of readers who encounter pre-formed, or almost pre-formed, groups of plays in the bookshop.

To clarify my parameters for a *stationer's collection* of dramatic texts and provide a tool for further research, the Appendix offers a table of play collections printed between *c.*1560 and 1659. This list of 123 collections draws on Farmer and Lesser's *DEEP*, and can be used, at a glance, for comparing collection patterns (and precedents) for commercial and non-commercial playbooks; determining which publishers repeatedly invested in and developed collections; identifying the format (i.e. folio, quarto, octavo, etc.) of collections; and establishing, with an eye to genre classifications, whether a collection contains a contents page that categorizes its texts. Because my emphasis is on how stationers collect, arrange, and present their texts, I include nonce collections (where stationers reissue separately printed texts as a collection, containing a unifying title page) and tract volumes (where separately printed texts are issued together but without a general title page). I do not, however, include *Sammelbände*, or collections of texts gathered by readers. While the preparation of a planned collection differs considerably from the process of gathering previously printed texts to form a nonce collection or tract volume, I am interested in *all* groups of texts (planned, nonce, or tract) that leave a stationer's premises as a collection.

Three key points about history plays in collection can be extrapolated from the table and a brief survey of the texts it features. First, prior to the 1619 Jaggard–Pavier collection, commercial history plays mainly appeared in collection as two-part plays: *1* and *2 Tamburlaine* (in 1590, 1593, and 1597); *1* and *2 Troublesome Reign of King John* (in 1591 and 1611), *1* and *2 Edward IV* (in 1599, 1600, 1605, 1613, 1619), and *The Conspiracy and Tragedy of Charles Duke of Byron* (in 1608), which dramatizes

---

[8] SRO3287; Arber, II, p. 596.

contemporary French history through the treasonous plots of Charles de
Gontaut, Duc de Biron (1562–1602).[9] In light of this pattern, the
1619 and 1623 ventures are distinctly significant: they bring together
not only a greater number of history plays but also those that dramatize
unrelated historical pasts. Lyons's work on seriality and historicity stresses
the continuities between the earlier two-part plays and the collections from
1619 and 1623, which is useful for understanding the print precedents
that shaped their publication.[10] However, it is also important to stress their
innovations, as nothing closely resembling these two play collections that
feature a considerable number of historical dramas had appeared in print.
Prior to 1619, the only commercial history plays to be published in
collections that were *not* exclusively two-part plays were Daniel's *Philotas*
(in 1605 as part of *Certain Small Poems*, and later in *Certain Small Works*,
1607 and 1611) and Jonson's *Sejanus* and *Catiline* (in 1616 as part of his
Works). None of these collections position history as an organizational
principle. The title page for *Certain Small Poems* suggests that the majority
of the collection is made up of 'Small Poems' and that *Philotas* – as a
'Tragedie' – represents a different 'kind' of text (the collection also includes
the 'Tragedie' of *Cleopatra*, but this is not advertised on the title page).[11]
In Jonson's *Works*, dramatic genre (especially something as slippery as
'history') does not order the collection. The plays are arranged chronologically, according to their order of composition, and the contents page
serves primarily to advertise their connection to specific (and mostly
aristocratic) patrons (see Figure 4.1).[12]

Second, it has not thus far been recognized that, before Jonson's *Works*
in 1616, *all* commercial plays in stationers' collections were histories – that
is, according to the parameters of this study, plays that were based on a
recognizable historical past. These collections mainly take the form of two-
part plays. *Tamburlaine*, published by Richard Jones, is the first clear
example of a commercial play in collection.[13] In addition to the fact that
these histories were theatrically linked as sequels in the playhouse, the
condition of history – of it being continuous and without clear-cut

---

[9] *The Troublesome Reign* was not actually a multi-part play in performance. It became a play
'collection' only through the insertion – in print – of an artificial division in the middle of the
play's action.

[10] Lyons, 'Serials', pp. 185–220.

[11] Samuel Daniel, *Certaine Small Poems* (London, 1605; STC 6239), A1r.

[12] Jonson, *Workes*, ¶3r.

[13] Earlier, in 1578, Jones published *1* and *2 Promos and Cassandra* as a two-part play collection. These
two plays may have been staged by a professional acting troupe, but their origins are uncertain.

The Catalogue.

Euery Man in his Humor,	To Mr. CAMBDEN.
Euery Man out of his Humor,	To the INNES of COVRT.
Cynthias Reuells,	To the COVRT.
Poëtaſter,	To Mr. RICH. MARTIN.
Seianus,	To ESME Lo. Aubigny.
The Foxe,	To the VNIVERSITIES.
The ſilent Woman,	To Sir FRAN. STVART.
The Alchemiſt,	To the Lady WROTH.
Catiline,	To the Earle of PEMBROK.
Epigrammes,	To the ſame.

The Forreſt,
Entertaynments,
Panegyre,
Maſques,
Barriers.

¶ 3

Figure 4.1 Catalogue from Jonson's *Works* (1616; STC 14751), ¶3r.

divisions or conclusions in its action – and the practices of non-dramatic historical publications likely contributed to their appearance as printed collections. 'History' as a branch of knowledge about the past is characterized by processes of gathering and ordering. Many non-dramatic histories, such as Holinshed's *Chronicles*, were ordered by year and later amended and expanded. The basic feature of history plays – that they dramatize the past – therefore situates them within a tradition of collection, not only in terms of sources, subjects, and narratives, but also material production. Early patterns of collecting history plays and reading non-dramatic histories potentially informed the design of the 1619 and 1623 collections, particularly as some of the publishers involved in these ventures invested in a number of ordered, historical texts.

Finally, one of my arguments in this chapter is that the contents page – or 'Catalogue' – in Shakespeare's Folio proposes a definition of the history play that is unprecedented in its specificity and exclusivity. Prior to the 1623 Folio, no other contents page from a play collection (commercial or non-commercial) features history as a prominent classificatory principle. Eleven collections contain contents pages: Norton's *All Such Treatises* (*c.*1570; see Figure 0.4), Gascoigne's *A Hundred Sundry Flowers* (1573) and *The Posies* [1575], Churchyard's *The First Part of Churchyard's Chips* (1575 and 1578), Seneca's *Ten Tragedies* (1581), Gascoigne's *Whole Works* (1587), Daniel's *The Poetical Essays* (1599) and *Certain Small Works* (1607 and 1611), and Jonson's *Works* (1616). None of these use 'history' as a clear category. Jonson's *Works* witnesses the only previous use of the term 'Catalogue' in a play collection, but history does not appear as a generic marker, nor do any other genre labels. As a title-page description, 'history' is used in only a few collections: *1* and *2 Promos and Cassandra* ('The Right Excellent and famous Historye of Promos and Cassandra: Deuided into two Commicall Discourses'), which seems, in this context, to evoke a fictional story, and *The Serpent of Division* (1590), which describes its prose text as 'the true History or Mappe of Romes ouerthrowe', but classifies the collection's play – *Gorboduc* – as a 'Tragedye'.[14] The term 'history' does not appear on any other title page for a play collection until 1619 and does not appear on a contents page until 1623.

[14] George Whetstone, *The Right Excellent and famous Historye of Promos and Cassandra* (London, 1578; STC 25347), A1r. John Lydgate, Thomas Norton, and Thomas Sackville, *The Serpent of Deuision [and] Gorboduc* (London, 1590; STC 17029), A1r. *1* and *2 Tamburlaine* are described on the title page as 'Tragicall Discourses', but a recognition of their historical subject is implied in Jones's preface 'To the Gentlemen Readers and others that take pleasure in reading Histories' (A1r–A2r).

These opening observations confirm the import of the 1619 and 1623 ventures for the history play. The rest of this chapter examines these collections in turn. By bringing together accounts of various national pasts that have different dramatic interests and relationships to historical records, the Jaggard–Pavier collection does not propose specific parameters for the genre, but prioritizes the reader's role in ordering, interpreting, and applying its histories. It offers a model of production that has more enduring relevance for the period than the 1623 Folio. This later collection, in contrast, 'fixes' history as a dramatic genre in a way that is not witnessed in any other collection before or, indeed, after its publication. As this chapter considers, the ventures weigh their histories and applications differently: the 1619 collection seems invested in a range of historical pasts and potentially advances a united 'British' identity for its readers, whereas the Folio seems to value English history and an English collective identity above others.

The 1619 Jaggard–Pavier Collection

In 1619, ten plays, all of which had been previously printed, were published as nine playbooks: *The Whole Contention* (containing *The First Part of the Contention* and *The True Tragedy of Richard Duke of York*), *Pericles*, *A Yorkshire Tragedy*, *The Merchant of Venice*, *The Merry Wives of Windsor*, *King Lear*, *Henry V*, *1 Sir John Oldcastle* and *A Midsummer Night's Dream*.[15] Some of the playbooks feature false title-page imprints, which obscure the fact that they were printed at the same time and involved the same group of stationers: William and Isaac Jaggard and Thomas Pavier. Five editions contain false dates, one contains no publication date, and at least two give false publication details.[16] It was not until Greg's seminal essay 'On Certain False Dates in Shakespearian Quartos' (1908) that these editions were rediscovered as a connected group of plays. Thanks to the work of scholars including Massai, Lesser and Stallybrass, and Hooks, the entrenched critical account that, beginning with the New Bibliographers,

---

[15] See STC 26101, 22341, 22297, 22300, 22293, 22291, 18796, 22303.

[16] The five plays with false dates are *Henry V* ('1608'), *Sir John Oldcastle* ('1600'), *A Midsummer Night's Dream* ('1600'), *The Merchant of Venice* ('1600'), and *King Lear* ('1608'); *The Whole Contention* is undated. False imprints are found in: *A Midsummer Night's Dream* ('Printed by Iames Roberts') and *The Merchant of Venice* ('Printed by J. Roberts'). The imprints for *The Merry Wives of Windsor* ('Printed for Arthur Johnson') and *King Lear* ('Printed for Nathaniel Butter') are not necessarily false; both Johnson and Butter may have been involved or cooperated in their publication.

proposed a narrative of piracy to explain the peculiarities of these 1619 playbooks is starting to change.[17] A court injunction from May 1619, in which the Lord Chamberlain, William Herbert, third earl of Pembroke, ordered that 'no playes that his Majesties players do play shalbe printed without consent of somme of them', has been routinely used to suggest that Pavier acted in an underhand way and tried to circumvent the injunction by including false publication details.[18] While the order suggests that the King's Men were attempting to control the circulation of their plays in print, there is no evidence to indicate that it applied to reprinted editions, the rights for which were already assigned to specific stationers.[19] Indeed, Pavier held the rights to five of these plays, meaning that he was entitled to publish them; and he possibly collaborated with other stationers – including Butter (with whom he had previously worked on Heywood's *If You Know Not Me*) – on the remaining editions for which the copyright was not derelict.[20] Because the playbooks do not imitate the typographical features of earlier editions and even prominently display the Jaggards' devices on each title page, the false imprints could not have been seriously intended to obscure publication details for members of the Stationers' Company, who would recognize these features.[21] Neither Pavier nor the Jaggards seem to have experienced any negative repercussions when the editions appeared, which strongly implies that this venture was not a piratical one. Rather than speculating about the unusual production circumstances in further detail, I concentrate on these plays as a collection that prioritizes ideas of 'history' as part of its selection and presentation strategies, and involves readers in this process.

Although none of the surviving copies are accompanied by a general printed title page, evidence suggests that early modern book buyers

[17] See Massai, *Editor*, ch. 4; Lesser and Stallybrass, 'Shakespeare'; Hooks, *Selling*, pp.112–24.
[18] William A. Jackson (ed.), *Records of the Court of the Stationers' Company, 1602 to 1640* (London: Bibliographical Society, 1957), p. 110. The source of the injunction was a letter written by Pembroke, which is no longer extant but survives as a summary in the records of the Stationers' Company.
[19] Massai, *Editor*, pp. 109–12.
[20] Marino, *Owning*, pp. 112–14. Pavier clearly owned the rights to *Henry V*, *The First Part of the Contention* and *The True Tragedy* (issued as *The Whole Contention*), *1 Sir John Oldcastle*, and *A Yorkshire Tragedy*, and, along with *Pericles*, these are the five editions on which his initials appear. Pavier may, at some point, have acquired the rights to *Pericles*, as the successors to his titles – Edward Brewster and Robert Bird – seem to have believed that the rights to this play were transferred to them by Pavier's widow (see Marino, *Owning*, p. 130). It is likely that the rights to *A Midsummer Night's Dream* and possibly *The Merchant of Venice* were derelict.
[21] The device on all of the editions, with the exception of *Midsummer*, is McKerrow #283, which Jaggard started to use in about 1610. *Midsummer* features McKerrow #136, which belonged to Jaggard from at least 1607. See McKerrow, *Devices*, pp. 49, 110; Marino, *Owning*, pp. 112–14.

encountered the plays as a collection in 1619 and I follow scholars such as Andrew Murphy in describing them as such.[22] Continuous signatures appear in *The Whole Contention* and *Pericles*, which indicates that the plays were intended to form a bibliographically continuous sequence; indeed, these three plays remain, in terms of their bibliographical identity, a collection. *The Whole Contention*, moreover, collects two distinct theatrical plays – *The First Part of the Contention* and *The True Tragedy* – under one title. The title page claims that it has been 'newly corrected and enlarged' and 'Diuided into two Parts'; but two plays have, in fact, been united, rather than a single play divided.[23] After *Pericles*, the continuous signatures are abandoned, which implies a revised publication design. The nine playbooks nevertheless seem to have remained together and were possibly bound as a collection at the point of their original sale. Lesser and Stallybrass have drawn attention to the absence of stab-stitch holes in many surviving copies, which suggests that the plays were purchased as part of a collection, rather than being loosely stitched together as individual playbooks in preparation for being bound by readers.[24] When the provenance of extant copies can be traced, it often reveals that the plays were preserved in collection during the seventeenth century – and some continue to be. However, they vary in the order in which they were arranged, making up a flexible collection.[25] It seems as if the 'third' edition of Heywood's *A Woman Killed with Kindness*, printed and published in 1617 by the Jaggards, was sometimes bound with the 1619 editions. Jeffrey Todd Knight found a 'ghost image' of Heywood's title page on the final verso of the Huntington Library's copy of *Henry V*, and Lesser and Stallybrass have noted an absence of stab-stitch holes in some extant copies of the edition, which implies they were also sold as part of a collection.[26] These plays represent 'the first attempt by a publisher to sell a bound book composed exclusively of plays from the professional

---

[22] Murphy, *Shakespeare in Print*, pp. 36–41.

[23] Shakespeare, *The Whole Contention between the two Famous Houses, Lancaster and Yorke* (London, [1619]; STC 26101), A1r.

[24] Lesser and Stallybrass, 'Shakespeare', pp. 119–33. For the significance of stab-stitching, see Aaron T. Pratt, 'Stab-Stitching and the Status of Early English Playbooks As Literature', *The Library*, 7th ser., 16:3 (2015), 304–28.

[25] Two known collections of the 1619 quartos survive in seventeenth-century binding: one at the Folger (STC 26101, copy 3 – the 'Gwynn copy') and one at Texas Christian University. See Lesser and Stallybrass, 'Shakespeare', pp. 123–25; Knight, 'Making', p. 326.

[26] Lesser and Stallybrass, 'Shakespeare', pp. 126–30. Jeffrey Todd Knight, 'Invisible Ink: A Note on Ghost Images in Early Printed Books', *Textual Cultures*, 5:2 (2010), 53–62. The 1617 quarto of *A Woman Killed with Kindness* is the second extant edition of the play, but its title page describes it as the 'third Edition', which suggests an earlier one has been lost.

theatres', and even with the Heywood addition, they form a largely Shakespearean collection of previously printed plays, most of which had been performed by the Chamberlain's Men/King's Men.[27] Because the inclusion of Heywood's earlier edition was not consistent and was not likely part of the original publication design, I concentrate in this chapter on the plays prepared and published in 1619.[28]

Buyers of the 1619 editions were, in effect, acquiring and assembling an early collection of history plays. While not all of the plays dramatize events that once took place or individuals who once existed (or were believed, at some point, to have taken place or existed), the editions' paratexts tend to emphasize a connection with 'history' as it relates to accounts of the past – especially when the playbooks are considered as a group. As Lyons summarizes:

> That five of the ten plays were explicitly advertised as 'histories' on their title pages [i.e. *Henry V, King Lear, Sir John Oldcastle, Pericles*, and *The Merchant of Venice*] and the remaining five were implicitly or explicitly linked to historical narratives suggests that dramatic 'kind' dominated both the selection and marketing of the Pavier quartos.[29]

The reading of history suggested by these quartos does not, however, prefigure the Folio's narrow categorization where history is synonymous with the English monarchical past, nor does it recall the subject matter of the bestselling single-text editions published by Wise and (later) Law, which had previously popularized Shakespeare as a writer of medieval monarchical history. Instead, the 1619 collection fashions 'Shakespeare' as a dramatist of different kinds of history and encourages readers to draw connections between unrelated historical pasts. It not only features English monarchical history (in *The Whole Contention* and *Henry V*), but also citizen, legendary, and classical histories. With a few important exceptions discussed later, most of the playbooks preserve the paratexts from their previous editions, which was common practice with reprints. However, as a collection, new interpretive links between the plays are introduced, which offer new frameworks and ways of reading the reproduced paratexts. The plays seem to advance an expansive notion of 'history' through the paratexts' engagement with ideas of truth, time, and authorship.

---

[27] Lesser and Stallybrass, 'Shakespeare', p. 130.

[28] For example, *A Woman Killed* is not part of the Gwynn copy at the Folger (STC 26101 copy 3), which is preserved in seventeenth-century binding.

[29] Lyons, 'Serials', p. 199.

First, paratextual parallels establish an emphasis on 'true' histories – both in the sense of an assurance of historical accuracy and of worthiness – which unites some of the collection's diverse pasts.[30] As discussed throughout this book, truth is a key, but slippery, concept for defining and validating 'history'. Creede's and Butter's publications advance claims of truthfulness, conflating the two dominant senses of historical accuracy and truthful sentiment and announcing their histories' connection to ongoing historiographical debate. In their wider output, neither Pavier nor the Jaggards invest in 'truth' as consistently as Creede and Butter; but the 1619 editions, as a group, seem to insist upon a reading that is attentive to the interplay between history and truth. The label 'true' appears on the title pages of *King Lear* (which features ancient British history, considered at length in Chapter 3), as well as *Pericles*, *A Yorkshire Tragedy*, and *1 Sir John Oldcastle*. The latter two dramatize citizen histories, and both contain attributions to Shakespeare, although neither were written by him. *A Yorkshire Tragedy* draws on a Jacobean murder case from April 1605, in which Walter Calverly killed his two sons and stabbed his wife. The title page underlines the play's presentation of real events by describing it as 'Not so New, as Lamentable and true', phrasing which also advertises the admonitory potential of the material.[31] Both the attribution and description appear in the first edition from 1608 (STC 22340), but in the 1619 collection this title page establishes connections with other plays, including *1 Sir John Oldcastle*, which also dramatizes a subject's life – in this case the life of the eponymous Lollard martyr during the reign of Henry V. This play is introduced on the title page as 'The first part | Of the true and honorable history' (see Figure 4.2), which again announces the worthiness of the subject, as well as its truthful representation and implied position as part of a sequence.[32] Only one part of *Oldcastle* is extant, however, and known to have been printed. In contrast, the title page of *Pericles* (STC 26101) seems to advertise its completeness alongside its truthfulness: it is 'the true Relation of the whole History, aduentures, and fortunes of the saide Prince', phrasing which suggests the play is linked to a known past that it dramatizes accurately and in its entirety.[33] One effect of these different applications is conceptually to bind together the

---

[30] Cf. ibid., p. 195.

[31] Thomas Middleton (?)/('W. Shakespeare'), *A Yorkshire Tragedie* (London, 1619; STC 22341).

[32] Michael Drayton, Richard Hathaway, Anthony Munday, and Robert Wilson ('William Shakespeare'), *The first part Of the true and honorable history, of the Life of Sir Iohn Old-castle, the good Lord Cobham* (London, 1600 [i.e. 1619]; STC 18796), A1r.

[33] Shakespeare [and George Wilkins], *Pericles, Prince of Tyre* (London, 1619; STC 26101), chi1r.

The firſt part

Of the true & hono-
rable hiſtory, of the Life of
Sir Iohn Old-caſtle, the good
Lord Cobham.

*As it hath bene lately aƈted by the Right
honorable the Earle of Notingham
Lord High Admirall of England,
his Seruants.*

Written by William Shakeſpeare.

London printed for T.P.
1600.

Figure 4.2 Title page from *1 Sir John Oldcastle* (Q2 1600 [1619]; STC 18796).

1619 plays and their flexible notions of truthfulness, which also establishes an overlap with ongoing historiographical discourses about the role of 'truth' in 'history'.

Second, the collection refashions its unhistorical plays as 'histories' – in the sense of an account of a recognizable past – through individual paratexts and the interpretative implications of binding these plays with others. *The Merchant of Venice* does not dramatize events that were once thought to have taken place, but it is described on its title page as 'The Excellent History of the Merchant of Venice', which mostly follows the phrasing of its first edition from 1600.[34] In the context of that edition, 'history' evokes a fictional story (and perhaps specifically, the story of a fictional life); but in 1619, alongside other 'true' histories and English monarchical histories, the term seems to signify an account of a real past. *A Midsummer Night's Dream* advertises its historicity through proximity rather than paratext. As Lyons identifies, its plot draws on the classical histories of Theseus and Hippolyta, and Pyramus and Thisbe.[35] By including this play in a collection that displays a clear interest in the historical past through plays such as *Henry V*, *The Whole Contention*, *King Lear*, *A Yorkshire Tragedy*, and *1 Sir John Oldcastle*, the historical setting and classical characters of *A Midsummer Night's Dream* are brought to the fore. Of all the 1619 plays, however, this edition (STC 22303) makes the least effort to advertise its historicity: the title page offers no description of the play's subject matter beyond its short title and it is the only one of the collection to contain a different woodcut, which seems to announce its separability from the other plays.[36]

Another example of the collection advancing the historicity of its non-histories can be seen in *The Merry Wives of Windsor*, a play in which the events are entirely fictitious and the theatrical character of Falstaff takes centre stage. A prominent position is given to Falstaff on the title page of the 1619 edition: 'A Most pleasant and excellent conceited Comedy of Sir Iohn Falstaffe, and the Merry Wiues of Windsor' (see Figure 4.3).[37] The spacing and layout of the title page closely resembles the collection's *1 Sir John Oldcastle* (STC 18796): the fourth title-line of each play begins with either 'Sir Iohn Old-castle' or 'Sir Iohn Falstaffe' (both in italics; see Figure 4.2). These parallels bring to mind the Oldcastle-Falstaff debacle

---

[34] Shakespeare, *The Excellent History of the Merchant of Venice* (London, 1600 [i.e. 1619]; STC 22297], A1r.
[35] Lyons, 'Serials', p. 200.   [36] See note 21 above.
[37] Shakespeare, *A Most pleasaunt and excellent conceited Comedy, of Sir Iohn Falstaffe and the merrie Wiues of Windsor* (London, 1619; STC 22300), A1r.

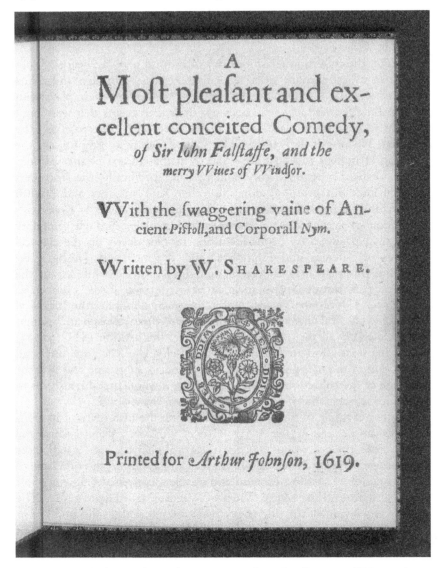

A

Moſt pleaſant and ex-
cellent conceited Comedy,
of Sir Iohn Falſtaffe, and the
merry VViues of VVindſor.

VVith the ſwaggering vaine of Ancient *Piſtoll*, and Corporall *Nym.*

Written by W. SHAKESPEARE.

Printed for *Arthur Iohnſon,* 1619.

Figure 4.3   Title page from *The Merry Wives of Windsor* (Q2 1619; STC 22300).

and the historicizing of Shakespeare's most unhistorical character in the
Henry IV plays, which is further underlined through the printed prologue
to *Oldcastle* that assures readers it 'is no pamper'd Glutton we present,
| Nor aged Councellour to youthfull sinne' (A2r). The identical spacing of

the title lines might even engender confusion and the continuing entanglement of the two figures (discussed earlier in Chapter 2). Labelled as a 'Comedy', *Merry Wives* seems to announce its connection to historical individuals and history plays such as *1* and *2 Henry IV*, *Henry V*, and *Oldcastle*, which feature either Falstaff as Hal's companion or Oldcastle, the Lollard martyr. Indeed, the play's link to *Henry V*, also part of the 1619 collection, is established through the plot description for *Merry Wives*, which includes the characters Pistol and Nym, who appear in *Henry V*. Although the first edition of *Merry Wives* also named these characters, the 1602 title-page summary is padded out with an additional description of the play's content: 'Entermixed with sundrie variable and pleasing humors, of Syr Hugh the Welch Knight, Iustice Shallow, and his wise Cousin M. Slender'.[38] Significantly, this extra detail is cut from the 1619 title page, which has the effect of prioritizing three named characters – Falstaff, Nym, and Pistol – and therefore securing a connection with *Henry V*, in which these characters feature or are discussed in detail (in contrast to the absent Shallow, Slender, and Sir Hugh).[39] Reshaped through its position in a collection, *Merry Wives* offers a citizen history as a prequel to the monarchical focus of *Henry V*, a continuity that is set up by the largely fictional Falstaff, who continues to be historicized through the Oldcastle entanglement.

Third, parallels in title-page phrasing and *mise en page* ask readers to make links between unrelated and widely separated historical pasts, an approach to history that can be witnessed throughout the period – although not in the design of Shakespeare's Folio Histories. Both *King Lear* and *Henry V* are described, in large type on their title pages, as a 'True Chronicle History' and a 'Chronicle History' (see Figure 4.4), respectively.[40] While this phrasing follows their first-edition title pages, binding these two plays together activates a new hermeneutic context. As discussed in Chapter 3, 'Chronicle History' was infrequently used as a print label for commercial plays and none of those on which it featured were issued in collection.[41] The material contiguity of *King Lear* and *Henry V* in the 1619 collection could remind readers of the chronicles in which both of

[38] Shakespeare, *A Most pleasaunt and excellent conceited Comedie, of Syr Iohn Falstaffe and the merrie Wiues of Windsor* (London, 1602; STC 22299), A2r.
[39] Cf. Lyons ('Serials', pp. 199–200), who suggests a connection between these plays in terms of historicity and seriality, but does not point out the changed title-page blurb for *Merry Wives*.
[40] Shakespeare, *The Chronicle History of Henry the fift* (London, 1608 [i.e. 1619]; STC 22291), A1r; *True Chronicle History of the life and death of King Lear, and his three Daughters* (London, 1608 [i.e. 1619]; STC 22293), A1r.
[41] See also Chapter 3, pp. 163–164.

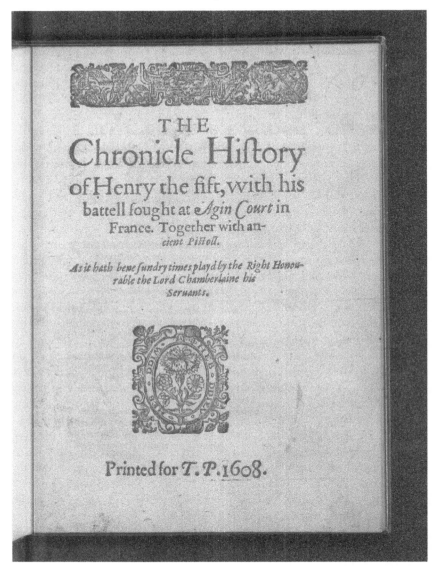

Figure 4.4   Title page from *Henry V* (Q3 1608 [1619]; STC 22291).

these plays find their sources, reinforcing a continuum between the leg-endary British history dramatized in the former and the relatively secure medieval English history of the latter. By uniting – through title-page paratexts and physical proximity – these separated historical pasts, the collection goes beyond the interest in seriality identified by Lyons and which can be seen with *Oldcastle, Henry V*, and *The Whole Contention* through their dramatization of related pasts. Indeed, the 1623 Folio's head titles for these histories – 'The Life of Henry the Fift' and 'The Tragedie of King Lear' – and the plays' inclusion under different generic categories draws attention to their temporal separation and suggests they represent different approaches to the past. The Folio division is less attentive to the Jacobean promotion of ancient British history that was so critical at the beginning of James's reign (as discussed in Chapter 3). In contrast, the 1619 collection could encourage a reading that acknowledges the significance and validity of Britain's originary narratives and reinforces a British, rather than English, national identity, where the 'Chronicle History' of Henry V (typically used to reflect on English military victories) is materially and conceptually linked to the 'Chronicle History' of King Lear/Leir.

Finally, all but one of the 1619 plays (*Henry V* is the exception) contain an attribution to Shakespeare, which therefore creates a history play collection by a single advertised author. Of course, two of these plays – *A Yorkshire Tragedy* and *1 Sir John Oldcastle* – are not thought to be by Shakespeare. In the case of the former, its first printed edition (STC 22340) and Register entry in 1608, both under Pavier's direction, feature the same attribution to Shakespeare, which makes the replication in the 1619 collection less noteworthy. This earlier edition nevertheless indicates Pavier's interest in 'Shakespeare' as a brand and the marketability of his name.[42] More significantly, the first edition of *Oldcastle* in 1600 was issued anonymously. It was very unusual to change an anonymously issued edition to an attributed one (seen also in Wise's second editions of *Richard II* and *Richard III*, discussed in Chapter 2). In this case, the play was clearly not by Shakespeare. Henslowe's *Diary* reveals that it was written by Drayton, Hathaway, Munday, and Wilson, and was intended as a rebuttal to Shakespeare's characterization of Falstaff (originally named Oldcastle) in the two parts of *Henry IV*.[43] While the play features Henry V, the dramatic emphasis is on Oldcastle as a subject, and it differs considerably from the monarchical focus of Shakespeare's plays. Perhaps the Jaggards and Pavier wanted to reinforce the Shakespearean focus of their project through the false attribution or encourage a recollection of

---

[42] SRO5440; Arber, III, p. 377.
[43] Henslowe records payment to the writers in October 1599; see Foakes (ed.), *Henslowe's Diary*, pp. 125–26 (F.65r).

(and possible confusion with) Shakespeare's *Henry IV* plays. As Jowett considers, the accompanying false date ('1600') may be an attempt to strengthen the Shakespearean attribution.[44] Whatever the precise motivation, this new attribution and the inclusion of both *Oldcastle* and *A Yorkshire Tragedy* within the collection fashions history as a dramatic genre that is attentive to both subjects and monarchs, as well as the interconnections between them. It advertises Shakespeare as a dramatist of histories based on the lives of citizens, which is somewhat inaccurate given his dominant emphasis on the actions of rulers, but it also draws attention to the citizens who do share the stage in his histories, such as Falstaff and Jack Cade, and encourages readers to concentrate on their stories.

The title page of *The Whole Contention* also contains a new attribution: 'Written by William Shakespeare, Gent' (see Figure 4.5). It not only marks the first time that these plays – *The First Part of the Contention* and *The True Tragedy* – had been attributed to Shakespeare in print, but also the first time that the dramatist's gentlemanly status had been advertised on a title page (or, indeed, within any part of a printed text). As *The Whole Contention* was printed when the continuous collection was still planned, this attributional precedent is revealing and implies that Shakespeare and his status were important features of the original design. Prior to 1619, both the Jaggards and Pavier displayed some interest in 'Shakespeare' as a marketing strategy: as mentioned, Pavier's 1608 edition of *A Yorkshire Tragedy* was attributed to Shakespeare, and *The Passionate Pilgrim*, published in 1599 and 1612 by the elder Jaggard, was the first collection of poetry to feature a title-page attribution to Shakespeare.[45] Although Lyons describes historicity and seriality as the main concerns of the venture, it seems to me that the Shakespearean identity of the collection is equally important and is not just a supplementary principle.[46] An interest in 'Shakespearean' 'history', which is shared – albeit in a different way – by the Folio, could be described as the driving emphasis of the collection. In contrast to the Folio, this interest is defined by an interplay of transtemporal and transnational 'histories' that pull away from an exclusive emphasis on English monarchical histories and where the lives of British subjects and fictional accounts that connote historicity come to the fore.

---

[44] John Jowett, 'Shakespeare Supplemented', in *The Shakespeare Apocrypha*, ed. Douglas A. Brooks (Lampeter: Edwin Mellen Press, 2007), pp. 39–73 (p. 45); Douglas A. Brooks, 'Sir John Oldcastle and the Construction of Shakespeare's Authorship', *Studies in English Literature, 1500–1900*, 38:2 (1998), 333–61.

[45] See Chapter 2, p. 129. See also Hooks, *Selling*, pp. 111–12.   [46] Lyons, 'Serials', p. 193.

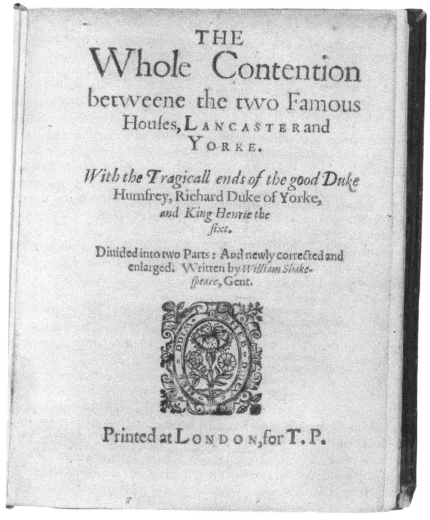

THE
Whole Contention
betweene the two Famous
Houfes, L ANCASTER and
Y ORKE.

With the Tragicall ends of the good Duke
Humfrey, Richard Duke of Yorke,
and King Henrie the
fixt.

Diuided into two Parts : And newly corrected and
enlarged. Written by *William Shake-*
fpeare, Gent.

Printed at L O N D O N, for T. P.

Figure 4.5   Title page from *The Whole Contention* ([1619]; STC 26101).

It is difficult to determine which of the stationers involved in the
1619 venture had most control over its design, including the selection
and presentation of its histories. Extant evidence does not clearly indicate
who took on the *role* of the publisher and there may have been a

collaborative investment.[47] We know that William and Isaac Jaggard printed all of the playbooks; their names are nowhere given, but their devices appear on every title page and the editions use their type throughout.[48] The Stationers' Register reveals that Pavier owned the rights to at least five of the plays and the title-page imprints for these editions display his initials, 'T.P.'[49] A well-established bookseller with an interest in historical texts, Pavier may have invested in all of the plays and therefore acted as the collection's publisher. Lyons takes this view, showing how Pavier's wider dramatic and non-dramatic output was characterized by seriality and historicity, but in doing so, mostly sidesteps the Jaggards. As Lyons demonstrates, Pavier invested in *The Spanish Tragedy* (1602, 1603, 1610) and its prequel, *The First Part of Jeronimo* (1605), as well as the anonymous play *Captain Thomas Stukeley* (1605), which follows the adventures of a historical individual, who fought and died at the Battle of Alcácer Quibir, and is a spinoff from Peele's *Battle of Alcazar*.[50] Pavier also invested in the second edition of *Jack Straw* (1604). As discussed in the Introduction, his presentation of the play – particularly through the inclusion of a woodcut bearing his initials – directs a sympathetic reading of the Peasants' Revolt and seems to prioritize the citizens' plight over the monarch's rule.[51] Pavier was a regular investor in commercial drama and, while the 1619 venture was his first collection, his prior output features plays that could be thematically linked on the basis of historical continuity. It is perhaps illustrative of Pavier's historical interests that all of the 1619 editions for which he owned the rights – *Oldcastle*, *Henry V*, *A Yorkshire Tragedy*, and *The Whole Contention* – dramatize a clearly recognizable past.

William and Isaac Jaggard may have also influenced the venture and its emphasis on history. Like Creede, the Jaggards were printer-publishers, sometimes working as trade printers and sometimes as publishers. They could have taken on a more central role in the 1619 editions than has been generally recognized.[52] Similar to Pavier, the Jaggards display an interest in playbooks and historical texts. William Jaggard had regular contact with theatre companies, because he had inherited the monopoly for playbill printing from James Roberts.[53] He collaborated with Pavier from the beginning of his career, acting as printer for *Jack Straw* (1604), *Captain*

47 Marino, *Owning*, p. 111.
48 Greg first established this point in 'Certain False Dates', pp. 113–31.   49 See note 20 above.
50 Lyons, 'Serials', pp. 193–98.   51 See Introduction, pp. 25–27.
52 For the importance of the Jaggards, see Hooks, *Selling*, pp. 112–24; Lesser and Stallybrass, 'Shakespeare', pp. 130–31; Marino, *Owning*, p. 111; and Massai, *Editor*, pp. 116–21.
53 STC, III, p. 90.

Thomas Stukeley (1605), and *Jeronimo* (1605). His interest in history is also independently maintained: as Hooks proposes, 'Jaggard seems to have had an abiding interest in history (both national and natural), civic duty, and moral improvement.'[54] The elder Jaggard wrote a book on the lord mayors of London (*A View of All the Right Honourable the Lord Mayors of this Honourable City of London*; STC 14343), which he published jointly with Pavier in 1601. He also published Anthony Munday's *Triumphs of a Reunited Britannia* (1605; STC 18279), which emphasizes, on its title page, Munday's position as a citizen and draper of London and suggests a clear parallel with Jaggard's book on the lord mayors and its interest in the London guilds. Munday's *Triumphs* celebrates the election of a new London mayor and 'the antiquitie of Brytaine' (A2r), made topical by James I's proposed union of England and Scotland. Histories of London's lord mayors, such as Munday's and Jaggard's, typically evoke Britain's legendary past because many of the city guilds based their originary narratives on ideas of Troynovant and Britain's Trojan ancestors. Both Munday's and Jaggard's texts are invested in ideas of British identity, which can also be seen through *King Lear* in the 1619 collection and its paratextual contiguity with *Henry V*.

In contrast to his father, Isaac Jaggard may not have been as interested in historical material: he did not write his own civic history, as William did, and, at the time of the 1619 collection, he was still a relatively junior stationer. As Massai proposes, Isaac may have acted as the publisher for Chapman's translation of *The Divine Poem of Musaeus* (1616, STC 18304), Heywood's *A Woman Killed with Kindness* (1617), and a translation of Boccaccio's *Decameron* (1620, STC 3172), all of which give his name in the imprint and seem to establish an interest in 'literary publication'.[55] Isaac's business practices were, however, conflated with his father's. For the texts listed above, William had printed the 1607 edition of *A Woman Killed*, while the other two were entered in the Register to the elder Jaggard.[56] Fuelling this dependency was the fact that William became blind in about 1612–13 and, because of this, Isaac was made free of the Stationers' Company by patrimony on 23 June 1613.[57] Although Isaac seems to have taken on a significant role in the publication of

---

[54] Hooks, *Selling*, p. 125.   [55] Massai, *Editor*, p. 117.
[56] For the Boccaccio translation, see SRO7237; Arber, III, p. 667; and for Chapman's translation, see SRO6703; Arber, III, p. 594. *A Woman Killed* was not entered in the Register; William printed the 1607 edition, which was sold by John Hodgets.
[57] Edwin Eliott Willoughby, *A Printer of Shakespeare: The Books and Times of William Jaggard* (London: Allan, 1934), pp. 102–3; Arber, III, p. 684.

Shakespeare's Folio (discussed in the next section), William's and Isaac's investments were collaborative in the period surrounding the 1619 collection, and the elder Jaggard's established interest in history may have been a driving factor.

It is difficult to hypothesize further about the individual contributions made by the two Jaggards and Pavier in planning the 1619 collection. The stationers clearly specialized in historical texts and shaped their publications through paratexts (as in *Jack Straw*) and through contributions to the main text (as in William's own *View of All the Right Honourable the Lord Mayors*). The preparation of copy for the 1619 collection also reveals an interest in historical accuracy. As Massai notes, *The Whole Contention* corrects the historical lineage described by York in *The First Part of the Contention*.[58] Earlier editions incorrectly identify Edmund of Langley (York's ancestor) as the second son of Edward III (rather than the fifth), as well as Thomas of Woodstock as the sixth, instead of the seventh (see Q1 1594; C4r–v). The 1619 edition carefully reconstructs the genealogy (see Q3; C4r–v). It is uncertain who was responsible for these changes, but Massai argues persuasively for the stationers' involvement as annotating readers – although further prising apart the agency of the Jaggards and Pavier, given their shared interest in history, is difficult. For this reason, I refer to these playbooks as the 'Jaggard–Pavier collection' to suggest that collaborative agency shaped the venture, to highlight the difficulty of distinguishing individual contributions, and to emphasize the plays' position as a flexible collection of Shakespearean histories, a point that is usually overlooked in favour of viewing them as separate, single-text editions. In this way, my discussion here also advances one of my book's overarching arguments: that while it is crucial to concentrate on the role of the publisher when evaluating the selection and print presentation of early modern texts, we need to be cautious for two key reasons. First, as the term 'publisher' is an anachronistic one for the period, it is sometimes unclear which stationer (or group of stationers) took on this *role* and the financial risk for a given venture; and second, it is likely that other agents – including trade printers – had influence over the presentation of texts.[59] In light of the ongoing working relationship between the Jaggards and Pavier and their individual specialisms, an evaluation of the 1619 collection is best served through concentrating on the model of collaboration that

[58] Massai, *Editor*, pp. 126–28.
[59] See also my discussion of Wise and Creede in Chapter 2, pp. 104–08.

this venture intimates, which also reinforces the myriad ways in which its histories could be read by stationers and the reading public .

One final printed feature has particular significance for my emphasis on the collection's construction of 'history': the false title-page dates. Although we cannot be sure why the false dates were incorporated, they are a paratextual feature that needs to be 'read', and they direct not only an interpretation of the histories themselves but also of the history of the material texts. False dates appear in *Henry V* ('1608'), *1 Sir John Oldcastle* ('1600'), *A Midsummer Night's Dream* ('1600'), *The Merchant of Venice* ('1600'), and *King Lear* ('1608'); and *The Whole Contention* is undated. These false or absent dates inform how the plays participate in, construct, and use history. They have the effect of limiting the contemporaneity of the plays because most are advertised as old editions, printed some ten to twenty years earlier. By appearing to reissue old editions alongside new reprinted editions (in the case of *Pericles*, *A Yorkshire Tragedy*, and *The Merry Wives of Windsor*, which are dated 1619), Pavier and the Jaggards encourage readers to believe they are acquiring a nonce collection or tract volume. It could have been part of the stationers' revised plans for the collection to create the impression of an established and antiquated group of (history) plays by Shakespeare.

This active positioning of the plays as old histories does not necessarily discourage their topical application to events from the late Jacobean period, but it requires readers to make these connections. The machinations of court favourites and political power struggles that feature in *The Whole Contention*, for example, would have been particularly ripe for appropriation in the context of James I's court and the recent execution of Walter Ralegh in 1618, which was seen by some as an attempt to placate Spain and further James's Hispanophile foreign policy.[60] Ralegh's disastrous expedition to Guiana in 1617, which involved the destruction of Spanish settlements, prompted his arrest when he arrived home and swiftly led to his execution. As John Chamberlain describes, Ralegh was 'bewrayed, or in a sort betrayed by Sir Lewes Stukeley (who had the charge of him)' and his examiners, including Sir Thomas Wilson, deliberately sought 'incriminating evidence'.[61] *The Whole Contention* begins with

---

[60] For the use of plays to reflect on Ralegh's execution, see Marina Hila, 'Dishonourable Peace: Fletcher and Massinger's *The False One* and Jacobean Foreign Policy', *Cahiers Élisabéthains*, 72:1 (2007), 21–30.

[61] McClure (ed.), *Chamberlain*, II, p. 165; Mark Nicholls and Penry Williams, 'Ralegh, Sir Walter (1554–1618)', *ODNB*, online ed., September 2015, https://doi.org/10.1093/ref:odnb/23039 (accessed 18 June 2020), para. 65.

(and advertises on its title page) the plot against 'the good Duke Humfrey' (A1r), which led to trumped-up charges of treason and his death. For readers sympathetic to Ralegh's plight and an anti-Spanish agenda, the playbook could be readily used to reflect on Jacobean court politics and compromising alliances that threaten state stability. Nevertheless, the false and absent dates preclude readers from supposing that the plays' publication was directly responsive to contemporary events (as the reprints of Butter's history plays clearly were) or designed to facilitate an application. The impulse for this kind of reading is left to readers.

Indeed, early buyers may have collaborated with the stationers in ordering the plays in collection, therefore blurring the boundary between collections put together by publishers (nonce and tract volumes) and those put together by readers (*Sammelbände*). Lyons suggests that the binding of the 1619 editions occurred in the Jaggards' shop – a view that is also taken up by Lesser and Stallybrass – and could have involved input from book buyers.[62] It is profitable, as Knight suggests, to view the playbooks as 'a user-driven compilation [rather] than a never-realized work'.[63] Evidence from extant copies of the 1619 editions indicates that they were bound in different orders, which highlights their flexibility as a collection and resemblance to *Sammelbände*. For example, a manuscript table of contents on the front flyleaf (verso) of Folger STC 26101 (copy 2) gives the following order of binding, which reflects the collection's organization prior to its disbanding in 1763: *A Woman Killed with Kindness*, *Henry V*, *The Whole Contention*, *The Merchant of Venice*, *King Lear*, *A Midsummer Night's Dream*, *The Merry Wives of Windsor*, *1 Sir John Oldcastle*, *A Yorkshire Tragedy*, and *Pericles*. Other copies reveal different arrangements. The Gwynn copy at the Folger (STC 26101 copy 3) is still preserved in its seventeenth-century binding and in the following order: *The Whole Contention*, *A Midsummer Night's Dream*, *Oldcastle*, *The Merchant of Venice*, *Henry V*, *King Lear*, *Pericles*, *Merry Wives*, and *A Yorkshire Tragedy*. Of these two examples, the first is particularly attentive to the historical subjects and sequences of the collection. *Henry V* is followed by the renamed *Whole Contention*, which dramatizes the civil wars that plagued the reign of Henry VI. Citizen histories are also grouped together: *The Merry Wives of Windsor* is followed by *1 Sir John Oldcastle*,

[62] Lyons, 'Serials', p. 203; Lesser and Stallybrass, 'Shakespeare', pp. 126–29. Knight suggests that the combinations of texts were likely the work of readers. See *Bound to Read: Compilations, Collections and the Making of Renaissance Literature* (Philadelphia: University of Pennsylvania Press, 2013), ch. 5.

[63] Knight, 'Making', p. 326.

two plays that are linked through the figures of Falstaff and Oldcastle and a shared emphasis on the lives of subjects, rather than monarchs. *A Yorkshire Tragedy* follows *Oldcastle* and continues the pattern of citizen histories. This example underlines the fact that different readers and book buyers display different interpretative agendas. For some, the historical emphasis of the collection may not have been particularly important. A collaboration over meaning took place in this 1619 collection – not only between the stationers, but between the stationers and book buyers – which promoted malleable readings of its 'old' history plays that could be variously weighed by participants as they explore their own notions and applications of 'history'.

Shakespeare's First Folio

In the Preface to his edition of Shakespeare's plays in 1765, Samuel Johnson discusses the superficiality of genre distinctions in the 1623 Folio:

> The players who in their edition divided our authour's works . . . seem not to have distinguished the three kinds, by any very exact or definite ideas . . . There is not much nearer approach to unity of action in the tragedy of *Antony and Cleopatra*, than in the history of *Richard the Second*. But a history might be continued through many plays; as it had no plan, it had no limits.[64]

For Johnson, the Folio's division is arbitrary. Because history as a dramatic genre is unruly – it has 'no plan', 'no limits', and 'might be continued through many plays' – we should expect the Folio plays to step outside and challenge their assigned categories. But while readers, like Johnson, could choose to make comparisons across the divisions, the Folio's paratexts nevertheless offer an unequivocal statement about the history play – one that has had a profound influence on many readers and critics who have not taken up Johnson's scepticism. This section briefly examines how the Folio's reading of history is underscored by the 'Catalogue', the absence of individual title pages, and the separate registers in each section, before considering who was responsible for the division of plays, and its impact, in conjunction with the dedication to the Herbert brothers, on ideas of history, timelessness, and timeliness.

The Catalogue is a crucial paratext that controls how readers encounter the Folio Histories. Prior to 1623, no play collection had featured a

---

[64] Samuel Johnson, *Mr Johnson's Preface to his Edition of Shakespear's plays* (London, 1765), pp. xv–xvi.

contents page that set out the parameters and importance of history as a dramatic genre. The Catalogue (and the collection as a whole) arranges its ten 'Histories' chronologically from *King John* to *Henry VIII* – that is, they are ordered according to the histories they present, rather than by the dates of their first performance or first publication (see Figure 4.6).[65] The titles have been shortened and standardized to reflect the fact that the plays now form a clear sequence of English monarchical histories.[66] Each title refers to one central monarch and follows a common formula: they are introduced as 'The Life of', followed by the monarch's name. Those plays which also include the monarch's death are described as 'The Life and Death of', while those plays which feature the same monarch over several parts are named according to their position in the series, as in *The First Part of King Henry the Sixth*. These uniform titles depart from those used in the early single-text playbooks: *The Second Part of King Henry the Sixth* (now the middle play in a three-part history) was originally published as *The First Part of the Contention Between the Two Famous Houses of York and Lancaster* (1594); and *The Life of King Henry the Fifth* was first issued as *The Chronicle History of Henry the Fifth* (1600) – the title it retained in the Jaggard–Pavier collection. As Lyons points out, the extended title-page descriptions that featured on single-text playbooks and often referred to other characters in the play (such as Hotspur, Falstaff, or Pistol) are absent in the Folio.[67] The streamlined titles direct attention towards the named monarch and seem to announce that the lives of English monarchs are the proper scope and subject matter for the genre, even if the actual dramatic focus of Shakespeare's plays was more varied.

None of the Folio plays contain individual title pages, a decision of their print presentation that further promotes a reading of the Histories as a continuous and fixed sequence. All the plays in Jonson's *Works* have their own title pages, which creates the impression that they are independent and separable from the collection, especially as most of these paratexts include details of first performance and company attribution. Similarly, each text in Daniel's *Certain Small Poems* (1605), which contains *Philotas* from the Children of the Queen's Revels, the closet drama *Cleopatra*, and a

---

[65] On the ordering and organization of plays in the Folio, see John Jowett, *Shakespeare and Text* (Oxford: Oxford University Press, 2007), pp. 86–88, and David Scott Kastan, *Shakespeare and the Book* (Cambridge: Cambridge University Press, 2001), ch. 2.

[66] See also Hooks, 'Making Histories', pp. 337–69.

[67] Lyons, 'Serials', p. 205. See also Emma Smith, 'Shakespeare Serialized: *An Age of Kings*', in *A Cambridge Companion to Shakespeare and Popular Culture*, ed. Robert Shaughnessy (Cambridge: Cambridge University Press, 2007), pp. 134–49.

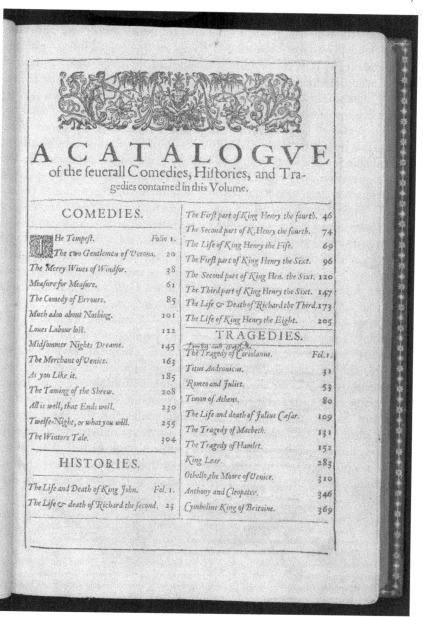

A CATALOGVE

of the feuerall Comedies, Histories, and Tragedies contained in this Volume.

COMEDIES.

He *Tempest*.	*Folio* 1.
The *two Gentlemen of Verona*.	20
The *Merry Wiues of Windfor*.	38
Meafure for Meafure.	61
The *Comedy of Errours*.	85
Much adoo about Nothing.	101
Loues Labour loft.	122
Midfommer Nights Dreame.	145
The *Merchant of Venice*.	163
As you Like it.	185
The *Taming of the Shrew*.	208
All is well, that Ends well.	230
Twelfe-Night, or what you will.	255
The *Winters Tale*.	304

HISTORIES.

The *Life and Death of King Iohn*.	*Fol.* 1.
The *Life & death of Richard the fecond*.	23

The *Firft part of King Henry the fourth*.	46
The *Second part of K. Henry the fourth*.	74
The *Life of King Henry the Fift*.	69
The *Firft part of King Henry the Sixt*.	96
The *Second part of King Hen. the Sixt*.	120
The *Third part of King Henry the Sixt*.	147
The *Life & Death of Richard the Third*.	173
The *Life of King Henry the Eight*.	205

TRAGEDIES.

Troylus and Creffida.	
The *Tragedy of Coriolanus*.	*Fol.* 1.
Titus Andronicus.	31
Romeo and Juliet.	53
Timon of Athens.	80
The *Life and death of Julius Cæfar*.	109
The *Tragedy of Macbeth*.	131
The *Tragedy of Hamlet*.	152
King Lear.	283
Othello, the Moore of Venice.	310
Anthony and Cleopater.	346
Cymbeline King of Britaine.	369

Figure 4.6   Catalogue from Shakespeare's First Folio (1623; STC 22273).

selection of non-dramatic texts, contains a separate title page. This collection is the first of the period to incorporate both commercial and non-commercial plays (see Appendix). *Philotas* is, however, bibliographically independent (with its own register), which seems to emphasize its material and conceptual separability as the only commercial play within the collection.[68] Shakespeare's Folio has a very different design. The varied performance origins of Shakespeare's plays – for example, *The True Tragedy of Richard Duke of York* (*3 Henry VI*) from Pembroke's Men and *Titus Andronicus* from 'the Earle of Darbie, Earle of Pembrooke, and Earle of Sussex their Seruants', according to the 1594 title page – are elided by the Folio's presentation.[69] As David Scott Kastan points out, no playing company (not even the King's Men) is named anywhere in the collection.[70] The Folio aims to create a coherent and closed canon of Shakespeare's plays that overlooks their different origins and conditions of composition and performance. In particular, the arrangement of the Histories and their lack of individual title pages ask readers to approach this grouping of plays as one historical narrative that converts the divisions between separate plays into mere intervals in the Folio's single overarching history of English monarchs after the Conquest.

Each of the three sections of the Folio – Comedies, Histories, and Tragedies – contains its own register and pagination, which seems to underline their construction as distinct dramatic categories. Lyons suggests that this bibliographical design facilitates the addition of new texts and encourages readers to see the Folio as a flexible collection.[71] To my mind, the separate signatures and pagination cement the Folio's tripartite division, and do not advertise it as a malleable collection like the Jaggard–Pavier editions.[72] Rather, the Histories' continuous signatures solidify the category, unite its different plays, and propose a single historical narrative. As Hooks puts it, 'the structural principle of the larger work transcends its individual parts'.[73] Indeed, it does not seem as if early modern readers

---

[68] Greg points out that, although *Philotas* is bibliographically independent, there is 'no evidence that the play was issued separately' (*Bibliography*, I, p. 349).

[69] Shakespeare, *The Most Lamentable Romaine Tragedie of Titus Andronicus* (London, 1594; STC 22328), A2r.

[70] Kastan, *Shakespeare and the Book*, p. 71. [71] Lyons, 'English Printed Drama', pp. 259–63.

[72] Cf. Charlton Hinman, *The Printing and Proofreading of the First Folio of Shakespeare*, 2 vols. (Oxford: Clarendon Press, 1963), II, pp. 504–29: Hinman shows that the decision to begin the sections with a new sequence of signatures was also connected to delays in accessing and securing the rights to texts. Similar to Lyons, he (I, p. 31) suggests that the separate signatures could represent a precautionary economic measure, in case the stationers found it difficult to shift copies of the complete folio.

[73] Hooks, 'Making Histories', p. 345.

divided up or part-purchased the Shakespeare Folio. The incorporation of other plays is witnessed only through publishers' interventions: the addition of *Troilus and Cressida* to some copies of the First Folio (between the Histories and Tragedies and identified as a 'Tragedie' through its head title) and the 'Apocrypha' to the Third and Fourth folios, which are discussed at the end of this chapter.[74] Collectively, therefore, the key features of the Folio's design – its Catalogue, lack of individual title pages, arrangement of its Histories, and the continuous register within each division – emphasize English history and seem to promote a collective English identity. Although Shakespeare wrote most of these plays during Elizabeth's reign, when England and Scotland were separately ruled nations, the significance of the Folio as a late Jacobean publication that separates its Scottish and British histories – *Macbeth*, *King Lear*, and *Cymbeline* – as 'tragedies' should not be overlooked. In contrast to the Jaggard–Pavier collection which promotes a continuity between *King Lear* and *Henry V* through their position as 'chronicle histories', the Folio divides them. An engrained Englishness – that also sidesteps the Welsh histories featured or discussed in *1* and *2 Henry IV*, *Henry V*, and *Cymbeline* – emerges as the dominant paratextual frame for readers.

Determining who was responsible for the 'Catalogue' and the Folio's influential division of plays is likely to remain speculative. The enterprise involved a collaboration between the King's Men and a syndicate of stationers who printed and published the collection. As shareholders in the King's Men, Shakespeare's former colleagues – John Heminges and Henry Condell – claim to have provided the playscripts (for the previously unprinted plays, but also, they broadly assert, for those that had already been published in 'stolne, and surreptitious copies', A3r) and prepared a dedication to William and Philip Herbert. Stationers William and Isaac Jaggard, Edward Blount, William Aspley, and John Smethwick are named in the colophon, which suggests they were responsible for producing the collection and securing the rights for unpublished and derelict copy.[75] The Jaggards (especially Isaac) and Blount are usually seen as the most invested in the Folio venture; the Register entry on 8 November 1623 for

---

[74] See Figure 4.6 for a manuscript addition of *Troilus and Cressida* to the Catalogue. Peter W. M. Blayney, *The First Folio of Shakespeare* (Washington, DC: Folger Library, 1991), pp. 17, 21–24.

[75] My emphasis is on the division of plays in the Folio. Much critical debate surrounds the preparation and annotation of copy and the agents involved as 'editors'. See Massai, *Editor*, pp. 149–58 for a summary.

Shakespeare's plays that 'are not formerly Entred to other men' is made out to Blount and Isaac Jaggard.[76] Their names also appear as part of the title-page imprint, whereas Aspley, Smethwick, and William Jaggard are named only in the colophon – although, as with the 1619 collection, distinguishing individual contributions is not straightforward.[77] The Folio's tripartite division may have been motivated by a marketing strategy that carefully negotiates the collection's literary position and which could have been proposed by the company or the syndicate of stationers. It occupies a middle ground between Jonson's presumptuous (as some saw it) labelling of his plays as 'Works' and an emphasis on performance origins seen in numerous single-text playbooks from the period.[78] The Folio's title page makes no reference to Shakespeare's texts as 'plays': the full description, 'Master William Shakespeares Comedies, Histories, and Tragedies | Published according to the True Originall Copies' (A1r), privileges genre rather than issues of form and theatrical provenance.

Of course, one of the reasons for organizing Shakespeare's plays in this way is the fact that he did write a significant number of plays based on English history after the Conquest. The Folio's organization is logical on the basis of Shakespeare's output; but it is also highly individual, representative of one dramatist rather than many. By the time of the Folio's production, Shakespeare's reputation as a dramatist of English history was already established – although it was more accurately a print identity than a stage identity. Performance evidence is limited, but it is unlikely that Shakespeare's histories, written some twenty to thirty years earlier, would have occupied a prominent position in the late Jacobean repertory of the King's Men. In print, however, Shakespeare's most successful plays continued to be *Richard II*, *Richard III*, and *1 Henry IV*: Wise published nine editions of these plays between 1597 and 1602, and Law invested in them throughout the Jacobean period, including the sixth edition of *Richard III* and seventh of *1 Henry IV* in 1622.[79] The Folio not only makes use of

[76] SRO7865; Arber, IV, p. 107.
[77] For accounts of the Folio's publication, see Blayney, *First Folio of Shakespeare*; Kastan, *Shakespeare and the Book*, ch. 2; Murphy, *Shakespeare in Print*, ch. 2; Gary Taylor, 'Making Meaning Marketing Shakespeare 1623', in *From Performance to Print in Shakespeare's England*, ed. Peter Holland and Stephen Orgel (Basingstoke: Palgrave Macmillan, 2006), pp. 55–72; Jowett, *Shakespeare and Text*, ch. 4; Ben Higgins, *Shakespeare's Syndicate: The First Folio, Its Publishers, and the Early Modern Book Trade* (Oxford: Oxford University Press, 2022).
[78] See also Chris Laoutaris, 'The Prefatorial Material', in *The Cambridge Companion to Shakespeare's First Folio*, ed. Emma Smith (Cambridge: Cambridge University Press, 2016), pp. 48–67 (pp. 49–51).
[79] Law carefully guarded his rights to *Richard II*, *Richard III*, and *1 Henry IV*. Hinman demonstrates that the printing of the Folio histories was held up, probably because the syndicate had difficulty

Shakespeare's print reputation and the broad subject consensus of these histories, it also seems to solidify the genre through the plays' arrangement and its paratextual strategies. Of the three genres outlined in the Catalogue, the Histories are given the most coherence through their standardized titles. While the head and running titles for the Comedies and Tragedies usually accord with their assigned genres, these plays are not presented with uniform titles in the Catalogue. None of the Comedies contain further generic identifiers or a formulaic title. And while three of the tragedies (*Coriolanus, Macbeth,* and *Hamlet*) are given the same formula ('The Tragedy of') in the Catalogue, the others are not; indeed, *Julius Caesar* is prefaced with 'The Life and death of', recalling the Histories' standard formula. The same attention to detail that shapes the Histories' paratextual definition in the Catalogue and privileges them in the centre of the collection is not so obviously repeated with the Tragedies and Comedies.

The King's Men could have been responsible for the Folio's division of plays and genre strategies. This is what Johnson assumes, when he claims in his Preface that 'the *players* . . . seem not to have distinguished the three kinds by any very exact or definite ideas' (my emphasis). The 1619 court injunction (mentioned earlier) indicates that the King's Men wanted to oversee and control the publication of their plays. It seems to have been at their instigation that steps were taken by William Herbert as Lord Chamberlain. Massai argues, however, that Isaac Jaggard may have prompted the company to undertake this cautionary measure and that the inspiration for the Folio project came from him.[80] Whatever the precise agency behind the injunction and the Folio venture, the fact that Heminges and Condell – the two company members directly associated with the project – had limited (if any) prior involvement with the book trade suggests that the syndicate of stationers must have taken on important roles in shaping the collection.

Blount's practices likely informed the presentation of the Folio. Other critics have evaluated his role in the venture, but his investment in William Alexander's *Monarchic Tragedies* has not yet been discussed in terms of its status as a non-commercial history-play collection and the influence it could have exerted on the Folio project.[81] Blount first published this collection in 1604 (STC 343), and it features two classical histories –

securing Law's permission to print *his* histories. See *Printing and Proofreading*, I, pp. 27–28, II, pp. 522–24.

[80] Massai, *Editor*, pp. 106–8.

[81] See Sonia Massai, 'Edward Blount, the Herberts, and the First Folio', in *Shakespeare's Stationers*, ed. Straznicky, pp. 132–46; Leah Scragg, 'Edward Blount and the Prefatory Material to the First Folio of Shakespeare', in *Bulletin of the John Rylands Library*, 79:1 (1997), 117–26.

Croesus and *Darius*. The plays have independent registers, and *Darius* was also issued separately. In 1607, Blount published this collection again (STC 344; see Appendix): this time, it contained reissues of *Croesus* and *Darius* from 1605, alongside first editions of *The Alexandraean Tragedy* and *Julius Caesar*, which have continuous signatures. These four classical histories are listed on the title page, which effectively serves the function of a contents page, and are labelled 'tragedies'. This classification highlights the collection's investment in classical models, which privilege comedy and tragedy as dramatic categories, regardless of a play's historical content. Shakespeare's Folio preserves this identification too: *Julius Caesar*, *Coriolanus*, and *Antony and Cleopatra* are all within the 'Tragedies' section. Blount's investment in a classical history-play collection, featuring a contents list and generic identifier, may have informed the paratextual strategies of the Folio, where the classical histories are kept separate from those based on English history. However, Blount's influence on the Folio's development and organization could be limited because, as Kastan and others have proposed, Blount potentially joined the Folio venture at a later date than the Jaggards.[82] Blount rarely invested in plays from the commercial stages. He sometimes entered them in the Register, but usually transferred the rights to another stationer, rather than publishing them himself. Revealingly, Blount entered *Antony and Cleopatra* on 20 May 1608 but, by the time of the Folio's production, seems to have forgotten that he owned the rights and re-entered the title in the Register on 8 November 1623.

Aspley, whose name appears only in the colophon, usually receives limited critical attention and is frequently dismissed as a 'minor partner' in the Folio, brought into the project because he held the rights to the two plays – *2 Henry IV* and *Much Ado About Nothing* – on which he had collaborated with Wise.[83] However, his early published output reveals a sustained interest in commercial drama, historical and newsworthy pamphlets, and a connection to the tripartite division later employed in the Folio.[84] Aspley invested in plays – including *The Malcontent* (1604), *Eastward Ho* (1605), and *Bussy D'Ambois* (1607) – from the boys' companies, and he published a range of topical texts, including union tracts such as John Gordon's *England and Scotland's Happiness* (1604) and *The*

---

[82] Kastan, *Shakespeare and the Book*, p. 61.
[83] Hooks, *Selling*, p. 108. Scragg, 'Edward Blount', p. 118.
[84] In the decade prior to the Folio, Aspley became the exclusive publisher of the sermons of John Boys (1571–1625) and he often favoured collaboration with other stationers (including Thomas Thorpe in the publication of *Shakespeare's Sonnets* in 1609).

Union of Great Britain (1604; STC 12061); William Biddulph's *The Travels of Certain Englishmen into Africa, Asia, Troy* &c (1609; STC 3051); and *The Great Turk's Defiance: Or his letter denunciatory to Sigismond the Third, now King of Polonia* (1613; STC 206). A critical connection has not yet been made between Aspley's involvement in the Folio and his role as the sole publisher of the anonymous *Warning for Fair Women* (1599) from the Chamberlain's Men. This play (as discussed in the Introduction) contains that striking induction involving three dramatic genres – Comedie, Hystorie, and Tragedie – which is echoed exactly in the Folio's division of plays. Although *A Warning for Fair Women* was only published once, its personification of these three 'kinds' is largely unmatched in other commercial plays from the period.[85] No other play collection before or after Shakespeare's Folio adopts this tripartite division. *A Warning for Fair Women* and the Folio are uniquely united in their use of these three categories as a frame – either in the form of a dramatic induction or paratext – for the main text(s) they contain. That Aspley is only named in the colophon of Shakespeare's Folio and is not part of the collected Register entry for the unregistered texts does seem to imply that his agency was limited. But the work of recent critics has reappraised the often-dismissed contributions of the 'colophon-only syndicate' and Aspley's early interest in plays (including those that explore ideas of genre), as well as historical and newsworthy texts, should not be overlooked in evaluating the Folio's structure.[86]

Nevertheless, of the syndicate, it is the Jaggards who have the clearest proven interest in history and history plays. It is likely that Isaac took the lead in the Folio project: his name appears (alongside Blount's) on the title page and only he is linked to the venture in the *Catalogus Universalis* for autumn 1622.[87] William's role may have been curtailed, in the latter stages, by his deteriorating health: he died shortly before the Folio appeared on the bookstalls. However, as Hooks has shown, the elder

---

[85] Robert Wilson's *The Cobbler's Prophecy* (1594) involves a similar exchange, but the characters are named according to the classical muses: Thalia, Clio, and Melpomine (C1v–C3v). It is also contained within the play and does not act as a frame for the whole.

[86] Massai (*Editor*, pp. 158–79) offers a reassessment of Smethwick's role, showing how he could have been responsible for preparing and annotating some of the plays. Neither his prior output nor his ownership of the rights for *Romeo and Juliet*, *Love's Labour's Lost*, and *Hamlet* reveal a clear interest in history.

[87] The *Catalogus Universalis* was ostensibly a biannual list of books exhibited at the Frankfurt book fair. In 1622, English editions of the list started to include a supplement of English books. The autumn 1622 edition confirms that Shakespeare's Folio was in progress by then and would contain 'Plays, written by M. William Shakespeare, all in one volume, printed by Isaack Iaggard, in fol.' The *Catalogus Universalis* of spring 1624 only gives Blount's name. See Blayney, *First Folio*, pp. 7–8, 26.

Jaggard remained a vocal and prolific stationer until his death, even if he, because of his blindness, was unable to print the texts himself.[88] Given their clear interest in historical and serial texts, the Jaggards could have played a key role in the division of Shakespeare's Folio plays. In particular, William's investment in texts that classify and order histories is especially relevant. As mentioned earlier, he wrote a book serializing the lord mayors of London during Elizabeth's reign. He also published texts that were advertised specifically as catalogues – such as *A Catalogue of the Kings of Scotland* (1610; STC 22008) and Ralph Brooke's *Catalogue and Succession of the Kings, Princes, Dukes, Marquesses, Earls, and Viscounts of this Realm of England, Since the Norman Conquest, to this Present Year, 1619* (1619, STC 3832; see Figure 4.7), the latter concentrating on the same national history as the Folio. These texts feature brief accounts of the lives of monarchs and/or aristocrats, arranged in chronological order and introduced by short headings that give the name of each individual: 'King Richard the second' is followed by 'King Henry the Fourth' and 'King Henry the fift' (Brooke, ¶¶6v– ¶¶¶2r). Because of the compendious, encyclopaedic nature of the catalogues that cover considerable periods of time up to the Jacobean present, they offer a reading of history that is continuous and attentive to sequences. Jaggard's prior investment in non-dramatic texts that use similar terms and display similar interests in classification could intimate his agency in the Folio's design. Although Jonson's *Works* features a contents page described as a 'Catalogue' and could be a model for Shakespeare's Folio, it does not order texts by genre or sequence its (two) histories.[89] The collaborative nature of Shakespeare's Folio project ultimately makes it impossible to identify those responsible for its division of plays. But the syndicate's wider investment patterns and paratextual practices potentially had a cumulative influence: Blount offered his classical histories to readers as 'tragedies'; Aspley invested in topical histories and a play featuring the same tripartite division of the later Folio; and the Jaggards published catalogues about historical subjects that were arranged in chronological order and privileged distinctive national pasts.

The Folio not only directs readings of its Histories through the Catalogue and the division, ordering, and presentation of plays, but also

---

[88] Hooks, *Selling*, pp. 124–32.
[89] While individual title pages in Jonson's *Workes* (1616; STC 14751) broadly identify each play as a comedy or tragedy, these categories are not clear cut. *Every Man In* and *Volpone* are described as comedies, whereas *Every Man Out* and *Poetaster* are each labelled a 'Comicall Satyre', which detracts from an impression of cohesion under two overarching categories. 'History' does not feature anywhere: *Sejanus* and *Catiline* are described as 'tragedies' on their title pages.

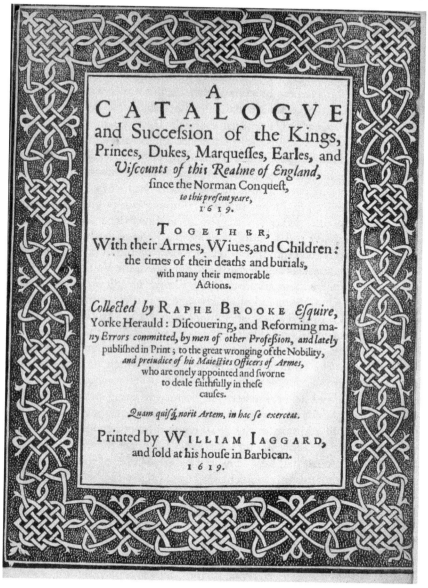

A

CATALOGVE

and Succeſsion of the Kings,
Princes, Dukes, Marqueſſes, Earles, and
Viſcounts of this Realme of England,
ſince the Norman Conqueſt,
to this preſent yeare,
1619.

TOGETHER,
With their Armes, Wiues, and Children :
the times of their deaths and burials,
with many their memorable
Actions.

Collected by RAPHE BROOKE *Eſquire,*
Yorke Herauld : Diſcouering, and Reforming ma-
ny Errors committed, by men of other Profeſsion, and lately
publiſhed in Print ; to the great wronging of the Nobility,
and preiudice of his Maieſties Officers of Armes,
who are onely appointed and ſworne
to deale faithfully in theſe
cauſes.

Quam quiſ̃q̃, norit Artem, in hac ſe exerceat.

Printed by WILLIAM IAGGARD,
and ſold at his houſe in Barbican.
1619.

Figure 4.7 Title page from Ralph Brooke's *Catalogue* (1619; STC 3832).

through its dedication to William and Philip Herbert, then the earls of
Pembroke and Montgomery, respectively. This paratext encourages two different approaches. On the one hand, it limits the Histories' contemporaneity by
associating them with the literary cachet of the Pembroke circle; but on the
other hand, it encourages a topical reading by linking them with the political
reputation of the Herbert brothers which, at this time, was aligned with
Protestant and anti-Spanish agendas. On the surface, the Folio's choice of
dedicatees may appear rather unusual, especially because James I would seem
to be the most likely candidate for a collection of plays from his official
company.[90] Heminges and Condell's dedication, however, speaks of an affinity
between the Herberts and the king's company. While its fulsome praise of the
Herberts and its modesty in the presentation of such 'trifles' (A2r) to the
brothers recall a *humilitas* topos that was commonplace in prefatory epistles,
other aspects of the dedication suggest an acknowledged and measurable
closeness. Heminges and Condell describe the Folio as both choosing and
finding its patrons and claim that in the Herberts' 'likings of the seuerall parts,
when they were acted, as before they were published, the Volume ask'd to be
yours' (A2v). The Herberts are advertised as recognizable theatrical and textual
patrons of the King's Men and of Shakespeare in particular, having 'prosequ-
uted both [the company] and their Author liuing, with so much fauour' (A2r).

It also appears that a *new* closeness developed between the Herberts and
the King's Men after Shakespeare's death, with the brothers emerging, in
many ways, as the company's de facto patrons, which provides another
reason for their selection as dedicatees.[91] This development picks up pace
between 1622 and 1623 – when the Folio was being printed. As Lord
Chamberlain, William Herbert made a few interventions on the company's behalf: in addition to the 1619 court injunction, Pembroke inter-
vened, in 1622, to allow the now-lost play 'Osmond the Great Turk' for
performance, after it had been censored by the Master of the Revels, John
Astley.[92] Shortly after this incident, in 1623, Henry Herbert (Pembroke's
kinsman) acquired the Revels office under slightly unusual circumstances
that imply, as Richard Dutton proposes, Pembroke's assistance.[93] Only a

[90] See Laoutaris, 'Prefatorial', p. 58; Marcus, *Puzzling Shakespeare*, p. 108; Massai, 'Blount', p. 138;
    Taylor, 'Making Meaning', pp. 67–69.
[91] See also Laoutaris, 'Prefatorial', pp. 57–63.
[92] William Herbert was appointed Lord Chamberlain on 23 December 1615 and held the post until
    1626, when he became Lord Steward and insisted the chamberlainship pass to his brother, Philip
    (who was Lord Chamberlain between 1626 and 1641).
[93] Richard Dutton, 'Patronage, Politics, and the Master of the Revels, 1622–1640: The Case of John
    Astley', *English Literary Renaissance*, 20:2 (1990), 287–319, and 'Herbert, Sir Henry (*bap.* 1594,

few weeks later, on 7 August 1623, James knighted Henry at Wilton, Pembroke's home, which strengthens the possibility that it was the Lord Chamberlain's authority that procured the post (and possibly the knighthood) for Henry and placed him in an influential position in which he could protect and promote the interests of the King's Men, whom he also favoured for court performances.[94] Although preparation for Shakespeare's Folio had been underway before this point, the preliminary materials were printed last and their presentation could reflect a growing closeness between the Herberts and the King's Men.

The literary cachet of the Herbert brothers would, however, have been enough to recommend them as dedicatees and direct an interpretation of the Folio's Histories. William and Philip Herbert were the sons of Mary Herbert, Countess of Pembroke, and sister to Philip Sidney. While a measurable connection between the King's Men and the Herbert brothers may have contributed to Heminges and Condell's choice, the marketability of the Herberts' name – their print capital – would have been apparent to the syndicate of stationers who took a lead role in shaping the venture. As Bergeron proposes, the dedication stands 'on the patronage fault line between past and future, between aristocratic and commercial support' – a blurring of private and public exchanges that I explored earlier through Wise's editions in Chapter 2.[95] In particular, the Folio's dedication to the Herberts finds a precedent in Blount's non-dramatic publications; indeed, Lorenzo Ducci's *Ars Aulica, or The Courtier's Art* (1607) features a dedication to the brothers written by Blount himself.[96] In this dedication, Blount assigns the text to the protection of the 'most Noble Brothers' and praises their 'indiuiduall and innated worths', the latter term implying not only a natural, inborn worthiness but also their birthright as part of the Sidney/Pembroke family.[97]

Blount's position as an 'upmarket literary stationer' possibly informed the Folio's selection of dedicatees and the paratext's printed presentation.[98] In addition to Alexander's *Monarchic Tragedies*, Blount was the publisher

d. 1673)', *ODNB*, online ed., January 2008, https://doi.org/10.1093/ref:odnb/13029 (accessed 16 September 2019), para. 4.

[94] N. W. Bawcutt (ed.), *The Control and Censorship of Caroline Drama: The Records of Sir Henry Herbert, Master of the Revels 1623–73* (Oxford: Clarendon Press, 1996), pp. 4–5.

[95] Bergeron, *Textual Patronage*, p. 142.

[96] Ibid., pp. 143–54; Scragg ('Edward Blount', pp. 117–26) has even proposed that Blount wrote the dedication to the Herberts in Shakespeare's Folio.

[97] Lorenzo Ducci, *Ars Avlica, or The Courtiers Arte* (London, 1607; STC 7274), A4r–v.

[98] Massai, 'Blount', p. 133. See also Kastan (*Shakespeare and the Book*, p. 62), who suggests that Blount could be credited for publishing the 'first Great Books course'.

of John Florio's translations of Montaigne's *Essays* (1603 and 1613) and, in collaboration with Waterson, Daniel's *Philotas* (incorporated in *Certain Small Poems*, 1605), which contains an important dedication to Prince Henry, signed by Daniel. It has not yet been recognized that this is the first dedication to a royal or aristocratic patron ever to be attached to a play from the commercial stages. In addition to defending his play (which attracted attention from the Privy Council and the 'censuring stage' for the title character's resemblance to Robert Devereux, second earl of Essex), Daniel considers the use and cyclical nature of history:

> These ancient representments of times past;
> Tell vs that men haue, doo, and always runne
> The selfe same line of action, and do cast
> Their course alike, and nothing can be donne.[99]

The dedication conflates, as part of its search to understand 'the tenure of our state' (A4v), a range of different times: the classical past of Philotas, the fading remnants of Elizabeth's reign, and the present time of Daniel's fallen fame and reputation. His pessimistic tone is (somewhat) tempered when he boldly looks to his dedicatee, Henry, as a 'most hopefull Prince, not as you are | But as you may be', whose future could involve 'glorious actions' that might be set down in the 'sure recordes of Bookes' to become another 'history' (A4r–v). Because of his experiences with prestigious publications and their paratextual features – including the dedication to the Herbert brothers and this unprecedented dedication to Prince Henry as part of a commercial playbook – Blount may have encouraged Heminges and Condell to use the Herberts as dedicatees. At the very least, the generous spacing and *mise en page* of the dedication's heading (prominently displaying the names and titles of the Herbert brothers) were probably informed by his earlier paratexts, which tend to prioritize the status of dedicatees and the enduring significance they assign to the texts in which they feature.[100]

An emphasis on the Herberts' literary reputation can be witnessed throughout the Folio's dedication and directs a reading of its Histories. The dedication is addressed to the 'Most Noble and Incomparable Paire of Brethren' (A2r) and assigns the brothers a nurturing role – one that has already shaped the plays' development on stage and which will transform their afterlife in print. One effect of this strategy is to elevate and separate texts from the specific context of their production. An emphasis on the

---

[99] Daniel, *Philotas*, in *Certaine Small Poems* (STC 6239), A4v, A5v.   [100] See *Ars Aulica*, A4r.

multi-generational Sidney–Pembroke family suggests a continuity between texts spanning the late Elizabethan and Jacobean periods that removes them from their contemporary moment. A reader approaching Shakespeare's Folio by paying attention to the Sidney–Pembroke connection that the dedication 'activates' could be encouraged to interpret the plays and the Folio venture as Jonson's commendatory verse implores: they are 'not of an age, but for all time' (A4v).[101] This way of reading also supplies an interpretation of the Folio's Histories. As discussed, the use of false dates and imprints in the Jaggard–Pavier collection creates the impression that the editions are old, unsold copies of Shakespeare's plays that have a kind of antiquated status. The topicality of the Folio Histories is similarly curtailed (albeit in a different way) when the monumentalizing imperative of the collection – promoted through the commendatory verses, address to readers, and the coterie associations of the dedication – is emphasized. The Histories can be read as old, classic plays about the *English* past that differ considerably from the new histories, including *Sir John van Olden Barnavelt*, *The Duchess of Suffolk*, *The Bondman*, and *A Game at Chess*, that were being performed on the London stages and reflected closely on late Jacobean politics.[102] Indeed, the presentation of those Folio Histories that had been previously printed contrasts significantly with the appearance of their earlier single-text editions, which resemble short, topical pamphlets. In these early editions, stationers, such as Millington, whose specialisms lay in newsworthy publications, invested in Shakespeare's texts because they could be applied to contemporary events, including the French Wars of Religion.[103] The 'Histories' are repurposed in the Folio as a lasting testament to Shakespeare's dramatic achievement, which positions them as established texts that lack the topicality of new plays.

---

[101] See also Paul Salzman, *Literature and Politics in the 1620s: 'Whisper'd Counsells'* (Basingstoke: Palgrave Macmillan, 2014), pp. 42–48, for an account of the Folio's 'rejection of topicality and assertion of lasting value' (p. 45). Salzman claims that the Folio's organization 'buries' plays (including *Richard II* and *Othello*) that could provoke contentious political readings, although I would suggest that the burying of *Richard II* is more accurately a consequence of the serialization of the Histories, which also serves other functions.

[102] Cf. the Dering Manuscript (Folger MS V.b.34), an adaptation of *1* and *2 Henry IV* into a single play, which was prepared by Sir Edward Dering in about 1623 from single-text copies of the plays. Indicative of the flexible contemporaneity of histories, the adaptation may have been inspired, as Jean-Christophe Mayer proposes, by 'the war-torn European world of the 1620s', which is underscored through several new pointed political allusions. See Mayer, 'Annotating and Transcribing for the Theatre: Shakespeare's Early Modern Reader-Revisers at Work', in *Shakespeare and Textual Studies*, ed. Kidnie and Massai, pp. 163–76 (p. 175).

[103] See Chapter 1, pp. 79-81.

My emphasis on the Folio's dedication, rather than on its address to readers and commendatory verses, is owing to the fact that the Herbert connection also activates another approach to the plays – especially the Histories. The dedication pulls in two directions: it suggests the *timelessness* of Shakespeare's plays, but it also suggests their *timeliness* by linking them with the Herberts' well-known political sympathies during the late Jacobean period. The interpretative malleability of paratexts is a factor in all publications, but becomes pronounced in collections featuring multiple texts, paratexts, and production agents. While Blount likely saw the dedication as authorizing the Folio's literary credentials, other readers – including the stationers with whom he collaborated and members of the book-buying public – may have been attentive to different interpretative imperatives.

During the late Jacobean period, the Herbert brothers were part of an anti-Spanish and anti-Catholic group of aristocratic peers, who supported direct involvement in the Thirty Years War and resistance to the proposed Spanish Match between Prince Charles and the Infanta Maria.[104] As Victor Stater discusses, Pembroke sought to limit Spanish influence 'at home and abroad', and as an 'early investor in colonial enterprises . . . he put money into many other schemes that would curb Spanish power'.[105] Both brothers invested in the Virginia Company – in fact, Pembroke was the Company's second-largest investor. Pembroke's politics were also recognized by his contemporaries: he was a popular figure in Parliament, where his anti-Spanish views found support from many of its members, and he argued against Parliament's dissolution in December 1621, by opposing Prince Charles and George Villiers, first duke of Buckingham. He had considerable power both in the Commons and the House of Lords, his properties affording him extensive control over several seats in the Commons.[106]

Pembroke's influence and political leanings were also acknowledged – and, as significantly, shaped – in print. He was the dedicatee of several

---

[104] See the most sustained account of the Herberts to date: Michael G. Brennan, *Literary Patronage in the English Renaissance: The Pembroke Family* (London: Routledge, 1988), as well as appendix A in Margot Heinemann's *Puritanism and Theatre: Thomas Middleton and Opposition Drama under the Early Stuarts* (Cambridge: Cambridge University Press, 1980). See also the entries for the Herberts in Franklin B. Williams, Jr, *Index of Dedications and Commendatory Verses in English Books before 1641* (London: Bibliographical Society, 1962), p. 94.

[105] Victor Stater, 'Herbert, William, third earl of Pembroke (1580–1630)', *ODNB*, online ed., January 2008, https://doi.org/10.1093/ref:odnb/13058 (accessed 16 September 2019), para. 19; see also Brennan, *Literary Patronage* , pp. 146–49.

[106] Stater, 'Herbert', para. 20.

publications promoting a militant Protestant agenda, including *A Gag for the Pope and the Jesuits* (1624), which, in its dedicatory epistle, claims that the pamphlet's objectives are supported by 'so noble an arme' as the earl of Pembroke's:

> [B]ut aboue all, my motiues arise from your Noble disposition towards Englands glory, and pious zeale to propagate the cause of Religion, which at this day is set vpon by viperous calumniation, as if either God meant not to performe his promise, concerning the stripping of the Strumpet naked.[107]

Both brothers were the dedicatees of Shute's English translation of *The Triumphs of Nassau* (1613; reprinted 1620), which recounts the successes of Maurice, Prince of Orange, a regular opponent of Spanish power and a Protestant figurehead in the Thirty Years War.[108] Indeed, the *personal* politics and religious sympathies of the Herberts (including how they may have changed over time) are in many ways subservient to how they were seen and constructed by others. The perception, during the late Jacobean period, of the Herbert brothers as strong advocates for anti-Spanish and anti-Catholic policies was shaped partly through their public support of ventures and parliamentary action that limited Spanish influence and partly through the nature of the dedications they received.[109]

The political import of the Herberts as playbook dedicatees can be witnessed in Philip Massinger's *The Bondman* (1624), which, as a single-text edition, encourages a direct connection between the dedication and its accompanying history play. Licensed for the stage on 3 December 1623 (at the same time as Shakespeare's Folio was published) and entered in the Register on 12 March 1624 by John Harrison and Edward Blackmore, *The Bondman* dramatizes Timoleon's defence of Syracuse against Carthage in 338 BCE, while also conflating different historical sources and periods.[110] The account of the slaves' rebellion, for example, draws on the Servile Wars in Sicily of 135–132 BCE, whereas the history of Timoleon dates from the fourth century BCE. Critics have described the play's ancient history – or 'Antient Storie' as advertised on the title page – as an example of 'opposition' drama that supports an anti-Spanish and anti-Catholic

---

[107] Anon., *A Gagge for the Pope and the Iesvits* (London, 1624; STC 20111), A2v–A3r.

[108] Jan Janszn Orlers, *The Trivmphs of Nassav*, trans. W. Shute (London, 1613: STC 17676 and 1620: STC 17677).

[109] See Brennan, *Literary Patronage*, chs. 7 and 9.

[110] As Emma Smith identifies, the 'first attested purchase of the First Folio' took place on 5 December 1623 by Sir Edward Dering. See Smith, *Shakespeare's First Folio: Four Centuries of an Iconic Book* (Oxford: Oxford University Press, 2016), p. 2.

agenda.[111] The opening act seems to allude to James's pacifist policies and refusal to provide military assistance to the Palatinate:

> O shame! that we that are a populous Nation,
> Ingag'd to liberall nature, for all blessings
> An Iland can bring forth; we that haue limbs
> And able bodies; Shipping, Armes, and Treasure,
> The sinnewes of the Warre, now we are call'd
> To stand vpon our Guard, cannot produce
> One fit to be our Generall.[112]

Jerzy Limon and Margot Heinemann argue that Massinger's drama expresses an informed resistance that favours military intervention in Europe.[113] The homogeneity of Massinger's politics has been usefully challenged by Benedict Robinson, who shows that the play 'refuses the religious rhetoric of militant Protestantism'.[114] But one of the ways in which the play – as a *printed book* – insists upon a militant Protestant reading is through Massinger's dedication to Philip Herbert, which links the play to the popular reputation of the Herberts. Massinger draws attention to Montgomery's 'Heroique disposition', claiming that when the play 'was first Acted, your Lordships liberall suffrage taught others to allow it for currant, it hauing receaued the vndoubted stampe of your Lordships allowance' (A3v). The nature of Montgomery's involvement with the play (and Massinger) is unclear, but the fact that it is his presence that – according to the dedication – gives the play its currency is significant, especially in light of the play's historical subject and the way in which this material is treated. As a printed book, *The Bondman* can be linked to the known politics of the Herberts, because this interpretation is encouraged through the dedication to Montgomery that assigns the play its interpretative and commercial 'currency': it is topical and of the present

---

[111] See Heinemann, *Puritanism*, ch. 12; Annabel Patterson, *Censorship and Interpretation: The Conditions of Writing and Reading in Early Modern England* (Madison: University of Wisconsin Press, 1984), pp. 81–99.

[112] Philip Massinger, *The Bondman* (London, 1624; STC 17632), B3r.

[113] See Heinemann, 'Drama and Opinion in the 1620s: Middleton and Massinger', in *Theatre and Government under the Early Stuarts*, ed. J. R. Mulryne and Margaret Shewring (Cambridge: Cambridge University Press, 1993), pp. 237–65 (pp. 237–45); and Jerzy Limon, *Dangerous Matter: English Drama and Politics in 1623/24* (Cambridge: Cambridge University Press, 1986), ch. 3 (esp. pp. 84–88). Heinemann disagrees with Limon's view that the political drama of 1623–24 was sponsored by Charles and Buckingham as part of a propaganda campaign (p. 262).

[114] Benedict S. Robinson, 'The "Turks", Caroline Politics, and Philip Massinger's *The Renegado*', in *Localizing Caroline Drama: Politics and Economics of the Early Modern English Stage, 1625–1642*, ed. Adam Zucker and Alan B. Farmer (Basingstoke: Palgrave Macmillan, 2006), pp. 213–37 (p. 217).

moment ('current, adj.', sense 3; *OED*) and has value as a commodity within a (monetary) system of exchange (sense 4; *OED*) because of the authorizing role performed by the dedication.[115] The playbook's other paratext, 'The Authors Friend to the Reader', further asserts that publication allows the play to be properly understood and profitable – both financially and in terms of the intellectual benefit it can offer to its consumers. The address is attentive to what the play costs: 'twelue-pence' for seeing it at the Cockpit and 'Six-pence more' for purchasing the playbook. But the address emphasizes that it is only through *reading* 'this worthy Story', which is printed 'for your sakes', that readers 'May Know, what they but Saw, and Heard before' (A4r).

A similar interpretative exchange can be seen in Shakespeare's Folio, where the public dedication makes a claim for an ongoing private connection between the Herberts and the King's Men, and activates the topical reputation of the brothers as an important frame through which to access and negotiate meaning. The Herberts not only authorize the collection as prestigious literary patrons, they also authorize political readings of the plays. Rather than applying exclusively to one play (as in *The Bondman*), the dedication can direct readings of the collection's categories. The Folio, for example, makes a strong claim for the importance of the English past. These vernacular histories could be seen as fashioning the nation as a significant political player on the world's stage and as a counter to Spanish influence and the political dependency that many feared would have followed from the Spanish Match. By concluding with *Henry VIII*, the Folio seems to lead providentially to the Tudor dynasty and the Protestant Reformation, promoting a political and doctrinal separation from Spain.[116] The fact that the Folio reached the bookstalls in the *immediate* aftermath of Prince Charles and Buckingham's return from Madrid in October 1623 without the Infanta Maria (an event that was greeted with celebration in England) provides a further spur for this reading.[117] The Folio's publication timing and design enhance the Herbert connection and link Shakespeare's English histories with Protestant and anti-Spanish

---

[115] *OED Online* (revised entry March 2021; accessed 11 April 2021).

[116] Other critics have also noted the 'iconoclastic impetus' of the Folio: Laoutaris ('Prefatorial', pp. 52–53) argues that the 'title page and facing poem together reproduce the function of post-Reformation tomb effigies which often looked directly at the viewer rather than upwards towards God' and suggests that 'the staunchly Protestant Herberts would have appreciated the post-reformation emblem'. See also Marcus, *Puzzling Shakespeare*, pp. 1–25.

[117] Charles and Buckingham returned to London on 5 October 1623; Shakespeare's Folio was entered in the Register on 8 November 1623, appearing on the bookstalls shortly after.

sympathies. They position the Folio within the late Jacobean marketplace where other history plays – such as *The Bondman* and reprints of Butter's Tudor histories *When You See Me You Know Me* (1621) and *1* and *2 If You Know Not Me* (1623) – were clearly intended to promote England's/Britain's role as an agent of Protestant political deliverance. A topical reading of the Folio therefore promotes an interpretative exchange between playbooks that are rarely considered together and are kept unprofitably apart by modern criticism because of their differences in size, format, and preparation.

Gary Taylor reaches a similar conclusion about the political leanings of the Folio's dedication, but suggests that it represents a change of tack. He proposes that James I was originally intended to be the dedicatee, but plans were revised as a result of a changing political environment.[118] In my view, the closeness of the Herberts and the King's Men and the literary reputation of the Pembroke circle indicate that the Herbert brothers were, from an early stage, mooted as the Folio's dedicatees. However, as is the nature of many aspects of the Folio's design, including its division of plays, the matter will remain unresolved. This uncertainty of agency also draws attention to the fact that a Protestant political reading is not suggested to the exclusion of others. The invocation of the Herberts offers the potential for situating the Folio's Histories within the context of their late Jacobean publication, but other paratextual materials and the presentation of the volume as a whole offer different interpretative incentives. The Folio celebrates the timelessness of Shakespeare's plays – explicitly through paratexts that deny the plays' confinement to any particular moment, and implicitly through the plays' presentation in a volume designed as a lasting monument to Shakespeare's work. The collection reflects the different agendas of its collaborators and seems to hedge its bets. Blount was known as a publisher of continental Catholic writers and it is unlikely that he associated the Folio with the anti-Spanish and anti-Catholic sympathies of the Herberts, investing instead in their literary reputation. The Folio's Histories encourage multiple readings: they can be seen as part of a canon of plays that are removed from the concerns of the present moment, or as easily appropriated texts that reflect on local, political issues dominating the late Jacobean period.

The one feature that unites these readings – in terms of the Folio's paratextual design – is the Englishness of the Histories. Although the clarity of the Folio's tripartite division is compromised by a careful reading

---

[118] Taylor, 'Making Meaning', pp. 67–68.

of its classical, ancient British, and Scottish histories (all categorized as 'Tragedies'), the way in which the Folio makes a book of itself is through its arrangement of plays and that unprecedented Catalogue. Paratextually, the Folio seems to suggest that the most important kind of history is English history, which is reinforced by the monumentalizing agenda of the project. The fact that the Folio ends with *Cymbeline, King of Britain* (the final play of the Tragedies) has, however, been seen as underscoring James I's succession and positioning the Folio as a collection invested in ideas of Britishness and British identity.[119] While *Cymbeline*'s place as the final play is significant (and perhaps reflects a strategy to open and close the Folio with plays that had not yet been seen in print), it does not detract from the central position of English history within the collection.[120] The Folio could have ordered its Histories to resemble chronicles such as Holinshed's, which would have seen the ancient British histories, *King Lear* and *Cymbeline*, as the first plays in the category. Instead, it is an English collective identity that takes prime position – and which persists in modern criticism that draws so heavily on the Folio's reading of history.

Conclusions

In the years following the publication of the 1623 Folio, its tripartite division was not taken up by any other play collection – and history did not appear again as a dramatic category on a title page or contents page. On the one hand, this absence could indicate that the promotion of history in Shakespeare's Folio had limited impact. On the other hand, it could suggest that the parameters assigned to history *were* influential and that later ventures did not adopt this classification because English monarchical history was not a significant part of their collections. Prior to Shakespeare's Folio, no play collection used two or more dramatic genres as part of its title, a situation that changed after 1623 (see Appendix). The Beaumont and Fletcher Folio, published by Humphrey Moseley in 1647, adopts a similar emphasis on genre divisions, but specifies only two categories through its title – *Comedies and Tragedies*. The collection was influenced by Shakespeare's Folio: it contains a dedication to Philip

---

[119] See Laoutaris, 'Prefatorial', p. 56, and Emrys Jones, 'Stuart *Cymbeline*', *Essays in Criticism*, 11:1 (1961), 84–99. See also Marshall, *Theatre and Empire* (pp. 67–78), who challenges the identification of Cymbeline with James, suggesting that their only similarity is that they were both styled kings of 'Britain'; and Marcus, *Puzzling Shakespeare* (ch. 3), who suggests that the play 'reveals signs of uneasiness with the Jacobean line' (p. 118).

[120] Jowett, *Shakespeare and Text*, pp. 86–88.

Herbert, which directly refers to the role of the Herbert brothers as patrons in Shakespeare's volume, and it also includes a 'Catalogue' of the plays.[121] 'History' is the notable omission from both the title and the catalogue, minimizing its significance as a dramatic category, but also perhaps confirming the 1623 parameters because none of the plays in the 1647 volume dramatize the lives of medieval English monarchs. Similarly, Moseley's 1651 collection of William Cartwright's works, which features plays and non-dramatic texts, is titled *Comedies, Tragicomedies, With other Poems* (Wing C709). An emphasis on dramatic categories is continued, with the exclusion of 'history' in a collection that does not feature the English monarchical past.

However, the fact that subsequent play collections were not as invested in putting forward ideas of genre through their paratexts suggests that the use of dramatic categories as general titles was somewhat superficial. The Beaumont and Fletcher Folio's interest in genre is not maintained beyond the title page. The collection is not organized by genre nor does the Catalogue divide its plays according to the two advertised categories; it simply lists all the plays as one group.[122] The same vague use of genre labels can be seen in the series of title pages prepared for nonce collections of Chapman's (Wing C1940A), Marston's (M816), and Ford's (F1466A) plays in 1652. It appears as if Richard Hearne printed (for Walter Chetwynd of Ingestre) three general title pages for collections that gathered together previously printed editions of the dramatists' plays. The overriding principle of collection is an authorial one and each collection contains an attribution to its dramatist alongside the same title – *Comedies, Tragicomedies, and Tragedies* – which takes on the function of an umbrella term that covers all of the included plays. While Shakespeare's Folio may have prompted the use of dramatic categories in collection titles, an attention to the parameters proposed by the 1623 venture is not substantially continued. Moreover, first-edition single-text playbooks used variants of 'history' on their title pages with much the same flexibility as before, seen in such wide-ranging texts as *The Costly Whore* in 1633 ('Comicall Historie'; STC 25582), *Perkin Warbeck* in 1634 ('Chronicle Historie'; STC 11157), and *The Great Duke of Florence* in 1636 ('Comicall Historie'; STC 17637). Reprints, such as *Doctor Faustus* ('Tragicall History'; 1624, 1628, 1631), tended to preserve their earlier classifications.[123] Even if collections eschewed it as a category, 'history' was

[121] Francis Beaumont and John Fletcher, *Comedies and Tragedies* (London, 1647; Wing B1581), A2r–v.
[122] Ibid., g2v. See also Berek, 'Genres', pp. 159–60.   [123] See STC 17435, 17435.5, 17436.

enduringly malleable as a dramatic label. Indeed, these last examples of 'history' all appear with a qualifier that serves to clarify the nature of the history offered by the play, which contrasts with the Folio's unqualified use. The epithets 'Tragicall', 'Comicall', and 'Chronicle' negate the Folio's threefold division of plays as each is aligned with 'history'.

For Shakespeare's plays in folio format, the 1623 Catalogue divisions stuck and its list of plays was preserved in later folios, even when more plays were added. Shakespeare's Third Folio (1664; published by Philip Chetwinde) and Fourth Folio (1685; published mainly by Henry Herringman, but also with Edward Brewster, Richard Bentley, and Richard Chiswell) include new plays said to be by Shakespeare, which are prominently advertised on the title page: *Pericles, The London Prodigal, Thomas Lord Cromwell, Sir John Oldcastle, The Puritan Widow, A Yorkshire Tragedy,* and *Locrine.*[124] These titles are, however, omitted from the Catalogue in both editions, which preserves the organization of the earlier folios. On the one hand, the Catalogue in the later editions makes that same clear statement about history as a dramatic genre. But, on the other hand, the fact that the new plays seem to be outside the Catalogue's tripartite division detracts from this clarity. All of the new plays had been previously printed with title-page attributions to Shakespeare or to 'W. S.' (as in *Locrine, Thomas Lord Cromwell,* and *The Puritan Widow*), which probably motivated their inclusion in the later folios. Significantly, three of these plays – *Pericles, Sir John Oldcastle,* and *A Yorkshire Tragedy* – had been part of the Jaggard–Pavier collection. In the later folios, they remain outside the volume's exclusive generic parameters, which serves to illustrate how differently the 1619 and 1623 collections approach ideas of genre and history, a point that is rarely recognized, as the dominant critical tendency is to stress the similarities between these collections and see the 1619 venture as a kind of precursor to the Folio.

It is, however, the Jaggard–Pavier collection's interest in the inclusivity of history, rather than the exclusivity suggested by the Folio, that has continuing relevance, and is one of the reasons why it is important to see this proto-collection as a significant, independent venture, rather than merely a precursor. Readers (both private and professional) continued to arrange their playbooks in volumes that suggest interconnections between

---

[124] Only *Pericles* is now regularly attributed to Shakespeare (and George Wilkins). Herringman's name is the only one to appear on all title-page imprints of the Fourth Folio. Brewster and Bentley appear alongside Herringman in one variant (Greg *), while all four stationers are named in another (Greg †). See Greg, III, p. 1119; Murphy, *Shakespeare in Print*, p. 55.

different histories. For example, beginning in the 1650s, publishers issued 'catalogues' of plays – meaning, in this case, stock lists of titles they had in their possession or general lists of plays (and sometimes other texts) that had been published in England.[125] Generic identifiers accompany individual titles in some of these catalogues.[126] In his 'Advertisement to the Reader' (appended to his 1671 catalogue), Francis Kirkman offers his own interpretation of the history play as a genre that has a wide scope and requires its readers to create their own meaning and definition:

> [B]y Playes alone you may very well know the Chronicle History of *England*, and many other Histories. I could enlarge much on this account, having for my own fancy written down all the Historical Playes in a succinct orderly method, as you may do the like.[127]

For Kirkman, as for other early play buyers and collectors, the history play incorporates English history and 'other Histories', and his account draws attention to the active participation that is involved in reading and organizing these plays. Kirkman assumes that readers will, like him, want to arrange their history plays in a 'succinct orderly method', but does not give prescriptive directions.

   Within his catalogue 'of all the Comedies, Tragedies, Tragi-Comedies, Pastorals, Masques and Interludes, that were ever yet Printed' (A1r) – a title that interestingly omits 'history' as a genre, despite the importance Kirkman assigns it in the advertisement – a variety of plays are labelled as histories (using the letter 'H'). Kirkman's organization does not suggest a systematic method, but the conflation of different readings and influences. For Shakespeare's plays, he adopts the 1623 Folio's classifications, but this model does not inform his treatment of other plays and his practices elsewhere are idiosyncratic. One interesting example is the classification of, what seems to be, Shakespeare's *King Lear* as a tragedy and the anonymous *King Leir* as a history (A4v–B1r). The different labels could suggest a reading that is attentive to the changes Shakespeare made to his source material (and the play's ending). But in Kirkman's case, it most likely relates to the editions the stationer was accessing or remembering: Shakespeare's Folio and the 1605 edition of the anonymous *Leir*. As part

---

[125] For publishers' catalogues, see also Hooks, *Selling*, ch. 4.
[126] See Archer's catalogue of 'all the Plaies that were ever printed', discussed briefly in the Introduction and appended to Massinger, Middleton, and Rowley, *The Old Law* (1656; M1048), a1r–b4v.
[127] Kirkman's advertisement and catalogue of all the plays 'that were ever yet Printed and Published' are appended to a translation of Pierre Corneille's *Nicomède* (London, 1671; Wing C6315), B4v. The catalogue (without the advertisement) had appeared ten years earlier in 1661.

of the Jaggard–Pavier collection, *King Lear* was, of course, a 'True Chronicle History', rather than a tragedy, which underscores the flexibility of genre labels and leads me to the final point with which I would like to conclude. The participation of plays in different genres is contingent upon how the material texts are presented through their paratexts and on how they are collected with others. The evidence of the Jaggard–Pavier collection and the subsequent practices of early readers and publishers advance a model for understanding history that moves beyond Shakespeare's Folio: it is flexible, subject to revision and the confluence of different influences, and can be variously weighed and interpreted depending on how plays are bound together.

Conclusion: 'A Historie of noble mention'

> Studyes haue, of this Nature, been of late
> So out of fashion, so vnfollow'd; that
> It is become more Iustice, to reviue
> The antick follyes of the Times, then striue
> To countenance wise Industrie.[1]

In 1634, Hugh Beeston published John Ford's *Perkin Warbeck*, an English history play first performed by Queen Henrietta Maria's Men. Critics have generally accepted the prologue's claims that studies 'of this Nature' have become 'So out of fashion, so vnfollow'd' as an indication of the history play's decline: *Perkin Warbeck* has been described as a 'fascinating oddity' within the Caroline period.[2] The prologue is, however, ambiguous. It is not entirely clear what is meant by studies 'of this Nature' – whether, for example, this description refers only to English histories, to distant histories that are removed from the 'antick follyes of the Times' or, instead, to honourable kinds of 'Historie of noble mention' (A4v). The playbook also contains discursive paratexts – a dedication and commendatory verses – that help to negotiate the play's meaning and impose a framework for reading. These print features are part of what makes *Perkin Warbeck* distinctive and different from earlier single-text English histories, such as those by Shakespeare, Heywood, and Rowley, which continued to be issued in individual editions during the Caroline period and lack any paratextual material beyond their title pages. This divergence in print features and investment patterns amongst Caroline histories makes a short consideration of them a useful point of conclusion. Farmer and Lesser

---

[1] John Ford, *The Chronicle Historie of Perkin Warbeck* (London, 1634; STC 11157), A4v.
[2] Alexander Leggatt, 'A Double Reign: *Richard II* and *Perkin Warbeck*', in *Shakespeare and His Contemporaries: Essays in Comparison*, ed. E. A. J. Honigmann (Manchester: Manchester University Press, 1986), pp. 129–39 (p. 138). See also Miles Taylor, 'The End of the English History Play in *Perkin Warbeck*', *Studies in English Literature, 1500–1900*, 48:2 (2008), 395–418.

propose that, during this period, a canon of Elizabethan and Jacobean plays was emerging – a canon that was not necessarily conceptually defined, but determined by marketability in the book trade and 'customers' attachment to particular "classics"'.[3] These 'Golden Age' playbooks (which include the histories of Shakespeare, Heywood, and Rowley) remained popular in print, whereas Caroline first editions seem to have been read for their novelty and currency.[4] *Perkin Warbeck*'s emphasis on its unusual status as a history could have the effect, in print, of aligning the new play with these earlier, established English histories. Its extensive paratexts, however, clearly identify it as a Caroline playbook and control readings of its subject much more explicitly than some earlier histories.

Perkin Warbeck dramatizes the monarchical claims of the title character, a pretender to the English throne, who challenged the authority of Henry VII by declaring he was Richard Plantagenet, Duke of York (the second son of Edward IV, who had disappeared in 1483). While the historical Warbeck confessed he was an impostor, Ford reshapes his sources to give a relatively sympathetic portrayal of Warbeck's career in which the protagonist is fully invested in his own claim that he is the rightful heir. Although the play concludes with Warbeck's execution and the state's purging 'of corrupted bloud' (L1r), it shows the pretender as heroically resolved in the pursuit of his claim. The playbook's discursive paratexts emphasize this interpretation: a series of commendatory verses applaud Ford's play, claiming that it eternizes both the writer and the historical Warbeck. Ralph Eure praises Ford for 'The GLORIOVS PERKIN, and thy Poet's Art | Equall with His, in playing the KINGS PART' (A3v). Similarly, George Crymes's commendatory verse glosses over Warbeck's rebellion and execution to celebrate the worthiness of his 'loftie spirit', conveyed through Ford's skill as a dramatist:

> Perkin is rediviu'd by thy strong hand,
> And crownd a King of new; the vengefull wand
> Of Greatnesse is forgot: His Execution
> May rest vn-mention'd, and His birth's Collusion
> Lye buried in the Storie: But His fame
> Thou hast eterniz'd; made a Crowne His Game.
> His loftie spirit soares yet.
>
> (A3v)

---

[3] Farmer and Lesser, 'Popularity', p. 28.
[4] Alan B. Farmer and Zachary Lesser, 'Canons and Classics: Publishing Drama in Caroline England', in *Localizing Caroline Drama*, ed. Zucker and Farmer, pp. 17–41 (esp. pp. 28–35).

While the paratexts in no way condone rebellion against a monarch, their praising and conjoining of Warbeck and Ford inevitably tempers criticism of the play's protagonist and encourages a reading that is sympathetic to Warbeck's own (albeit misguided) ideals. It is a playbook that could be used to explore ideas of resistance and opposition. The fact that Henry Herbert allowed the publication of *Perkin Warbeck* on the proviso that the overseers 'observ[e] the Caution in the License' perhaps indicates that he read the play as having subversive potential.[5] Herbert's assessment would, however, have been based only on the main play: until 1637, paratexts were not subject to licensing, meaning that they could be an important transactional site for negotiating a play's application to the times and its use of history. They provided a platform for direct and unregulated commentary, in contrast to the main text – that is until the Star Chamber Decree of 1637 added 'Titles, Epistles, Prefaces, Proems, Preambles, Introductions, Tables, [and] Dedications' to the list of items that required authorization prior to publication.[6] The decree indicates a growing awareness of paratexts' ability to position a text, potentially in controversial ways.

The example of *Perkin Warbeck* introduces three important points about the Caroline publication of history plays with which I would like to conclude. This study has concentrated on the publication of history plays during Shakespeare's lifetime and in the years immediately following his death, when the Folio was being prepared and published. Chapters have considered how agents other than Shakespeare and his fellow dramatists read and constructed history plays, including the interpretative implications these actions had and continue to have. It is, however, useful to address a few Caroline developments, particularly because they were shaped by practices from the earlier periods, because they help to clarify this study's approach, and because they connect Chapter 4's emphasis on paratexts in collections with patterns in single-text history plays. First, Caroline single-text editions regularly use their dedications, addresses to readers, and commendatory verses to put forward readings of the histories they contain, offering in some cases a more direct interpretation than the paratexts accompanying collected editions could achieve. While an assessment of playbook paratexts has formed the basis of this study's four main chapters, these materials have often been limited to title pages, which have then been considered alongside an analysis of a publisher's wider output.

---

[5] Bawcutt (ed.), *Records*, p. 53.
[6] See Item II from the 1637 Star Chamber Decree; printed in Arber, IV, pp. 528–36.

The kind of paratextual address featured in *Tamburlaine* (1590) or *The Wonder of Women* (1606) – both considered in the Introduction – do not become a regular part of single-text, commercial playbooks until roughly the Caroline period. To illustrate, between 1626 and 1642, approximately 121 first editions were published and, of these, 79 (or 65 per cent) contain a dedication, address to readers, and/or commendatory verse. In comparison, of the 111 first editions printed between 1603 and 1625, 50 (or 45 per cent) contain one or more of these paratexts, the rate of inclusion increasing towards the end of the Jacobean period.[7] This gradual development, suggestive of the growing status of plays from the commercial stages, applies to all genres of first-edition playbooks. However, as the examples of *Perkin Warbeck* and Massinger's late Jacobean playbook, *The Bondman*, demonstrate, discursive paratexts could play a vital role in shaping a history play's contemporaneity and an understanding of its own history.

To give another Caroline example, Massinger's *The Roman Actor*, first performed by the King's Men in 1626 and published in 1629 by Robert Allott, features a number of paratextual addresses that seem designed to highlight the play's application to Caroline concerns, including a growing unease over Charles I's absolutist views, his attitude towards parliamentary debate, and the dominance of court favourites, particularly Buckingham. The play is set during the reign of the Emperor Domitian (who ruled from 81 to 96 CE) and portrays the emperor as a tyrannical, absolutist ruler. It draws on Jacobean histories, such as *Sejanus* and *A Game at Chess*, and incorporates a series of inset plays that explore the ability of drama to enact or encourage change.[8] The play ends by emphasizing the dangers of tyrannical government and offers a warning to rulers: 'Good Kings are mourn'd for after life' but those who are governed 'onely by their will' die 'Vnlamented'.[9] The playbook's publication in 1629 may have been occasioned by its potential for a topical reading: in March of that year, an

---

[7] My calculations only consider first-edition 'commercial' plays, most of which are single-text editions. When a collection (such as Shakespeare's Folio) includes a first-edition text, the collection as a whole has been counted as one. The relevant paratexts for this comparison are dedications, addresses, and commendatory verses, because they are used most frequently to position plays and direct readers' interpretation. Changing the parameters – for example, taking account of actor and character lists – yields different results: between 1603 and 1625, 61 of the 111 first editions (55 per cent) contain paratexts in addition to a title page, which increases, between 1626 and 1642, to 108 out of 121 first editions (or 89 per cent). Statistics have been calculated using *DEEP* and the finding lists from Berger and Massai's *Paratexts in English Printed Drama*, II, pp. 954–1009.

[8] See Patterson, *Censorship*, pp. 95–99; Martin Butler, 'Romans in Britain: *The Roman Actor* and the Early Stuart Classical Play', in *Philip Massinger: A Critical Reassessment*, ed. Douglas Howard (Cambridge: Cambridge University Press, 1985), pp. 139–70.

[9] Philip Massinger, *The Roman Actor* (London, 1629; STC 17642), K4v.

outspoken critic of Buckingham's royal influence, Sir John Eliot, was arrested for insubordination towards Charles. As Annabel Patterson proposes, this event may have informed the publication of *The Roman Actor*, given that one of the tyrannical vices exposed in the play is the suppression of dissenting views.[10] The playbook's presentation strategies support this idea because they seem invested in blurring the boundary between text and paratext by merging the play's history with the paratexts' presentist concern with the actions of Caroline readers. The paratexts claim that Massinger has revitalized his Roman history, making it current and useful. Ford's commendatory address, for example, suggests that Massinger's representation of historical individuals may inspire action in its readers:

> ... thy abler Pen
> Spoke them, and made them speake, nay Act agen
> In such a height, that Heere to know their Deeds
> Hee may become an Actor that but Reades.
>
> (A4r)

While Ford is drawing on conventional tropes, praising Massinger for his ability to write dialogue that brings his Roman history to life, the verses also imply that this history can shape actions in wider political life (which is the quest of its inset plays), and turn the playbook's readers into both theatrical and political actors.

My second point is that first-edition Caroline playbooks draw attention to the involvement of the play's dramatist in publication with much greater frequency than Elizabethan and Jacobean playbooks. Most of the history plays examined in this study do not reveal any traces of their authors' role in the process; instead, it is likely that publication agents took the lead or were entrusted with the task by dramatists and/or companies, which is why they are my main focus. There are, of course, exceptions in the playbooks of, for example, Jonson, Marston, and Dekker – the latter clearly worked with Butter in the publication of *The Whore of Babylon*. Nevertheless, much of the interest in history plays as printed books and the different ways in which they could be positioned to respond to other dramatic and non-dramatic texts was stationer driven. By the Caroline period, dramatists regularly seem to be involved as overseers and to contribute prefatory materials that offer readings of their plays. This new conspicuousness is not, however, uniform or even consistent for one dramatist. New plays were still published without paratexts and without

---

[10] Patterson, *Censorship*, p. 96.

any indication of the author's cooperation or knowledge. The reason why this (partial) development is noteworthy is because it reveals changing structures of investment in the Caroline book trade – which is something that Farmer and Lesser also discuss in their study of the period.[11] With dramatists and theatre companies becoming more involved in publication, patterns in investment shift slightly. They are more fragmented than they were in earlier periods: fewer stationers specialize in history plays, as Butter did, the tendency being to focus instead on specific dramatists.

Further attempts were also made to restrict publishers' freedoms. In a letter to the Stationers' Company, dated 10 June 1637, Philip Herbert (as Lord Chamberlain) commanded stationers 'to take Order for the stay of any further Impression of any of the Playes or Interludes of his Majesties servantes without their consentes' and clarified the reasons for his involvement:

> I am informed that some Coppyes of Playes belonging to the King and Queenes servantes the Players, and purchased by them at Deare rates, haueing beene lately stollen or gotten from them by indirect meanes are now attempted to bee printed and that some of them are at the Presse and ready to bee printed, which if it should bee suffered, would directly tend to their apparent Detriment and great preiudice and to the disenabling of them to doe their Majestes service.[12]

The Stationers' Company was required to prohibit the publication of playbooks by its members unless they had 'some Certificate in writeing vnder the handes of Iohn Lowen and Ioseph Taylor for the Kings servantes and of Christopher Bieston for the Kings and Queenes young Company'.[13] This order indicates that the King's Men and Beeston (the impresario in control of Queen Henrietta Maria's Men and Beeston's Boys) wanted to control the publication of their plays. While a similar request had been issued by William Herbert in 1619, it was only for the King's Men. Gurr singles out the 1637 order as 'the first record of the companies using officialdom to protect their rights over their playbooks', and it was followed by another order on 7 August 1641 from the new Lord Chamberlain, Robert Devereux, third earl of Essex, but this time only for

---

[11] Farmer and Lesser, 'Canons', pp. 17–41.
[12] E. K. Chambers (ed.), 'Dramatic Records: The Lord Chamberlain's Office', *Collections Vol. II Part III*, Malone Society Publications, vol. 71 (Oxford: Oxford University Press, 1931), pp. 321–416 (pp. 384–85).
[13] Ibid., p. 385.

plays from the King's Men.[14] These orders are not, however, a testament
to their effectiveness. The very fact that they were needed suggests non-
compliance. They do nevertheless demonstrate that companies, impresa-
rios, and dramatists were hoping to reallocate stationer privileges and
become the main agents overseeing the publication of commercial plays.

Stationers retained pivotal and exclusive roles in the publication of
reprints – both as single-text editions and collections. Humphrey
Lownes issued another reprint of Heywood's two-part plays *1* and *2*
Edward IV in 1626. The second edition of Shakespeare's Folio, preserving
its tripartite division, was published in 1632; and Nathaniel Butter and
John Norton, both based in St Paul's Churchyard, dominated the Caroline
market for reprinted single-text history plays. Butter continued to invest in
his provenly successful early Jacobean histories: Heywood's *If You Know
Not Me, You Know Nobody* (Part 1: Q7 1632, Q8 1639; Part 2: Q4 1633)
and Rowley's *When You See Me You Know Me* (Q4 1632). From 1632,
Norton, operating at the south door of St Paul's, started to publish
editions of Shakespeare's *Richard II* (Q6 1634), *Richard III* (Q8 1634),
and *1 Henry IV* (Q8 1632, Q9 1639), titles previously held by Matthew
Law during the Jacobean and early Caroline periods.[15] None of these
history-play reprints contain individual prefatory addresses, dedications, or
commendatory verses. Shakespeare's Folio contains paratexts for the entire
collection, rather than individual ones that direct the reading of each play.
This pattern is to be expected. Most reprints follow their first editions,
even if some paratexts have lost relevance or the application has changed.
What is significant, however, is the division that was emerging between the
printed appearance of first editions and the reprints of older histories. Most
first editions printed during the Caroline period contain quite elaborate
and discursive paratextual materials and, when considering the absence of
these in, for example, Butter's, Norton's, and Lownes's editions, a visual
disparity is apparent. This development corresponds to Farmer and
Lesser's observations about the split in the Caroline book trade. Patterns
in playbook paratexts enhance this division and, for history plays, it has the
added effect that reprinted histories – specifically, those of English
monarchs – seem to recall older theatrical traditions and acquire an
established status.

---

[14] Gurr, *Shakespearian Playing Companies*, p. 382. See also Loewenstein, *Possessive Authorship*,
    pp. 37–38.
[15] A printer by trade, Norton had been hired by Law to print *Richard III* (Q7) in 1629 and, following
    his marriage to Law's daughter, Alice, appears to have inherited these copyrights. For a profile of
    Norton's interest in Shakespeare's histories and their politics, see Farmer, 'Norton', pp. 147–76.

Finally, perhaps owing to the split in the book market, the range of history plays appearing on the London bookstalls during the Caroline period was particularly diverse. It is essential to take account of both first-edition and reprint markets, as it is only by doing so that we can recover an accurate picture of the publications available to readers.[16] Reprinted histories predominantly featured medieval English and Tudor pasts. It is in this group that *Perkin Warbeck* attempts to position itself as a new classic. Other Caroline first editions, especially those that were written and first staged during the period, tend to reveal an interest in classical and distant historical pasts, as in *The Roman Actor*. Indeed, Massinger adopts a similar strategy in *Believe as You List* (written in 1630–31), a play which originally dramatized the life of King Sebastian of Portugal but, owing to Henry Herbert's censorship, was moved to a classical setting (second century BCE) and lightly reshaped to recount the history of the Seleucid king, Antiochus III the Great.[17] Other examples include Thomas Nabbes's *Hannibal and Scipio* (1637), a play first performed by Queen Henrietta Maria's Men in 1635, and Lodowick Carlell's *1* and *2 Arviragus and Philicia* (1639) from the King's Men, which features ancient British history. An examination of these markets therefore indicates continuing interest in plays dramatizing and using the past – which, for first editions, was often registered directly in paratexts that assess the 'Actions of Antiquitie'.[18]

Buyers' collecting practices demonstrate that these plays were read alongside each other. A *Sammelband*, assembled in *c*.1635 and now held in the Folger, contains Caroline first editions alongside reprinted editions (also mostly Caroline). The selection of texts prioritizes classical and English history plays, including, in the following order: *The Roman Actor* (1629), *Catiline* (1635), *Caesar and Pompey* (1631, by Chapman), *The Tragedy of Nero* (1633, anonymous), *1* and *2 The Troublesome Reign of King John* (1622), *1 Henry IV* (1632), *Richard III* (1629), *1* and *2 Edward IV* (1626), and *1* and *2 If You Know Not Me, You Know Nobody* (1632; 1633).[19] This *Sammelband* shows that readers united different historical

---

[16] Farmer and Lesser ('Canons', p. 20) also show that the years from 1629 to 1640 record the 'highest edition totals of the entire early modern period'.

[17] See Bawcutt (ed.), *Records*, pp. 171–72. In several places in the manuscript (the play was not printed until 1849), the original names survive, including the use of 'Sebastian' for Antiochus on folios 9a (line 634) and 13a (line 1127). See Philip Massinger, *Believe as You List*, ed. Charles Sisson, Malone Society Publications, vol. 60 (Oxford: Oxford University Press for the Malone Society, 1927), pp. 22, 38.

[18] *Perkin Warbeck*, A2r.

[19] Folger Shakespeare Library STC 4619. The dates correspond to the imprints on each play in the *Sammelband*, which was likely bound up shortly after the publication of the latest edition (i.e., Jonson's *Catiline*). See Knight, 'Making', pp. 318–22.

pasts through their binding practices, although this example does maintain a division between classical and English pasts that is enhanced by the absence of paratextual materials in the English histories. Patterns in the Caroline book trade (including the division in the market between first and reprint editions) perhaps contributed to an emerging canon of *English* histories – as single-text reprints and as part of Shakespeare's Folio collections. The 'established' status of the English monarchical history play – secured by Caroline publication patterns and marketability – and the cultural capital subsequently accrued by Shakespeare have helped to define the history play in ways that have continuing relevance today.

*

Rather than providing a teleological narrative of the genre's development, *Publishing the History Play in the Time of Shakespeare* has concentrated on local readings of history plays suggested by the strategies of selection and presentation that inform the publication process. It has argued that history plays do not have fixed characteristics or ideologies; they do not 'belong' to the genre; and they do not use the past in clearly defined or consistent ways. Plays do not have a single political application or relationship to their time of composition. Instead, these readings and ways of categorizing, historicizing, and politicizing are brought to the plays by the individuals who engage with them during their performance and print afterlives. While history-play criticism has by now a long-standing interest in discussing the wider social, political, and historical contexts of early modern drama, it often depends on single, author-centric readings of the plays. Studies tend to focus on how the dramatist (usually Shakespeare) has adapted historical sources to examine the past and reflect on an early modern present. I have not aimed to uproot this emphasis on the dramatist, but to offer a different – and largely unexplored – perspective on the history play that has crucial consequences for other approaches. By bringing the methodologies of book history and bibliographic studies to bear on an analysis of history plays, I have been able to show how the publication process controls our access to and understanding of the genre through strategies of selection (print contexts) and presentation (print paratexts). Rather than depending on the notion of implied readers, my emphasis on the publication process provides evidence of historical readers and their interpretations of the genre and of specific plays. Genre is not something static or unchanging in the life of a text, and an analysis of publication practices recovers a range of synchronic, transitory readings (some of which have had lasting consequences) that do not depend on a reified author's interpretation but are responsive to the reception and use of history plays.

This study has therefore concentrated on the role of publishers – the first professional readers of history plays. Publishers are at the nexus of production and reception, which makes them so useful for exploring genre. They are agents of reception, who 'read' history plays and respond to patterns in the book trade, and they are also agents of production, who shape playbook presentation and content in ways that direct the responses of other readers. Because publishers are collectors and categorizers of texts, they are closely invested in ideas of genre – even if this is not explicitly articulated in playbook paratexts. Their patterns of investment 'bind' together (conceptually and sometimes materially) different history plays and, through these practices, we can explore how plays were selected and used by some of their most influential historical readers. I do not, however, consider the influence of publishers to the exclusion of other agents, such as trade printers who could also shape the printed presentation – and therefore interpretation – of playbooks. An overarching emphasis on both the distinctive and overlapping roles of stationers helps us to see that plays dramatizing different national pasts were read together, that history plays were marketed alongside non-dramatic texts, and that they were important participants in the period's historical culture. Indeed, it would be beneficial for critical studies that explore topics of national identity, sovereignty, and government in the period and typically concentrate on Shakespeare's English histories to broaden their scope, as the practices of early modern stationers reveal and capitalize on the connections that exist between a diverse range of histories.

The publication process also sheds light on another key feature of history plays: their timeliness. Stationers only invested in history plays (or any speculative text) because of a predicted 'currency' – that the texts would appeal to readers and make a profit. History plays needed to be 'current', an expectation of production that draws attention to a conceptual overlap between ideas of timeliness and timelessness. Some history playbooks advertise their timeliness through newsworthy subjects and/or print paratexts that encourage topical applications (as in *The Whore of Babylon*), but so too do publications (such as Shakespeare's First Folio) that position their histories and dramatists as having a degree of timelessness – which is simply another form of 'currency' and contemporaneity that is rooted in and reflective of a specific moment, albeit one that aspires to greater longevity.

Publishers' practices were determined by multiple factors and agendas, and it is crucial to recognize that some of these did not involve a careful reading of a history play or an understanding of its political force. Their investments were controlled, for example, by the availability of playscripts, the ownership of titles, and by external efforts to allocate the rights to copy (such as those by several lord chamberlains). Wise's investment in Shakespeare's English histories can be linked to the contemporaneity of this kind of history during the 1590s, but also to Shakespeare's name and the connection of the Chamberlain's Men to George Carey. The 1619 Jaggard–Pavier collection similarly displays an interest in ideas of history, but also in 'Shakespeare' as an organizational principle. And despite the Folio's efforts to singularize and fix the genre, it offers, as a collection, multiple ways of reading the plays, shaped by the different strategies of those who collaborated in its production. Like early modern and modern writers (ranging from Sidney and Florio, to Derrida, Jauss, Rackin, and Griffin) who theorize directly about 'kinds' of writing and ideas of genre, publishers are motivated by their own agendas – which, in their case, are contingent upon the marketability of plays and the influence of collaborative networks of exchange.

These agendas have had significant consequences for history plays – and, of course, for all plays. The way in which a play makes a book of itself informs subsequent readers' responses, and the selection of plays for publication has largely determined our access to early modern drama. In particular, *Publishing the History Play in the Time of Shakespeare* has warned against the assumption that printed plays are representative of performance repertories. Our view of the Queen's Men as a company specializing in history plays has been defined through publication. Shakespeare's prominence as a dramatist of English monarchical history has been established through patterns of print investment from Wise, to the Jaggards and Pavier, to the Folio syndicate. It is essential to recognize that the theatre and the book trade are two separate environments that reflect very different kinds of participation in history as a dramatic genre. It has been the aim of this book to evaluate one of these and to explore how the publication process has written its own history of these plays and their accounts of the past.

Plays in Collection, 1560–1659

Featured in this table are all printed collections that include at least one play, commercial or non-commercial. The abbreviations in the 'Type of Collection' column, which refers to the kinds of texts within the collection, are expanded as: NCP = non-commercial play; CP = commercial play; ND = non-dramatic text; (N) = nonce or tract collection. Those collections which contain one or more commercial plays are highlighted in grey, which illustrates a rough chronology of collections that can be compared to patterns for non-commercial plays (although this visual distinction should not be taken to suggest a rigid boundary between these types of collections). Two-part plays are assigned uniform titles (i.e. '1 & 2') to indicate this status at a glance. The inclusion of contents pages is indicated by the relevant column, which also gives the general heading assigned to these contents in the printed book. When all of a collection's texts are named on the title page (which therefore acts as a contents list), 'TP' is given in the 'Contents' column. This indicator does not, however, appear for two-part plays. To assist in locating the collections, STC and/or Wing numbers are provided for each edition and issue (details for the latter are given by either '/x' in the STC/Wing column or a footnote). The stationer(s) who likely invested in the collection and took on the role of the publisher are indicated in the final column. Latin plays are not included in this list.

Date	Collection Title	Author(s)	Type of Collection	Contents	STC/ Wing	Format	Publisher(s)
[c.1560]	A Merry Jest of Robin Hood and of His Life	Anon.	NCP/ND	TP	13691	4°	William Copland
[c.1570]	All Such Treatises	Thomas Norton (and Thomas Sackville for Gorboduc)	NCP/ND (N)	Yes (no heading)	18677	8°	John Day (1)
1573	A Hundred Sundry Flowers	George Gascoigne	NCP/ND	Yes ('contents')	11635	4°	Richard Smith
[1575]	The Posies	George Gascoigne	NCP/ND	Yes ('Flowers', 'fruites', 'Hearbes', 'Weedes')	11636/7	4°	Richard Smith
1575	The First Part of Churchyard's Chips	Thomas Churchyard	NCP/ND	Yes ('Contentes')	5232	4°	Thomas Marsh
1578	The First Part of Churchyard's Chips	Thomas Churchyard	NCP/ND	Yes ('Contentes')	5233	4°	Thomas Marsh
1578	1 & 2 Promos and Cassandra	George Whetstone	CP?/ NCP?		25347	4°	Richard Jones
1581	Ten Tragedies	Seneca (English translations)	NCP	Yes ('Names')	22221	4°	Thomas Marsh
1587	The Whole Works	George Gascoigne	NCP/ND	Yes ('Flowers', 'fruites', 'Hearbes', 'Weedes')	11638/9	4°	Richard Smith
[c.1590]	A Merry Jest of Robin Hood and of His Life	Anon.	NCP/ND	TP	13692	4°	Edward White (1)

Year	Title	Author(s)			STC	Format	Printer/Publisher
1590	The Serpent of Division [and Gorboduc]	John Lydgate; Thomas Norton; Thomas Sackville	NCP/ND	TP ('History'; 'Tragedy')	17029	4°	John Perrin
1590	1 & 2 Tamburlaine the Great	Christopher Marlowe	CP		17425	8°	Richard Jones
1591	The Countess of Pembroke's Ivychurch	Abraham Fraunce	NCP/ND	TP	11340	4°	William Ponsonby
1591	1 & 2 The Troublesome Reign of King John¹	Anon.	CP		14644	4°	Sampson Clarke
1592	A Discourse of Life and Death; Antonius	Mary Herbert; Robert Garnier; Philippe de Mornay	NCP/ND	TP (Life and Death'; 'Tragedie')	18138	4°	William Ponsonby
1592	Speeches Delivered to Her Majesty This Last Progress	Anon.	NCP		7600	4°	Joseph Barnes
1593	1 & 2 Tamburlaine the Great	Christopher Marlowe	CP		17426	8°	Richard Jones
1594	Delia and Rosamond Augmented; Cleopatra	Samuel Daniel	NCP/ND	TP	6243.4	16°	Simon Waterson
1595	Delia and Rosamond Augmented; Cleopatra	Samuel Daniel	NCP/ND	TP	6243.5	8°	Simon Waterson
1597	1 & 2 Tamburlaine the Great	Christopher Marlowe	CP	[no title leaf]	17427	8°	Richard Jones
1598	Delia; Rosamond; Cleopatra (imperfect copy)	Samuel Daniel	NCP/ND		6243.6	12°	Simon Waterson

¹ The Troublesome Reign is actually a single play that has been presented – in print – as a two-part play through the insertion of an artificial division (including a title page and print prologue) in the middle of the play's action. It is useful to include here because the playbook constructs itself as a collection through its print strategies.

Date	Collection Title	Author(s)	Type of Collection	Contents	STC/ Wing	Format	Publisher(s)
1598	*The Countess of Pembroke's Arcadia*	Philip Sidney	NCP/ND		22541	2°	William Ponsonby
1599	*The Countess of Pembroke's Arcadia*	Philip Sidney	NCP/ND		22542	2°	Robert Waldegrave
1599	*The Poetical Essays*	Samuel Daniel	NCP/ND	Yes ('Argumentes of these Essayes')	6261	4°	Simon Waterson
1599	*1 & 2 Edward the Fourth*	Thomas Heywood	CP		13341	4°	John Oxonbridge
1600	*1 & 2 Edward the Fourth*	Thomas Heywood	CP		13342	4°	John Oxonbridge and Humphrey Lownes (1)
1601	*The Works*	Samuel Daniel	NCP/ND		6236/7	2°	Simon Waterson
1602	*1 & 2 A Satire of the Three Estates*	David Lindsay	NCP		15681[2]	4°	Robert Charteris
1604	*His Part of King James his Royal and Magnificent Entertainment*	Ben Jonson	NCP		14756	4°	Edward Blount
1604	*The Monarchic Tragedies*	William Alexander	NCP		343	4°	Edward Blount
1605	*The Countess of Pembroke's Arcadia*	Philip Sidney	NCP/ND		22543/a	2°	Simon Waterson; Matthew Lownes listed for (a)
1605	*1 & 2 Edward the Fourth*	Thomas Heywood	CP		13343	4°	Nathaniel Fosbrooke
1605	*Certain Small Poems*	Samuel Daniel	CP/NCP/ ND		6239	8°	Simon Waterson and Edward Blount (latter included for *Philotas*)[3]

[2] There are two issues of this collection: the first exists in two states (STC 15681 and 15681.5); the second (STC 15682) is dated 1604 and titled *The Works of the Famous and Worthy Knight, Sir David Lindsay.*

[3] *Philotas* is bibliographically independent, but there is no evidence it was issued separately (Greg, I, p. 340).

Year	Title	Author	CP/NCP/ND	General title	STC	Format	Publisher
1607	*Certain Small Works*	Samuel Daniel	CP/NCP/ND	Yes ('Poems')	6240	8°	Simon Waterson
1607	*Philotas; A Panegyric Congratulatory; A Defence of Rhyme*	Samuel Daniel	CP/NCP/ND	[no general title]	6263	12°	Edward Blount
1607 [1608]	*The Monarchic Tragedies* / *The Characters of Two Royal Masques*	William Alexander / Ben Jonson	NCP / NCP	TP ('Tragedies')	344 / 14761	4° / 4°	Edward Blount / Thomas Thorpe
1608	*The Conspiracy and Tragedy of Charles Duke of Byron*	George Chapman	CP		4968	4°	Thomas Thorpe
1610	*The Order and Solemnity of the Creation of the High and Mighty Prince Henry*	Samuel Daniel	NCP/ND		13161	4°	John Budge
1611	*1 & 2 The Troublesome Reign of King John*	Anon. (attributed to 'W. Sh.')	CP		14646	4°	John Helme
1611	*Certain Small Works*	Samuel Daniel	CP/NCP/ND	Yes ('Poems')	6242/3	12°	Simon Waterson
1613	*1 & 2 Edward the Fourth*	Thomas Heywood	CP		13344	4°	Humphrey Lownes (1)
1613	*The Countess of Pembroke's Arcadia*	Philip Sidney	NCP/ND		22544/a	2°	Simon Waterson; Matthew Lownes listed for (a)
1613	*The Triumphs of Truth; The Entertainment on Michaelmas Day 1613*	Thomas Middleton	NCP	TP	17904	4°	Nicholas Okes
1613	*A Relation of the Late Royal Entertainment*	Thomas Campion	NCP	TP	4545	4°	John Budge

Date	Collection Title	Author(s)	Type of Collection	Contents	STC/ Wing	Format	Publisher(s)
1616	The Monarchic Tragedies	William Alexander	NCP		345	8°	William Stansby
1616	The Works	Ben Jonson	CP/NCP/ ND	Yes ('Catalogue')	14751[4]	2°	William Stansby
[1619]	The Whole Contention Betweene the Two Famous Houses, Lancaster and York; Pericles [with other plays likely bound in a tract volume; see Chapter 4]	William Shakespeare	CP		26101	4°	William and Isaac Jaggard and Thomas Pavier
1619	1 & 2 Edward the Fourth	Thomas Heywood	CP		13345	4°	Humphrey Lownes (1)
1621	The Countess of Pembroke's Arcadia	Philip Sidney; William Alexander	NCP/ND		22545[5]	2°	Dublin Society of Stationers
1621	Honourable Entertainments	Thomas Middleton	NCP		17886	8°	George Eld
1622	1 & 2 The Troublesome Reign of King John	Anon. (attributed to 'W. Shakespeare')	CP		14647	4°	Thomas Dewe
1623	The Whole Works	Samuel Daniel	CP/NCP/ ND		6238	4°	Simon Waterson

[4] There are two issues of this collection: the first (STC 14751) exists in two states, and the second (STC 14752) lists Richard Meighen as bookseller.
[5] There are five issues, which vary in imprint details: the other four are STC 22545.5 (1622, for Waterson and Lownes); 22545-7 (1622, for Waterson); 22546 (1622, for Lownes): 22546a (1622, for Lownes).

1623	Comedies, Histories, and Tragedies	William Shakespeare	CP	Yes ('Catalogue' of Comedies, Histories, and Tragedies)	22273	2°	W. and I. Jaggard; E. Blount, J. Smethwick, W. Aspley
1625	The Conspiracy and Tragedy of Charles Duke of Byron	George Chapman	CP		4969	4°	Thomas Thorpe
1626	1 & 2 Edward the Fourth	Thomas Heywood	CP		13346	4°	Humphrey Lownes (1)
1627	The Countess of Pembroke's Arcadia	Philip Sidney; William Alexander	NCP/ND		22547[6]	2°	Simon Waterson
1627	The Two First Comedies	Thomas Newman (trans.); Terence	NCP	TP	23897	8°	George Miller
1630	Aristippus; The Conceited Pedlar	Thomas Randolph	NCP	TP	20686	4°	John Marriot
1630	Aristippus; The Conceited Pedlar	Thomas Randolph	NCP	TP	20686.5	4°	John Marriot
1630	Aristippus; The Conceited Pedlar	Thomas Randolph	NCP	TP	20687	4°	Robert Allott
1631	Aristippus; The Conceited Pedlar	Thomas Randolph	NCP	TP	20688	4°	Robert Allott
1631	The Works. Second Volume	Ben Jonson	CP	[no general title]	14753.5[7]	2°	Robert Allott

[6] There are three issues, which vary in imprint details: the other two are STC 22548 (1629, with Waterson as bookseller) and 22548a (1629, with Moore as bookseller).

[7] The collection was issued again in 1640 with a general title page, alongside Volume 3 of The Works (STC 14754 and 14754a).

(cont.)

Date	Collection Title	Author(s)	Type of Collection	Contents	STC/Wing	Format	Publisher(s)
1632	*Comedies, Histories, and Tragedies*	William Shakespeare	CP	Yes ('Catalogue', of Comedies, Histories, Tragedies)	22274[8]	2°	Robert Allott
1632	*Six Court Comedies*	John Lyly	CP		17088/9	12°	Edward Blount
1633	*The Countess of Pembroke's Arcadia*	Philip Sidney; William Alexander; Richard Beling	NCP/ND		22549	2°	Simon Waterson, Robert Young; Thomas Downes (1)
1633	*Poems*	Robert Gomersall	NCP/ND		11993	8°	John Marriot
1633	*Certain Learned and Elegant Works*	Fulke Greville	NCP/ND	Yes ('Names')	12361	2°	Henry Seile
1633	*The Works*	John Marston	CP	TP (Workes … Being Tragedies and Comedies')[9]	17471/2	8°	William Sheares (1)
1634	*The Rogue; Calisto and Meliboea*	Mateo Aleman	NCP/ND (N)	TP ('Life' and 'Tragi-Comedy')	291/.5	2°	Robert Allott
[1635?]	*Aristippus; The Conceited Pedlar*	Thomas Randolph	NCP	TP	20690	4°	Dublin Society of Stationers

8 There are five different issues, which vary in the imprint: STC 22274b (gives Aspley as publisher); 22274c (gives Hawkins as publisher); 22274d (gives Meighen as publisher); 22274e (gives Smethwick as publisher).
9 The list of plays is only included in STC 17472.

			NCP	TP			
1635	Aristippus; The Conceited Pedlar	Thomas Randolph	NCP		20689	4°	Robert Allot
1635	Dramatic Poems	Samuel Daniel	CP/NCP (N)		6243.8[10]	4°	John Waterson
1637	Pleasant Dialogues and Dramas	Thomas Heywood	NCP/ND	Yes ('Table')	13358	8°	Richard Hearne
1637	Recreations with the Muses	William Alexander	NCP/ND	Yes ('Table')	347	2°	Thomas Harper
1638	The Countess of Pembroke's Arcadia	Philip Sidney; William Alexander; Richard Beling; James Johnstoun	NCP/ND		22550	2°	John Waterson and Robert Young
1638	The Spring's Glory, with Other Poems, Epigrams, Elegies, and Epithalamiums	Thomas Nabbes	NCP/ND		18343/a	4°	Charles Greene
1638	Poems with the Muses' Looking Glass; Amyntas	Thomas Randolph	CP/ND		20694	4°	Francis Bowman
1639	Plays, Masques, Epigrams, Elegies, and Epithalamiums	Thomas Nabbes	CP/NCP/ ND (N)		18337	4°	John Dawson (2) (printer); Nicholas Fussell (bookseller)
1639	1 & 2 Arviragus and Philicia	Lodowick Carlell	CP		4627	12°	Richard Sergier (2) and John Crooke (1)
1640	The Works [Volume 1]	Ben Jonson	CP/NCP/ ND	Yes ('Catalogue')	14753	2°	Richard Bishop
1640	The Works. Second [and Third] Volume	Ben Jonson	CP/NCP/ ND		14754/ a[11]	2°	Richard Meighen, Thomas Walkley

[10] This collection is a reissue of all the plays (on quires 2A to 2T) from *The Whole Works* (1623), with a new general title page.

[11] There are two issues: STC 14754 adds a general title page to the plays from the 1631 collection (see above) and contains Volume 3 of the *Works*. STC 14754a contains Volume 3 and the second edition of *The Devil is an Ass*, but lacks *Bartholomew Fair* and *The Staple of News*.

(cont.)

Date	Collection Title	Author(s)	Type of Collection	Contents	STC/Wing	Format	Publisher(s)
1640	Q. Horatius Flaccus His Art of Poetry	Ben Jonson, Horace	NCP/ND		13798[12]	12°	John Benson
1640	*Poems with the Muses' Looking Glass; Amyntas*	Thomas Randolph	CP/ND	.	20695l.5	8°	Francis Bowman
1640	*Poems*	Thomas Carew	NCP/ND		4620	8°	Thomas Walkley
1640	*The Fancies Theatre*	John Tatham	NCP/ND		23704[13]	8°	Richard Best
1641	*The Prisoners and Claracilla*	Thomas Killigrew	CP	TP ('Tragae-Comedies')	14959/ K452	12°	Andrew Crooke (1)
1642	*Poems*	Thomas Carew	NCP/ND		C564	8°	Thomas Walkley
1643	*Poems with the Muses' Looking Glass; Amyntas*	Thomas Randolph	CP/NCP/ ND		R241[14]	8°	Francis Bowman (?)
1645	*Poems*	John Milton	NCP/ND		M2160	8°	Humphrey Moseley
1646	*Poems &c*	James Shirley	NCP/ND		S3481	8°	Humphrey Moseley
1646	*Fragmenta Aurea*	John Suckling	CP/ND		S6126	8°	Humphrey Moseley
1647	*Erotopaignion, or The Cyprian Academy*	Robert Baron	NCP/ND		B889/90	8°	W. Wilson (printer); J. Hardesty, T. Huntington, T. Jackson (2) (booksellers)
1647	*Comedies and Tragedies*	Francis Beaumont and John Fletcher	CP/NCP	Yes ('Catalogue of all the Comedies and Tragedies')	B1581	2°	Humphrey Moseley and Humphrey Robinson

[12] There are four issues, all under STC 13798, which vary in title-page imprint and the issue of *The Gypsies Metamorphosed* contained in the collection.

[13] A second issue – Wing T229 – has a cancel title page dated 1657 and lists William Burden as publisher. The play – *Love Crowns the End* – also has a cancel title page.

Year	Title	Author		TP	Wing	Format	Publisher
1648	Fragmenta Aurea	John Suckling	CP/ND		S6127	8°	Humphrey Moseley
1649	The Country Captain and The Variety	William Cavendish	CP		N877	12°	Humphrey Moseley and Humphrey Robinson
1651	Poems, with a Masque	Thomas Carew	NCP/ND	TP ('Comedies?')	C565/A	8°	Humphrey Moseley
1651	Comedies, Tragicomedies, With other Poems	William Cartwright	CP/NCP/ND		C709	8°	Humphrey Moseley
1652	Poems with the Muses' Looking Glass; Amyntas; Jealous Lovers; Aristippus	Thomas Randolph	CP/NCP/ND		R242/3	8°	Francis Bowman (R243)
1652	Comedies, Tragicomedies, and Tragedies	George Chapman	CP (N)		C1940A	4°	Richard Hearne (?)
1652	Comedies, Tragicomedies, and Tragedies	John Marston	CP (N)		M816	4°	Richard Hearne (?)
1652	Comedies, Tragicomedies, and Tragedies	John Ford	CP (N)		F1466A	4°	Richard Hearne (?)
1653	Poems	Francis Beaumont and John Fletcher	NCP/ND		B1602[15]	8°	Lawrence Blaiklock
1653	Five New Plays	Richard Brome	CP	TP ('Plays')	B4870[16]	8°	Humphrey Moseley, Richard Marriot, Thomas Dring (1)
1653	Six New Plays	James Shirley	CP	TP ('Plays')	S3486[17]	8°	Humphrey Moseley, Humphrey Robinson

[15] There are three issues: Wing B1603 lists William Hope as publisher and is dated 1653; B1604 is dated 1660, also names Hope as publisher, and adds Fletcher as author.

[16] There are two issues: Wing B4781 is dated 1654 and lists 'J.F.' as printer and Sweeting as bookseller.

[17] There are two issues under the same Wing number; the second adds *The Gentleman of Venice* and *The Politician* (both dated 1655).

(cont.)

Date	Collection Title	Author(s)	Type of Collection	Contents	STC/Wing	Format	Publisher(s)
1654	Two Tragedies	Thomas May	? (N)	TP ('Tragedies')	M1416	12°	Humphrey Moseley
1654	1 & 2 The Nuptials of Peleus and Thetis	James Howell	NCP		H3097	4°	Henry Herringman
1655	The Countess of Pembroke's Arcadia	Philip Sidney	NCP/ND		S3768	2°	W. Dugard (printer); G. Calvert and T. Pierrepont (booksellers)
1655	The History of Philosophy	Thomas Stanley; Aristophanes	NCP/ND		S5237/8	2°	Humphrey Moseley and Thomas Dring (1)
1655	1 & 2 The Passionate Lovers	Lodowick Carlell	CP		C581/A	8°	Humphrey Moseley
[1655?]	Actaem and Diana; with A Pastoral Story of the Nymph Oenone	Robert Cox	NCP(?)	TP	C6711[18]	4°	Robert Cox; Archer listed on C6711
1655	Three New Plays	Philip Massinger	CP	TP ('Playes')	M1050	8°	Humphrey Moseley
1656	Don Zara Del Fogo	Samuel Holland	NCP/ND		H2437[19]	8°	Thomas Vere
1656	Three Excellent Tragedies	Thomas Goffe	NCP	TP ('Tragedies')	G1006	8°	George Bedell and Thomas Collins (1)
1657	Two New Plays	Lodowick Carlell	CP	TP ('Playes')	C582	8°	Humphrey Moseley
1657	Two New Plays	Thomas Middleton	CP	TP ('Playes')	M1989	8°	Humphrey Moseley
1657	Two Plays	James Shirley	CP (N)	TP ('Playes')	S3490	4°	Joshua Kirton

[18] There are two issues: Wing C6711 gives Archer as publisher and also adds the play *Simpleton the Smith*.
[19] Two further issues vary in the preliminaries: Wing H2445 (1656) and H2443 (1660).

1658	Fragmenta Aurea	John Suckling	CP/ND		S6128[20]	8°	Humphrey Moseley
1658	Small Poems of Diverse Sorts	Aston Cokayne	CP/NCP/ND		C4898[21]	8°	William Godbid
1658	Two Plays	Jasper Mayne	CP	TP ('Comedy', 'Tragy-Comedy')	M1480[22]	4°	Richard Davis
[1659]	Honoria and Mammon; The Contention of Ajax and Ulysses	James Shirley	NCP		S3475[23]	8°	'for the use of the author'
1659	Five New Plays	Richard Brome	CP	TP ('Playes')	B4872	8°	Henry Brome and Andrew Crooke (1)
1659	The Last Remains of Sir John Suckling	John Suckling	CP(?)/ ND		S6130[24]	8°	Humphrey Moseley

[20] A second issue with the same Wing number contains *The Last Remains of Sir John Suckling*, which includes *The Sad One*.

[21] There are five other issues, which vary in the imprint: Wing C4894 (1658); C4894A (1659); C4897 and C4897A (1662); and C4895 (1669).

[22] There are three issues, all with the same Wing number: one was issued without *The Amorous War*, one contains the first edition of the play, and one contains either the first or second edition of the play.

[23] Three issues vary in preliminaries: S3475 claims the book was printed for the use of the author; S3474 and S3473 (1659) give John Crooke (1) as publisher.

[24] This collection was included in the second issue of the 1658 *Fragmenta Aurea* (see above).

Bibliography

Manuscripts

Kew, National Archives, State Papers Domestic, Elizabeth I; SP 12/278
London, British Library, Additional MS 27632
London, British Library, Additional MS 31022 (R)
London, British Library, Additional MS 33785
London, British Library, Additional MS 81083
London, British Library, Stowe 158
London, Worshipful Company of Stationers and Newspaper Makers, Liber C

Primary Texts

[Place of publication is London, unless otherwise specified.]
Alexander, Gavin (ed.), *William Scott, The Model of Poesy* (Cambridge: Cambridge University Press, 2013)
Alexander, William, *The Monarchick Tragedies* (1605, STC 343 and 1607, 344)
Anon., *The Famovs Victories of Henry the fifth* (1598; STC 13072)
   The Famous Victories of Henry the Fifth, prep Chiaki Hanabusa, Malone Society Publications, vol. 171 (Manchester: Manchester University Press for the Malone Society, 2007)
Anon., *A Gagge for the Pope and the Iesvits* (1624; STC 20111)
Anon., *An Homilie Against Disobedience and Wylfull Rebellion* (1570; STC 13680)
Anon., *The Life and death of Iacke Straw* (1604; STC 23357)
Anon., *The True Chronicle History of King Leir* (1605; STC 15343)
Anon., *A Continuation of More Newes from the Palatinate [13 June 1622]* (1622; STC 18507.51A)
Anon., *The Mutable and wauering estate of France, from the yeare of our Lord 1460, vntill the yeare 1595* (1597; STC 11279)
Anon., *Newes from Brest* (1594; STC 18654)
Anon., *News from Lough-foyle in Ireland* (1608; STC 18784)
Anon., *Newes From Most Parts of Christendome [25 September 1622]* (1622; STC 18507.79)
Anon., *The certaine Newes of this present Weeke [23 August 1622]* (1622; STC 18507.72)

254

Anon., *A Plaine Demonstration of the Vnlawful Svccession of the Now Emperovr Ferdinand the Second, because of the incestuous Marriage of his Parents* ('the Hage' [i.e. London], 1620; STC 10814)

Anon., *The True Tragedie of Richard the third* (1594; STC 21009)

Anon., *Sir Thomas Smithes Voiage and Entertainment in Rushia* (1605; STC 22869)

Anon., *A Warning for Faire Women* (1599; STC 25089)

Anon./[George Peele?], *The Historie of the two valiant Knights, Syr Clyomon Knight of the Golden Sheeld, sonne to the King of Denmarke; And Clamydes the white Knight* (1599; STC 5450a)

Anon./Henri IV of France, *The Copie of a Letter sent by the French king* (1595; STC 13119)

Anon./Henri IV of France, *The Kings Declaration and Ordinance, Containing the Cause of His Warre* (1600; STC 13121)

Anon./'I. H.', *The Divell of the Vault* (1606; STC 12568)

Anon./'J. G. E.', *Englands Hope, Against Irish Hate* (1600; STC 7434.7)

Anon./'R. A.', *The Valiant Welshman* (1615; STC 16)

Anon./'R. S.', *The Iesuites play at Lyons in France* (1607; STC 21513.5)

Anon./'W. S.', *The Lamentable Tragedie of Locrine* (1595; STC 21528)

Barlow, William, *The Svmme and Svbstance of the Conference* (1604; STC 1456)

Barnes, Barnabe, *The Divils Charter* (1607; STC 1466)

Barret, Robert, *The Theorike and Practike of Moderne Warres* (1598; STC 1500)

Beaumont, Francis and John Fletcher, *Comedies and Tragedies* (1647; Wing B1581)

Bell, Thomas, *The Downefall of Poperie* (1604; STC 1818 and 1818.5)

Bignon, Jérôme, *The True Maner of Electing of Popes*, English translation (1605; STC 3057.7 and 3058)

Blundeville, Thomas, *The true order and Methode of wryting and reading Hystories* (1574; STC 3161)

Brabantina, Charlotte, *The Conuersion of a most Noble Lady of France In Iune last past* (1608; STC 11262)

Brooke, Ralph, *A Catalogve and Succession of the Kings, Princes, Dukes, Marquesses, Earles, and Viscounts of this Realme of England, since the Norman Conquest, to this present years, 1619* (1619; STC 3832)

Browne, Thomas, *Christian Morals* (1716)

Camden, William, *Britannia* (1586; STC 4503)

Carey, Robert, *Memoirs of the Life of Robert Cary, Baron of Leppington, and Earl of Monmouth; Written by Himself* (R. and J. Dodsley, 1759)

Cecil, William, *A Trve Report of Svndry Horrible Conspiracies* (1594; STC 7603)

Clapham, Henoch, *A Briefe of the Bibles Historie* (1603, STC 5333; 1608, STC 5334) *Errour on the Left Hand* (1608; STC 5342)

Coke, Edward, *La Sept Part Des Reports Sr. Edw. Coke* (1608; STC 5511)

Corneille, Pierre, *Nicomède* (1671; Wing C6315)

Daniel, Samuel, *Certaine Small Poems* (1605; STC 6239)
The First Fowre Bookes of the ciuile warres (1595; STC 6244)
The Civile Wares (1609; STC 6245)

Davies of Hereford, John, *Bien Venu* (1606; STC 6329)

Dekker, Thomas, *The Whore of Babylon* (1607; STC 6532)

Dekker, Thomas [and Thomas Middleton], *The Magnificent Entertainment* (1604; STC 6510)

Drayton, Michael, Richard Hathaway, Anthony Munday, and Robert Wilson ('William Shakespeare'), *The first part Of the true and honorable history, of the Life of Sir Iohn Old-castle, the good Lord Cobham* (1600 [1619]; STC 18796)

Ducci, Lorenzo, *Ars Avlica, or The Courtiers Arte* (1607; STC 7274)

Fernández, Jerónimo, *The Honour of Chivalrie*, trans. Oratio Rinaldi and 'L.A.' (1598; STC 1804)

Field, Theophilus (ed.), *Albvm, Sev nigrum amicorum* (1600; STC 19154)
 An Italians dead bodie, Stucke with English Flowers (1600; STC 19154.3)

Florio, John, *Florios Second Frvtes* (1591; STC 11097)

Ford, John, *The Chronicle Historie of Perkin Warbeck* (1634; STC 11157)

Freeman, John, *The Apologie for the Conformable Ministers of England For their Subscription to the present Church Gouernment* (1609; STC 11366.5)

Galloway, Bruce R. and Brian P. Levack (eds.), *The Jacobean Union: Six Tracts of 1604* (Edinburgh: Clark Constable, 1985)

Greene, Robert ('R. G.'), *The Comicall Historie of Alphonsus, King of Aragon* (1599; STC 12233)
 The Honorable Historie of frier Bacon, and frier Bongay (1594; STC 12267)
 The Scottish Historie of Iames the fourth (1598; STC 12308)

[Greene, Robert]/Anon., *The First part of the Tragicall raigne of Selimus* (1594; STC 12310a)

Hall, Edward, *The Vnion of the two noble and illustrate famelies of Lancastre and Yorke* (1548; STC 12721)

Harington, John, *A Briefe View of the State of the Church of England* (1653; Wing H770)

Harrison, Stephen, [Thomas Dekker, and John Webster], *The Archs of Trivmph* (1604; STC 12863)

Harry, George Owen, *The Genealogy of the High and Mighty Monarch, James* (1604; STC 12872)

Hayward, John, *The First Part of the Life and raigne of King Henrie the IIII* (1599; STC 12995)

Heywood, Thomas, *An Apology for Actors* (1612; STC 13309)
 The English Traueller (1633; STC 13315)
 If you know not me, you know no bodie (1605, STC 13328 and 1639, STC 13335)
 The Second Part of If you know not me, you know no bodie (1606, STC 13336 and STC 13336.5)
 The Rape of Lvcrece (1608; STC 13360)

Holinshed, Raphael, *The First and second volumes of Chronicles ... First collected and published by Raphaell Holinshed, William Harrison, and others: Now newlie augmented and continued ... to the yeare 1586 by Iohn Hooker alias Vowell Gent. and others* (1587; STC 13569)

Holland, Abraham ('A. H.'), 'A Continved Inqvisition against Paper-Persecutors', in John Davies of Hereford ('I. D.'), *A Scovrge for Paper-Persecutors* (1625; STC 6340)

Jaggard, William, *A view of all the Right Honourable the Lord Mayors of this Honorable Citty of London* (1601; STC 14343)

James I of England and Ireland (James VI of Scotland), *Basilikon Doron* (Edinburgh, 1599, STC 14348; and London, 1603, STC 14353)

'By the King [19 May 1603]' (1603; STC 8314)

'By the King [20 October 1604]' (1604; STC 8361)

The Kings Maiesties Speech [19 March 1604] (1604; STC 14390)

His Maiesties Speech to Both the Houses of Parliament [31 March 1607] (1607; STC 14395)

Triplici nodo, triplex cuneus, or An Apology for the Oath of Allegiance (1607, STC 14400; 1609, STC 14401)

Johnson, Samuel, *Mr Johnson's Preface to his Edition of Shakespear's plays* (1765)

Jonson, Ben, *The Diuell is an Asse* (1631; STC 14753.5)

King James his Royall and Magnificent Entertainment (1604; STC 14756)

Seianvs His Fall (1605; STC 14782)

The Staple of Newes (1631; STC 14753.5)

The Workes of Beniamin Jonson (1616; STC 14751)

Lavater, Ludwig, *Three Christian Sermons*, trans. William Barlow (1596; STC 15322)

Of Ghostes and Spirites (1596; STC 15321)

Lefèvre, Raoul, *The Auncient Historie of the destruction of Troy*, trans. William Caxton and William Phiston (1597; STC 15379)

Lodge, Thomas, *The Wovnds of Ciuill War* (1594; STC 16678)

Lodge, Thomas and Robert Greene, *A Looking Glasse for London and England* (1594; STC 16679)

López de Gómara, Francisco, *The Pleasant Historie of the Conquest of the West India, now called new Spaine*, trans. Thomas Nicholas (1596; STC 16808)

Lydgate, John, Thomas Norton, and Thomas Sackville, *The Serpent of Deuision [and] Gorboduc* (1590; STC 17029)

Marlowe, Christopher, *The troublesome raigne and lamentable death of Edward the second* (1594; STC 17437)

The Massacre at Paris ([1594]; STC 17423)

Tamburlaine the Great (1590; STC 17425)

Marlowe, Christopher and Thomas Nashe, *The Tragedie of Dido Queene of Carthage* (1594; STC 17441)

Marston, John, *The Wonder of Women, or the Tragedie of Sophonisba* (1606; STC 17488)

Massinger, Philip, *Believe as you List*, ed. Charles Sisson, Malone Society Publications, vol. 60 (Oxford: Oxford University Press for the Malone Society, 1927)

The Bondman (1624; STC 17632)

The Roman Actor (1629; STC 17642)

Massinger, Philip, Thomas Middleton, and William Rowley, *The Old Law* (1656; Wing M1048)

McClure, Norman Egbert (ed.), *The Letters and Epigrams of Sir John Harington; Together with The Prayse of Private Life* (Philadelphia: University of Pennsylvania Press, 1930)

    The Letters of John Chamberlain, 2 vols. (Philadelphia: American Philosophical Society, 1939)

Meres, Francis, *Palladis Tamia* (1598; STC 17834)

Middleton, Thomas (?)/('W. Shakespeare'), *A Yorkshire Tragedie* (1619; STC 22341)

Munday, Anthony, *The Trivmphs of re-vnited Britania* (1605; STC 18279)

Nashe, Thomas, *Christs Teares Over Ierusalem* (1593, STC 18366 and 1594, STC 18367)

    Haue with you to Saffron-walden (1596; STC 18369)

    Pierce Pennilesse His Supplication to the Diuell (1592; STC 18371)

    The Terrors of the night (1594; STC 18379)

Norton, Thomas, *All such treatises as haue been lately published by Thomas Norton* ([1570]; STC 18677)

Norton, Thomas, and Thomas Sackville, *The Tragedie of Ferrex and Porrex* (1565, STC 18684)

    The Tragidie of Gorbodvc ([1570]; STC 18685)

Orlers, Jan Janszn, *The Trivmphs of Nassav*, trans. W. Shute (1613, STC 17676 and 1620, STC 17677)

Peele, George, *The Famous Chronicle of king Edward the first* (1593; STC 19535)

Persons, Robert ('R. Doleman'), *A Conference About the Next Svccession to the Crowne of Ingland* ('N.' [i.e. Antwerp], 1594 [1595]; STC 19398)

Playfere, Thomas, *The Meane in Movrning* (1596; STC 20015)

    A Most Excellent and Heavenly Sermon (1595, STC 20014 and STC 20014.3)

    The Pathway to Perfection (1596; STC 20020)

Pricket, Robert, *The Lord Coke His Speech and Charge* (1607; STC 5492)

Puttenham, George, *The Arte of English Poesie* (1589; STC 20519.5)

Roberts, Henry, *Englands Farewell to Christian the fourth* (1606; STC 21079)

    Honours Conquest (1598; STC 21082)

    Pheander: The Mayden Knight (1595; STC 21086)

    The Trvmpet of Fame (1595; STC 21088)

Rowley, Samuel, *When you see me, You know me* (1605; STC 21417)

Savile, Henry and Tacitus, *The Ende of Nero and Beginning of Galba; Fower Bookes of the Histories of Cornelivs Tacitvs; The Life of Agricola* (Oxford: 1591; STC 23642)

Serres, Jean de, *Historical Collection of the Most Memorable Accidents and Tragicall Massacres of France, vnder the Raignes of Henry 2, Francis 2, Charles 9, Henry 3, Henry 4 now liuing* (1598; STC 11275)

Shakespeare, William, *Comedies, Histories, and Tragedies* (1623; STC 22273)

    The First part of the Contention betwixt the two famous Houses of Yorke and Lancaster (1594; STC 26099)

The Whole Contention between the two Famous Houses, Lancaster and Yorke [and *Pericles, Prince of Tyre*] ([1619]; STC 26101)

The History of Henrie the Fovrth (1598, STC 22280 and 1599, STC 22281)

Henry IV Part 1, ed. David Bevington (Oxford: Oxford University Press, 1987)

The Second part of Henrie the fourth (1600; STC 22288 and 22288a)

Henry IV Part 2, ed. René Weis (Oxford: Oxford University Press, 1997)

The Chronicle History of Henry the fift (1608 [1619]; STC 22291)

True Chronicle Historie of the life and death of King Lear and his three Daughters (1608, STC 22292 and 1608 [1619], STC 22293)

King Lear, ed. R. A. Foakes (Arden Shakespeare, 1997)

A Pleasant Conceited Comedie Called Loues labors lost (1598; STC 22294)

The Excellent History of the Merchant of Venice (1600 [1619]; STC 22297)

A Most pleasaunt and excellent conceited Comedie, of Syr Iohn Falstaffe and the merrie Wiues of Windsor (1602, STC 22299 and 1619, STC 22300)

A Midsommer nights dreame (1600 [1619]; STC 22303)

The Tragedie of King Richard the second (1597, STC 22307; 1598, STC 22308; and 1608, STC 22310 and 22311)

The Tragedy of King Richard the third (1597, STC 22314 and 1598, STC 22315)

The Tragedy of King Richard III, ed. John Jowett (Oxford: Oxford University Press, 2000)

King Richard III, ed. James R. Siemon (Arden Shakespeare, 2009)

An Excellent conceited Tragedie of Romeo and Iuliet (1597; STC 22322)

The Most Lamentable Romaine Tragedie of Titus Andronicus (1594; STC 22328)

Shakespeare, William et al., *The Passionate Pilgrime* (1599; STC 22342)

Sidney, Philip, *The Correspondence of Sir Philip Sidney*, ed. Roger Kuin, 2 vols. (Oxford: Oxford University Press, 2012)

The Defence of Poesie (1595; STC 22535)

Stow, John, *The Annales, or Generall Chronicle of England*, rev. Edmund Howes (1615; STC 23338)

A Survay of London (1598, STC 23341; and 1603, STC 23343)

[Thornborough, John], 'John Bristoll', *The Ioiefvll and Blessed Revniting* (Oxford, [1605?]; STC 24036)

Tilenus, Daniel, *Positions Lately Held by the L. Du Perron, Bishop of Eureux, against the sufficiency and perfection of the Scriptures* (1606; STC 24071)

The True Copy of two Letters ... Wherein the principall poynts in controuersie with the Papists, are leanedly and fully confuted (1605; STC 24072)

Whetstone, George, *The Right Excellent and famous Historye of Promos and Cassandra* (1578; STC 25347)

Wilkinson, Edward, *E.W. His Thameseidos* (1600; STC 25642)

Wilson, Robert, *The Coblers Prophesie* (1594; STC 25781)

The pleasant and Stately Morall of the three Lordes and three Ladies of London (1590; STC 25783)

Secondary Texts

Anderson, Jennifer and Elizabeth Sauer (eds.), *Books and Readers in Early Modern England* (Philadelphia: University of Pennsylvania Press, 2002)

Archer, Harriet, *Unperfect Histories: The Mirror for Magistrates, 1559–1610* (Oxford: Oxford University Press, 2017)

Archer, Ian W., 'Palavicino, Sir Horatio (c.1540–1600)', *ODNB*, online ed., January 2008, https://doi.org/10.1093/ref:odnb/21153 (accessed 16 September 2019)

Astington, John H., 'Playing the Man: Acting at the Red Bull and Fortune', *Early Theatre*, 9:2 (2006), 130–43

Atkin, Tamara, *Reading Drama in Tudor England* (London: Routledge, 2018)

Atkin, Tamara and Laura Estill (eds.), *Early British Drama in Manuscript* (Turnhout: Brepols, 2019)

Baron, S. A., 'Butter, Nathaniel (*bap.* 1583, *d.* 1664)', *ODNB*, online ed., January 2008, https://doi.org/10.1093/ref:odnb/4224 (accessed 17 April 2021)

Bawcutt, N. W. (ed.), *The Control and Censorship of Caroline Drama: The Records of Sir Henry Herbert, Master of the Revels 1623–73* (Oxford: Clarendon Press, 1996)

Bayer, Mark, 'Staging Foxe at the Fortune and the Red Bull', *Renaissance and Reformation*, 27:1 (2003), 61–94

Berek, Peter, 'Genres, Early Modern Theatrical Title Pages, and the Authority of Print', in *The Book of the Play: Playwrights, Stationers, and Readers in Early Modern England*, ed. Marta Straznicky (Amherst and Boston: University of Massachusetts Press, 2006), pp. 159–75

'*Locrine* Revised, *Selimus*, and Early Responses to *Tamburlaine*', *Research Opportunities in Renaissance Drama*, 23 (1980), 33–54

'*Tamburlaine*'s Weak Sons: Imitation As Interpretation before 1593', *Renaissance Drama*, 13 (1982), 55–82

'Tragedy and Title Pages: Nationalism, Protestantism, and Print', *Modern Philology*, 106:1 (2008), 1–24

Bergeron, David M., '"Bogus History" and Robert Greene's *Friar Bacon and Friar Bungay*', *Early Theatre*, 17:1 (2014), 93–112

'King James's Civic Pageant and Parliamentary Speech in March 1604', *Albion*, 34:2 (2002), 213–31

Textual Patronage in English Drama, 1570–1640 (Aldershot: Ashgate, 2006)

Bevington, David, 'Tragedy in Shakespeare's Career', in *The Cambridge Companion to Shakespearean Tragedy*, ed. Claire McEachern (Cambridge: Cambridge University Press, 2003), 50–68

Bevington, David (ed.) at al., *English Renaissance Drama: A Norton Anthology* (New York: Norton, 2000)

Bezio, Kristin M. S., *Staging Power in Tudor and Stuart English History Plays: History, Political Thought and the Redefinition of Sovereignty* (Farnham: Ashgate, 2015)

Blayney, Peter W. M., *The Bookshops in Paul's Cross Churchyard*, Occasional Papers of the Bibliographical Society, No. 5 (London: Bibliographical Society, 1990)

The First Folio of Shakespeare (Washington, DC: Folger Library, 1991)

'The Publication of Playbooks', in *A New History of Early English Drama*, ed. John D. Cox and David Scott Kastan (New York: Columbia University Press, 1997), pp. 383–422

The Stationers' Company and the Printers of London, 1501–1557, 2 vols. (Cambridge: Cambridge University Press, 2013)

The Texts of 'King Lear' and Their Origins, Volume I: Nicholas Okes and the First Quarto (Cambridge: Cambridge University Press, 1982)

Bourdieu, Pierre, *The Field of Cultural Production: Essays on Art and Literature*, ed. Randal Johnson (Cambridge: Polity, 1993)

Bowers, Fredson, *On Editing Shakespeare and the Elizabethan Dramatists* (Philadelphia: University of Pennsylvania Library for the Philip H. and A. S. W. Rosenbach Foundation, 1955)

Boys, Jayne E. E., *London's News Press and the Thirty Years War* (Woodbridge, Suffolk: Boydell, 2011)

Brennan, Michael G., *Literary Patronage in the English Renaissance: The Pembroke Family* (London: Routledge, 1988)

Brooks, Douglas A., *From Playhouse to Printing House: Drama and Authorship in Early Modern England* (Cambridge: Cambridge University Press, 2000)

'Sir John Oldcastle and the Construction of Shakespeare's Authorship', *Studies in English Literature, 1500–1900*, 38:2 (1998), 333–61

Brownlee, Victoria, 'Imagining the Enemy: Protestant Readings of the Whore of Babylon in Early Modern England, c.1580–1625', in *Biblical Women in Early Modern Literary Culture, 1550–1700*, ed. Victoria Brownlee and Laura Gallagher (Manchester: Manchester University Press, 2015), pp. 213–33

Bullough, Geoffrey, *Narrative and Dramatic Sources of Shakespeare*, 8 vols. (London: Routledge and Kegan Paul, 1957–75)

Burgess, Glen, Rowland Wymer and Jason Lawrence (eds.), *The Accession of James I: Historical and Cultural Consequences* (Basingstoke: Palgrave Macmillan, 2006)

Butler, Martin, 'Romans in Britain: *The Roman Actor* and the Early Stuart Classical Play', in *Philip Massinger: A Critical Reassessment*, ed. Douglas Howard (Cambridge: Cambridge University Press, 1985), pp. 139–70

Theatre and Crisis, 1632–1642 (Cambridge: Cambridge University Press, 1984)

Campbell, Lily B., *Shakespeare's 'Histories': Mirrors of Elizabethan Policy* (San Marino, CA: Huntington Library, 1947)

Cavanagh, Dermot, Stuart Hampton-Reeves, and Stephen Longstaffe (eds.), *Shakespeare's Histories and Counter-Histories* (Manchester: Manchester University Press, 2006)

Chambers, E. K., *William Shakespeare: A Study of Facts and Problems*, 2 vols. (Oxford: Clarendon Press, 1930)

Chambers, E. K. (ed.), 'Dramatic Records: The Lord Chamberlain's Office', *Collections Vol. II Part III*, Malone Society Publications, vol. 71 (Oxford: Oxford University Press for the Malone Society, 1931), pp. 321–416

Champion, Larry S., '"What Prerogatiues Meanes": Perspective and Political Ideology in *The Famous Victories of Henry V*', *South Atlantic Review*, 53:4 (1988), 1–19

Clegg, Cyndia Susan, '"By the choise and inuitation of al the realme": *Richard II* and Elizabethan Press Censorship', *Shakespeare Quarterly*, 48:4 (1997), 432–48

Press Censorship in Jacobean England (Cambridge: Cambridge University Press, 2001)

'The Stationers' Company of London', in *The British Literary Book Trade, 1475–1700*, ed. James K. Bracken and Joel Silver, Dictionary of Literary Biography, vol. 170 (Detroit: Gale Research, 1996), 275–91

Coldiron, A. E. B., *Printers without Borders: Translation and Textuality in the Renaissance* (Cambridge: Cambridge University Press, 2015)

Colie, Rosalie, 'Genre-Systems and the Functions of Literature', in *The Resources of Kind: Genre-Theory in the Renaissance*, ed. Barbara K. Lewalski (Berkeley and Los Angeles: University of California Press, 1973), pp. 1–31

Connolly, Annaliese, 'Peele's *David and Bethsabe:* Reconsidering Biblical Drama of the Long 1590s', *Early Modern Literary Studies*, Special Issue 16 (2007), 9.1–20

Dadabhoy, Ambereen, 'Two Faced: The Problem of Othello's Visage', in *Othello: The State of Play*, ed. Lena Cowen Orlin (London: Arden Bloomsbury, 2014), pp. 121–47

Danson, Lawrence, *Shakespeare's Dramatic Genres* (Oxford: Oxford University Press, 2000)

Davis, Alex, *Renaissance Historical Fiction: Sidney, Deloney, Nashe* (Cambridge: D. S. Brewer, 2011)

De Grazia, Margreta and Peter Stallybrass, 'The Materiality of the Shakespearean Text', *Shakespeare Quarterly*, 44:3 (1993), 255–83

Derrida, Jacques, 'The Law of Genre', trans. Avital Ronell, *Critical Inquiry*, 7:1 (1980), 55–81

Dillon, Janette, 'The Early Tudor History Play', in *English Historical Drama, 1500–1660: Forms outside the Canon*, ed. Teresa Grant and Barbara Ravelhofer (Basingstoke: Palgrave Macmillan, 2008), pp. 32–57

'Is There a Performance in This Text?', *Shakespeare Quarterly*, 45:1 (1994), 74–86

Shakespeare and the Staging of English History (Oxford: Oxford University Press, 2012)

Di Salvo, Gina M., '"A Virgine and a Martyr both": The Turn to Hagiography in Heywood's Reformation History Play', *Renaissance and Reformation*, 41:4 (2018), 133–67

Dowling, Margaret, 'Sir John Hayward's Troubles over his *Life of Henry IV*', *The Library*, 4th ser., 11:2 (1930), 212–24

Duncan-Jones, Katherine, '*Christs Tears*, Nashe's "Forsaken Extremities"', *Review of English Studies*, 49:194 (1998), 167–80

Dutton, Richard, 'Herbert, Sir Henry (*bap.* 1594, *d.* 1673)', *ODNB*, online ed., January 2008, https://doi.org/10.1093/ref:odnb/13029 (accessed 16 September 2019)

'*King Lear, The Triumphs of Reunited Britannia* and "The Matter of Britain"', *Literature and History*, 12:2 (1986), 139–51

Mastering the Revels: The Regulation and Censorship of English Renaissance Drama (Basingstoke: Macmillan, 1991)

'Patronage, Politics, and the Master of the Revels, 1622–1640: The Case of John Astley', *English Literary Renaissance*, 20:2 (1990), 287–319

Eisenstein, Elizabeth L., *The Printing Press As an Agent of Change*, 2 vols. (Cambridge: Cambridge University Press, 1980)

Erne, Lukas, 'The Popularity of Shakespeare in Print', *Shakespeare Survey 62* (2009), 12–29

Shakespeare and the Book Trade (Cambridge: Cambridge University Press, 2013)

Shakespeare As Literary Dramatist, 2nd ed. (Cambridge: Cambridge University Press, 2013)

Erne, Lukas and Devani Singh (eds.), *Bel-vedére or The Garden of the Muses: An Early Modern Printed Commonplace Book* (Cambridge: Cambridge University Press, 2020)

Farmer, Alan, 'John Norton and the Politics of Shakespeare's History Plays in Caroline England', in *Shakespeare's Stationers: Studies in Cultural Bibliography*, ed. Marta Straznicky (Philadelphia: University of Pennsylvania Press, 2013) pp. 147–76

'Play-Reading, News-Reading, and Ben Jonson's *The Staple of News*', in *The Book of the Play: Playwrights, Stationers, and Readers in Early Modern England*, ed. Marta Straznicky (Amherst and Boston: University of Massachusetts Press, 2006), pp. 127–58

Farmer, Alan B. and Zachary Lesser, 'Canons and Classics: Publishing Drama in Caroline England', in *Localizing Caroline Drama: Politics and Economics of the Early Modern English Stage, 1625–1642*, ed. Adam Zucker and Alan B. Farmer (Basingstoke: Palgrave Macmillan, 2006), pp. 17–41

'The Popularity of Playbooks Revisited', *Shakespeare Quarterly*, 56:1 (2005), 1–32

'Vile Arts: The Marketing of English Printed Drama, 1512–1660', *Research Opportunities in Renaissance Drama*, 39 (2000), 77–165

'What Is Print Popularity? A Map of the Elizabethan Book Trade', in *The Elizabethan Top Ten: Defining Print Popularity in Early Modern England*, ed. Andy Kesson and Emma Smith (Farnham: Ashgate, 2013), pp. 19–54

Ferguson, Arthur B., *The Chivalric Tradition in Renaissance England* (Washington, DC: Folger Shakespeare Library, 1986)

Clio Unbound: Perception of the Social and Cultural Past in Renaissance England (Durham, NC: Duke University Press, 1979)

Fincham, Kenneth and Peter Lake, 'The Ecclesiastical Policy of King James I', *Journal of British Studies*, 24:2 (1985), 169–207

Finkelpearl, P. J., 'Davies, John (1564/5–1618)', *ODNB*, online ed., September 2004, https://doi.org/10.1093/ref:odnb/7244 (accessed 16 September 2019)

Fowler, Alastair, 'Genre and the Literary Canon', *New Literary History*, 11.1 (1979), 97–119

Frazer, Paul, 'Shakespeare's Northern Blood: Transfusing *Gorboduc* into *Macbeth* and *Cymbeline*', in *Shakespeare in the North: Place, Politics and Performance in England and Scotland*, ed. Adam Hansen (Edinburgh: Edinburgh University Press, 2021), pp. 41–59

Freebury-Jones, Darren, 'Determining Robert Greene's Dramatic Canon', *Style*, 54:4 (2020), 377–98

Fulton, Thomas C., '"The True and Naturall Constitution of That Mixed Government": Massinger's *The Bondman* and the Influence of Dutch Republicanism', *Studies in Philology*, 99:2 (2002), 152–77

Fussner, F. Smith, *The Historical Revolution: English Historical Writing and Thought 1580–1640* (New York: Columbia University Press, 1962)

Gajda, Alexandra, 'The Earl of Essex and "Politic History"', in *Essex: The Cultural Impact of an Elizabethan Courtier*, ed. Annaliese Connolly and Lisa Hopkins (Manchester: Manchester University Press, 2013), pp. 237–59

Galloway, Bruce, *The Union of England and Scotland 1603–1608* (Edinburgh: John Donald, 1986)

Gants, David L., 'Creede, Thomas (*b.* in or before 1554, *d.* 1616)', *ODNB*, online ed., September 2004, https://doi.org/10.1093/ref:odnb/6666 (accessed 16 September 2019)

Genette, Gérard, *The Architext: An Introduction*, trans. Jane E. Lewin (Berkeley and Los Angeles: University of California Press, 1992)

'Introduction to the Paratext', trans. Marie Maclean, *New Literary History*, 22:2 (1991), 261–72

Gibson, James M., 'Shakespeare and the Cobham Controversy: The Oldcastle/Falstaff and Brooke/Broome Revisions', *Medieval & Renaissance Drama in England*, 25 (2012), 94–132

Gilchrist, Kim, *Staging Britain's Past: Pre-Roman Britain in Early Modern Drama* (London: Bloomsbury Arden, 2021)

Gillies, John, 'The Scene of Cartography in *King Lear*', in *Literature, Mapping, and the Politics of Space in Early Modern Britain*, ed. Andrew Gordon and Bernhard Klein (Cambridge: Cambridge University Press, 2001), pp. 109–37

Grant, Teresa, 'Drama Queen: Staging Elizabeth in *If You Know Not Me You Know Nobody*', in *The Myth of Elizabeth*, ed. Susan Doran and Thomas S. Freeman (Basingstoke: Palgrave Macmillan, 2003), pp. 120–42

'History in the Making: The Case of Samuel Rowley's *When You See Me You Know Me* (1604/5)', in *English Historical Drama, 1500–1660: Forms outside the Canon*, ed. Teresa Grant and Barbara Ravelhofer (Basingstoke: Palgrave Macmillan, 2008), pp. 125–57

Grant, Teresa and Barbara Ravelhofer, 'Introduction', in *English Historical Drama, 1500–1660: Forms outside the Canon*, ed. Teresa Grant and Barbara Ravelhofer (Basingstoke: Palgrave Macmillan, 2008), pp. 1–31

Grant, Teresa and Barbara Ravelhofer (eds.), *English Historical Drama, 1500–1660: Forms outside the Canon* (Basingstoke: Palgrave Macmillan, 2008)

Greenblatt, Stephen, *Shakespearean Negotiations: The Circulation of Social Energy in Renaissance England* (Oxford: Clarendon Press, 1988)

Greg, W. W., *Some Aspects and Problems of London Publishing between 1550 and 1650* (Oxford: Clarendon Press, 1956)

'On Certain False Dates in Shakespearian Quartos', *The Library*, 2nd ser., 34 (1908), 113–31

Grene, Nicholas, *Shakespeare's Serial History Plays* (Cambridge: Cambridge University Press, 2002)

Griffin, Andrew, 'Thomas Heywood and London Exceptionalism', *Studies in Philology*, 110:1 (2013), 85–114

Griffin, Benjamin, *Playing the Past: Approaches to English Historical Drama, 1385–1600* (Woodbridge, Suffolk: D. S. Brewer, 2001)

Guneratne, Anthony R., *Shakespeare and Genre: From Early Modern Inheritances to Postmodern Legacies* (New York: Palgrave Macmillan, 2011)

Gurr, Andrew, *The Shakespeare Company, 1594–1642* (Cambridge: Cambridge University Press, 2004)

The Shakespearian Playing Companies (Oxford: Clarendon Press, 1996)

Hadfield, Andrew, *Shakespeare, Spenser, and the Matter of Britain* (Basingstoke: Palgrave Macmillan, 2004)

Hammer, Paul E. J., 'Shakespeare's *Richard II*, the Play of 7 February 1601, and the Essex Rising', *Shakespeare Quarterly*, 59:1 (2008), 1–35

Hansen, Adam, 'Writing, London, and the Bishops' Ban of 1599', *The London Journal*, 43:2 (2018), 102–19

Hattaway, Michael, 'Dating *As You Like It*, Epilogues and Prayers, and the Problems of "As the Dial Hand Tells O'er"', *Shakespeare Quarterly*, 60:2 (2009), 154–67

'The Shakespearean History Play', in *The Cambridge Companion to Shakespeare's History Plays*, ed. Michael Hattaway (Cambridge: Cambridge University Press, 2002), pp. 3–24

Heinemann, Margot, 'Drama and Opinion in the 1620s: Middleton and Massinger', in *Theatre and Government under the Early Stuarts*, ed. J. R. Mulryne and Margaret Shewring (Cambridge: Cambridge University Press, 1993), pp. 237–65

Puritanism and Theatre: Thomas Middleton and Opposition Drama under the Early Stuarts (Cambridge: Cambridge University Press, 1980)

Helgerson, Richard, *Forms of Nationhood: The Elizabethan Writing of England* (Chicago: University of Chicago Press, 1992)

'Shakespeare and Contemporary Dramatists of History', in *A Companion to Shakespeare's Works: Volume II: The Histories*, ed. Richard Dutton and Jean E. Howard (Oxford: Blackwell, 2003), pp. 26–47

'Tasso on Spenser: The Politics of Chivalric Romance', *Yearbook of English Studies*, 21 (1991), 153–67

Herman, Peter C., 'Hall, Edward (1497–1547)', *ODNB*, online ed., November 2018, https://doi.org/10.1093/ref:odnb/11954 (accessed 16 September 2019)

'Henrician Historiography and the Voice of the People: The Cases of More and Hall', *Texas Studies in Literature and Language*, 39 (1997), 261–83

Hertel, Ralf, *Staging England in the Elizabethan History Play: Performing National Identity* (London: Routledge, 2014)

Higgins, Ben, *Shakespeare's Syndicate: The First Folio, Its Publishers, and the Early Modern Book Trade* (Oxford: Oxford University Press, 2022)

Hila, Marina, 'Dishonourable Peace: Fletcher and Massinger's *The False One* and Jacobean Foreign Policy', *Cahiers Élisabéthains*, 72:1 (2007), 21–30

Hill, Tracey, *Anthony Munday and Civic Culture* (Manchester: Manchester University Press, 2004)

Pageantry and Power: A Cultural History of the Early Modern Lord Mayor's Show 1585–1639 (Manchester: Manchester University Press, 2011)

Hinman, Charlton, *The Printing and Proofreading of the First Folio of Shakespeare*, 2 vols. (Oxford: Clarendon Press, 1963)

Hoak, Dale, 'Edward VI (1537–1553)', *ODNB*, online ed., May 2014, https://doi.org/10.1093/ref:odnb/8522 (accessed 16 September 2019)

Hoenselaars, Ton (ed.), *Shakespeare's History Plays: Performance, Translation and Adaptation in Britain and Abroad* (Cambridge: Cambridge University Press, 2004)

Holderness, Graham, *Shakespeare Recycled: The Making of Historical Drama* (Hemel Hempstead: Harvester Wheatsheaf, 1992)

Shakespeare's History (Dublin: Gill and Macmillan, 1985)

Holderness, Graham, Nick Potter, and John Turner, *Shakespeare: The Play of History* (Basingstoke: Macmillan, 1987)

Hooks, Adam G., 'Making Histories: or, Shakespeare's *Ring*', in *The Book in History, The Book as History: New Intersections of the Material Text*, ed. Heidi Brayman, Jesse M. Lander, and Zachary Lesser (New Haven and London: Yale University Press, 2016), pp. 341–74

Selling Shakespeare: Biography, Bibliography, and the Book Trade (Cambridge: Cambridge University Press, 2016)

'Shakespeare at the White Greyhound', *Shakespeare Survey 64* (2011), 260–75

'Wise Ventures: Shakespeare and Thomas Playfere at the Sign of the Angel', in *Shakespeare's Stationers: Studies in Cultural Bibliography*, ed. Marta Straznicky (Philadelphia: University of Pennsylvania Press, 2013), pp. 47–62

Hope, Jonathan and Michael Witmore, 'The Hundredth Psalm to the Tune of "Green Sleeves": Digital Approaches to Shakespeare's Language of Genre', *Shakespeare Quarterly*, 61:3 (2010), 357–90

Hopkins, Lisa, 'The Danish Romance Play: *Fair Em, Sir Clyomon and Sir Clamydes*, and *Hoffman*', *Early Modern Literary Studies*, Special Issue 27 (2017), 1–17

Drama and the Succession to the Crown, 1561–1633 (Farnham: Ashgate, 2011)

Houliston, Victor, 'The Hare and the Drum: Robert Persons's Writings on the English Succession, 1593–6', *Renaissance Studies*, 14:2 (2000), 235–50

'Persons [Parsons], Robert (1546–1610)', *ODNB*, online ed., September 2004, https://doi.org/10.1093/ref:odnb/21474 (accessed 16 September 2019)

Howard, Jean E. and Phyllis Rackin, *Engendering a Nation: A Feminist Account of Shakespeare's English Histories* (London: Routledge, 1997)

Hunt, Arnold, *The Art of Hearing: English Preachers and Their Audiences, 1590–1640* (Cambridge: Cambridge University Press, 2010)

Hunter, G. K., *The Oxford History of English Literature, Volume 6: English Drama, 1586–1642: The Age of Shakespeare* (Oxford: Clarendon Press, 1997)

'Truth and Art in History Plays', *Shakespeare Survey 42* (1990), 15–24

Jauss, Hans Robert, 'Literary History As a Challenge to Literary Theory', trans. Elizabeth Benzinger, *New Literary History*, 2:1 (1970), 7–37

Jones, Emrys, 'Stuart *Cymbeline*', *Essays in Criticism*, 11:1 (1961), 84–99

Jowett, John, *Shakespeare and Text* (Oxford: Oxford University Press, 2007)

'Shakespeare Supplemented', in *The Shakespeare Apocrypha*, ed. Douglas A. Brooks (Lampeter: Edwin Mellen Press, 2007), 39–73

Jowett, John and Gary Taylor, 'Sprinklings of Authority: The Folio Text of *Richard II*', *Studies in Bibliography*, 38 (1985), 151–200

'The Three Texts of *2 Henry IV*', *Studies in Bibliography*, 40 (1987), 31–50

Kamps, Ivo, *Historiography and Ideology in Stuart Drama* (Cambridge: Cambridge University Press, 1996)

'The Writing of History in Shakespeare's England', in *A Companion to Shakespeare's Works: Volume II: The Histories*, ed. Richard Dutton and Jean E. Howard (Oxford: Blackwell, 2003), pp. 4–25

Karremann, Isabel, *The Drama of Memory in Shakespeare's History Plays* (Cambridge: Cambridge University Press, 2015)

'A Passion for the Past: The Politics of Nostalgia on the Early Jacobean Stage', in *Passions and Subjectivity in Early Modern Culture*, ed. Brian Cummings and Freya Sierhuis (Farnham: Ashgate, 2013), pp. 149–64

Kastan, David Scott, *Shakespeare after Theory* (London: Routledge, 1999)

Shakespeare and the Book (Cambridge: Cambridge University Press, 2001)

Shakespeare and the Shapes of Time (Basingstoke: Palgrave Macmillan, 1982)

Kathman, David, 'London Inns As Playing Venues for the Queen's Men', in *Locating the Queen's Men, 1583–1603: Material Practices and Conditions of Playing*, ed. Helen Ostovich, Holger Schott Syme, and Andrew Griffin (Farnham: Ashgate, 2009), pp. 65–76

Kesson, Andy, *John Lyly and Early Modern Authorship* (Manchester: Manchester University Press, 2013)

'Was Comedy a Genre in English Early Modern Drama?', *British Journal of Aesthetics*, 54:2 (2014), 213–25

Kesson, Andy and Emma Smith, 'Introduction: Towards a Definition of Print Popularity', in *The Elizabethan Top Ten: Defining Print Popularity in Early Modern England*, ed. Andy Kesson and Emma Smith (Farnham: Ashgate, 2013), pp. 1–15

Kewes, Paulina, *Authorship and Appropriation: Writing for the Stage in England, 1660–1710* (Oxford: Clarendon Press, 1998)

'The Elizabethan History Play: A True Genre?', in *A Companion to Shakespeare's Works: Volume II: The Histories*, ed. Richard Dutton and Jean E. Howard (Oxford: Blackwell, 2003), pp. 170–93

'Henry Savile's Tacitus and the Politics of Roman History in Late Elizabethan England', *Huntington Library Quarterly*, 74:4 (2011), 515–51

'History and Its Uses: Introduction', *Huntington Library Quarterly*, 68:1–2 (2005), 1–31

'The Puritan, the Jesuit and the Jacobean Succession', in *Doubtful and Dangerous: The Question of Succession in Late Elizabethan England*, ed. Susan Doran and Paulina Kewes (Manchester: Manchester University Press, 2014), pp. 47–70

Kim, Jaecheol, 'The North–South Divide in *Gorboduc*: Fratricide Remembered', *Studies in Philology*, 111:4 (2014), 691–719

King, John N., 'John Day: Master Printer of the English Reformation', in *The Beginnings of English Protestantism*, ed. Peter Marshall and Alec Ryrie (Cambridge: Cambridge University Press, 2002), pp. 180–208

Kirk, Andrew M., *The Mirror of Confusion: The Representation of French History in English Renaissance Drama*, new ed. (London and New York: Routledge, 2014)

Kirwan, Peter, *Shakespeare and the Idea of Apocrypha: Negotiating the Boundaries of the Dramatic Canon* (Cambridge: Cambridge University Press, 2015)

Knight, Jeffrey Todd, *Bound to Read: Compilations, Collections and the Making of Renaissance Literature* (Philadelphia: University of Pennsylvania Press, 2013)

'Invisible Ink: A Note on Ghost Images in Early Printed Books', *Textual Cultures*, 5:2 (2010), 53–62

'Making Shakespeare's Books: Assembly and Intertextuality in the Archives', *Shakespeare Quarterly*, 60:3 (2009) 304–40

Knighton, C. S., 'Barlow, William (*d.* 1613)', *ODNB*, online ed., January 2008, https://doi.org/10.1093/ref:odnb/1443 (accessed 13 June 2020)

Knutson, Roslyn L., 'Filling Fare: The Appetite for Current Issues and Traditional Forms in the Repertory of the Chamberlain's Men', *Medieval & Renaissance Drama in England*, 15 (2003), 57–76

Playing Companies and Commerce in Shakespeare's Time (Cambridge: Cambridge University Press, 2001)

'The Repertory', in *A New History of Early English Drama*, ed. John Cox and David Scott Kastan (New York: Columbia University Press, 1997), pp. 461–80

'What's So Special about 1594?', *Shakespeare Quarterly*, 61:4 (2010), 449–67

Knutson, Roslyn L., David McInnis, and Matthew Steggle (eds.), *Loss and the Literary Culture of Shakespeare's Time* (Cham: Palgrave Macmillan, 2020)

Krantz, Susan E., 'Thomas Dekker's Political Commentary in *The Whore of Babylon*', *Studies in English Literature, 1500–1900*, 35:2 (1995), 271–91

Lake, Peter, *How Shakespeare Put Politics on the Stage: Power and Succession in the History Plays* (New Haven: Yale University Press, 2016)

Lake, Peter and Steven Pincus (eds.), *The Politics of the Public Sphere in Early Modern England* (Manchester: Manchester University Press, 2007)

Laoutaris, Chris, 'The Prefatorial Material', in *The Cambridge Companion to Shakespeare's First Folio*, ed. Emma Smith (Cambridge: Cambridge University Press, 2016), pp. 48–67

Leggatt, Alexander, 'A Double Reign: *Richard II* and *Perkin Warbeck*', in *Shakespeare and His Contemporaries: Essays in Comparison*, ed. E. A. J. Honigmann (Manchester: Manchester University Press, 1986), pp. 129–39

Lesser, Zachary, *Renaissance Drama and the Politics of Publication: Readings in the English Book Trade* (Cambridge: Cambridge University Press, 2004)

Lesser, Zachary and Peter Stallybrass, 'The First Literary *Hamlet* and the Commonplacing of Professional Plays', *Shakespeare Quarterly*, 59:4 (2008), 371–420

'Shakespeare between Pamphlet and Book, 1608–1619', in *Shakespeare and Textual Studies*, ed. Margaret Jane Kidnie and Sonia Massai (Cambridge: Cambridge University Press, 2015), pp. 105–33

Levy, F. J., 'Hayward, Daniel, and the Beginnings of Politic History in England', *Huntington Library Quarterly*, 50:1 (1987), 1–34

Tudor Historical Thought (San Marino, CA: The Huntington Library, 1967)

Lidster, Amy, 'At the Sign of the Angel: The Influence of Andrew Wise on Shakespeare in Print', *Shakespeare Survey 71* (2018), 242–54

'Challenging Monarchical Legacies in *Edward III* and *Henry V*', *English: Journal of the English Association*, 68:261 (2019), 126-42

'Publishing *King Lear* (1608) at the Sign of the Pied Bull', in *Old St Paul's and Culture*, ed. Shanyn Altman and Jonathan Buckner (London: Palgrave Macmillan, 2021), pp. 293–318

'"With much labour out of scattered papers": The Caroline Reprints of Thomas Heywood's *1* and *2 If You Know Not Me You Know Nobody*', *Renaissance Drama*, 49:2 (2021), 205–28.

Limon, Jerzy, *Dangerous Matter: English Drama and Politics in 1623/24* (Cambridge: Cambridge University Press, 1986)

Lockey, Brian C., *Law and Empire in English Renaissance Literature* (Cambridge: Cambridge University Press, 2006)

Lockyer, Roger, *The Early Stuarts: A Political History of England, 1603–1642*, 2nd ed. (London: Longman, 1999)

Loewenstein, David and Michael Witmore (eds.), *Shakespeare and Early Modern Religion* (Cambridge: Cambridge University Press, 2015)

Loewenstein, Joseph, *Ben Jonson and Possessive Authorship* (Cambridge: Cambridge University Press, 2002)

Lyons, Tara L., 'English Printed Drama in Collection before Jonson and Shakespeare', unpublished PhD thesis, University of Illinois (2011)

'Richard Jones, *Tamburlaine the Great*, and the Making (and Remaking) of a Serial Play Collection in the 1590s', in *Christopher Marlowe, Theatrical Commerce and the Book Trade*, ed. Kirk Melnikoff and Roslyn L. Knutson (Cambridge: Cambridge University Press, 2018), pp. 149–64

'Serials, Spinoffs, and Histories: Selling "Shakespeare" in Collection before the Folio', *Philological Quarterly*, 91:2 (2012), 185–220

MacCaffrey, Wallace T., 'Carey, Henry, first Baron Hunsdon (1526–1596)', *ODNB*, online ed., September 2014, http://www.oxforddnb.com/view/article/4649 (accessed 16 September 2019)

Maguire, Laurie E., 'The Craft of Printing (1600)', in *A Companion to Shakespeare*, ed. David Scott Kastan (Oxford: Blackwell, 1999), pp. 434–49

Shakespearean Suspect Texts: The 'Bad' Quartos and Their Contexts (Cambridge: Cambridge University Press, 1996)

Manley, Lawrence and Sally-Beth MacLean, *Lord Strange's Men and Their Plays* (New Haven and London: Yale University Press, 2014)

Marcus, Leah S., *Puzzling Shakespeare: Local Reading and Its Discontents* (Berkeley: University of California Press, 1988)

Marino, James J., *Owning William Shakespeare: The King's Men and Their Intellectual Property* (Philadelphia: University of Pennsylvania Press, 2011)

Marshall, Tristan, *Theatre and Empire: Great Britain on the London Stages under James VI and I* (Manchester: Manchester University Press, 2000)

Massai, Sonia, 'Edward Blount, the Herberts, and the First Folio', in *Shakespeare's Stationers: Studies in Cultural Bibliography*, ed. Marta Straznicky (Philadelphia: University of Pennsylvania Press, 2013), pp. 132–46

Shakespeare and the Rise of the Editor (Cambridge: Cambridge University Press, 2007)

'Shakespeare, Text and Paratext', *Shakespeare Survey 62* (2009), 1–11

Massai, Sonia and Heidi Craig, 'Rethinking Prologues and Epilogues on Page and Stage', in *Rethinking Theatrical Documents in Shakespeare's England*, ed. Tiffany Stern (London: Arden Shakespeare, 2020), pp. 91–110

Mayer, Jean-Christophe, 'Annotating and Transcribing for the Theatre: Shakespeare's Early Modern Reader-Revisers at Work', in *Shakespeare and Textual Studies*, ed. Margaret Jane Kidnie and Sonia Massai (Cambridge: Cambridge University Press, 2015), pp. 163–76

'The Decline of the Chronicle and Shakespeare's History Plays', *Shakespeare Survey 63* (2010), 12–23

'The "Parliament Sceane" in Shakespeare's *King Richard II*, XVII–XVIII: *Bulletin de la société d'études anglo-américaines des XVIIe et XVIIIe siècles*, 59 (2004), 27–42

'Shakespeare and the Order of Books', *Early Modern Literary Studies*, Special Issue 21 (2013), 5:1–24

McCullough, Peter, 'Print, Publication, and Religious Politics in Caroline England', *The Historical Journal*, 51:2 (2008), 285–313

McInnis, David and Matthew Steggle, 'Introduction: *Nothing* Will Come of Nothing? Or, What Can We Learn from Plays That Don't Exist?', in *Lost Plays in Shakespeare's England*. ed. David McInnis and Matthew Steggle (Basingstoke: Palgrave Macmillan, 2014), pp. 1–14

McKenzie, D. F., *Bibliography and the Sociology of Texts* (Cambridge: Cambridge University Press, 1999)

McKerrow, R. B., 'Booksellers, Printers, and the Stationers' Trade', in *Shakespeare's England: An Account of the Life and Manners of His Age*, 2 vols. (Oxford: Clarendon Press, 1916), II, pp. 212–39

McMillin, Scott, 'The Queen's Men in 1594: A Study of "Good" and "Bad" Quartos', *English Literary Renaissance*, 14:1 (1984), 55–69

McMillin, Scott and Sally-Beth MacLean, *The Queen's Men and Their Plays* (Cambridge: Cambridge University Press, 1998)

McMullan, Gordon, 'The Colonization of Early Britain on the Jacobean Stage', in *Reading the Medieval in Early Modern England*, ed. Gordon McMullan and David Matthews (Cambridge: Cambridge University Press, 2007), pp. 119–40

Melnikoff, Kirk, *Elizabethan Publishing and the Makings of Literary Culture* (Toronto: University of Toronto Press, 2018)

'Jones's Pen and Marlowe's Socks: Richard Jones, Print Culture, and the Beginnings of English Dramatic Literature', *Studies in Philology*, 102:2 (2005), 184–209

Minton, Gretchen E., 'Apocalyptic Tragicomedy for a Jacobean Audience: Dekker's *Whore of Babylon* and Shakespeare's *Cymbeline*', *Renaissance and Reformation*, 36:1 (2013), 129–52

Moore, Helen, 'Jonson, Dekker, and the Discourse of Chivalry', *Medieval & Renaissance Drama in England*, 12 (1999), 121–65

'Roberts [Robarts], Henry (fl. 1585–1617), author', *ODNB*, online ed., September 2004, https://doi.org/10.1093/ref:odnb/23753 (accessed 14 May 2020)

Moretti, Franco, *Graphs, Maps, Trees: Abstract Models for a Literary Theory* (London: Verso, 2005)

Morrissey, Mary, *Politics and the Paul's Cross Sermons, 1558–1642* (Oxford: Oxford University Press, 2011)

Munro, Lucy, *Archaic Style in English Literature, 1590–1674* (Cambridge: Cambridge University Press, 2013)

Murphy, Andrew, *Shakespeare in Print: A History and Chronology of Shakespeare Publishing* (Cambridge: Cambridge University Press, 2003)

Murphy, Donna N., '*Locrine, Selimus*, Robert Greene, and Thomas Lodge', *Notes and Queries*, 56:4 (2009) 559–63

Nicholls, Mark and Penry Williams, 'Ralegh, Sir Walter (1554–1618)', *ODNB*, online ed., September 2015, https://doi.org/10.1093/ref:odnb/23039 (accessed 18 June 2020)

Oberer, Karen, 'Appropriations of the Popular Tradition in *The Famous Victories of Henry V* and *The Troublesome Raigne of King John*', in *Locating the Queen's Men, 1583–1603: Material Practices and Conditions of Playing*, ed. Helen Ostovich, Holger Schott Syme, and Andrew Griffin (Farnham: Ashgate, 2009), pp. 171–82

Ostovich, Helen, Holger Schott Syme, and Andrew Griffin (eds.), *Locating the Queen's Men, 1583–1603: Material Practices and Conditions of Playing* (Farnham: Ashgate, 2009)

Parvini, Neema, *Shakespeare's History Plays: Rethinking Historicism* (Edinburgh: Edinburgh University Press, 2012)

Patterson, Annabel, *Censorship and Interpretation: The Conditions of Writing and Reading in Early Modern England* (Madison: University of Wisconsin Press, 1984)

Pearce, N. D. F. and Christopher Burlinson, 'Heath, John (*b. c.*1585), epigrammatist', *ODNB*, online ed., September 2004, https://doi.org/10.1093/ref:odnb/12838 (accessed 9 April 2021)

Peters, Julie Stone, *Theatre of the Book, 1480–1880: Print, Text and Performance in Europe* (Oxford: Oxford University Press, 2000)

Pinciss, G. M., 'Thomas Creede and the Repertory of the Queen's Men, 1583–1592', *Modern Philology*, 67:4 (1970), 321–30

Pitcher, John, 'Daniel, Samuel (1562/3–1619)', *ODNB*, online ed., September 2004, https://doi.org/10.1093/ref:odnb/7120 (accessed 16 September 2019)

Pollard, Alfred W., *Shakespeare Folios and Quartos: A Study in the Bibliography of Shakespeare's Plays, 1594–1685* (London: Methuen, 1909)

Shakespeare's Fight with the Pirates and the Problems of the Transmission of His Text (London: Alexander Moring, 1917)

Pratt, Aaron T., 'Stab-Stitching and the Status of Early English Playbooks As Literature', *The Library*, 7th ser., 16:3 (2015), 304–28

Pugliatti, Paola, *Shakespeare the Historian* (Basingstoke: Palgrave Macmillan, 1996)

Rackin, Phyllis, *Stages of History: Shakespeare's English Chronicles* (Ithaca: Cornell University Press, 1990)

Read, Conyers, 'Walsingham and Burghley in Queen Elizabeth's Privy Council', *English Historical Review*, 28:109 (1913), 34–58

Ribner, Irving, *The English History Play in the Age of Shakespeare*, rev. ed. (London: Methuen, 1965)

Richards, Jennifer, *Voices and Books in the English Renaissance: A New History of Reading* (Oxford: Oxford University Press, 2019)

Richards, Jennifer and Fred Schurink, 'The Textuality and Materiality of Reading in Early Modern England', *Huntington Library Quarterly*, 73:3 (2010), 345–61

Roberts-Smith, Jennifer, '"What makes thou upon a stage?": Child Actors, Royalist Publicity, and the Space of the Nation in the Queen's Men's *True Tragedy of Richard the Third*', *Early Theatre*, 15:2 (2012), 192–205

Robinson, Benedict S., 'Thomas Heywood and the Cultural Politics of Play Collections', *Studies in English Literature, 1500–1900*, 42:2 (2002), 361–80

 'The "Turks", Caroline Politics and Philip Massinger's *The Renegado*', in *Localizing Caroline Drama: Politics and Economics of the Early Modern English Stage, 1625–1642*, ed. Adam Zucker and Alan Farmer (Basingstoke: Palgrave Macmillan, 2006), pp. 213–37

Robinson, Marsha S., *Writing the Reformation: 'Actes and Monuments' and the Jacobean History Play* (Aldershot: Ashgate, 2002)

Rostenberg, Leona, 'Nathaniel Butter and Nicholas Bourne, First "Masters of the Staple"', *The Library*, 5th ser., 12:1 (1957), 23–33

Salzman, Paul, *Literature and Politics in the 1620s: 'Whisper'd Counsells'* (Basingstoke: Palgrave Macmillan, 2014)

Samuel, Edgar, 'Lopez [Lopes], Roderigo [Ruy, Roger] (*c.*1517–1594)', *ODNB*, online ed., January 2008, https://doi.org/10.1093/ref:odnb/17011 (accessed 16 September 2019)

Schelling, Felix E., *The English Chronicle Play: A Study in the Popular Historical Literature Environing Shakespeare* (New York: Macmillan, 1902)

Schillinger, Stephen, 'Begging at the Gate: *Jack Straw* and the Acting Out of Popular Rebellion', *Medieval & Renaissance Drama in England*, 21 (2008), 87–127

Schwyzer, Philip, 'The Jacobean Union Controversy and *King Lear*', in *The Accession of James I: Historical and Cultural Consequences*, ed. Glen Burgess, Rowland Wymer and Jason Lawrence (Basingstoke: Palgrave Macmillan, 2006), pp. 34–47

Scragg, Leah, 'Edward Blount and the Prefatory Material to the First Folio of Shakespeare', *Bulletin of the John Rylands Library*, 79:1 (1997), 117–26

Shapiro, James, *1606: William Shakespeare and the Year of 'Lear'* (London: Faber, 2015)

Sharpe, Kevin, *Reading Revolutions: The Politics of Reading in Early Modern England* (New Haven: Yale University Press, 2000)

Sherman, William H., *Used Books: Marking Readers in Renaissance England* (Philadelphia: University of Pennsylvania Press, 2008)

Smith, Emma, *The Making of Shakespeare's First Folio* (Oxford: Bodleian Library, 2015)

Shakespeare's First Folio: Four Centuries of an Iconic Book (Oxford: Oxford University Press, 2016)

'Shakespeare Serialized: An Age of Kings', in *A Cambridge Companion to Shakespeare and Popular Culture*, ed. Robert Shaughnessy (Cambridge: Cambridge University Press, 2007), pp. 134–49

Smith, Helen, '"To London all"? Mapping Shakespeare in Print, 1593–1598', in *Shakespeare and Textual Studies*, ed. Margaret Jane Kidnie and Sonia Massai (Cambridge: Cambridge University Press, 2015), pp. 69–86

Smith, Helen and Louise Wilson, 'Introduction', in *Renaissance Paratexts*, ed. Helen Smith and Louise Wilson (Cambridge: Cambridge University Press, 2011), pp. 1–14

Smuts, R. Malcolm, 'States, Monarchs, and Dynastic Transitions: The Political Thought of John Hayward', in *Doubtful and Dangerous: The Question of Succession in Late Elizabethan England*, ed. Susan Doran and Paulina Kewes (Manchester: Manchester University Press, 2014), pp. 276–94

Smyth, Adam, *Material Texts in Early Modern England* (Cambridge: Cambridge University Press, 2018)

Spikes, Judith Doolin, 'The Jacobean History Play and the Myth of the Elect Nation', *Renaissance Drama*, 8 (1977), 117–49

Stater, Victor, 'Herbert, William, third earl of Pembroke (1580–1630)', *ODNB*, online ed., January 2008, https://doi.org/10.1093/ref:odnb/13058 (accessed 16 September 2019)

Stern, Tiffany, *Documents of Performance in Early Modern England* (Cambridge: Cambridge University Press, 2009)

'Epilogues, Prayers after Plays, and Shakespeare's *2 Henry IV*', *Theatre Notebook*, 64:3 (2010), 122–29

'"On each Wall and Corner Poast": Playbills, Title-pages, and Advertising in Early Modern London', *English Literary Renaissance*, 36:1 (2006), 57–89

'Sermons, Plays, and Note-Takers: *Hamlet* Q1 As a "Noted" Text', *Shakespeare Survey 66* (2013), 1–23

Stern, Tiffany (ed.), *Rethinking Theatrical Documents in Shakespeare's England* (London: Arden Shakespeare, 2020)

Stilma, Astrid, 'Angels, Demons and Political Action in Two Early Jacobean History Plays', *Critical Survey*, 23:2 (2011), 9–25

Straznicky, Marta, 'Introduction: Plays, Books, and the Public Sphere', in *The Book of the Play: Playwrights, Stationers, and Readers in Early Modern England*, ed. Marta Straznicky (Amherst and Boston: University of Massachusetts Press, 2006), pp. 1–20

Straznicky, Marta (ed.), *The Book of the Play: Playwrights, Stationers, and Readers in Early Modern England* (Amherst and Boston: University of Massachusetts Press, 2006)

Shakespeare's Stationers: Studies in Cultural Bibliography (Philadelphia: University of Pennsylvania Press, 2013)

Strong, Roy, *Henry Prince of Wales and England's Lost Renaissance* (New York: Thames and Hudson, 1986)

Syme, Holger, 'The Meaning of Success: Stories of 1594 and Its Aftermath', *Shakespeare Quarterly*, 61:4 (2010), 490–525

'Thomas Creede, William Barley, and the Venture of Printing Plays', in *Shakespeare's Stationers: Studies in Cultural Bibliography*, ed. Marta Straznicky (Philadelphia: University of Pennsylvania Press, 2013), pp. 28–46

Taylor, Gary, 'Historicism, Presentism and Time: Middleton's *The Spanish Gypsy* and *A Game at Chess*', *Sederi*, 18 (2008), 147–70

'History, Plays, Genre, Games', in *The Oxford Handbook of Thomas Middleton*, ed. Gary Taylor and Trish Thomas Henley (Oxford: Oxford University Press, 2012), pp. 47–63

'Making Meaning Marketing Shakespeare 1623', in *From Performance to Print in Shakespeare's England*, ed. Peter Holland and Stephen Orgel (Basingstoke: Palgrave Macmillan, 2006), pp. 55–72

Taylor, Miles, 'The End of the English History Play in *Perkin Warbeck*', *Studies in English Literature, 1500–1900*, 48:2 (2008), 395–418

Teramura, Misha, 'Brute Parts: From Troy to Britain at the Rose, 1596–1600', in *Lost Plays in Shakespeare's England*, ed. David McInnis and Matthew Steggle (Basingstoke: Palgrave Macmillan, 2014), pp. 127–47

Tillyard, E. M. W., *Shakespeare's History Plays* (London: Chatto & Windus, 1944)

Tipton, Alzada, 'Caught between "Virtue" and "Memorie": Providential and Political Historiography in Samuel Daniel's *The Civil Wars*', *Huntington Library Quarterly*, 61:3/4 (1998), 325–41

Velz, John W. (ed.), *Shakespeare's English Histories: A Quest for Form and Genre* (Binghamton, NY: Medieval & Renaissance Texts & Studies, 1996)

Vitkus, Daniel J., *Three Turk Plays from Early Modern England* (New York: Columbia University Press, 2000)

Walker, Greg, *The Politics of Performance in Early Renaissance Drama* (Cambridge: Cambridge University Press, 1998)

Wall, Wendy, *The Imprint of Gender: Authorship and Publication in the English Renaissance* (Ithaca: Cornell University Press, 1993)

Walsh, Brian, '"Deep Prescience": Succession and the Politics of Prophecy in *Friar Bacon and Friar Bungay*', *Medieval & Renaissance Drama in England*, 23 (2010), 63–85

Shakespeare, the Queen's Men and the Elizabethan Performance of History (Cambridge: Cambridge University Press, 2009)

'Truth, Poetry, and Report in *The True Tragedy of Richard III*', in *Locating the Queen's Men, 1583–1603: Material Practices and Conditions of Playing*, ed. Helen Ostovich, Holger Schott Syme, and Andrew Griffin (Farnham: Ashgate, 2009), pp. 123–33

Unsettled Toleration: Religious Difference on the Shakespearean Stage (Oxford: Oxford University Press, 2016)

Walsham, Alexandra, 'Bell [*alias* Burton], Thomas (*b. c.* 1551, *d.* in or after 1610)', *ODNB*, online ed., January 2008, https://doi.org/10.1093/ref:odnb/2026 (accessed 8 April 2020)

Whipday, Emma, *Shakespeare's Domestic Tragedies: Violence in the Early Modern Home* (Cambridge: Cambridge University Press, 2019)

White, Paul Whitefield, '"Histories out of the scriptures": Biblical Drama in the Repertory of the Admiral's Men, 1594–1603', in *Loss and the Literary Culture of Shakespeare's Time*, ed. Roslyn L. Knutson, David McInnis, and Matthew Steggle (Cham: Palgrave Macmillan, 2020), pp. 191–214

Willoughby, Edwin Eliott, *A Printer of Shakespeare: The Books and Times of William Jaggard* (London: Allan, 1934)

Winston, Jessica, 'National History to Foreign Calamity: *A Mirror for Magistrates* and Early English Tragedy', in *Shakespeare's Histories and Counter-Histories*, ed. Dermot Cavanagh, Stuart Hampton-Reeves, and Stephen Longstaffe (Manchester: Manchester University Press, 2006), pp. 152–65

Woods, Gillian, 'The Contexts of *The Trial of Chivalry*', *Notes and Queries*, 54:3 (2007), 313–18

Woolf, D. R., *The Idea of History in Early Stuart England* (Toronto: University of Toronto Press, 1990)

'News, History and the Construction of the Present in Early Modern England', in *The Politics of Information in Early Modern Europe*, ed. Brendan Dooley and Sabrina A. Baron (Abingdon: Routledge, 2001), pp. 80–118

Reading History in Early Modern England (Cambridge: Cambridge University Press, 2000)

The Social Circulation of the Past: English Historical Culture, 1500–1730 (Oxford: Oxford University Press, 2003)

Worden, Blair, 'Afterword', in *Doubtful and Dangerous: The Question of Succession in Late Elizabethan England*, ed. Susan Doran and Paulina Kewes (Manchester: Manchester University Press, 2014), pp. 295–303

'Historians and Poets', *Huntington Library Quarterly*, 68:1–2 (2005), 71–93

'Which Play Was Performed at the Globe Theatre on 7 February 1601?', *London Review of Books*, 25:13 (10 July 2003)

Wormald, Jenny, 'The Creation of Britain: Multiple Kingdoms or Core and Colonies?', *Transactions of the Royal Historical Society*, 2 (1992), 175–94

Wright, Gillian, 'The Politics of Revision in Samuel Daniel's *The Civil Wars*', *English Literary Renaissance*, 38:3 (2008), 461–82

Yamada, Akihiro, *Thomas Creede: Printer to Shakespeare and His Contemporaries* (Tokyo: Meisei University Press, 1994)

Reference Works

Arber, Edward (ed.), *A Transcript of the Registers of the Company of Stationers of London, 1554–1640 A.D.*, 5 vols. (London, 1875–77; Birmingham, 1894)

Bergel, Giles and Ian Gadd (eds.), *Stationers' Register Online*, CREATe, University of Glasgow, http://stationersregister.online

Berger, Thomas L. and Sonia Massai (eds.), with Tania Demetriou, *Paratexts in English Printed Drama to 1642*, 2 vols. (Cambridge: Cambridge University Press, 2014)

Chambers, E. K., *The Elizabethan Stage*, 4 vols. (Oxford: Clarendon Press, 1923)

Dahl, Folke, *A Bibliography of English Corantos and Periodical Newsbooks, 1620–1642* (London: Bibliographical Society, 1952)

Farmer, Alan B. and Zachary Lesser (eds.), *DEEP: Database of Early English Playbooks*. Created 2007, http://deep.sas.upenn.edu

Foakes, R. A. (ed.), *Henslowe's Diary*, 2nd ed. (Cambridge: Cambridge University Press, 2002)

Greg, W. W., *A Bibliography of the English Printed Drama to the Restoration*, 4 vols. (London: Oxford University Press for the Bibliographical Society, 1939–59)

Greg, W. W. and E. Boswell (eds.), *Records of the Court of the Stationers' Company: 1576–1602* (London: Bibliographical Society, 1930)

Ioppolo, Grace (dir.), *The Henslowe–Alleyn Digitisation Project*, King's Digital Lab, King's College London, https://henslowe-alleyn.org.uk

Jackson, William A. (ed.), *Records of the Court of the Stationers' Company, 1602 to 1640* (London: Bibliographical Society, 1957)

Knutson, Roslyn L., David McInnis, Matthew Steggle, and Misha Teramura (eds.), *Lost Plays Database* (Washington, DC: Folger Shakespeare Library, 2018), www.lostplays.folger.edu

Lemon, Robert and Mary Anne Everett (eds.), *Calendar of State Papers: Domestic Series, of the Reigns of Edward VI, Mary, Elizabeth, and James I (1547–1625)*, 12 vols. (London: Longman et al., 1856–72)

McKerrow, Ronald B., *Printers' and Publishers' Devices in England and Scotland, 1485–1640* (London: Printed for the Bibliographical Society at the Chiswick Press, 1913)

Pollard, A. W. and G. R. Redgrave (eds.), *A Short-Title Catalogue of Books Printed in England, Scotland, and Ireland and of English Books Printed Abroad, 1475–1640*, 2nd ed., rev. W. A. Jackson, F. S. Ferguson, and K. F. Pantzer, 3 vols. (London: Bibliographical Society, 1976–91)

Shakespeare Documented, convened by Folger Shakespeare Library (created 2016), https://shakespearedocumented.folger.edu

Wiggins, Martin, in association with Catherine Richardson, *British Drama 1533–1642: A Catalogue*, 8 vols. (Oxford: Oxford University Press, 2011–)

Williams, Franklin B., Jr., *Index of Dedications and Commendatory Verses in English Books before 1641* (London: Bibliographical Society, 1962)

Index

Milton Keynes UK
Ingram Content Group UK Ltd.
UKHW022343200224
438080UK00012B/59